GIFT EXCHANGE

Since Marcel Mauss published his foundational essay *The Gift* in 1925, many anthropologists and specialists of international relations have seen in the exchange of gifts, debts, loans, concessions, or reparations the sources of international solidarity and international law. Still, Mauss's reflections were deeply tied to the context of interwar Europe and the French colonial expansion. Their normative dimension has been profoundly questioned after the age of decolonization. A century after Mauss, we may ask: what is the relevance of his ideas on gift exchange and international solidarity? By tracing how Mauss's theoretical and normative ideas inspired prominent thinkers and government officials in France and Algeria, from Pierre Bourdieu to Mohammed Bedjaoui, Grégoire Mallard adds a building block to our comprehension of the role that anthropology, international law, and economics have played in shaping international economic governance from the age of European colonization to the latest European debt crisis.

Grégoire Mallard is Associate Professor of Anthropology and Sociology at the Graduate Institute (Geneva). He is the author of *Fallout: Nuclear Diplomacy in an Age of Global Fracture* (2014) and co-editor of *Contractual Knowledge: One Hundred Years of Legal Experimentation in Global Markets* (2016). His publications focus on prediction, knowledge, and ignorance in global governance.

Cover picture: photo of a stock of the Compagnie forestière Sangha-Oubangui from author's private collection.

Gift Exchange

THE TRANSNATIONAL HISTORY OF A POLITICAL IDEA

GRÉGOIRE MALLARD
Graduate Institute of International and Development Studies

CAMBRIDGE
UNIVERSITY PRESS

CAMBRIDGE
UNIVERSITY PRESS

University Printing House, Cambridge CB2 8BS, United Kingdom

One Liberty Plaza, 20th Floor, New York, NY 10006, USA

477 Williamstown Road, Port Melbourne, VIC 3207, Australia

314–321, 3rd Floor, Plot 3, Splendor Forum, Jasola District Centre, New Delhi – 110025, India

79 Anson Road, #06–04/06, Singapore 079906

Cambridge University Press is part of the University of Cambridge.

It furthers the University's mission by disseminating knowledge in the pursuit of education, learning, and research at the highest international levels of excellence.

www.cambridge.org
Information on this title: www.cambridge.org/9781108489690
DOI: 10.1017/9781108570497

When citing this work, please include a reference to the DOI 10.1017/9781108570497

First published 2019

A catalogue record for this publication is available from the British Library.

Library of Congress Cataloging-in-Publication Data
NAMES: Mallard, Gregoire, 1977– author.
TITLE: Gift exchange : the transnational history of a political idea / Gregoire Mallard.
DESCRIPTION: Cambridge, United Kingdom ; New York, NY : Cambridge University Press, 2019. | Series: Cambridge studies in law and society | Includes bibliographical references and index.
IDENTIFIERS: LCCN 2018042538| ISBN 9781108489690 (hardback) | ISBN 9781108453486 (paperback)
SUBJECTS: LCSH: Gifts – Political aspects. | Diplomatic gifts. | Mauss, Marcel, 1872–1950. Essai sur le don. | BISAC: LAW / General.
CLASSIFICATION: LCC GT3040 .M35 2019 | DDC 341.3/3–dc23
LC record available at https://lccn.loc.gov/2018042538

ISBN 978-1-108-48969-0 Hardback
ISBN 978-1-108-45348-6 Paperback

Contents

Figures

Acknowledgments

The genesis of this book is a perfect illustration of the role of serendipity in the process of formulation and reformulation of research questions. Little did I know that I would follow in the footsteps of Marcel Mauss's acclaimed biographer Marcel Fournier and write a book on Mauss's anthropology of the gift when, ten years ago, my wife, Eléonore Lépinard, and I rented his Montreal apartment for a year and worked under the gaze of the bronze bust of Emile Durkheim that he had placed on his desk. With this book, I have confirmed my wife's suspicion that I remain inexorably fascinated by great dead white men – like Honoré de Balzac, Jean Monnet, or indeed Marcel Mauss – and that, instead of writing a book titled *Queering Marcel Mauss* – a task too intimidating, although highly relevant – I would spend several years researching Mauss's role within the group of solidarist and socialist thinkers who participated in the political affairs of the last century. For that, I will blame Marcel Fournier, as it is in his library that I first read Mauss's political writings, where I first found the missing link between the anthropology of gift-giving practices, the modern forms of international credit exchanges, and the intellectual history of the concept of solidarity that I was looking to explore. And I will thank Eléonore, who accepts me with all my deficiencies, and whose companionship remains a proof that gifts can be given without always being immediately given back.

Unfulfilled intellectual interests never die, and I found with this story an opportunity to revive an old flame of mine: I first became interested in the French nebula of solidarist intellectuals and sociologists during a class taught by Vincent Viet more than fifteen years ago at the École Normale Supérieure (Cachan) on the history of labor relations in France. These young sociologists' intellectual passion, political involvement, and thirst for emancipation formed a riveting narrative of collective ambition and accomplishments. But, in the following decade, I rarely returned to the belle époque and interwar period. Instead, I wrote my first monograph, *Fallout*, on the changing international legal environment, evolving conceptions of sovereignty, and new forms of contractual agreements that regulated the nuclear trade in the second half of the twentieth century. I largely ignored the interwar period, as there was very little to regulate in terms of nuclear trade. Still, as *Fallout* focuses on a group of thinkers and politicians gathered around Jean Monnet, one of the main architects of the postwar European and global nuclear orders, I ventured from time to time into Monnet's early attempts to establish a financial and commercial European order within the League of Nations. As I researched the role of Jean Monnet and other important figures (like Konrad Adenauer and John Foster Dulles) in the (failed) establishment of an interwar financial order, I stumbled again on these French solidarists whose involvement in issues of international finance I had wanted to study. I also discovered that some characters who, like Jacques Soustelle, had exercised great responsibility in French postwar nuclear policy, had in fact started their career as PhD students working under the supervision of Mauss. Such oddities begged for more research.

Of course, the direction of this socio-historical inquiry has taken many turns, and what started as a book on the solidarists, European solidarity, and financial history, ended up as a book on Marcel Mauss, his essay *The Gift*, his followers, international law, and financial history up to this day.

Many colleagues and friends helped me navigate these various twists, and I would like to thank especially: Robert Mauss, who authorized me to consult Mauss's archives, and Christophe Labaune, who helped me explore the rich material at the Collège de France, as well as the staff of the Archives Nationales in Saint Denis, where I consulted the papers of Albert Thomas, Léon Blum, and Jacques Soustelle in particular. Jean-Michel Servet generously told me about the adventures of the Maussian economists around the French Caisse des dépôts et consignations, and he also read the whole manuscript and provided very useful feedback. Very special thanks go to Mohammed Bedjaoui, who opened his home to me, and gave me more than ten hours of recorded interviews and a presentation of his private papers. I also owe special thanks to Filipe Calvao, Sheila Galvin, and Davide Rodogno, who took the time to read and comment upon an early draft of the whole manuscript in June 2016. Deval Desai and Pierre Pénet read the full draft, as the manuscript was nearing completion in March 2018 and they gave me incredibly constructive comments. Furthermore, graduate students and colleagues at the Graduate Institute gave me additional comments during the class "Marcel Mauss and International Relations," which I gave at the Graduate Institute in spring 2017.

Additional thanks also go to all those who commented on parts of the chapters and/or who engaged in Maussian discussions: Kristin Avram, Gopalan Balachandran, Eric Brousseau, Alain Chenu, Leo Coleman, Ariel Colonomos, Mathew Craven, Yves Dezalay, Yvan Droz, Neil Gross, Marc Flandreau, Juan Flores-Zendeja, Marcel Fournier, Anna Gelpern, Neil Gross, Mitu Gulati, Terence Halliday, Volker Heins, Anne Holthoefer, Adil Khan, Marcelo Kohen, Dan Lainer-Vos, Claire Lemercier, Michael Loriaux, Frédéric Mérand, Alessandro Monsutti, Stephen Nelson, Reut Paz, Kim Priemel, Jérôme Sgard, Gregory Shaffer,

Isabelle Shulte-Tenckhoff, Augustin Simard, Jean Terrier, and Christine Unrau. As always, Madeleine Arenivar did a superb job editing my prose; she should be praised for her patience. I would also like to thank my editor at Cambridge, Matt Gallaway, for being such a responsive, efficient, and positive fellow traveler in the process of transforming an inchoate manuscript into a real book.

At last, this book has been published in Open Access with the support of the Swiss National Science Foundation (grant # 10BP12_183395), and I would like to thank the organization for making its diffusion easier and wide.

Abbreviations

AIJD	Association Internationale des Juristes Démocrates
CDC	Caisse des Dépôts et Consignations
CEPII	Centre d'Etudes Prospectives et d'Informations Internationales
DSA	Debt Sustainability Assessment
EBRD	European Bank for Reconstruction and Development
EC	European Commission
ECB	European Central Bank
ECJ	European Court of Justice
EDC	European Defense Community
EEC	European Economic Community
EFEO	École Française d'Extrême-Orient
EHESS	École des Hautes Etudes en Sciences Sociales
EMS	European Monetary System
ENA	École Nationale d'Administration
ENAA	École Nationale d'Administration d'Algerie
ENS	École Normale Supérieure
ENSAE	École Nationale de la Statistique et de l'Administration Economique
EP	European Parliament
EPHE	École Pratique des Hautes Etudes
ESM	European Stability Mechanism
EU	European Union
FLN	Front de Libération Nationale [Algeria]
GDP	gross domestic product
GPRA	Gouvernement provisoire de la République algérienne
ICJ	International Court of Justice
ICSID	International Center for the Settlement of Investment Disputes
IEP	Instituts d'Etudes Politiques
ILC	International Law Commission
ILO	International Labor Organization
IMF	International Monetary Fund
NIEO	New International Economic Order

OAS	Organisation armée secrète
OPEC	Organization of Petroleum Exporting Countries
PCJ	Permanent Court of Justice
RPF	Rassemblement du Peuple Français
SFIO	Section Française de l'Internationale Ouvrière
SMP	Securities Markets Programme
SRM	Single Resolution Mechanism
TFEU	Treaty on the Functioning of the European Union
UDMA	Union démocratique du manifeste algérien
UDSR	Union démocratique et socialiste de la Résistance
UGEMA	Union Générale des Etudiants Musulmans Algériens
UK	United Kingdom
UN	United Nations
UNCTAD	United Nations Conference on Trade and Development
UNGA	United Nations General Assembly
US	United States
USRAF	Union pour le Salut et le Renouveau de l'Algérie Française
WTO	World Trade Organization

1

The History of a Political Idea

Gifts, Trusts, Reparations, and Other Fetishes of International Solidarity

The Gift is probably the best-known essay by a French anthropologist. It was written by Emile Durkheim's nephew Marcel Mauss for the first volume of *L'Année sociologique* published after Durkheim's death.[1] The universal theory of gift-giving practices it provides has been at the center of many postwar disputes between French social theorists,[2] from Claude Lévi-Strauss[3] to Pierre Bourdieu[4] and Jacques Derrida,[5] as well as many central United States (US) theorists.[6] This influence might explain why it is still required reading for anthropology students in France, the United States, and many other places.

At the same time, as Lygia Sigaud has demonstrated, there are many "discontinuities in the interpretation of *The Gift*." In particular, she notices a "general indifference to Mauss's preoccupations with rights and obligations"[7] in the postwar reception of *The Gift*, and a contemporary focus on the moral and non-utilitarian webs of meaning associated with everyday (market) exchanges.[8] This focus on everyday forms of "commodity fetishism"[9] – when commodities are granted the personal qualities of the former possessors and the moral power of the community which produced them – although associated with remarkable developments in contemporary social theory,[10] contrasts deeply with Mauss's interest in understanding international exchanges between sovereign entities and in pursuing a dialogue with legal theorists on the role of evolving conceptions of sovereignty in changing forms of trade and commerce.

Indeed, this book argues, Mauss conceived of his essay as the coronation of a decade-long interest in the history of international contractual obligations among sovereign groups (tribes, empires, nations, etc.), expressed when the latter exchange *prestations* (a term difficult to translate into English, which refers to the services given), "apparently freely given, yet coercive and interested."[11] Mauss's focus on the question of sovereignty, its origins and manifestation, as well as on gift exchanges conceived as visible fetishes of international solidarity, has been lost to most sociologists and anthropologists who have applied his model to the local rather than international level.

Why is this so? What was Mauss's real focus when he wrote his famous essay on the origins of international solidarity, and why have we forgotten it? What were the academic conversations and public controversies in which his essay intervened? Was it merely an essay in the anthropology of law, contracts, and exchanges, or was it also a political tract that placed anthropology at the forefront of debates on global governance? How did Mauss conceive of the relationship between his anthropological essays more generally, and his political reflections, in which he discussed the best ways of restoring order and solidarity in a shattered European political landscape, marked by Germany's defeat and French expansion in its new colonies? If the two sides of his work were so linked, what was the legacy of his anthropological approach to international solidarity in debates about global governance before and after decolonization?

This book tries to answer these questions by historicizing the production and reception of Mauss's ideas on gift exchange, especially as the latter have intersected with other ideas developed by international law scholars and colonial administrators about international financial and global commercial governance, both within Europe and between Europe and the rest of the world. The argument is situated at the confluence between the sociology of political ideas and expert knowledge, sociological studies of global governance, and the intellectual history of colonization and decolonization, particularly (but not only) in the French context.

Building upon recently published scholarship which highlights the role of the early twentieth-century "return of the gift" – to cite Harry Liebersohn[12] – as a political discourse, grounded in the new discipline of anthropology, this book indeed starts from the premise that the anthropology of gift exchange was not just a scholarly preoccupation with the local mores of distant and "archaic" societies. In fact, when Mauss articulated a discourse on the exchange of gifts, he built upon, and reframed, the work of political and legal theorists who sought to answer centuries-old questions: What is the good form of government? How can political societies of different natures solve the problem of international order while maintaining the freedom of, and the solidarity between, their members? How can an international society sustain itself over time and develop a sense of solidarity among its interacting sovereigns when their constitutional politics differ drastically in kind?

In showing how different generations of anthropologists, colonial administrators and legal scholars used Mauss's model of gift exchange to answer these questions, this book shows how Mauss, his followers and his critics applied the notion of gift exchange in various contexts to reflect upon international relations between sovereign entities; and how they thus placed anthropology on equal footing with international law and economics in debates about good global governance. In particular, it recovers and traces Francophone expert struggles over what good governance has meant since the interwar era in the French field of power – broadly conceived – through the lens of a series of contemporary distinctions between different political imaginaries of solidarity, shaped by different disciplines and articulated around different conceptions of Europe's role in the management of global affairs.

1 THE IDEA OF GIFT EXCHANGE AND THE PROBLEM OF INTERNATIONAL ORDER

This book positions itself in the growing literature on global governance that is concerned with understanding the intellectual underpinnings of evolving international legal arrangements in the twentieth century before and after decolonization: in particular, the relation between the evolution of international law and the changing institutional architecture of global governance. It seeks to locate Mauss's specific contribution with *The Gift*, and that of some of his followers and disciples who drew inspiration from that essay, in what Michel Foucault would call the domain of "governmentality,"[13] and, more specifically, the type of discursive techniques that proliferated in the twentieth century to govern the international circulation of goods, commodities, financial obligations, and other material exchanges which tied together nations in a dense web of contractual obligations. It adds a new building block to our comprehension of the role played by various disciplines (anthropology, international law, economics) to the shaping of discourses and practices associated with the rise of European solidarity, the end of colonialism, and the beginning of globalization, by looking at the role of French-speaking anthropologists and their epigones in these debates – whose importance is often overlooked in recent intellectual histories of global governance.[14]

Methodologically, it follows what Foucault called a "genealogical approach,"[15] as it traces the evolution of the model of the gift in the long twentieth century back to Mauss's writing. By model, I mean the formulation of a general law which expresses a relation of causality: here, between the circulation of material things and the creation of a moral sense of obligation between contracting parties. Indeed, unlike other monographs on legal intellectual history, which focus on one distinct period,[16] this book thus traces the genealogy of various conceptualizations of gift exchanges within French anthropology and their relation to debates on global governance over more than a hundred years: from the European division of colonial territories in the late nineteenth century, to the attempts to recreate conditions of European solidarity with the League of Nations, the transformation of the United Nations under the pressure of decolonization, and attempts to create a more equitable New International Economic Order (NIEO) as popularized by Third World chief jurist and diplomat Mohammed Bedjaoui (1929–) during the oil crises of the 1970s.[17]

The recent book *The Return of the Gift: European History of a Global Idea* by Harry Liebersohn prepares the groundwork for such an endeavor.[18] Liebersohn's work is particularly interesting, for it traces how the circulation of gifts became an object of problematization in the discourses on colonial governance and what we could call today North–South relations of those late eighteenth- and early nineteenth-century British philosophers concerned with the establishment of a modern form of "good government" at the time of the expanding colonial administration of ethnically diverse populations by the chartered companies, like the East India

Company. The administrators-turned-ethnologists in these companies sought to better understand the logic of the colonial subjects' economic practices for the purpose of extracting more resources without risking political revolts.[19] In so doing, they rehabilitated the ideology of "gift giving as an exchange of favors to create bonds of obligation and loyalty, which was a pervasive feature of English as well as Indian society, with patronage between more or less powerful politicians, between authors and aristocrats," but which nonetheless came under the attack of utilitarian "intellectuals of nineteenth-century Europe."[20]

In particular, exchanges of gifts as a way of creating social and legal obligations across societies and nations (or "races," in the language of the time) appeared to British utilitarian thinkers like James Mill to "be a vestige of the old order" abolished in continental Europe by the French Revolution, "and a disturbance in a modern democratic society."[21] Utilitarian intellectuals, like Jeremy Bentham, drew sharp distinctions between their own practices of government – enlightened, rational, modern, formal – and the practices – personal, unpredictable, premodern, based on the material exchange of gifts – of those whose rule they replaced in the overseas territories where colonial private interests were expanding. Even if some of the utilitarian apostles of bureaucratic rulemaking agreed with Max Weber that, while the modern administration of the economy liberated political subjects, it also carried the risk that individuals would experience life in an "iron cage,"[22] most of them believed it was necessary to break down the authority of interpersonal networks. Thus, the model of the gift disappeared from the realm of political theory in most of the nineteenth century, although it survived in the everyday practice of colonial administrators.

Before the turn of the century, the importance of the gift survived only in "amateur" rather than professional anthropological discourses produced by administrators of the East India Company: the latter not only practiced the exchange of gifts with Indian authorities so as to establish the legitimacy of their presence (and thus fell under the British utilitarians' accusations of corruption and undue personal enrichment), but they also turned themselves into field ethnographers, forming what Marc Flandreau calls the "bureaucratic modality"[23] of mid-nineteenth-century British anthropology. Still, these amateur nineteenth-century anthropologists kept their gift exchange practices outside the field of political theory, and the institutionalization of anthropology had yet to take place in the greatest colonial power of the nineteenth century – the British Empire.

The model of gift exchange found its way back to theories of good government, as Liebersohn shows, through early twentieth-century anthropology rather than in political theory or economics: more precisely, through anthropological writings published in English by German anthropologists expatriated in the United Kingdom and the United States, and by Frenchmen like Mauss. Although *fin-de-si ècle* British anthropology was largely at the service of financial investors and bond-issuing companies,[24] some exceptions did exist: Franz Boas (1858–1942), Richard

Thurnwald (1869–1954), and Bronislaw Malinowski (1884–1942) were the three among the most important fieldwork anthropologists – in contrast to Mauss, who forever remained an armchair anthropologist and philologist – whose writings aimed to rehabilitate the gift as a model of good global governance. Before the writings of Mauss, they each tried to demonstrate that there was nothing premodern in this form of government, and that in fact, those "modern" political societies which denied the legitimacy of obligations formed out of the material circulation of gifts were not only less reflexive but also more unjust and threatening to individuals than those which had an appreciation for the wisdom of the obligations created through interpersonal exchange.[25]

After Mauss, the anthropologists' scholarly preoccupation with gift exchange marked the return in political discourses of a particular answer to the centuries-old questions raised by political theorists: what is the good form of government? Can we – and if so, how to – design institutions capable of imposing a quasi-legal obligation to bond the contracting parties of an international exchange? How could this sense of obligation be shared when contracting parties (nations, ethnic minorities, empires, colonies, etc.) shared no other cultural, technical, religious, legal, and moral characteristics in common, other than the exchange itself? Mauss proposed that the observation of the exchange of gifts in many different societies could serve to draw lessons applicable to understand and improve the relations between European and non-European political societies.

Analyzing the legacy of Mauss's ideas on gift exchange in such a manner thus requires that we follow in the footsteps of Steven Shapin and Simon Shaffer who, along with Bruno Latour, have developed a socio-history of ideas, in which academic disciplinary discourses (including physics but also anthropology) are treated as original solutions to the problem of knowledge as well as providing solutions to the political problem of order; and political discourses are treated as also providing solutions to the epistemic problems of knowledge, not just to the political problem of order.[26] This "symmetrical" methodological perspective on *The Gift* starts from the assumption that Mauss's political and anthropological writings were intrinsically connected, and that his main source of political concern and theoretical reflection had in fact an international rather than domestic dimension.[27] In other terms, Mauss's anthropology was an attempt to answer the political question of order in general and international order in particular, and his political writings on sovereign debt crises[28] or international obligations attempted to demonstrate the veracity of his anthropological thesis about the centrality of gift exchanges in the making of war and peace, conflict and order, brutality and civilization.

Whereas Liebersohn's story starts with the British rejection of the model of the gift in nineteenth-century political theory and ends with its return in early twentieth-century Anglophone anthropology,[29] this book starts with Mauss's political and anthropological writings and follows the legacy of this idea in French (or rather, Francophone) political, anthropological, and legal discourses deployed by a wide range of public intellectuals, from French colonial apologists to Third World intellectuals and legal theorists, who wrote about economic cooperation between the North and South in the context of French colonization and decolonization. It thus shares with Liebersohn's a key premise: that Mauss's ideas on the gift were part of a transnational discussion between anthropologists, legal scholars, political theorists, and statesmen on the management of international commercial and financial relations in general, and colonial relations in particular; and at the same time, that it is imperative to capture the association between anthropological, legal, and political ideas in a diachronic perspective, focused in one context (either Anglophone or Francophone), while being attentive to the cross-pollination between the two traditions.

In doing so, the argument intervenes in a growing literature on the place that anthropology and the social sciences have served in the making of colonial rule as well as in the operation of international markets. Within the latter field, since the seminal writings of Tal Asad, Bernard Cohn, and up until the more recent history of anthropological writings and their relation with financial globalization by Marc Flandreau, historians have focused mostly on the Anglophone or German-speaking literature produced in anthropology.[30]

Historians of French anthropology, like Alice Conklin, Benoît de L'estoile, Federico Neiburg, and Lygia Sigaud, to cite just a few, have mostly focused on the relation between colonial administration and the French anthropologists' work in the field of museography, as the latter justified their fact-collecting missions by claiming to help the colonial subjects safeguard a cultural heritage – as in the preparation of the famous 1931 Colonial Exhibition in Paris.[31] But Maussian anthropologists not only helped foster and shape a taste for "the primitive," through their counseling role in the preparation of colonial exhibitions or the private collection of non-Western artifacts, African masks and other fetishes, they also developed a discourse on the power that gift exchanges have to hold societies together. While building on French historians' narratives, this book digs deeper into the history of the discipline of anthropology and its relation with colonial administration. Indeed, it shows how the core of French anthropology's classics – like Mauss's foundational essay *The Gift* – is filled with preoccupations that reflect broader social considerations deeply enmeshed with the politics of European powers inside and outside Europe.

This book thus fills a gap in the history of French anthropology, as it identifies the traces of Mauss's interventions in the political debates of the time, the echoes and discursive shifts, the repetitions and euphemisms, and all other influences that can be traced between Mauss's texts and those of his contemporaries, beyond his immediate community of intimates and colleagues, and across generations, extending for instance to the study of anti-colonial thinkers in the age of independences.[32] In so doing, the book also draws on a series of monographs by French political historians who have explored the trajectories and writings of these intellectuals, academics and legal scholars with whom Mauss interacted.[33] But, strangely enough, most of these historians have left the figure of Mauss outside of their investigation, and thus, have not paid attention to the importance of the model of the gift in the political reflections of Mauss's contemporaries – maybe because, in contrast to Jaurès, Blum, or Thomas, Mauss remained an academic throughout the years, and did not reach commanding positions in any government.

In exploring this link, this book thus unearths important changes in the perceptions of gift exchanges from the prewar to the interwar and the postwar eras, from the question of the Congo to the question of Algeria, and the attempts to decolonize previous models of gift exchange. This deep relation between the model of the gift, the colonial imaginary, and anthropology of "inter-societal" relations may also explain, so I claim here, that these very ties then made some aspects of Mauss's work unacceptable at the time of decolonization, leading his work to be reinterpreted accordingly. If the publication of Mauss's *The Gift* may have signaled the return of the gift, it was also the moment when it reached its zenith, as Mauss's solution to the problem of international order was later discarded by many disciplines, including the adjacent disciplines of economics and international law, at the time of decolonization. Assuming the philosophy of the gift may again come back in the near future, the title of this book could have been "the eclipse of the gift."

This book offers a new interpretation of Marcel Mauss's *The Gift* and of its legacy in the social sciences as well as in international public law and finance – all fields addressing the politics of sovereignty and engaging in debates about global governance. Taken together, the following chapters will portray a very unorthodox picture of the epistemic and political goals that Mauss's model of the gift was meant to achieve. From the 1970s onward, *The Gift* was thus read as providing a universal law explaining how interpersonal and disinterested relations can emerge from the circulation of gifts at the local level,[34] most notably by a Francophone movement of social scientists, economists, sociologists, and anthropologists, who in the early 1980s founded the Mouvement Anti-Utilitariste en sciences sociales (associated around their review MAUSS) devoted to the empirical study of gift-making practices and the history of Mauss's ideas (their production and reception).[35] This book inevitably challenges their interpretations of Mauss's model of the gift, as these social scientists drew from Mauss the idea that even in modern capitalistic economies, pockets of "gift exchange" modeled after noncontractual and non-interested relations (such as the "social economy" and "non-monetized exchange systems")[36] continued to exist, and that they needed to be unearthed and lauded for the good they provided to both local and larger communities.[37] This debate also crossed the Atlantic to the United States, where institutional economists like George Akerloff[38] took inspiration from *The Gift* to theorize about the incompleteness of contracts and the necessity of preserving social relations based on trust in the economic sphere – thanks to the protection of "gift economies" within otherwise distinct "market economies."[39]

Not only were these concerns only secondary (if present at all) to Mauss when he wrote *The Gift*, but my argument also suggests that he may not have been in agreement with the reading that MAUSS and their Anglophone epigones (like bestselling anthropologist David Graeber) made of his text.[40] In fact, this book challenges the notion of the gift economy conceived as a coherent self-enclosed sphere where local economies are ruled by non-market norms, motivations, and mechanisms. In contrast, it claims that Mauss's model of the gift (developed not only in *The Gift* but also in *The Nation* and his political writings) serves to understand heterogeneous systems of international trade and finance which intersect across multiple sovereignties, traversed by various systems of law and varied forms of political sovereignty, in which contracting parties follow self-interested as well as disinterested motivations. As Mauss famously wrote, the gift or the "system of total prestations" is a "total social fact,"[41] which partakes in economic logics as much as it belongs to the realms of law, morality and politics, and whose specificity lies in its hybridity: indeed, the system of "prestations" may be what various political societies can hold in common when they differ in every other respect (law, politics, culture, morality, techniques, etc.).

To understand what his notion of gift exchange truly meant, and why Mauss and some of his students remained obsessed with the question of international solidarity when they promoted the study of gift exchanges, it is necessary to understand how this obsession came to be, and how it can guide our reflections on the contemporary and future organization of international relations in their economic, political, and legal dimensions. These are the key objectives of the following chapters.

2 OVERVIEW OF THE BOOK'S CHAPTERS

After this introduction, Chapter 2 presents the broad methodology, the scope of the analysis, as well as the cast of intellectuals whose writings are surveyed in the other chapters and their overall relations of co-optation, conflict, and competition in the French academic and colonial fields. Methodologically, this book not only seeks to trace the genealogy of theories of gift exchange in anthropological, legal, economic, and political discourses, and to relate the latter with sociological changes affecting the place of anthropology in the French academic field; rather, it also claims to provide some important lessons on how to conduct a historical sociology of intellectual debates from the colonial to the postcolonial contexts. Indeed, it moves beyond a purely intellectual history project by drawing on sociological concepts first operationalized by Christophe Charle and Pierre Bourdieu in the sociology of intellectuals and intellectual fields.[42] Although a classical Bourdieuan field-theoretical approach is useful to characterize how Mauss and his network of peers situated themselves in the French field of power, it shows why it is important to move beyond this purely national perspective and to pay special attention to the transnational ties existing between the colonial and the international fields, as in the neo-Bourdieuan scholarship developed by George Steinmetz.[43]

After surveying the contours of the metropolitan and colonial fields in which Mauss became an important player at the time of the publication of *The Gift*, Chapter 3 then situates Mauss's thinking on the international solidarity created by the exchange of gifts, which he published in *The Gift* in 1925 as part of the 1923–4 volume of *L'Année sociologique*, within the intellectual trajectory of the Durkheimian school of sociology, and the specific understanding of the notion of "solidarity" that it developed in a context in which the notions of European order were deeply questioned. It focuses more specifically on the relation between Mauss's anthropological reflections and his political writings on European financial issues and the question of German reparations in the early 1920s. Indeed, Mauss's essay *The Gift* addressed similar themes as those he discussed with colleagues and friends on the politics of European financial solidarity, sovereign debt cancellation and the question of German reparations paid to the Allies. Mauss was fully involved in the collective effort led by French solidarist thinkers, legal scholars, and politicians who were responsible for inclusion of the reparations provisions in the Versailles Treaty, which tried to settle the peace. In arguing that anthropology shows that the material exchange of gifts has always created a sense of reciprocal obligation among the sovereign parties to the exchange, Mauss proposed a most optimistic vision of the power of gift exchanges to restore European cooperation, financial solidarity and sustainable peace after the traumatic experience of the Great War. Through the accumulation of historical and ethnographic precedents, Mauss's legal anthropology also took a jurisprudential turn, as he sought to convince his readers that the policy of partial sovereign debt cancellation – where the idea of a moratorium on payments figured prominently – which he promoted, was grounded on a vast survey of anthropological facts. Indeed, Mauss made clear both in his 1925 essay and in his political writings of 1922 and 1924 that the Allies needed to give the Germans time to recover economically before they could give back to the neighboring populations who had suffered during the Great War.

In many ways, the story of German reparations and European solidarity proved Marcel Mauss wrong: the exchange of services ("prestations") and goods does not always create a sense of moral obligation and solidarity between the exchanging parties. Even though one could argue that, on the contrary, Mauss's repeated warnings to his contemporaries went unheeded, and the specific rituals he claimed were necessary for this sense of European solidarity to emerge were disregarded many times by the French and German nationalists, Chapter 4 shows that Mauss himself took this political failure as an opportunity to reflect more generally on the conditions that could lead international economic exchanges to either destroy or strengthen moral and political solidarities between sovereign parties. To show how Mauss's earlier reflections on European solidarity were generalized to the broader colonial context, Chapter 4 first explores the range of colonial discourses that emerged before the Great War from within the socialist and solidarist circles in which Mauss participated. It focuses in particular on the criticisms raised against the abuses of the chartered companies in the Congo which were voiced by Mauss's socialist friends in the French national Parliament and by the French Committee for the Protection and Defense of Indigenous Populations (hereafter, the Indigenous Committee), in whose activities Mauss participated in the 1900s. Second, it presents a more reflexive and less-known phase in Mauss's thinking about the power of gifts to foment a sense of "inter-societal"[44] (or international) solidarity in the colonial context. Mauss's publication record suggests that he abandoned his reflections on gift exchange after his 1925 publication of *The Gift*. But now that we can read Mauss's manuscript *The Nation* (which Mauss continued to edit at least until after his election to the Collège de France in 1931, although it remained unpublished in its full version until 2013), thanks to the formidable work of transcription which was conducted by Jean Terrier and Marcel Fournier, we can better understand how Mauss's earlier reflections on solidarity found in *The Gift* related to debates about French interwar colonial policy, in which Mauss also participated by training colonial administrators at his Institute of Ethnology. With his writings and teaching, Mauss presented a coherent research program and a progressive political agenda which moved away from the mercantilist exploitation of the colonies, but which nonetheless participated in solidifying the French administrative and colonial presence overseas thanks to the benevolent management of a "giving" French Empire.

Chapter 5 focuses on the legacy of Mauss's ideas on gift exchange from the colonial context to the postwar struggles of decolonization in Algeria. As Marcel Mauss died in 1950, he did not live to see the limits and subversion of the discourse of gift exchange in colonial administration, and the outcome of the wars of decolonization, marked by two historical turning points: 1954 and the peace between France and (a divided) Vietnam; 1962 and the peace with an independent Algeria. But some of his students did. Two in particular updated their master's reflections on the conditions that could preserve the French imperial solidarity between the metropolis and its overseas territories in the postwar era: Germaine Tillion and Jacques Soustelle. Chapter 5 shows how Mauss's concepts of gift exchange and integration were deployed and reframed by Germaine Tillion and Jacques Soustelle in the Algerian context in a new sense: departing from Mauss's *The Nation*, they proposed that the Algerian territories should remain integrated with the French metropolis in the short and long term, so as to form a new stage of integration beyond the national (and thus purely inter-national) and to allow the exchange of gifts between the metropolis and Algeria to continue for the benefit of both parties. In their view, such consolidation of the economic and financial ties between Algeria and the French metropolis should be guaranteed by a change in the constitutional and political organization of the French Republic itself, so that the two societies could truly merge their institutions in a post-national sovereign Republic. To propose a multicultural, transnational, and postcolonial understanding of integration was a radical departure from the creation of a society of independent nations, which had been the League of Nation's objective in the interwar period and the goal that Mauss espoused.

Chapter 5 also explains why a new generation of anti-colonial anthropologists who came of age in the Algerian field of power during the Algerian war reacted so strongly against the normative use of the idea of gift exchange by older colonial administrators and anthropologists to argue in favor of the continued French presence overseas in debates on global governance. If Soustelle managed to impulse a highly unlikely constitutional reform when de Gaulle came back to power and tasked Soustelle with writing the Constitution of the Fifth French Republic, his writings on gift exchange in the context of the Algerian War lead to a counter-attack by liberal political scientists, who asked the French metropolis to stop framing the colonial and Algerian issues in terms of gift exchange, and to redirect trade and investments away from Algeria, in accordance to purely market-based criteria. The model of gift exchange not only came under attack from metropolitan political scientists, but also from ethnologists like Pierre Bourdieu, who criticized Soustelle's language of generosity and transnational gift exchange between the metropolis and Algeria as a kind of deceitful rhetoric meant to hide the reality of colonial relations marked by a century-long process of acculturation, alienation, and exploitation. With Bourdieu's writings on Algeria, anthropologists of gift exchanges left the terrain of the politics of global governance and sovereignty (to the benefit of international law scholars) and turned to the practices they characterized as gift exchanges at the local level. The anthropology of the gift, which had been intricately linked to the defense of the French colonial destiny, was thus invested with new meanings, and relocated at the local rather than international level in order to survive as a legitimate epistemic model for anthropologists, sociologists, and ethnographers.

If the international and transnational dimensions of solidarity created by the exchange of gifts were evacuated from the discourse of French anthropology shortly before Algeria's independence, Chapter 6 shows how international public law further distanced its normative ideals from the model of gift exchange in the postcolonial context. The strong normative implication of the discourses praising gift exchanges in the context of French colonial rule, which anthropologists and colonial administrators had developed from the 1920s to the 1960s, led to their rejection by "Third World"[45] foreign policy elites and international public lawyers in the context of the financial and economic dimensions of state "succession" entailed in the transitions from colonial empires to newly independent states. Chapter 6 traces that process by analyzing how Algerian intellectuals formed in France when the debate about decolonization was raging, argued with and against Soustelle's theory of postcolonial integration to criticize the policy of bilateral "cooperation" between the former colonial power and the newly independent states which the French state wanted to impose on its former dominions in Africa after 1962. Chapter 6 focuses on the trajectory of Algeria's foremost foreign policy architect and prominent international law scholar, Mohammed Bedjaoui, and his struggle in favor of the establishment of the NIEO, which included, but was not limited to, the repudiation by newly independent nations of all debts they may have contracted during colonial times. In contrast to other histories of the NIEO, which focus on the writings of Anglophone authors,[46] this chapter traces back the intellectual origins of the NIEO to the Francophone interwar context and the debates on gift exchange which opposed colonial administrators, anthropologists, and economists in the Algerian and metropolitan fields of power. It explains the intellectual and political origins of the Algerian rebellion against the continuation of privileged "cooperation" between former metropolises and colonies, by surveying the work of these Algerian diplomats who promoted the NIEO and advocated the globalization of gift exchanges through "global negotiations" (on oil exchange and debt relief for instance) between North and South, in an attempt to "decolonize" Mauss's model of the gift.

Still, the efforts of the promoters of the NIEO to give a new global validity to Mauss's model of the gift were dashed by the advent of neoliberalism and the deregulation of markets it imposed. The latter eventually marked the downfall of the gift ideology as a principle of global economic governance. Chapter 7 draws some conclusions by highlighting the role of broader changes in the global governance architecture associated with neoliberalism, which may explain why Mauss's original fixation on the problems of colonial trade and European financial solidarity were lost to future generations of anthropologists and economists after the collapse of the Bretton Woods system and the transition to a world of fluctuating market-based parities between currencies after President Nixon decided to let the dollar float in 1973. Indeed, Mauss's analysis of the role of gift exchanges made sense mostly within a system where states were formally in full control of exchange parities, and where the currencies were indexed on the price of gold. In a world in which speculative market logics were introduced in the heart of financial statecraft and policymaking, Mauss's analysis of gift-making practices by state representatives no longer made sense in any useful way.

Thus, we can explain why Mauss's reflections on gift exchange are no longer associated with his broader thoughts on the origins of international solidarity, and the interwar disputes about colonial governance. There are, of course, explanations of the misinterpretations that crowd the history of *The Gift* that pertain to the logics of the French academic field more narrowly conceived: misinterpretation from one generation to the next is not a surprise in the French academic scene, where many ambitious young men ritualistically claim a founding father as the precursor to their own theory, at the same time as they kill the adopted ancestor through disfigurement and misrepresentation.[47] In this case, the reasons for the collective amnesia are deeper: when conventional market logics came to dominate all international economic relations in the late 1970s, thus putting an end to the glorification of gift exchange, it was no longer illogical to consider that Mauss's primary relevance to the problems of the time was to help anthropologists and economists distinguish between different kinds of market logics (socially embedded logics vs. speculative and antagonistic logics).[48] Thus, this chapter situates the reasons for the loss of relevance of Mauss's ideas on international gift exchange and global governance in the creation of the new international financial order of the neoliberal globalizing world. It also explains why these reflections on gift exchange have never been as relevant as they are today for our reflection on the future of political, legal, and financial relations in Europe, after the successive financial crises which have affected the eurozone since 2008.

2

The Cast

Marcel Mauss and His Legacy in the French Fields of Power

Many commentators of *The Gift* have found the objectives that Mauss sought to accomplish with this publication hard to fathom. In fact, to understand the constellation of meanings surrounding this obscure text, we have to situate it in its proper socio-political context: the author was Marcel Mauss; the publication outlet was a sociology journal called *L'Année sociologique*; the year of publication was 1925; and the city in which it was published was Paris. All of these four markers are important to better understand which goals Mauss sought to accomplish with this publication.

This chapter thus first reviews the situation of Mauss relative to his immediate circles of interpersonal relations at the time he published *The Gift*, before taking a higher-level perspective, by describing the logics of the French fields of power in the interwar period. Indeed, this chapter shows that, although a classical Bourdieuan field-theoretical approach to intellectual fields is useful to characterize how Mauss and his peers situated themselves in the French field of power, it is also key to situate them at the intersection of the colonial and the metropolitan fields, whose tensions and conflicts determined how *The Gift* was later received.[1]

1 SITUATING THE GIFT IN ITS IMMEDIATE CONTEXT OF RECEPTION

The Gift was the product of an accomplished and still rising institution-builder, Marcel Mauss, who benefited, in the words of Pierre Bourdieu,[2] from the right type of social capital – economic capital recycled into academic and intellectual capital thanks to his uncle's mentorship. In 1925, his centrality in the academic field was no longer contested either inside or outside France, especially in the Anglo-American academic worlds. His discipline was in a period of exceptional growth, which resulted both from external political factors – the expansion of the French Empire as a result of the 1919 peace of Versailles – and more local factors – the infatuation of Parisian art collectors for "primitive" fetishes. Mauss was part of these multiple circles which overlapped and accumulated over the years (see Figure 1): the worlds of socialists that agitated the Latin Quarter during the time of the Dreyfus affair, the

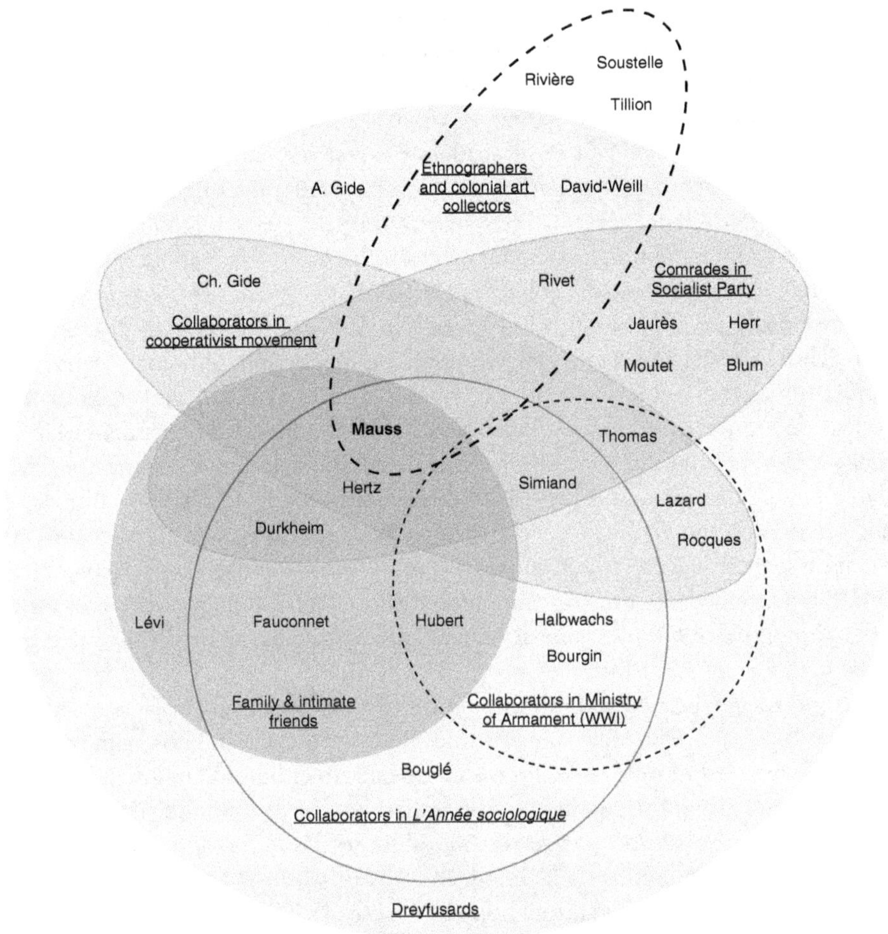

FIGURE 1 Marcel Mauss's circles of friends and collaborators

policymakers and industrial planners during the war, the elites from high finance who were involved in international financial negotiation during the German reparations debate, as well as the colonial administrators and beneficiaries of the colonial expansion who gathered important artistic collections in the interwar period. These partially overlapping circles constituted the readership that Mauss targeted with his polemical essay on the nature of the gift.

In order to better understand the goals that Mauss sought to accomplish with the publication of *The Gift*, let us start with the first marker: the author. Marcel Mauss was born on May 10, 1872 to a Jewish family which had lived in Alsace-Lorraine, the most eastern part of France, until his father moved to the small town of Epinal (situated in Moselle, France) in order to keep his family French, as Alsace and

Lorraine had been annexed by the German Reich after the defeat of the Second Empire of Louis-Napoleon Bonaparte in early 1871. Marcel's father died at an early age, leaving the young Mauss to become a "rich young man,"[3] as his uncle, the sociologist Emile Durkheim (1858–1917), wrote to Mauss (his elder sister's child).

To sum up Mauss's education and academic career very succinctly: at 21, he came to Bordeaux to prepare the *agrégation* of philosophy under the tutelage of his uncle, Emile Durkheim – who, being his elder by only fourteen years, was halfway between an uncle and an older brother – and he successfully passed this competitive exam in 1895. Then, in contrast to some of his friends, like Paul Fauconnet (1874–1938), who became a professor of philosophy in a French *lycée*, Mauss enrolled in PhD studies with Sylvain Lévi (1863–1938), an eminent Indologist and philologist who was a professor at the École Pratique des Hautes Etudes (EPHE) and then at the Collège de France, and who developed a particular fondness for his student Marcel Mauss.[4] Although he did not complete his dissertation on prayer, thanks to Lévi, Mauss found a lecturing position at the EPHE in 1901 to teach "The history of religion among non-civilized peoples." With the interruption of the Great War, which he spent as a translator in the British army, Mauss continued to teach at the EPHE, but also became the Director of the Institute of Ethnology (created in 1926) at the Sorbonne, and in 1931, after several unsuccessful bids, he finally obtained the "chair of sociology" – the first one ever created – at the Collège de France. He taught there until 1940, when he was put into retirement two years early as a result of the anti-Jewish laws passed by the Vichy regime. He spent the war in Paris, with his wife (whom he married in 1934, but with whom he had no children), and died in 1950.

The second part of the equation is also important: the journal in which *The Gift* was published, *L'Année sociologique* (*L'Année*). Indeed, *L'Année* gives an indication of the first circle of scholars and intellectuals with whom Mauss interacted (see Figure 1), whom he impacted throughout the course of his life. Emile Durkheim was teaching in Bordeaux in 1898 when he founded *L'Année*, a biannual review which published mostly book reviews surveying the most recent works in German, American, British, and French sociology, history, and anthropology, as well as a few long essays – like the one Mauss wrote with his friend Henri Hubert titled "The Nature and Function of Sacrifice,"[5] or *The Gift*. The scarcity of the essays published in *L'Année*, coupled with the international diversity of the books that were reviewed, certainly played a key role in the wide reception granted to *The Gift* in the Anglophone world. Indeed, many prestigious authors, like James Frazer (1854–1941), the famous author of *The Golden Bough*,[6] whom Mauss had met and befriended in Oxford in 1898,[7] eagerly expected to receive their copy of *L'Année* to read their own book's review: what author would not want to have his book reviewed by young talented Frenchmen who also fought for progressive intellectual causes? As they focused their editorial efforts on producing many book reviews – long before the *London* or *New York Review of Books* obtained the recognition they have today – Durkheim and Mauss not only turned *L'Année* into a formidable vitrine for Anglo-

American intellectual production in France, but they were also able to present the French "school of sociology" to the outside world – especially the Anglo-American worlds.

Mauss's essays were given particular attention as he played a leading role in the editorial team. First, although his uncle was critical of Mauss's versatility, which had prevented him from writing a single-authored monograph before the First World War, Mauss wrote about 2,500 pages out of the 11,000 pages that were published in *L'Année* before the war – almost a fourth of the contributions.[8] Second, Durkheim relied on his nephew to recruit young progressive Parisian intellectuals attracted by sociology to write for *L'Année*. Young French academic talent could be found, then as well as now, at the *École Normale Supérieure* (ENS), and although not a graduate of the ENS himself, Mauss befriended most of the young ENS students during the Dreyfus affair (see Figure 1). The students had publicly asked for the revision of the trial of Captain Dreyfus: a Jewish officer from the same eastern part of France as Mauss, who was declared a traitor and sent to a labor camp by a military tribunal with almost no evidence (and which eventually turned out to be based on forgeries). Although Mauss was on a study trip abroad – first in Oxford and then in the Netherlands, before he returned to take (and then teach) classes at the EPHE in Paris – when the Dreyfus affair broke out,[9] when he came back, he met most of the most ardent Dreyfusard intellectuals; he participated in many of their initiatives[10] and he enrolled most of them in *L'Année*.[11]

Among these Dreyfusard intellectuals whose writings or personal papers I have surveyed to research this book, we can cite: Albert Thomas (1878–1932), a star student of the ENS who was convinced by the famous librarian of the ENS, Lucien Herr (1864–1926, whom Durkheim had befriended in 1883),[12] to join the Dreyfusards, and who would later have a strong influence on the group, in particular during the First World War when he became Minister of the Armament and enrolled the whole editorial team of *L'Année* to work on the war preparation effort. François Simiand (1873–1935) was a philosophy student at the ENS who turned to the analysis of law, society, and economics under the influence of Durkheim and who soon joined the editorial team of *L'Année* in charge of socioeconomic questions, before becoming, according to Mauss, the "intellectual master"[13] of his Minister Albert Thomas during the Great War.[14]

Henri Hubert (1872–1927) was another ENS graduate and laureate of the *agrégation* of history, whom Mauss met when the two attended Sylvain Lévi's class at the EPHE,[15] and whose common fight for Dreyfus led Durkheim to call him a "family member"[16] – he would later become first the assistant to, and then the curator of, the Museum of Archeology of Saint-Germain-en-Laye. Like Simiand, Hubert spent the war planning industrial defense preparedness, with a specialization on the production of tanks, and later remained in close contact with Thomas, establishing connections and exchanging ideas between the latter and Mauss.[17]

Not all the ENS students who worked for *L'Année* were close to Mauss: some kept their distance from his overbearing presence, like Célestin Bouglé (1870–1940), who first conceived the project of creating *L'Année*[18] and who founded and directed the Center of social documentation at the library of the ENS. From there, he had a strong influence on the next generation of anthropologists, like Claude Lévi-Strauss, and sociologists, like Mauss's younger cousin Raymond Aron (1905–83), who worked for Bouglé in the 1930s. Maurice Halbwachs (1877–1945) was another ENS student who had fallen into Durkheim's orbit, but not under Mauss's influence. Halbwachs defended a dissertation on housing expropriation practices in Paris, at the same time as he developed a Durkheimian sociology of the working class – before entering the Ministry of Armament under Albert Thomas from 1915 to 1917.[19] During the interwar period he turned to topics involving collective memory[20] while teaching in the newly liberated University of Strasbourg (in Alsace).[21] Hubert Bourgin (1874–1955) was yet another ENS student who had met Thomas and Mauss when they fought for Dreyfus, and also spent the war in the Ministry of Armament.[22] These were the men who worked to establish *L'Année*.

During the Dreyfus affair, this group of politicians, professors, and students multiplied initiatives in the field of publishing and continued education for workers of the Latin Quarter where they studied and taught: they created the Société nouvelle de librairie Bellais where they diffused many tracts on socialism and socialist cooperatives; they created the École Socialiste in the Latin Quarter[23] and the Bourse du travail des cours sur le mouvement syndical, which they put in motion from 1898 to 1910. Mauss even attempted to develop joint actions with socialist and non-socialist cooperatives, the latter led by the legal scholar and political economist Charles Gide (1847–1932) – the uncle of André Gide (1869–1951), the famous gay novelist and leading editor who received the Nobel Prize in literature in 1947. Charles Gide was a lawyer by training but also a professor of political economy who would be elected in 1923 to the first chair in cooperative studies created at the Collège de France – and who would later help Mauss get elected to the same prestigious institution. Before the Great War, Charles Gide helped non-socialist cooperatives successfully merge at the European level with the socialist cooperatives coordinated by Mauss,[24] and after the Great War, Mauss and Charles Gide crossed paths again, when Gide acted as France's representative to the Reparations Commission, while Mauss was an editor of the socialist journal *Le Populaire*, who wrote on the issue of German reparations, as I will explain in the next chapter.[25]

For a short period, the famous poet, editorialist, and pamphleteer Charles Péguy (1873–1914) joined these young progressive intellectuals, but he soon left the Librairie Bellais after a political and personal disagreement with Mauss and Herr – other sentimental reasons might have been at play, as Péguy later regretted that he could no longer see the young Mauss, whose "elegance and carnation were the dream of [his] sleepless nights, the image of [his] feverish desires."[26]

The fashionably dressed dandy whose dissolute life was seriously judged by his uncle Durkheim,[27] Mauss made quite an impression on his fellow comrades. In addition to being a young professor at EPHE, he was thus what we would call today an energetic "community organizer," although one who preferred to coordinate cooperatives across regions and even countries from his base in the Latin Quarter, rather than one who spent time in the South Side of Chicago.

Now, and third, the year of publication of *The Gift* is also important: 1925. In the small intellectual Parisian milieu, 1925 differed from the prewar years in important respects. By that time, the Great War had taken its toll on Mauss's generation, and the Third International had split the international socialist movement in two, leaving on one side those who believed in a reformist strategy whereby social change would be accomplished within the existing constitutional framework (thanks to elections); and on the other side, those who followed Lenin and wanted to export the Soviet Revolution to the whole world.

Before the war, Mauss had been a fellow traveler of the French socialist party founded by Durkheim's friend, Jean Jaurès (1859–1914), whom Durkheim had met when Jaurès was a student at the ENS, where Durkheim prepared for the *agrégation* in philosophy. Mauss had met Jaurès first in Bordeaux, thanks to Durkheim, and then again during the Dreyfus affair.[28] The two men met with a former student of the ENS, Léon Blum (1872–1950), by then a young rapporteur at the Conseil d'Etat (the highest court in administrative law) who wrote the legal defense of Emile Zola when the latter was attacked for libel after publishing his famous Dreyfusard article "J'accuse . . . !"[29] Mauss later contributed (with Jaurès) to the creation of the journal *L'Humanité*, and from the beginning sat on its board of trustees as one of two representatives of the new political party, the "Section Française de l'Internationale Ouvrière" (SFIO), created by Jaurès in 1905 (see Figure 1).[30] These socialists had deep ties to the ENS,[31] leading French historians of the socialist movement in France to call their form of socialism "*socialisme normalien*":[32] even Blum had been admitted to the ENS before being expelled for poor attendance, distracted by his high school best friend André Gide, with whom Blum conducted his poetic and literary endeavors before turning to politics.[33]

If effervescence characterized the early years of the twentieth century for these young French socialists, the early 1920s were very different from the prewar decade: when Mauss published *The Gift* in 1925, he was 53, no longer a young man. In fact, the war had turned him into the dean of the Durkheimian school of sociology, as most of the prewar collaborators of *L'Année sociologique* had died or had left academia. Jean Jaurès was the first French casualty of the war: he was assassinated by a young nationalist a few days before the war broke out, as he was on his way to write an op-ed in *L'Humanité* in which he planned to defend the cause of peace and call on European socialist parties to unite against the coming war. To cite just a few others, we can mention Mauss's cousin and Emile Durkheim's son, André Durkheim (1892–1915), in whom the elder Durkheim had placed his hopes for an intellectual heir, and who was soon joined in death by his father who died of grief in 1917; or Robert Hertz (1881–1915), who was one of Mauss's best friends among the collaborators of *L'Année*, and was killed in Verdun. Hertz had been one of the ardent figures of *socialisme normalien* and like Mauss before him,[34] he had gone to study the anthropological school in the United Kingdom – the British later recognized him, through the voice of Edward Evans-Pritchard (1902–73), as the next Durkheim.[35] He was gone too.

With the Great War not only did many collaborators of *L'Année* disappear, but some dreams associated with their cooperativist utopia also died. The utopia they had pursued before the war was strongly influenced by the ideology of "solidarism," which was developed by a nebula of jurists and legal scholars interested in the notions of solidarity, debt and contract, in which, indeed, one could count Durkheim and Charles Gide,[36] but in which Léon Bourgeois (1851–1925) was the most prominent and influential intellectual at the time: Bourgeois was a lawyer by training, an essayist, and the founder of the "Radical Socialist" Party, who became the head of the French government in 1895 – a position he kept only for a short period of time, due to parliamentary opposition to his attempt to pass a progressive income tax (finally created during the Great War). Bourgeois was influential in late nineteenth-century France for diffusing the notion that every individual was born with a "social debt" which they needed to pay back in order to maintain the existence of the social bonds (or solidarity) between individuals of the same nation. Such a moral and social philosophy, expressed in simple terms, asked those who had received more to give back more to society than those who had received less. This principle may seem self-evident now, but it was not so at the time: remember that Bourgeois's government fell after parliamentary opposition against his proposal to introduce progressive income tax – something that is widely accepted today. After the war, Bourgeois was nominated to be the first President of the League of Nations in 1919 after a long-lasting effort in favor of obligatory arbitration of interstate conflicts in the Hague conferences, an activity for which he received the Nobel Peace Prize in 1920, even though some could have argued that the Great War had precisely proven that arbitration was not binding enough to stop conflicts from escalating.

As Mauss was involved in the socialist party created by Durkheim's friend Jean Jaurès rather than in Bourgeois's radical party, claims that his intellectual agenda reflected a solidarist inspiration may look like an oddity. But solidarism worked as a loose ideology before the Great War,[37] and as Marcel Prélot writes, Jaurès' socialism, and that of the generation he inspired, was a "quasi-solidarism"[38] – just as the solidarist position of Charles Gide was "quasi-socialism," if socialism, as envisioned by Emile Durkheim, was a "tendency to organize" relations between individuals, firms, contractual partners, and other forms of modern beings associated with the industrial life under the democratic rule of law.[39]

Furthermore, the socialists and solidarists argued ardently that the cause of peace in Europe was their main priority: they planned to avert a war in Europe by uniting workers across borders and by calling for a general transborder strike of workers in case of an imminent risk of war in Europe. For instance, the French socialists sent a delegation of the Parliamentary Group for Arbitration to Bern, Switzerland, in May 1913 for a conference on Franco-German entente,[40] which included important socialist figures like Jean Jaurès and Marcel Sembat (1862–1922) – a close friend of Marcel Mauss and Bronislaw Malinowski,[41] who wrote on international affairs for *L'Humanité* before becoming the Minister of Public Work during the war with Léon Blum as his chief of staff.[42] For them, international solidarity between European nations was of higher value than a global communist revolution: at least, that is what French socialists believed until Jaurès's assassination, which, on the eve of the war, was the electroshock that woke them up from their dogmatic dreams.

Mauss's prewar actions as a public intellectual had been in fact characteristic of this broad solidarist philosophy. For a decade before the Great War, Mauss defended the cause of European solidarity by intervening in the European "cooperativist" movement, which mushroomed outside the party system and outside the state's purview to challenge a strict understanding of market operations. These cooperatives abided by a notion of solidarity which was conceived in terms very close to Léon Bourgeois's normative (and utterly positive) understanding of social solidarity and anchored on such legal notions as the "quasi-contract":[43] solidarity was made manifest by an active mutualization of wealth, contracts, and duties in the sphere of exchange (rather than that of production) by the social groups themselves.[44] By forming cooperatives in independence from their state's diktats, individuals found a way to express their solidarity against the disaggregating forces of contemporary markets. As Bouglé later wrote, in this conception of solidarity, individuals consider that "the State stops being the lawgiver who brings the tables of the law from some distant Sinaï: it is in the river of everyday life, in the current of private law, that the State finds its reason to intervene."[45]

The primary purpose of the cooperativists whom Mauss represented was thus not to appropriate the means of production and challenge the state's authority, which is why Marxists and socialists like Mauss clashed on the value of cooperation for the workers' cause. The Marxist parties – one of which was headed by Karl Marx's son-in-law, Paul Lafargue (1842–1911), whom Mauss confronted directly[46] – prioritized the goal of bringing down the capitalist system in France, and Germany over all other objectives. Whereas Mauss defended the multiplication of consumer cooperatives, or wholesales, the orthodox Marxists condemned these cooperatives for delaying the coming revolution by allowing workers to collectively bargain cheaper prices.[47] Mauss defended wholesales and cooperatives of workers for exactly the same reason: workers benefited from higher living standards by reducing their costs of living and mutualizing resources against the risks of modern life (work accidents, early death due to poor health in urban centers, unemployment, etc.). Furthermore, by participating in cooperatives, workers developed international ties with other cooperatives in Europe, which helped them create solidarities across national boundaries and in relative autonomy from their state's purview.[48]

But even if Marxists and non-Marxist socialists clashed before the war, the SFIO had managed to keep various socialist families together before 1914. With the proof that pan-European workers' movements had failed to stop the war, and with the Bolshevik Revolution of 1917, the split between Marxists and non-Marxists in the French socialist movement was made official and irreversible – at least until the mid 1970s. In 1920, the prewar SFIO was split as a direct result of the Bolshevik Revolution, and more than half of the socialist party left to form the French Communist party and took with them Jaurès and Mauss's old journal *L'Humanité* in their suitcases. Thus, the leading post-1920 intellectuals of the remaining SFIO, Blum and Mauss, kept the keys of the old SFIO and took over another much smaller socialist journal, *Le Populaire*, to express their minority views on international politics and the need to counter the Soviet Revolution: this journal was partially funded by Blum, Belgian cooperatives, and private donors, and issued 2,225 copies a day when it was first published in April 1921, in contrast to *L'Humanité*, which issued 200,000 copies a day in 1920.[49] As far as Mauss was concerned, he still believed in the solidarist notions of solidarity, quasi-contracts or tacit contracts, which not only found their way into his scientific essays, like *The Gift*, but also infiltrated his political writings, as in Mauss's 1924 essay on Bolshevism, in which he criticized the lack of Soviet recognition for the existence of "tacit international contracts"[50] between nations bound by debt relations, but he no longer represented the majority view in the left wing of the political spectrum. Thus, the year 1925 marked a time of maturity for Mauss, if maturity can be signaled by the proliferation of younger intellectuals expressing views more radical than one's own on the main problems of the time.

Fourth, and last, Paris was the place of publication of *The Gift*. Paris had recently been the center of the world, as the diplomatic negotiations that settled the Great War had taken place there for more than a year. In the mid 1920s, it remained a city of contrasts: it was the capital of an ailing nation, which depended on German reparations to reconstruct the villages and industrial plants destroyed by the war in the former fighting zone; but it was also the capital of booming empire, with newly gained colonies from the Germans – in Togoland and Cameroon – and a new zeal for large-scale ethnographic explorations of the ethnically diverse populations living in its colonies. Paris was becoming the city of the Colonial Exhibitions, of the new artistic movements, with the excitement for the new "Negro art," which first attracted the small group of artists, collectors, anthropologists, and curators gathered around Mauss and Paul Rivet (1876–1958) – a doctor and ethnographer who specialized in South America, Rivet was assistant curator at the Museum of Natural History in

1925, but was soon selected to be the director of the Museum of Ethnology of the Trocadero in 1928 (which became the Musée de l'Homme in 1937).

Mauss was a direct witness, if not a player, in this artistic revolution. The bridge between the academic and artistic worlds and the world of collectors was facilitated by Rivet's assistant at the Museum of Ethnology: Georges-Henri Rivière (1897–1985). Rivière, on top of his job at the Museum of Ethnology,[51] was also the private adviser of David David-Weill (1872–1951), the director and heir of the Lazard Frères bank in Paris, whose immense wealth was put to the service of art collection, which he donated generously to many Parisian museums (like the Museum Guimet on South Asian art).[52] Thanks to these political, academic, and aesthetic transformations in Parisian life, Mauss's reflections on gift exchange inspired intellectuals and politicians beyond the first circle of socialist and Dreyfusard thinkers with whom he crossed paths before the war. In the mid 1920s, Mauss became actively involved in the institutionalization of ethnology in Paris, at the nexus between academia and French colonial administration. The young ethnologists who worked at the Museum of Ethnology were formed at Mauss's newly founded Institute of Ethnology in Paris, which finally came into being in 1926 with Mauss and Rivet as its two secretary-generals (see Figure 1).

The creation of the Institute of Ethnology in 1926 allowed ethnologists to serve as a bridge between the aging generation of colonial administrators and reformers to the newcomers in the field of colonial administration. The management of the Institute gathered many eminent scientists, most of whom were well doted in colonial capital: it was codirected by Marcel Mauss, with Paul Rivet and Lucien Levy-Bruhl (1857–1939), a cousin of Alfred Dreyfus, who had befriended both Durkheim and Jaurès at the ENS. But it also comprised colonial administrators, especially in the Council of the Institute, which included prestigious professors at the Collège de France, like Louis Finot (1864–1935), a close friend of Sylvain Lévi, who directed the French School of the Far East (EFEO), one of the most important institutions for the colonial administration of Indochina, and Colonial Governors, like Maurice Delafosse (1870–1926), who also taught at the Colonial School.[53]

At the Institute of Ethnology, and then at the Museum, Mauss's students learned how to collect, identify, date, classify, and display the artifacts and fetishes they brought back from their ethnological missions, and they mingled with the art collectors of the worlds of high finance, like the Rothschilds and Lazards, who funded their missions abroad. Rivière, whose sister later conducted ethnographies in Algeria[54] with Mauss's doctoral student Germaine Tillion (1907–2008), organized more than 60 exhibitions at the Museum in less than a decade, some with Mauss's students, like the South Americanist Alfred Métraux (1902–63), or the Maya specialist Jacques Soustelle (1912–90) – who replaced Rivière as assistant to Rivet in 1937 when Rivière became the director of the Museum of Popular Arts and Traditions. Soustelle was also a graduate of the ENS and among the most talented of Mauss's PhD students.

This Parisian collaboration, which was based on the exchange of gifts between art collectors, ethnologists, and curators, was fruitful for all. Without it, Mauss's famous essay might never have been published, as it was thanks to a generous gift by David David-Weill that Mauss published the 1925 volume of *L'Année sociologique* – the first one published since the end of the war – in which *The Gift* was printed. David-Weill and other art collectors also funded many of the big ethnographic missions pushed forward by Mauss, like the Dakar-Djibouti Mission (1931–33) led by Marcel Griaule (1898–1956), another of Mauss's PhD students who toured French Africa from West to East in search of all the artifacts he could put his hands on.[55] For Mauss, this was a new world, well suited with his Parisian dandyism, full of energy and optimism for the possibilities offered to French ethnology by the French imperial expansion.

2 MAUSS'S RELATIVE MARGINALITY IN THE FRENCH METROPOLITAN FIELD OF POWER

To move beyond the immediate circle of colleagues and friends whom Mauss targeted with the publication of *The Gift*, and to view the development of their ideas from a higher viewpoint, it makes the most sense to draw on the field-theoretical approach first developed by Christophe Charle and Pierre Bourdieu in the sociology of intellectuals and intellectual fields. Armed with their concepts, we can study how such a publication as *The Gift* helped Mauss redraw social boundaries between disciplines in the French academic field; and which resources and forms of capital circulated in the academic field at the critical time when the disciplines of anthropology and ethnology were becoming institutionalized under Mauss's leadership.[56]

It is remarkable how much the anthropologists, economists and international law scholars who developed Mauss's ideas on gift exchange and who were part of the overlapping circles already described looked alike in terms of their social capital: most of them were men – until Mauss's students, indeed all of them were men – often from a bourgeois or at least urban background, and they graduated from the top French public schools like the ENS. Furthermore, they most often represented a subcategory of elites whom Pierre Bourdieu, drawing on the sociology of religion, has called the "heresiarchs":[57] those elites with enough social capital to reach the top echelons of state power, but still not quite to the top, as one key dimension of their identity kept them in a situation of vulnerability.

Most of Mauss's peers (as cited in Figure 1) were indeed religious minorities, like the Gides (uncle and nephew, both Protestant), or Durkheim, Blum, Lazard, and Mauss, who were all well assimilated Jews or "*Juif d'Etat*"[58] as Pierre Birnbaum has called these "secularized Jews devoted to the public service of their country who . . . identified completely with the laic universalism of the modern French state,"[59] and who attained positions as high civil servants. Their sense of attachment to the elite was fragile, as they knew their standing in the circles of state insiders could be subject to the moods and whims of the long-established Catholic or aristocratic elites who sometimes allied with the mobs to threaten these newcomers. When they did rise to the top, as Léon Blum did in 1936, when he became the head of the French government as the leader of the Front populaire party coalition, they were still vulnerable to the attacks of both mobs and political–administrative elites: in February 1936, Blum survived a lynching when his car got stuck in a nationalist protest, and immediately after his election, he was attacked in the French Parliament by right-wing parliamentarians for being the first Jew elected as the leader of the French government. In 1940, the Vichy government arrested him and put him on trial for treason, before turning him over to the Nazi authorities at the end of the war – which he miraculously also survived, when his group of political hostages deported to Buchenwald was freed by the Allies.[60]

To give another illustration, one can cite Mauss's friend, Max Lazard (1875–1953), whom he also thanked for a generous gift toward publication in the volume of *L'Année sociologique* in which *The Gift* was published.[61] As in the case of Mauss's trajectory, it is clear that Max Lazard's career was largely determined by the quantity and quality of social capital he received at birth: he was the son of Simon Lazard, one of the founders of the Paris bank Lazard Frères, and the cousin of David David-Weill, who managed the affairs of the Paris branch during the interwar period (see Figure 1). Marcel Mauss and Max Lazard's professional development ran along parallel courses, accounted for by a common social background. Both came from Jewish families from Alsace-Lorraine; they were deeply patriotic and attached to the French Republic at the same time as they were very much open to the British and US academic worlds (something not taken for granted at a time when German academia entertained a strong attraction among French colleagues); they fought for Dreyfus's rehabilitation and conceived it to be their duty to intervene in public debates as experts with knowledge grounded in their discipline; they had key access to insider knowledge thanks to their network of peers as well as their social and family relations. Still, Mauss and Lazard made different choices, and their endowment in terms of economic, social, and cultural capital may account for such differences. Max Lazard did not follow an ambitious uncle in Bordeaux, but found his way to New York thanks to the generous help of his father and uncle's business partners, where he completed a PhD on economic cycles causing unemployment at Columbia University.[62] Later, like many of Mauss's friends and peers, he entered Albert Thomas's cabinet at the Ministry of Armament and then followed Thomas to Geneva when Thomas became the head of the newly created International Labor Organization (ILO).

One of Marcel Mauss's PhD students, Jacques Soustelle, aptly expressed the feeling of vulnerability – or fragile legitimacy – which many of these men felt based on their religious, or rather ethnic, affiliation (as religion was also ethnicity in France): as a Protestant growing up near Lyon, Soustelle read the history of the

Reformation when he was 10 and thus learned very early on "that [he] belonged to a minority, that France was his nation [*patrie*] and that French was his language, but that the French state had often been their enemy."[63] Very few among Mauss's close circle of friends did not have dramatic firsthand experience of this enmity of the French state during the course of their life. For Mauss's generation, first came the Dreyfus affair, when anti-Semitism was ardently fought for in the nationalist press and in the courtrooms. Then came the Vichy regime, which first downgraded the civic rights of Jews, and then actively participated in organizing their extermination during the Nazi occupation. The Second World War in particular took a strong toll within Mauss's circle of colleagues for the precise reason that many of them belonged to religious minorities, especially Jews: most importantly, ten anthropologists who were members of the Musée de l'Homme group, one of the first Resistance groups created in occupied France in 1940, were arrested and executed by the Nazis in 1942: Anatole Lewitsky, Boris Vildé, Léon-Maurice Nordmann, Georges Ithier, Jules Andrieu, René Sénéchal, and Pierre Walter; only Yvonne Odon and Georges-Henri Rivière survived. For her part, Germaine Tillion, another of Mauss's PhD students, joined the group upon her return from Algeria to Paris in 1940 – she was arrested with her mother in 1942 and deported to Ravensbruck (where her mother died),[64] and from where she survived to publish the first ethnographic analysis of the concentration camp system. Paul Rivet, who, as director of the Musée de l'Homme, shared responsibilities in the group, survived the chase by the Nazis thanks to his exile in Colombia and then Mexico, where his former assistant Jacques Soustelle brought him to participate in the activities of the Free France until his return to Paris in 1945.[65] Although not Jewish himself, Maurice Halbwachs was killed by the Nazis in the Buchenwald concentration camp in March 1945, after being arrested for harboring his son (who committed acts of resistance and was Jewish according to the Nazis, since his mother was).

Mauss himself survived the Nazi occupation, even living in the occupied zone, without experiencing deportation, which in itself was an oddity: Marcel Fournier, Mauss's biographer, believes that Mauss benefited from the active protection of either German anthropologists, who appreciated his work on the Germanic tribes and the Celts, or that of the Minister of Labor and Cooperation in the Vichy government, Marcel Déat (1894–1955), who had worked with Lucien Herr and Célestin Bouglé at the library of the ENS before adhering to Blum's SFIO, before creating a new party representing "neo-socialists," with the active support of Mauss.[66] Still, although Mauss was neither assassinated nor deported by the Nazis, he suffered tremendously from the war years, as did his close entourage: with the first decrees passed by the Vichy government and the Nazis in the occupied zone, he was forbidden from teaching either at the Collège de France or at the Institute of Ethnology, and had to resign from all his functions; later he even had to leave his apartment when it was requisitioned by the Nazis.

As the following chapters will detail, a concern for the perils and dangers looming over the head of Mauss and his immediate circle of friends was never absent from Mauss's mind, and manifested itself in more minor publications at the time he wrote *The Gift*: although anti-Semitism was not explicitly mentioned in Mauss's essay, and contemporary readers would be hard pressed to find any suggestions that the selection of cases of gift exchanges that he surveyed in his essay betrayed a worry for the revival of anti-Semitism in the interwar context, the next chapter shows that such a concern was made clear in his other political and academic essays which he published right before the publication of *The Gift*. To find an explicit rebuke of the anti-Semitic representation of Jews as greedy individuals unable to give, which Mauss found in social science essays and "political apologies of the most vulgar type,"[67] one had to read Mauss's book reviews in the same volume of *L'Année sociologique* in which *The Gift* was published – something that the new edition of *The Gift* prepared by Jane Guyer will make easier for English-speaking readers[68] – in which he denounced the anti-Semitism of German scholars who distinguished "between the societies and classes in which *altruistic* exchanges are common, and the societies and classes which are *parasites* of the exchange systems (aristocracies, plutocracies, Jews)."[69] Mauss's editorial choice explains why contemporary readers, most of whom will not read *The Gift* in the large volume of *L'Année sociologique* in which it was published, are not conscious that, indeed, these anti-Semitic writings on gift exchange were very much present in Mauss's mind, and he made a point of attacking them throughout his life.

3 MAUSS'S CENTRALITY IN THE COLONIAL FIELDS

Although a classical Bourdieuan field-theoretical approach is useful to characterize how Mauss and his network of peers situated themselves in the French field of power in the interwar period,[70] it is also important to move beyond this purely national perspective, as the specific discipline – anthropology – and the specific group of intellectuals – Mauss's circles – on which it focuses requires us to pay attention not only to the purely metropolitan French academic and political fields, but also to the transnational ties existing between the colonial and the international fields.[71] Indeed, as George Steinmetz writes in his post-Bourdieuan history of the German colonial field, any historian of intellectual fields should avoid "the dangers of error due to a nation-state-based approach which are exacerbated in the case of imperial sociologists, many of whom spend a great deal of time overseas in research sites or historical archives, interacting with scholars and laypeople from the colonized population and from other metropolitan nations."[72]

In this regard, the creation of the Institute of Ethnology in 1926 not only gave Mauss a way to increase visibility of his approach to ethnography in the French metropolitan academic field, but it was also supposed to give a rightful place to ethnology in the colonial field, from which it had been absent until then. Ethnology had not been a priority for the French Republic before the war.[73] Since the establishment of the Third Republic in the early 1880s, the Paris-based Colonial School had been the main center of training for colonial administrators.[74] As William Cohen writes, in 1914, "the administrative section of the Colonial School was the first functioning program specifically established to train men [of the metropolis] for civil service positions,"[75] who were required to gain at least one year of formal training from the Colonial School. Students were trained in a purely formal and universalist manner, with no attention paid to the local context into which these men would be sent.

Before the war, students in the Colonial School learned accounting, history of French colonization, and Roman law,[76] as their professors in the School assumed that "there cannot be ten different ways to organize a family, to conceive of property or of a contract."[77] The emphasis was on legal knowledge: students had to enroll in a Bachelor of Arts in law in parallel to their training at the Colonial School.[78] Language requirements were particularly limited (Arabic being the dominant language taught in the School), and sometimes oriented toward languages of little value in the colonial territories. Maurice Delafosse, a former bush administrator was one of the only teachers of African customs, language and history at the Colonial School.[79] Furthermore, most of the trainees were metropolitan citizens, as the administration of the School had bowed to the recriminations of the sociologist Gustave Le Bon (1841–1931), who claimed that training colonial subjects in Paris (as the British had done in London) would only excite their passion for national independence and their desire for a modern lifestyle far from their material conditions of life.[80] Thus, it was an understatement to say that the Colonial School had little use or regard for the kind of knowledge that ethnography could bring to its curriculum. In the early 1920s, Robert Delavignette, who took over the direction of the Colonial School after the departure of Georges Hardy (1884–1972), a former colonial officer in Morocco, still lamented the fact that "ethnographic reports were considered taboo [by most colonial administrators in the field] and buried away in the administrative files."[81]

As far as the field of power in Algeria was concerned, strong resistance also prevented ethnologists from gaining a say in the training of French administrators in Algeria, although the sources of blockage were different in Algeria and in West Africa, as Algeria was a settler colony with a large presence of citizens of the French Republic. Until after the Second World War, the University of Algiers, which provided a large contingent of French administrators in Algeria (judges, lawyers, law clerks, etc.) was strongly segregated between those students who studied French administrative, criminal or civil law in Algeria and who were mostly of European descent; and those students of Arab or Berber descent who remained concentrated in sub-tracks specialized in the study of customary law – Muslim law in the case of Algeria, but also local codes from Kabylia.[82]

In none of the curricula did ethnology appear as legitimate. Muslim law students from Algiers – where the only school of law in Algeria was created in 1879 – were expected to confine themselves to the study of Muslim law in order to become *oukils* authorized to plead a case before a *cadi* in a Muslim court, and students in French law who studied in Algiers did not take an ethnology test.[83] As a result, in 1910, only seven out of the 300 lawyers located in Algeria were of Muslim descent (representing a mere 4 percent),[84] and forty-five years later, in 1955, that proportion had hardly improved, with fewer than twenty lawyers of Muslim descent out of 400 registered lawyers in Algeria.[85]

In Algeria, the segregation of the state officials was thus not grounded on any legal discrimination, but on the self-perpetrating prejudices of the educational system and the professional organizations that controlled entry into the legal profession in the colonial field in Algeria: namely, the bar associations of the main cities of Algeria (Algiers, Oran, and Constantine), which maintained a strong boundary between the study of both systems of law: French and customary law. In fact, the Algiers bar association systematically ignored the jurisprudence of the Court of Algiers,[86] which, in 1882, had decided that admission to the bar was not dependent upon acquisition of French citizenship by Algerian Muslims: as obtaining the latter required Algerian Muslims to renounce their observance of Muslim laws, the Court had reasoned that it amounted to forced conversion (or at least, a turn toward secularism) unwelcome to most.[87] But in the 1920s and 1930s, the Paris or Algiers bars still denied the right to exercise to law graduates from Madagascar, Algeria, and Indochina, who were not full citizens of the French Republic.[88] And the situation worsened in the 1930s, in the context of an increasingly competitive legal market, marked by the economic downturn and the naturalization of many European Jewish refugees who practiced law in their country of origin. By then, the bar associations in both metropolis and overseas territories lobbied for even more restrictive conditions on access to legal professions, thus further strengthening the boundary between the serious study of French law and the less interesting study of local legal systems, which they left to the colonial subjects, and to ethnologists indeed in the Institute of Ethnology.[89]

Confronted with such lack of interest in the contribution that ethnology could bring to the training of French administrators and lawyers in Algeria or West Africa, Mauss started writing letters to the Ministry of the Colonies in the early 1900s, when he lamented "the paucity of interest for ethnography on the part of the state, the public and the learned societies," which explained why the "entirety of ethnographic work is done by the British and the Americans"[90] – but to no avail. Already in 1902 and 1907, after his trips to the Netherlands and the United Kingdom, Marcel Mauss had written memorandums addressed to the Minister of the Colonies in which he appealed (in vain) to the patriotism of the minister to create a "Bureau of French Ethnology similar to the American Bureau created at the Smithsonian."[91] For Mauss, the terrible state of ethnological knowledge in France explained the "multitude of mistakes found in the French literature on the supposed barbarism of the Negroes of Congo," which stood in "sharp contrast with the work done in Germany by [Adolf] Bastian (who died in the field)."[92]

In the absence of a national home for ethnology, Mauss feared that French anthropologists and colonial administrators would have to continue to rely on the German institutes to find ethnographic facts, as the latter "not only collect data among populations of German colonies, but also in other parts of the world, including in the French colonies"[93] – a fact he underlined to alarm the French Ministry that German ethnography may have ambitioned to administer the local populations under French tutelage. As Mauss added in his prewar letters, "there is an abysmal difference between our negligence and the model organization of the Germans and Americans,"[94] which could not be blamed on financial constraints, "as the Institutions created in Berlin are only those of Prussia, a country much smaller than France."[95]

But in 1926, the situation had changed. The selection of the name "Ethnology" rather than "Anthropology" for Mauss's new Institute was indicative of the division of labor between the two disciplines in the French metropolitan academic field at the time. For years, Mauss fought against the state funding of scientific chairs in raciology and somatology, which was the only chair created in France for anthropology before the creation of the Institute of Ethnology. Anthropology was less important to Mauss than ethnology, as the former was based on the observation of "racial traits that can endure a long time after a civilization has lost its mental, social and national singularity,"[96] so its development, and particularly that of somatology, was not urgent. In contrast, cultural ethnography and museographic sciences were eminently pressing tasks for Mauss, as cultural practices and artifacts could disappear in one generation after the French occupation of new territories, which is why Mauss, Rivet, and others took to heart the mission to revive the Museum of Ethnology of the Trocadero at the same time as they created the Institute of Ethnology, as Alice Conklin and other historians have showed.[97] At the same time, Mauss pushed for the creation of a French science of "ethnography," which he defined "as the science which describes and classifies races, peoples, civilizations, or rather, that part of the science which focuses on the races, peoples and civilizations of an inferior rank, which differs from that other part called 'history' or 'folklore,' which describes the peoples of the East and of ancient Europe."[98]

This last sentence should have any contemporary anthropologist who declares to be a Maussian think twice before taking at face value Mauss's definition of the discipline. Of course, our Maussian colleagues in anthropology today do not think of themselves as being involved in the study of "the races, peoples and civilizations of an inferior rank," and Mauss retains a definitive attraction among anthropologists because of his universal erudition and his attention to complex linguistic phenomena.[99] But, for Mauss, the reasons for the development of "descriptive sociology" (or "ethnology") in the colonies or in Algeria were not only scientific but also (and maybe more importantly for the minister) practical ones. Ethnology had practical implications for the art of colonial government that anthropology lacked: the measurement of crania may be of interest to racist criminologists interested in the science of eugenics but it does not tell you how to extract taxes from local populations without breaking implicit or secret sacred obligations for which tax collectors can be sanctioned by death. Mauss took considerable pains to convince the Ministry of the Colonies of the practical benefits that could derive from the development of ethnology in France.[100] Even though, as Mauss wrote to the minister in 1913, "the utilitarian consequences" stemming from the creation of a "purely scientific Bureau or Institute of ethnology will be indirect, they will be considerable."[101] Indeed, as Mauss emphasized time and again in his memorandums on the topic, "nowhere is it truer that in colonial policy that 'knowledge is power.'"[102] As Mauss wrote:

> it is of utmost political importance that we be informed of the state of mind of the millions and millions of Negroes whom we pretend to administer without knowing them, either in the Congo, Guinea, Sudan, Madagascar, as well as the salvage tribes of Annam, Laos and Tonkin, who are understood only by a few zealous military men, who nonetheless lack the time and resources to produce adequate descriptions of their mores.[103]

It was thus a major breakthrough for Mauss to obtain the creation of an Institute of Ethnology in Paris in 1926, and that the Institute of Ethnology later managed to obtain an important say on the knowledge deemed legitimate by the political and administrative authorities for the selection of future administrators in the French colonial field. At the Institute, in the late 1920s and early 1930s, Mauss thus gave for instance a class titled "Ethnological Lessons for the Use of Colonial Administrators, Missionaries and Explorers,"[104] and in 1927, Mauss even obtained the opportunity to teach a twenty-four-week class on ethnology at the Colonial School.[105] Mauss's multipositionality, and the interlocking of advisory boards in the various training centers of colonial administrators, certainly helped him build the legitimacy of the newly founded Institute of Ethnology in the eyes of the Ministry of the Colonies and the Colonial School. Even if ethnographic training at the Colonial School did not always translate into its use in the field,[106] the role of ethnology in the curriculum of the Colonial School changed with the collaboration Georges Hardy started with Mauss and his Institute of Ethnology. Hardy greatly raised the prestige of his school by strengthening the academic content of its curriculum and by organizing preparatory classes in the "grands lycées," which previously only trained students to the *grandes écoles* like the ENS and the École Polytechnique.[107] Thus, entry into the Colonial School became a valued alternative for the smart young students who had failed the competitive exam for either of these alternatives, and who did not want to go in French law schools straight out of high schools. These smart students were likely to be attracted by Mauss's charismatic erudition: at the Colonial School, thanks to the fact that Mauss himself, and later his most brilliant students (like Jacques Soustelle and Marcel Griaule) taught classes in ethnography, trainees could engage with the most interesting research in anthropology, sociology, and ethnography. Maussian ethnology had moved to the center of the orthodoxy in colonial sciences, along with French law and colonial economics.

As George Steinmetz writes, "the socio-spatial contours of imperial socio-scientific fields," such as the one under study here "are shaped by the analytic object itself – by the empires being studied."[108] Thus, George Steinmetz's reflections on the necessity for historical sociologists interested in the study of empires to not only contextualize the struggles of important thinkers in the metropolitan field of power, but also in the colonial fields, rings particularly pertinent, as the men and women who studied under Mauss's supervision the past, present, and future of colonial relations in the French context not only drew upon the social capital they accumulated in the metropolis to move on with their career in the metropolitan field of power, but also on what Steinmetz has called "colonial capital"[109] (a form of capital valued in the state structures outside the metropolis, whose certification was grounded on the demonstrated knowledge of the mores of colonial subjects) to ground the legitimacy of their claims to colonial administration.

Rather than studying the circulation of social capital in one field only, we historical sociologists interested in the relation between the academic and political fields should then study the intersection between institutional logics in multiple fields: in the Algerian and West African colonial fields for instance (see Figure 2), various ministries (like the Ministry of Interior or the Ministry of Colonies), various private interests (like colonial banks and chartered companies that operated in the Congo for instance), as well as various institutions of higher learning (like the Colonial School or the Institute of Ethnology) had gained a stake in the colonial game, and the study of their interactions should be located in the specific fields in which these institutions operated.

As a result of such differentiation between various fields of power in the French colonial age, the "colonial capital" with which aspiring colonial administrators and anthropologists started their careers was spent with varying effects depending on whether they used it to fight ideological and administrative battles in the fields of power in the metropolis, in Algeria, or in the colonial field in West Africa, for instance. These men and women who circulated around Mauss not only institutionalized ethnology in the French metropolis, they also moved in an environment that is best described as a colonial field: it can neither be reduced to the purely French metropolitan field, nor to an international anonymous space. And this colonial field can in fact be subdivided in various sub-fields: the colonial field in West Africa, where careers of colonial administrators typically started at the Paris-based Colonial School, where Mauss started to teach ethnology in the late 1920s; and the Algerian field of power, where many more passageways existed with the metropolitan field, thus enabling an intense circulation between academic, political, economic, and

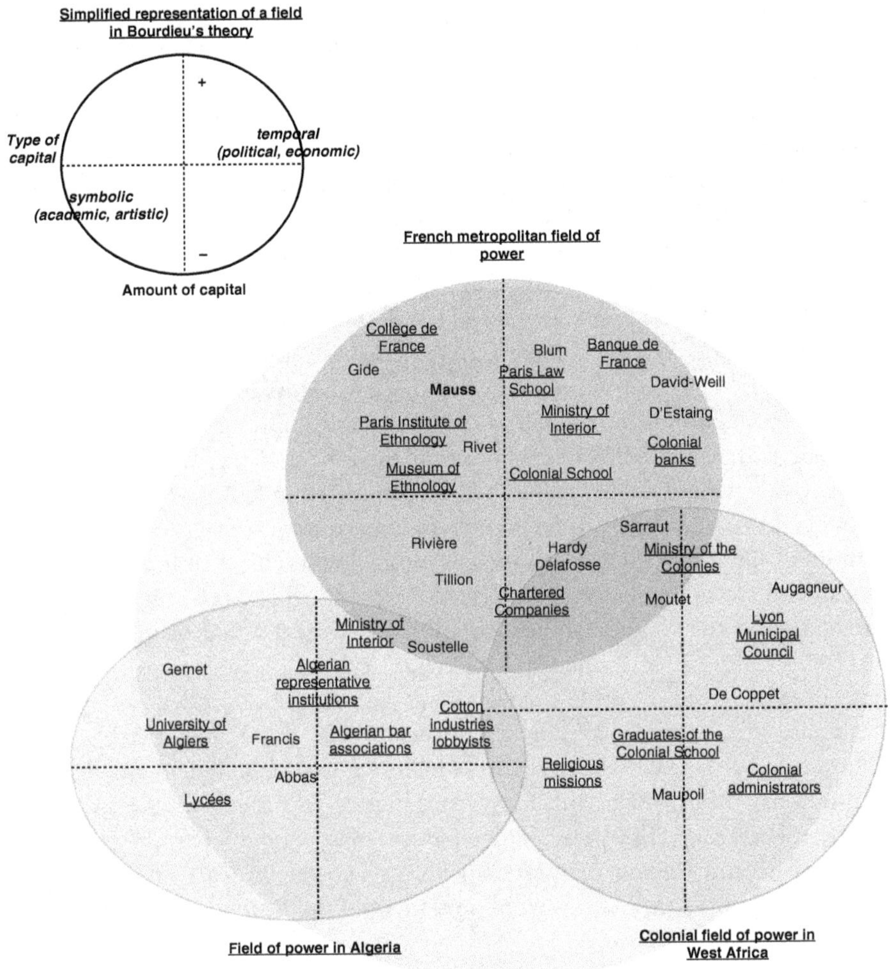

FIGURE 2 The colonial, Algerian, and metropolitan fields of power in the interwar period

administrative elites from the metropolis and Algeria. The Algerian field itself was not reducible to the other colonial fields, as its administrative elements fell under the authority of the Ministry of Interior and other Ministries in charge of deciding essential questions in the three Algerian departments that France claimed to belong to the French Republic itself. Representing where various institutions are situated in these various fields in the interwar period, Figure 2 can help sociologists and historians, although only schematically, highlight the existence of institutional forces beyond the immediate level of Mauss's circle of interpersonal relations.

Rejecting the metropolis-centered view of fields is key to explain some critical discontinuities in the lives and careers of ethnologists who were trained by Mauss and carried on with his thoughts on gift exchange, as their lives moved beyond the colonial and metropolitan fields. In particular, George Steinmetz's perspective of fields can help us explain why these intellectuals and administrators could accumulate high levels of social capital in the colonial fields – including Algeria, West Africa, East Africa and Madagascar, and Indochina – that could later be translated in the metropolitan field, at least during specific periods, and why their colonial capital suddenly became irrelevant after decolonization.

Here, the career of Jacques Soustelle not only illustrates how ethnographic knowledge was used to accumulate political and social capital in the colonial and metropolitan fields, but also why the sudden destruction of the colonial field after the Second World War so dramatically affected the life opportunities of these ethnologists/colonial administrators who drew on Mauss to think about international and colonial relations in terms of gift exchange. During the Second World War, it was first thanks to his connections from the ENS and the Musée de l'Homme and the ethnographic fieldwork that he had conducted in Mexico (whose indigenous populations from Yucatan Soustelle had long observed) that Jacques Soustelle "converted" his anthropological/academic capital into political cash: in 1939, when the war with Germany started, Soustelle was nominated in Mexico to become the head of propaganda services for the Central American region, a post he then used to raise funds for the Free France after General de Gaulle's June 18 call.[110] In 1942 Soustelle entered de Gaulle's government in exile in London as Head of Information, before becoming the head of the intelligence service in November 1943, after the government moved from London to Algiers; then Minister of Information in May 1944, and Minister of the Colonies in November 1945. His career, judged from that point of view, was strongly embedded in the French metropolitan field of power, at least until he started accumulating, due to the specific circumstances of the Second World War, some capital in the Algerian field.

Soustelle's political career extended far beyond the boundaries of the metropolitan state: for more than thirty years, he consistently transferred the academic capital he accumulated in the metropolitan field into political capital valued in the colonial and Algerian fields of power; and vice versa. For instance, when the Gaullists lost the 1946 elections, Soustelle convinced de Gaulle to form a broader trans-party movement (the Rassemblement du Peuple Français (RPF) in 1947), which he led as secretary general and director of the parliamentary group for the next eight years, until Pierre Mendès France named him governor general in Algeria in January 1955. Soustelle's recognition as a skilled politician and an eminent anthropologist certainly intervened in Mendès France's decision to appoint him as the highest civilian authority in Algeria, just two months after the beginning of the insurrection launched by the Algerian Front de libération nationale (FLN) on November 1, 1954.[111] Then, Soustelle helped de Gaulle by fomenting a coup in Algiers in May 1958, which brought the Fourth

Republic to its knees and de Gaulle back to power (and Soustelle back to the government as Minister of the Sahara and Atomic Energy).

But after de Gaulle dramatically shifted gears on the issue of Algerian independence, Soustelle left the government, and, after 1961, spent eight years in clandestine exile and permanent movement to hide from de Gaulle's private intelligence officers-killers (the so-called *barbouzes*), as the war between Gaullists and pro-French Algeria supporters raged within the French intelligence circles – until the events of May 1968 diminished the authority of de Gaulle. Back from his exile in 1968, Soustelle could still count on the active support of Parisian academics, like Claude Lévi-Strauss, to land a job back in academia and at the French Academy,[112] but he was no longer able to influence either national or international politics.

4 THE COMPETITION BETWEEN DISCIPLINES IN THE COLONIAL FIELDS OF POWER

By situating the development of anthropology and international law in relation to both the French colonial fields of power and the metropolitan field of power, the next chapters will explain how anthropologists, who specialized in knowing the mores of the colonial subjects whose lives their state or concessionary companies administered, used their specific knowledge and their accumulated colonial capital to push for specific arrangements between the metropolis and its overseas territories, sometimes in alliance with, at other times in opposition to, other professionals such as jurists (specialists of international and/or colonial law), economists (specialists of colonial trade and finance) and the bureaucrats and policymakers involved in colonial affairs.[113] Indeed, the colonial fields in which Maussian ethnologists gained a stake were not empty, but already populated by different experts, who fiercely defended their jurisdiction over colonial policy. Once they gained entry into the colonial fields, ethnologists needed to form alliances not only with colonial administrators who were politically close to them, like Léon Blum, or his Minister Marius Moutet, or some governor generals like Marcel de Coppet, but also with other experts coming from other disciplines like international law, colonial law, or public finance.

The notion of a colonial field is thus helpful to situate the space in which these debates and conflicts between disciplines took place, for instance, between ethnologists and economists as well as high civil servants in charge of the colonial trade policy, like Edmond Giscard d'Estaing (1894–1982) who had long opposed the socialist views defended by Léon Blum or Maurice Viollette on the necessity for France to engage a "generous" colonial policy based on gift exchange between the metropolis and its overseas territories.[114] Men like Edmond Giscard d'Estaing had very different trajectories from Mauss's students: for instance, he was an inspector of finance who was the High Commissioner of the Rhineland under French occupation during the early 1920s before becoming the administrator of French banks in

Indochina, and then the father of Valéry Giscard d'Estaing (1926–), who preceded François Mitterrand (1916–96) as President of the French Republic. His views on colonial trade were quite typical of the opinions and expertise found in the French Treasury.[115] Edmond Giscard d'Estaing often found himself arguing against the logic of the gift exchange and the integration of colonial subjects (Algerian subjects in particular) in the body politic of the French Republic, which was defended by some of Mauss's students, like Jacques Soustelle. For Giscard father, if the metropolis wanted to be generous, it had to find the best investment opportunities for its capital rather than prioritize sending it to Algeria, where investments could be wasted.

When they intervened in the debates on colonial policy, high civil servants who had a training in finance, like François Bloch Lainé (1912–2002), an economist who became France's Treasury Director in 1947, and whose great uncle was none other than Léon Blum, did not look at the ethnographic facts collected by ethnologists or colonial administrators, but at instruments of macroeconomic policy, such as France's balance of payments. On this basis, they often came in direct conflict with Mauss's students, as they argued that the logic of continued gift exchange between the metropolis and its colonies turned "the logic of the Colonial Pact upside down" as "France provided the metropolitan francs which allowed its colonies to keep a dramatically unbalanced balance of payments,"[116] as a result of their imports of industrial goods produced in the French metropolis. To understand the shifting meanings of the notion of gift exchange, it is thus essential to contextualize the debates in which ethnology positioned itself in the range of disciplines that claimed a stake in the colonial field.

In the interwar period, ethnologists not only had to defend their legitimacy against economists and trade specialists, but also against international law scholars, some of whom were sympathetic to the Durkheimian ethnologists gathered around Mauss, while others paid little attention to the local legal contexts in which the French state imposed its legal norms and rules when it expanded its influence to Algeria or West Africa. As Martti Koskenniemi demonstrates, after the Great War, some international law scholars had been influenced by the Durkheimian sociological approach, like Georges Scelle (1878–1951),[117] who was a collaborator of *L'Année sociologique*, and who taught both at the University of Paris and the Institut des Hautes Etudes Internationales, an institute founded in Geneva with the support of the Rockefeller Foundation[118] to serve as an observatory for the study of the emerging world society – now the Graduate Institute, where I happen to find myself teaching and writing. Confident in the ability of the League of Nations to generate international solidarity through cultural, legal, and economic exchanges, Scelle taught that political–legal ties of a quasi-federal nature would almost naturally emerge among member states of the League of Nations if exchanges between a plurality of political societies proliferated – in ways that were reminiscent of the Maussian notion that political societies moved up the scale of integration as they practiced gift exchanges, as I will show later. Like Mauss's students at the Institute of Ethnology, Durkheimian international law scholars did not oppose colonialism: they found in the League of Nations, and the mandates it granted to the French and British Empires in Africa and beyond, an opportunity to bring diverse political societies toward higher levels of civilization, so as to foster world peace and international solidarity.[119]

In contrast, the ethnological lessons that Mauss and his students could draw on gift exchanges by studying the interactions between legal norms in the colonial context, were much less appreciated, if recognized as legitimate at all, by international law scholars who worked in the French Ministry of Foreign Affairs before the Second World War. For many of those jurisconsults, international law was merely an instrument to be used in the service of European great powers: for them, paying attention to the legal norms recognized by colonial subjects amounted almost to an unpatriotic gesture aimed at hurting the absolute rights of the colonial power.[120] For instance, Jules Basdevant (1877–1968), a professor of international public law at the University of Paris and Sciences-Po Paris, who worked for the Ministry of Foreign Affairs as a jurisconsult in the 1930s – a position he quit in 1940 when Pétain came to power – and a member of the International Court of Justice (ICJ) from 1946 to 1964, was quite typical of this generation of jurisconsults.[121] Like Albert de la Pradelle (1871–1955), who taught at the University of Grenoble, before founding the Paris-based Institut des Hautes Etudes Internationales, and many other jurisconsults, Basdevant "made no secret of his distaste of the solidarists' sweeping generalizations"[122] about history's progress toward a more integrated international society, and their unlimited hope in the power of economic interdependence to generate new quasi-constitutional legal norms between a plurality of political communities. In his work as jurisconsult, Basdevant was not only ardently in favor of France's colonial mission, but he was also particularly oblivious of the legal and contractual obligations that colonial subjects had recognized (and had been recognized) as theirs: for instance, from 1918 to 1920, when he was charged with the official task of publishing the French Record of treaties and conventions, he excluded most of the treaties signed by the French state with African and Asian sovereigns (with the exception of those signed with Ethiopia and Liberia), even those signed by the representatives of the Third Republic with the Algerian emirs (like Abd El-Kader), Nigerian kings (like Samori Touré, the grandfather of Seku Touré, the first president of independent Guinea) or East Asian emperors, which had been ratified and even published in the *Journal Officiel*.[123] Basdevant's symbolic act of exclusion perfectly reflected the colonial mindset of some French jurists, for whom the only purpose of these conventions had been to secure the nonintervention of other European great powers when the French Republic claimed African territories as its own.[124]

To understand the reception of Mauss's ideas in the colonial field, it is thus necessary to reconstruct the logics of these various fields during the times when Mauss was writing and publishing. Furthermore, if one wants to understand how the reception of his ideas on gift exchange evolved over time, it is important to describe the mechanisms of intergenerational struggle that worked these fields from within. Indeed, from the interwar period to the postwar era, these fields experienced dramatic changes. For instance, after the Second World War, the emergence of strong law schools outside Paris, in which new disciplines like political science, geography, or Weberian political sociology were combined with international law, changed how international law was being taught, and challenged the association between the study of international law and the defense of French colonialism. In this approach to international law, there was little use for the lessons that ethnologists could draw from their study of legal customs, but rather, the emphasis was placed on understanding the relations between legal rules, the life of domestic and international bureaucracies, and the agendas of political parties that pushed for the reform or conservation of existing legal rules.

The strength of this new approach to international law was evident for instance in the Law School of the University of Grenoble, in which Claude-Albert Colliard (1913–90) served as dean for a long time, and where Mohammed Bedjaoui came to study until he graduated in 1956, with a doctorate in international law. Colliard was, in the words of Bedjaoui, the "perfect example of the radical socialists of the Third Republic, who hated colonialism"[125] – a subject he also taught at Sciences-Po Grenoble, from which Bedjaoui also graduated, and where he took Colliard's course "Imperialism and the Economy."[126] In his realist approach to international law, ethnology, and the ethnographic study of cultural, social and economic exchanges between political societies, had no place – but this no longer meant that those who sponsored this approach adhered to a pro-colonial ideology, in contrast to interwar international law scholars like Jules Basdevant. Affirming the exclusive rights of states to author international law (against the pluralist Durkheimian precepts found in the study of law as practiced in the colonial field) stood in harmony with the goal of achieving recognition of statehood for independent colonies,[127] and thus, with the study of the administrative and legal criteria that international legal scholars had so far used to define statehood. In this new postwar academic context, ethnology in general, and the ethnography of gift exchange, had to change to remain relevant to the political debates of the time and the pressing question of colonial reform.

5 THE IMPERIAL INVENTION OF "THIRD WORLD" INTELLECTUALS

At last, this book hopes to convince sociologists and historians to adopt the neo-Bourdieuan view of fields in order to explain continuities that were masked by the sudden process of decolonization for the former colonial subjects: for instance, the French (second-class) citizens from the colonies (or Algeria) who experienced high social mobility in the French academic or colonial fields before decolonization, and who remained in positions that straddled two fields of power after national independence – both in the former metropolis, where they kept many ties, and in their newly independent states, where they often rose to the top tiers of power. For instance, the intellectual trajectory of Bedjaoui and those of his mentors Ferhat Abbas (1899–1985) and Ahmed Francis (1912–68) – a doctor who had studied medicine in Paris (obtaining a doctoral degree in 1939) and who had practiced in Setif, like Abbas – were deeply rooted within the French fields of international public law and colonial policy.

In other histories of international law in which such intellectuals figure prominently, such as in Balakrishnan Rajagopal's *International Law from Below*,[128] there is a tendency to treat such intellectual and political elites from "the Global South" as "Third World" elites, as if their trajectory was tied only to their newly independent nation-state and to the Third World more generally. Doing so may lead historians of international law to ignore the processes of capital transmission and accumulation that had started in the French metropolitan field of law before the beginning of national independence.

The historiography on the New International Economic Order (NIEO) provides a good example of how historians can forget that key notions associated with this broad program found their historical and intellectual origins in the French academic fields. After Algerian independence, the mid 1970s were an intense period of Algerian diplomatic activity, which in turn explains why no international lawyer from the Third World exercised a similar influence and role as Mohammed Bedjaoui on the definition of the NIEO program.[129] For twenty years, and until hopes to reform the economic international system waned after Margaret Thatcher was elected Prime Minister in the United Kingdom and Ronald Reagan President of the United States, Mohammed Bedjaoui indeed played a leading role in formulating the legal doctrine behind the economic program of the NIEO.[130] As Special Rapporteur to the International Law Commission (ILC) he steered the work of eminent legal scholars who, through their participation in the ILC, reported to the UN General Assembly on points of law for which the General Assembly had sought clarification.[131] For this reason, the publication of his acclaimed book *Towards a New International Economic Order*, published in 1978 by UNESCO,[132] was not only the work of a learned scholar of international public law but also the platform on which a "Third World Lawyer tried to structure the struggle of the Group of 77,"[133] as Balakrishnan Rajagopal writes.

But, in fact, Bedjaoui's reach extended beyond the confines of international organizations and reached far into the Franco-Algerian bilateral relation: after serving as Algeria's Minister of Justice until the late 1960s, he became the Algerian Ambassador to France (1970–9) when the nationalization of French oil interests in Algeria was undertaken, before he moved on to other prestigious postings, first as Ambassador to the UN in New York (1979–82), and then Judge at the ICJ for almost twenty years. Furthermore, it is impossible to understand his career and his intellectual trajectory without placing them in the history of the French metropolitan and colonial fields of law before and after Algeria's independence. Indeed, the few Algerian lawyers and legal scholars who, like Bedjaoui, used their legal status, expertise, and skills to defend Algerian independence after the Second World War were all trained in the metropolis, and evolved in the metropolitan field of law, whether they were of European, Arab, or Caribbean descent.

The very low number of Muslim lawyers practicing French law before 1962 explains that the mobilization of the legal profession (or rather, the "legal complex" to use the concept developed by Terence Halliday, Lucien Karpik, and Malcolm Feeley in their study of political lawyering)[134] in favor of Algeria's independence, which provided its legal experts to the Francophone anti-colonial movement, did not originate from the colonial field but rather from the metropolitan field. Halliday, Karpik, and Feeley do not make the distinction between the colonial and metropolitan fields of power that George Steinmetz makes. But this duality is an important factor explaining how political lawyers mobilized in the Francophone anti-colonial movement, and the difference one finds for instance between the mobilization of Algerian and Indian lawyers prior to their respective independences.[135] In the latter case, political lawyering existed in the colonial field – with the Indian Supreme Court becoming an important guardian of political liberties – where class and ethnic identity did not determine the legal status of the practicing lawyers or the content of their decisions when sitting in court.[136] On the contrary, as Ataouia Kralfa shows in her analysis of the bar associations in Algeria, most of the practicing lawyers in the colonial field in Algeria were located in positions that were strongly determined by their class, race, and gender, and they had little room to maneuver around these socio-ethnic boundaries.[137]

The division of the French academic field, with strong and autonomous metropolitan institutions, and weak and subordinate colonial institutions in Algeria, thus protected those anti-colonial students who, like Mohammed Bedjaoui, left Algeria to study and have an academic career in metropolitan France. This was particularly true in the more practical side of the field of law after the Second World War. French historians of the legal field like Sylvie Thénault have showed that the lawyers who represented FLN terrorists who were arrested in Algeria in the 1950s were more protected from the repression of French authorities when they were based in Paris than when they belonged to the Algerian field of law.[138] After 1954, lawyers of either European or Muslim descent who practiced in Algeria and who defended the FLN were fiercely chased by the French administration, and often placed in detention camps, like Amar Bentoumi (1923–2013), who left Algeria in 1957 to join the Algerian Provisional Government (in French, GPRA) after escaping the French watch, before becoming Algeria's first Minister of Justice in 1962 – before Mohammed Bedjaoui.[139] Metropolitan lawyers, like Jacques Vergès (1924–2013), a French lawyer of Caribbean and Vietnamese origin, enjoyed more freedom than his Algerian colleagues to delegitimize French law by using the courtroom to publicly denounce the torture of political prisoners – what Vergès called the defense "strategy of rupture"[140] that he and other FLN defenders practiced after 1957. Lawyers in Algeria, some of them close to the Communist party, were also arrested and placed in detention camps, like Elie Guedj, Albert Smadja, Louis Grange, and Kaddour Sator. Several of them were even killed, like Amokran Ould Aoudia (1925–59), murdered by the French secret services as he walked out of his law firm.[141] Assassination attempts were also ordered against them when traveling to Algiers, as in the case of Tunisian-born Gisèle Halimi (1927–).[142]

In fact, this division between the metropolitan and colonial fields of law, which structured legal practice in France before the independence of Algeria, had a strong impact on the evolution of the field of law in the early years of the Algerian Republic. The fact that Algerian Muslims were forced into separate tracks, with a specialization in the study of local customary law rather than French law (or international law, for that matter), meant that very few of the Algerian Muslims trained in Algeria before the war could administer justice after 1962, and that among the French judges who sat in Algerian courts, very few had developed some knowledge of the legal customs that Algerian Muslims of various ethnicities followed. Thus, an independent Algeria had to train and then hire an entire cadre of judges and Algerian magistrates. As Mohammed Bedjaoui said in a personal interview in spring 2017, as Minister of Justice from 1963 to 1970, he faced the "immense challenge of replacing the colonial legislation with the Algerian legislation,"[143] and the French judges with Algerian judges. Indeed, French Algeria had "reserved all positions of judges to French citizens" as they had "represented a sector of sovereignty that Algerians should not control."[144] Until these positions were filled, the Algerian Republic could either choose to use the judicial "cooperation" planned by the Evian Agreements, and rely on French *coopérants* to be the lawful officers and judges of the independent Algerian state, or find its judges elsewhere.[145]

After Algeria's independence, Bedjaoui thus immediately recruited the few Algerian presidents of bar associations who had impeccable anti-colonial credentials to serve as the judges, like Abdel Khader Francis, a lawyer and president of the local bar from the district of Relizane to the west of Algiers, who was the brother of Ahmed Francis, Algeria's first Minister of the Economy and Finance. And rather than drawing on former French judges who had held positions in Algeria (in the French colonial field), he tried to recruit French *coopérants* from the French metropolitan field but not as judges: he used them instead in lower administrative and clerical functions, as well teachers and administrators in the University of Algiers, where he became dean of the Law School during the same period as he was Minister of Justice (1963–70).[146] It was a process of decolonization of the administration of justice that took some time in the making, but that was essential to the dissolution of the colonial field of power in Algeria.

The following chapters thus pay particular attention to both continuities and displacements in the colonial and metropolitan fields of power before and after decolonization. They show why it is important to consider former colonial subjects who were treated as second-class citizens before decolonization and former colonial administrators/ethnographers who ruled over the fate of these populations as part of a post-national field during and after the colonial period. In particular, they demonstrate how the logics of the colonial field before and after decolonization were key not only to understand the trajectories of Mauss and his collaborators within the broader field of power, but also to reconstruct the changing reception of their published work, especially as the latter touched upon the main themes that Mauss sought to address in his reflections on exchange of gifts: that is, the origins and development of a sense of financial solidarity between European and non-European nations.

3

The Gift and European Solidarity

Marcel Mauss and the Politics of Reparation in Interwar Europe

In 1923 and 1924, as Marcel Mauss was preparing the rebirth of *L'Année sociologique* in which he would publish *The Gift*, the European public was captivated by the sovereign debt crises which threatened the stability of European economies. At stake was the sustainability of the interwar legal order created by the Treaty of Versailles, signed in June 1919 between Germany and the Allied Powers, and strengthened by the League of Nations and the Reparations Commission, which calculated the amount of debt that Germany owed to the Allies – France especially. Barely five years after the end of a war of unprecedented human cost for the European continent, the specter of division and armed conflict was again haunting European nations.

The main questions that contemporaries of Mauss asked about German reparations were not very different from those that sovereign debt managers and central bankers ask today about Greece's debt: Were they sustainable or too high for the German economy? Should their amount be reduced or the schedule of their payments renegotiated? Should the creditors extend a temporary suspension of payments (a moratorium) to Germany so that the German economy would have a chance to recover, after which Germany could repay in full what it owed to its creditors? But the traumatic memory of a conflict that had claimed almost ten million lives made it impossible for Mauss's contemporaries to answer these questions on purely technical aspects. Whether Europeans agreed, or not, to settle the financial issues which had been central to the resolution of the conflict determined whether they would live another war – an even more destructive war – in their lifetime or not.

If contemporary historians like Sally Marks now argue that German reparations were sustainable for the German economy, and that their odious character was merely a myth, exploited by postwar German political elites to consolidate political power and justify their opposition to the postwar settlement,[1] the dominant view in France at the time was that reparations were a sanction against the Germans' wartime behavior. The French and German publics saw the attribution of reparations as the ascription of a moral, or as Martti Koskenniemi argues, a "metaphysical guilt"[2] placed on the German state, and thus no renegotiation could be opened, for the latter would have betrayed the memory of the fallen soldiers of the Allied nations. For Germany to be reintegrated in the concert of civilized European nations, its government had to pay the reparations owed to the populations of France and Belgium whose regions had been destroyed by the fury of the conflict.

Such a public perception led many historians to argue that the Treaty of Versailles was too punitive, too one-sided in its assignment of responsibility and guilt, pointing to the seemingly "unprecedented" reparations as restraining conditions that strangled postwar economic development and cooperation: John Torpey for instance, sees in the "reparations" provisions of the Versailles Treaty an "unambiguous form of 'victor's justice,' which were resented accordingly."[3] Some historians believe they were the source of the political disorder which led to the rise of the Nazis and the outbreak of the Second World War in Europe.[4] They implicitly relay the views expressed at the time by German intellectuals, legal scholars, and politicians who also presented the Allies' requests as a series of "Diktats,"[5] and who considered that these German reparations constituted an "odious debt" which the vanquished nation – although it signed the Versailles Treaty – did not consent to pay.[6]

Mauss was deeply engaged in the debate on German reparations. In his op-eds in *Le Populaire*, Mauss blamed the nationalists in the French government for framing German payments as sanctions: he wrote, "the ones who carry the blame are the idiots who implemented the Versailles Treaty: the French Minister of Finance, Mr. Klotz, the right-wing press . . . the stupid crowds who believed in their claims that 'Germany will pay' whatever formidable sum the French requested."[7] According to his view, it was possible to reschedule payments or cancel some part of the German reparations if such renegotiation helped restore European solidarity and order.

Many socialist and progressive leaders in France shared Mauss's view of the reparations. Some, like Mauss's colleague Léon Blum, the leader of the French socialist party at the time, tried to define a third way in the socialist journal *Le Populaire*, as he rejected the type of unilateral cancellation of debts decided by the Soviets which had shocked Mauss's contemporaries, as well as the strict adherence to treaties espoused by nationalists.[8] For Mauss and Blum, had the Germans decided to unilaterally cancel their reparations obligations, they would have ruined the trust of European nations in international cooperation and would have invited war in response. But these French socialists also denounced the lack of flexibility of the French government in the implementation of the economic stabilization program decided by Germany's creditors. Mauss and Blum argued instead in favor of "giving time" to Germany, so that it could reconstitute its finances, honor its financial commitments in the future, and bring the other debt-ridden European economies back on track with peace and prosperity. The future of the European continent, and its centrality in world affairs, was at stake.

Furthermore, socialists around Mauss valued the concept of reparations in which they saw the manifestation of a new type of quasi-contractual relations between the peoples of Europe. In 1923, Léon Blum told German socialists that the reparations were the first pan-European redistribution policies consistent with the new notion of *justice réparative*. As he said, "The principle of reparations reflects one of the idealist inspirations of the Treaty of Versailles. It is neither a punitive sanction," Blum added, "nor a war bounty, but a reparation for damages caused."[9] For him, the philosophy of reparations embodied in the Versailles Treaty reflected a new progressive conception of the state, whose legitimacy derived from its ability to safeguard the payment of social debts that its citizens had explicitly or tacitly contracted when forming a nation. Blum insisted that "this is the first time this principle is applied, and it is the basis for a new Law," and adding that "the commitment of Germany toward France and Belgium is only a consequence of the commitment of France and Belgium toward its own victims, which is entirely new." Blum gave a powerful argument to illustrate that claim: "until then," he continued "a man whose house was burned by the war had no right to claim reparation from the state, which could object that there is a risk of war, when it is a supreme imperative. This notion of reparation is a new right, a rule of collective solidarity, a principle of national insurance, in which the socialists could only place their hopes."[10]

Mauss fully agreed with his fellow socialists. Whereas international financial relations had been completely absent from Mauss's prewar reflections, they rose to the top of his political and intellectual agenda after the Great War. In the early 1920s, Mauss thus spared no effort accusing the nationalists on both sides of the Rhine of misrepresenting the logic of reparations and sovereign debt relations, which embodied the values of multilateralism and dispassionate management in global affairs: it was the first time indeed that a multilateral Reparations Commission was granted the responsibility to determine the amount to be paid by Germany to the different allies (France, but also Belgium, the UK, etc.) in a quasi-scientific manner.[11] The Reparations Commission should be heard, so Mauss argued, especially when it proposed to reschedule the payment of German reparations in order to make that debt sustainable and place the German economy on the path of economic recovery and reintegration in the concert of honorable European nations. There had to be a third way between communist disorder and market discipline, along the lines that Blum and the French socialists defined.

The reparation question included in the Versailles Treaty was thus at the very heart of Mauss's concerns at the time he wrote *The Gift*: in particular, the question of how European solidarity could be rebuilt by having Germany pay reparations to the Allies, and how Europe's economic recovery could erase the scars left by the Great War and reinstitute Europe at the center of global affairs. This proximity raises the following questions: did the anthropology of the gift that Mauss tried to elaborate at the same time as he wrote on international economic governance help him develop a specific understanding of the problem of international order that other kinds of discourses, like economics or international law, failed to reveal? If so, what perspective did the anthropology of the gift open for Mauss's contemporaries interested in the question of international order?

After tracing the origins of Mauss's conception of European solidarity back to his wartime experiences, this chapter describes the intellectual and administrative origins of the philosophy of reparative justice, which influenced some of the authors of the post-1919 international economic order. By analyzing how Mauss and the French socialists who participated in the war effort, especially at the Ministry of Armament, interpreted the meaning of the new financial international order erected by the reparations provisions contained in the Versailles Treaty, the chapter makes it clear that Mauss used his anthropological essay to back up his arguments in favor of debt rescheduling and a moratorium on payments with anthropological facts: especially facts about the temporal conditions that must be respected in order for reparations and other policies of debt forgiveness to create international solidarity in a postwar context.

The Gift, so I argue, was a way for Mauss to mobilize anthropology in a juridical battle to establish precedents that would prove that the gifts are always given back if some unspecific amount of time separates the gift from the counter-gift. Indeed, Mauss established that the type of debt exchange that he advocated in the context of the German reparations debate had a long presence in European (in particular Germanic) legal culture and practices of gift-making. In that sense, *The Gift* can be read as a normative justification of the policies of sovereign debt rescheduling that Mauss initially advocated with regard to German reparations and inter-allied debts: anthropological knowledge helped Mauss argue that the idea of a debt moratorium extended to Germany was in fact a perfectly normal measure to restore a European sense of solidarity, rather than an exceptional favor, and the most secure way to preserve the European continent from another major conflict.

1 THE WARTIME EXPERIENCE OF ALLIED FINANCIAL SOLIDARITY

A traditional historian of ideas would certainly start a chapter on the notions of solidarity, contracts, and reparations with a survey of the important predecessors who influenced Mauss's conception of contractual law and social obligations, which can be traced in *The Gift* and in Mauss's earlier essays: for instance, in his 1921 article on an "ancient form of contract among the Thraces," in which he first demonstrated that ancient European societies had developed a "system of total prestations,"[12] very similar to the one described by Franz Boas in his ethnography of the Kwakiutls' "potlatch," which led him to conclude that the logic of gift exchange that he later claimed to have uncovered was indeed universal. Such a historian would then emphasize the intellectual debt that Mauss owed to his uncle, Emile Durkheim, who defined the notion of solidarity in sociological terms in his famous book *De la division du travail social*,[13] but also the inspiration Mauss drew from Alfred Fouillée, another sociologist and philosopher of law; or from Léon Bourgeois and Charles Gide, who, like Durkheim, differentiated between societies depending on their forms of the solidarity – "mechanic" or "organic," depending upon how societies organized the division of labor.[14] This is not the perspective that I adopt in this chapter.

Instead of a pure intellectual and disciplinary history of ideas, I would like to contextualize the key notions such as debt obligations, reparations, quasi-contracts, which Mauss introduces in *The Gift*, by identifying their meanings when they circulated within the political debates of his time, which related to the question of Allied solidarity during the Great War; and afterwards, with the question of German reparations to the Allies. If Mauss and his friends had helped workers create cooperatives and wholesales before the Great War, the protracted conflict soon revealed the necessity of European nations to launch a total war, in which all economic sectors, all genders, and all ethnicities were to be mobilized. As the war mobilization escalated, the young Durkheimian intellectuals soon helped industrialists create cooperatives, and bankers as well, with the patriotic goal of helping the democratic Allies win the Great War against the German autocrats and their allies. It is interesting to see how the notions of solidarity and cooperation, far from disappearing from the vocabulary of the socialists and Durkheimians who had been the most fervent advocates for peace before the war, took on this new meaning during and after the Great War: the international solidarity manifested by the alliance treaties was translated into a gigantic effort of contractualization and mutualization of the economic wartime effort of the French, British, and American war industries against Germany and its own allies.

During the war, Albert Thomas and his Ministry of Armament realized one of the most important reorganizations of industrial production and international trade in modern history, which was directly inspired by the prewar cooperativist movement in favor of wholesales and mutualization of contracts.[15] This effort was largely concentrated on the war industries and their financing, as the latter had to meet strict production goals for the allied armies to keep up with Germany's efforts. For these industries to be able to increase their productivity, Thomas forced workers and industrialists to sit at the table to negotiate conventions fixing salaries, production targets, and labor conditions. The Ministry also negotiated procurement plans with Allies to ensure access to raw materials and industrial goods not produced in France as well as to ensure the stability of its currency, in order to be able to meet its financial obligations throughout the course of the war.[16] Thus, the state did not substitute itself for the private initiative, but it helped private interests organize themselves at the industry level so as to optimize the division of labor and the organization of trade for the allies' interest – thus creating a sense of solidarity between the classes within the same society and across societies.

Even if Mauss did not directly participate in planning the war effort, as he found a role as a translator attached to the twenty-seventh division of the British army, he obtained firsthand knowledge of the initiatives undertaken at the Ministry of Armament to turn the cooperativist philosophy into concrete action. "*L'Année* holds the keys" to the Ministry of Armament, as Durkheim anxiously wrote to Mauss in August 1915.[17] By 1915, the Durkheimians were heavily involved in the industrial planning effort. Simiand and Halbwachs were trying to find new optimized ways to reconfigure the international division of labor between the Allies in an attempt to create what we would today call "global commodity chains," by bringing, for instance, British coal with Algerian minerals into the same chain of production.[18] Long gone were the days when Hubert, Simiand, Mauss, and Durkheim divided the book reviews among their little group for *L'Année sociologique*.

Simiand was not the only trained economist inspired by solidarism and socialism to join Thomas at the Ministry of Armament. Among other legal scholars of solidarist inspiration, we can cite Israel William Oualid (1880–1942), born in Algiers' Jewish community, who, like all other Durkheimians, had been a member of the League of Human Rights founded during the Dreyfus affair, and who would later write important work on the costs of the Great War with Charles Gide, as well as works on money, tariffs, and exchange rates.[19] Arthur Fontaine (1860–1931), a former student of Polytechnique and chief inspector of work, who entertained a brilliant Parisian life with parties attended by artists and novelists like Charles Gide's nephew André Gide,[20] and who later worked to found the International Labor Organization (ILO) with Albert Thomas, also joined the group.[21] Among these men, Mauss entertained a rich correspondence throughout the war with his best friend and coauthor, Henri Hubert, mobilized in 1915, whom Albert Thomas wrote had become the "soul of the automobile service" in the Ministry, before engaging in economic and political negotiation with Russia in 1917, and then overseeing the restitution of works of art by the Germans to the Belgians and French after the war.[22]

Last, one other economist joined Thomas's team: Max Lazard, the son of Simon Lazard of Lazard Frères,[23] who had known Simiand and Mauss at least since 1908.[24] Max Lazard entered Thomas's cabinet before being sent to Washington to organize the purchase of war materials on behalf of the French war industries (which had thus mutualized their calls for materials), and then working together with Arthur Fontaine on drafting the articles of the Versailles Treaty that established the ILO, which he joined with Thomas and Fontaine after its creation. As reflected in his correspondence, Mauss remained in close touch with Max Lazard before and after the war, as the two men continued to contribute financially to the same socialist cooperative until at least 1927.[25] They mixed at social events with some cooperativists *de passage* in Paris, like Robert Hunter (1874–1942), an American sociologist, philanthropist, and activist involved in the fight against child labor.[26] Even when Thomas was replaced at the top of the Ministry of Armament in 1917 by Louis Loucheur (1872–1932), another Polytechnicien and self-made man in the construction sector in France, some of the Durkheimians like Halbwachs left, but the Ministry kept the same orientation.

During the war, Paris was thus not an uninteresting place to live in, and the Ministry of Armament not a bad location to start planning the shape of the postwar financial order in Europe. If, as recorded by Marcel Proust, the nightlife had dramatically changed compared to the glorious days of the *belle époque*, as many of the young aristocrats who entertained parties and salons had been killed in the trenches, the daily life of Ministry officials was full of stimulating intellectual opportunities for the young sociologists and economists interested in participating in the reorganization of the war economy. It was also full of opportunities for the young Durkheimian sociologists to develop new friendships with the French bankers associated with the financing of war procurement: indeed, the officials of the Ministry of Armament also had to make sure that the French state could meet the payments due to the Anglo-American Allies in exchange for weapons and other military materials. In this regard, the presence of Max Lazard, whom Mauss knew well, in the Ministry ensured that the other Durkheimians would have access to some of the prominent members of the newly founded inter-allied Commission on Exchanges, charged with the stabilization of the franc during the war, and who included André Lazard (1869–1931), Max Lazard's brother, among its members.

If Mauss knew Max Lazard well before the war, he may, although it is not certified, have met André Lazard, as the latter also spent the first two years of the war working as a translator in the headquarters of the British army of General Haig. Mauss later acknowledged in *The Nation* that a friend of his at the Commission on Exchanges provided him with key insider knowledge about currency stabilization, and it could have been André Lazard.[27] In 1916, after joining the service of Governor General Hubert Lyautey (1854–1934) in Morocco and then Lyautey's services at the Ministry of War, when the latter became Minister,[28] André Lazard was sent back to work at the Lazard bank, which was the Banque de France's operator of the exchange market, and at the newly founded Commission on Exchanges. The presence of the Lazard Frères owners in this Commission was perfectly justified by the fact that the question of exchanges was indeed deeply related to the market of gold, and that the bank Lazard Frères had carved out a very specific role for itself in that market: at the turn of the nineteenth century, the bank invested in a new line of business – the transfer of gold from the US to France (and vice versa).[29]

With the prewar system known as the "gold standard," any transaction could indeed be monetized either in local currency or in gold. Importers thus had an interest in paying in gold rather than in local currency if the price of the latter was higher than the amount of gold they would have to ship to the exporting country. Around the time of the Dreyfus affair, the first generation of Lazard bankers, a family of French Jews who had left the eastern region of France after its annexation by the Germans in 1871, had established a network of banks in Paris, San Francisco, New York, and London, and started operating on the gold market in 1884, for "other reasons than profit,"[30] according to Alexandre Weill, one of the bank's founders. Prestige was one of these reasons: indeed, in the 1880s, the Banque de France had started to invest massively in the acquisition of gold, in order to foster the activities of its importing and exporting industries, so that they might one day benefit from the relative differences between the price of gold and the local currencies where they exported or imported goods. Thanks to their investment in the purchase, transport, and sale of gold, the Lazard banking network thus created a privileged relationship with this very prestigious client: the Banque de France, which relied on its discretion to conduct its "gold policy."[31]

For the Lazard bank, helping the French central bank even when it was not the most profitable line of business was not a disinterested act, although it was also a manifestation of the banking partners' patriotism: as the founder of the Weill dynasty (later the David-Weill dynasty) liked to remind his family, a serious financial establishment could not always seek short-term profits, but it had to shoulder its clients in times of crisis, in the hope of being given back profits in times of opulence. As Alexandre Weill wrote, "reciprocity [between a creditor and its client] imposes itself. If we give this, we must obtain that. *Donnant, donnant*, this is the law of business."[32] As he added, "When profit margins are reduced, we have to keep serving our clients with the same zeal as before, and we can even take advantage of these business cycles, as we may gain new clients rejected by the indifference of other financial institutions."[33] This precept was all the more true when the client was as prestigious as the Banque de France, and in the transition from peacetime to wartime.

The Lazard bank faithfully applied this principle when the war with Germany broke out in 1914. At the onset of the war, the bank J.P. Morgan had obtained agreement from the British government to serve as the sole intermediary for all purchases of food and war material in the United States – organizing a kind of "wholesale" whose task was to obtain better prices than could be obtained by individual British bidders. Understandably, J.P. Morgan wished to play the same role for the French government.[34] But the Paris and New York Lazard branches objected to the fee that J.P. Morgan had negotiated for all transactions (soon amounting to billions of US dollars) – which was duly relayed by the French press. Very quickly, the Lazard Frères bank succeeded in securing their role as the main transporter of the gold that the Banque de France loaned to the French government to pay the collateral on US and British sales of war material. Throughout the war, they didn't charge any fee for the services they offered to the French government, despite the fact they obtained a quasi-monopoly on the exchange of gold.[35]

This offer was not the only gift that the Lazard bank offered to the French nation. Lazard Frères also helped the French government launch large national subscriptions (*emprunts nationaux*). Indeed, as real patriots, they fully supported the mission defined by the French Prime Minister Ribot:

> We have to bring the reserves we have. At this time, egoism is not only synonym with cowardice and treason, but it would also be the worst foolhardiness. What should these reserves become if France shall not be victorious? They would become the ransom asked from us rather than the price of victory. This is why the army of French savings shall arise: like the army that fights, it is the army of France.[36]

In fact, this willingness to form close ties with the French central bank, and to gain prestige from a reciprocal relationship formed by the mutual exchange of services and gifts, was continued by Alexandre Weill's son, David Weill (later David David-Weill), when the franc became the target of speculative attacks in the mid 1920s. But we will come back to this other episode later. What matters here is that within "the army of French savings," the Lazard bank partners certainly had reached the rank of a four-star General by the end of the war, and the Lazard brothers provided a unique source of information on the operations of Franco-American operators in high finance for the Durkheimian officials in the Ministry of Armament – and through them, for Mauss, who became extremely interested in financial affairs during and after the war.

Indeed, if, after the war, Mauss remained interested in the question of workers' cooperatives and was consulted as an expert on the subject by Albert Thomas (the Director of the ILO in Geneva until his premature death in 1932),[37] he moved on to discuss mostly topics related with high finance in a series of publications in *La vie socialiste* and *Le populaire*, the latter a journal partially funded by the new leader of the SFIO (Léon Blum), Belgian cooperatives, and private donors.[38] With the disbanding of the Commission on Exchanges following the end of the war, one the main questions that preoccupied Mauss and other Durkheimian friends of his, like Henri Hubert, was whether or not France would be able to meet the financial obligations it had contracted for the service of its war debts; and whether or not France's monetary policy would dramatically increase the price of those debts. This is why Mauss and his friends praised the work of the Reparations Commission, which, after the Versailles Treaty was signed, was endowed with the responsibility to help France and other bankrupt European nations shoulder their debt and stabilize their currency in order to avoid the eruption of another deadly conflict.

2 GUILT AND RESPONSIBILITY IN THE GERMAN REPARATIONS SCHEME

Today, it may not appear evident that the work of the Reparations Commission prefigured the postwar role of the International Monetary Fund (IMF) as stabilizer of currency parities,[39] which is why it is important to come back to the history of the legal concept of reparations in the peace negotiations: it is necessary if we want to understand why Mauss found it crucial to write about the debt swaps that the Reparations Commission organized between European nations, and to hail it as an exemplary model of global governance in the field of international economic relations. Indeed, many historians continue to see in the "reparations" provisions of the Versailles Treaty a form of victor's justice, which imposed an odious and unsustainable debt on a vanquished nation; and they see in the Reparations Commission the arm of the creditor nations, like France, whose revengeful instincts were revealed when the latter invaded Germany's richest regions when Germany defaulted on its debt servicing obligations.[40]

During the Great War, it is true that many French nationalists conceived of reparations as a rightful penalty against the crime of aggression committed by the German Emperor against the Belgian and French armies rather than as a mechanism of macroeconomic stabilization. That interpretation was particularly fashionable among the French jurisconsults in the Commission on the Responsibilities of the Authors of War and the Enforcement of Penalties (hereafter, Commission on Responsibilities), formed at the end of the war to prepare parts of the Versailles Treaty. The German responsibility in causing the war was debated in the Commission on Responsibilities, which concluded that Germany was indeed responsible for the war and recommended the prosecution of the German emperor for the violation of "international morality and the sanctity of treaties" – a demand that was included in the section on penalties (articles 227–230) of the Versailles Treaty.[41]

The discussion of this notion of responsibility actually started in the early days of the war when the French government tasked none other than Emile Durkheim to write an official document challenging the German doctrine according to which the outbreak of the war had been Russia's responsibility.[42] As Durkheim wrote to his nephew in December 1914, he believed that his brochure established the "irrefutable demonstration" of Germany's responsibility in starting the war.[43] Then, in a publication commissioned by the French government on the role of war in the German "mentality," Durkheim went even further: he wrote that the responsibility of the German state in the declaration of war was not only imputable to a series of fateful tactical decisions by the German leadership which forced the Austro-Hungarian Empire to declare war on Serbia and thus on Russia, but it also corresponded to broader general traits in the "German mentality"[44] – a claim he found less irrefutable, as he later told Mauss.[45] In many ways, the notion of responsibility found in these essays, written at the beginning of the war, was still ambiguous enough to be interpreted as criminal guilt or as simple financial responsibility in the civil law sense.

In the Commission on Responsibilities, the French were represented by a politician and a legal scholar with political leanings far from the Durkheimian: André Tardieu (1875–1945) and Ferdinand Larnaude (1853–1942). Tardieu, an editorialist and right-wing politician who would go on to become President of the Council (Prime Minister) of France, served as adviser to Prime Minister Georges Clemenceau (1841–1929) in the peace negotiations. As the deputy of the Territory of Belfort, a small department that had been carved out from the larger regions of

Alsace and Lorraine,[46] and which had symbolized the heroic resistance of the French against the Germans in the 1871 war, Tardieu was ardently nationalist – and even anti-Semitic – as well as imperialist; in fact, he was involved in various scandals of the French administration of the Congo before the war, which placed him in direct confrontation with Jean Jaurès and Albert Thomas, as discussed in the next chapter. Politically, Larnaude stood halfway between Tardieu and Bourgeois: although the latter had been one of Larnaude's mentors, Larnaude's strong anti-German feelings brought him closer to Albert de Lapradelle, a jurisconsult for the Minister of Foreign Affairs with whom Larnaude participated in a committee working to define the legal notion of reparations.

For Tardieu, Larnaude, and other French jurisconsults, the French demands that Germany pay some reparations after the war manifested the continued "national union" against the enemy and the clear expression of the French state's will to win the economic peace after winning the war. It was motivated by the duty to sanction Germany for its unacceptable behavior during the war and its criminal responsibility in the multiplication of war crimes (invasion of a neutral country,[47] state terrorism against civilian populations, use of gas, and chemical warfare).[48] In the deliberations of the Commission on Responsibilities, Larnaude and Tardieu repeatedly argued that the reference to Germany's "responsibility" as a state should in fact be discussed in the context of international prosecution of the crimes committed by the German army.[49] The final Commission Report argued that a failure to punish violations of the laws and customs of war in defense of absolute sovereignty would "shock the conscience of civilized mankind," emphasizing that "the public conscience insists upon a sanction"[50] (which was how they framed the question of reparations).[51] Thus, in this sense, responsibility was conceived as the mark of criminal guilt.

When the Council of Four (Allied heads of state), which decided the final wording of the Treaty,[52] presented it to the French and British public opinion, the nationalist interpretation of German reparations (as a blame and sanction against Germany's conduct) seemed to prevail: the press, outraged over German war crimes, called for retribution and ascribed moral guilt to Germany for the atrocities of the war. Calls to "Hang the Kaiser"[53] and punish war criminals played an especially prominent role in the British parliamentary elections of 1918.[54] The British proposal to prosecute the German Emperor also met with enthusiastic approval from the French Premier, Georges Clemenceau,[55] who presented the peace settlement to his compatriots as a complete vindication of France's 1870 defeat: France legally recovered the territories that it had lost in 1870 (Alsace and Lorraine) and obtained new colonial territories (like Cameroon and half of Togo, the other half going to the British, which also gained German colonies in East Africa, when Japan obtained German colonies in the Pacific), as well as reparations from the Germans.

But even if Tardieu and Larnaude rejected the notion that reparations could be tied to France's alleged "responsibility" to compensate for war damages,[56] or that reparations would express some form of social solidarity between citizens of the same nation (France) or continent (Europe), another more progressive and positive understanding of the "duty to repair" existed at the time, in which reparations were indeed tied to a notion of solidarity that was to become the basis of a new right for citizens in Europe: the right to have one's properties restored if destroyed because of a war. The ambiguity over the meaning of "reparations" and their consequences – in large part a product of the decentralized process of negotiation of the Versailles Treaty[57] – was thus due to the presence of conflicting forces in the French field of power, which resulted in a power struggle over the meaning of the financial obligations created by the Treaty.

Against the nationalist interpretation, the notion of responsibility was associated with generous calls to act responsibly in favor of European postwar financial solidarity – which is how Mauss and his friends, like Gide, Blum, or Hubert, understood the concept of responsibility. Solidarists read in the sixteen articles (231–247, and all the annexes) of the Versailles Treaty the description of a collective institutional machinery set up to decide the amount of, and monitor the payment of, German reparations, so that Germany could be reintegrated in the European community of responsible states. On the one hand, solidarists admitted that these articles established "the responsibility [rather than guilt] of Germany and her allies for causing all the loss and damage to which the Allied and Associated Governments and their nationals have been subjected as a consequence of the war imposed upon them by the aggression of Germany and her allies" (article 231). But on the other hand, the Versailles Treaty also planned the establishment of a Commission of Reparations, to determine the extent to which Germany could "make complete reparation for all such loss and damage done to the civilian population of the Allied and Associated Powers and to their property during the period of the belligerency"[58] (article 232).

Furthermore, the Versailles Treaty also specified that Germany would "make a special issue of bearer bonds" (article 232) to restore the properties of civilians, the final amount of which, as well as the schedule of payments, depended on the recommendation of the Reparations Commission (article 233),[59] which shall "give to the German Government a just opportunity to be heard." This last sentence was especially important, as it meant that the reparations philosophy did not hinge on the German admission of guilt, but instead, the recognition of some collective responsibility among European nations in repairing the war damages caused by states to Allied populations especially, as the latter had suffered to a much greater extent from the war destructions than the Germans.[60]

For the solidarists, the notion of reparation was thus based on the notions of financial responsibility and solidarity found in other legal texts, such as a law passed by the French Parliament that tied together these notions of responsibility. This law, passed on October 22, 1915, stated in part: "The Republic proclaims the equality of all Frenchmen and the solidarity of nations in supporting the costs of war; the damages caused in France to the movable properties and real estate property, by acts of warfare, open the right to a complete reparation."[61] As Charles Gide later commented, this law expressed a form of "national solidarity, which had never before been expressed in such an affirmative way by France" – after previous wars, like in 1870, "it was said that the victims of the war might be compensated for their loss, but nothing was done, and nobody had raised to the possibility of complete reparation."[62] As Louis Loucheur (Albert Thomas's successor as Minister of Armament in 1917 and then Minister of Liberated Territories in 1921 and 1922), explained to Chancellor Rathenau in mid June 1921, the reparations provisions in the Versailles Treaty were a direct emanation of the same philosophy that had inspired the French 1915 law establishing the state's new duty to repair.[63]

Léon Bourgeois and Louis Loucheur moved the analysis of reparations architecture away from the political debates about alleged German "guilt" and back to the progressive elaboration of a body of international law concepts, such as collective responsibility, duty to repair, collective insurance. They were actively involved in this effort to promote recognition of a European social debt to the civilian victims of the war: Europe had a debt to those Belgians and Frenchmen whose private wealth was destroyed because their possessions were located on the battlefield. Léon Bourgeois, who was the rapporteur on the Versailles Treaty to the French Parliament, saw in the principle of reparations a formidable advance for European civilization precisely because the treaty clearly distinguished reparations from indemnities, as the Allies did not ask "any indemnity from Germany in compensation for the military expenses."[64] As Bourgeois added, the American delegation had opposed the inclusion of war costs, as the Germans had only accepted reparations for civilian losses in their "pre-armistice agreement."[65] Eventually, they settled for a sum which was close to 160 billion francs – to compensate the French civilian population mostly for damages directly caused by bombardments (85 billion) and pensions to war invalids and widows (60 billion) – and they excluded the payment of an indemnity (to reimburse war costs) which would have amounted to another 143 billion francs.[66]

For solidarists, special financial measures included in the Versailles Treaty thus simply ensured that the Allied populations would not suffer more than the German population from the financial burden created by war debts – which would have been the case in the absence of reparations, as most destruction had happened on Belgian and French soil.[67] For them, the reparations scheme illustrated the broad philosophy of financial responsibility that the architects of peace asked all European nations to observe. Indeed, according to the peace settlement with Germany (and Austro-Hungary), each state was asked to act responsibly in order to maintain the collective order and to accept some redistribution to equalize the burden of war debts. The notion of financial responsibility was not only found in the Versailles Treaty signed between the Allies and Germany, but also in other peace treaties, like the Treaty of Saint-Germain-en-Laye, signed in September 1919 by the Allies and the successor states to the former Austro-Hungarian Empire. These peace treaties established the idea that old debt contracts between the defeated central European empires should be honored by the new nations formed after the war. Past debt contracts could be restructured only in extreme circumstances, if the people had not consented to the borrowing and the proceeds had not benefited the people at the time debt was contracted.[68] All the newly created states in Central Europe had thus to accept to pay debts that they had not contracted, in order for Europe to remain financially stable. Alexander Sack (1890–1955), a Russian émigré who worked in France on the question of sovereign debt restructuring in the context of state succession, found only one example of cancelled debt in Europe: that of Poland (a new state created out of the association of territories formerly under either German or Russian authority and control), which was relieved from a small part of the debt (an amount to be fixed by the Reparations Commission) contracted by the Germans to fund their occupation and colonization of Polish lands (article 254).[69]

This reading of the financial provisions contained in the peace treaties was thus in line with the general solidarist ideology of Charles Gide and Marcel Mauss, for whom to repudiate debts in a unilateral way – as the Bolsheviks had done – would have been a crime against the principle of reciprocity, or interdependence.[70] For Mauss, when Bolsheviks rejected the Tsarist debts and confiscated the property rights of foreign nationals on Russian soil, they had failed to honor "the tacit international contracts"[71] – in solidarist parlance, the quasi-contracts – and had destroyed the national and international trust in the Soviet regime, leading to the "disappearance of the sources of all social life: trust and good faith"[72] – a conclusion with which Max Lazard was in total agreement, as he wrote to Mauss.[73] For Mauss, the negative international reaction to Russia's revolution was thus the logical consequence of Russia's inconsequent ignorance of the founding principles of international law (good faith and avoidance of unilateral acts), since "a State has only the right to apply its laws to its citizens and to the foreign nationals who are residents, but it has to avoid giving the appearance of committing any injustice and any violations against tacit international contracts, e.g. against public and private international law."[74]

It is important to contextualize these debates about financial responsibility in the political discussions of the German reparations and Europe's financial order, as our analysis of Mauss's notion of gift exchange, which he introduced in this context, may be misguided by more recent utilizations of Mauss's concepts in the context of present-day debates about international economic governance, which are marked by the ever-widening opposition between left-wing thinkers and anthropologists, and the multilateral financial institutions, like the IMF, which impose unrealistic conditionalities on debtor states, in Europe and elsewhere. But, in fact, a world separates the present-day calls for unilateral debt cancellation proposed by left-wing thinkers such as David Graeber or Eric Toussaint – the Belgian historian and president of the Committee for the Abolition of Illegitimate Debts, who was selected in 2015 by the left-wing President of the Greek Parliament, Zoe Konstantopoulou, to conduct the "citizen audit" of the Greek debt[75] – in the context of the present-day Greek sovereign debt crisis, and the calls in favor of "financial responsibility" expressed by Mauss and Gide in the immediate post-Versailles context. Even if present-day anthropologists like Graeber claim to be inspired by Mauss, when they argue for instance in favor of unilateral debt cancellation, the latter wrote extensively on the sacred duty of all nations to honor their debt.

3 THE EUROPEAN SOVEREIGN DEBT RESTRUCTURATION MECHANISMS IN QUESTION

If the Great War hit hard the group of Durkheimians, with the death of Durkheim father and son, it also failed to disband them, and the economic aftermath of the war focused their attention on the same question: whether the wartime industrial cooperation and financial solidarity between Allies could survive the end of the war, or whether the defeated Germany could be included in the circle of Allies in order to restore a sense of European solidarity, in particular against the Soviet threat. These questions were indeed central in the writings of the Durkheimians – Mauss in particular – that focused on the role of German reparations in the restoration of international solidarity and economic prosperity in the European continent, where new nations had carved a space for themselves on the debris of the Central European empires.

Among those who argued that the Versailles Treaty served to establish a framework for the financial organization of international solidarity in Europe after the war, Marcel Mauss became particularly active: from 1920 to 1924, Mauss published more than forty editorials in *Le Populaire*, in which he defended his reading against those in the right-wing government, who, like Louis-Lucien Klotz (the Minister of Finance from 1917 to 1920 and a Jewish native of Alsace, like Mauss himself) or André Tardieu, had claimed that reparations were due to France because of Germany's guilt in starting the war and later conducting atrocities.[76] As Mauss wrote about Klotz, he was "the only Jew who does not understand a word of finance," and he suspected that George Clemenceau, the French President, "perhaps displaying satanic tendencies," had nominated him as Minister of Finance to "expiate the sins of Israel and of the nation"[77] and turn him into a scapegoat for the German public, who would later associate the requirement that Germany pay formidable sums to France with a transnational Jewish plot.

In contrast, Mauss consistently lauded the work of the multilateral Reparations Commission gathered in Brussels in December 1920 to recalculate the amount of the reparations. The Reparations Commission included many among Mauss's friends and cooperativist collaborators, like Charles Gide and Louis Loucheur representing France, and Jean Monnet (1888–1979), who was also a friend of André Lazard, representing the League of Nations as its first Secretary General.[78]

The French team led by Gide also included Charles Rist (1874–1955), a professor of law and economics who coauthored with Gide the *Histoire des Doctrines Economiques*, and whose book on *La Déflation* was lauded by Mauss in *L'Année*;[79] as well as Arthur Fontaine, the labor inspector and philanthropist, who joined Albert Thomas and Max Lazard at the ILO in Geneva after the war. Mauss was convinced that the French government should follow the recommendations of the Reparations Commissions, which had become the official institutional conduit for the harmonization of national accounts in Europe as well as for negotiations of sovereign debt rescheduling in a globalizing world economy conducted across the Atlantic.[80]

At a time of reopening European markets and European-wide investments in reconstruction efforts, members of the Reparations Commission believed that it should fully participate in the establishment of a common legal architecture governing financial flows – in the same way the IMF played the role of ensuring currency stabilization from the end of the Second World War to the dismantlement of the Bretton Woods system that occurred with the end of dollar–gold convertibility. For Charles Gide and his collaborators, reparations were meant to fairly balance the price of the war among the warring parties so that European solidarity could be reconstituted on sustainable grounds.[81] As Charles Gide and Albert Thomas's former collaborator Israel William Oualid noted, "[a]mong the damages resulting from the war, we have the debts that each warring party has contracted, which weigh to a greater extent on the victors than on the vanquished."[82] This imbalance in the weight of the war debts between victors and vanquished was precisely what the German reparations were supposed to eliminate: there was no point asking Germany too much to pay, or too little.

The debt imbalances resulting from the unequal distribution of war destructions in Europe meant a kind of macroeconomic system of debt redistribution should be found for each sovereign debt to be sustainable. As Mauss wrote, in Brussels:

> illustrious experts (Irving [Fisher] from New York, [Charles] Gide from Paris, [Arthur Cecil] Pigou from Cambridge) agreed on the substantive claims that it was necessary: 1) to fix a rational reparations policy based on a reasonable estimate of the credit and debit of each warring party; 2) to devalue depreciated moneys in proportion of that estimate; 3) in the meantime, to find enough international capital in order [for central banks] to let enough gold circulate to restore the gold standard.[83]

Thus, the Reparations Commission conducted what the IMF now calls debt sustainability assessment (DSAs) as a preliminary step before any negotiation of the amount of German reparations it was legally mandated by the Versailles Treaty to ascribe to the Germans. This turned the Commission into an essential mechanism of financial transfer and macroeconomic regulation. The holistic and forward-looking strategy adopted by the Reparations Commission to treat the problem of reparations meant that economists integrated reparations within the broader context of Europe's sovereign debt problem – or rather, they inferred the reparations from the overall credit and debit of each European nation, including an overall estimate of all the wartime debts contracted to domestic and international actors. The numbers were the product of a collective study commissioned by James Shotwell (1874–1965), an economic and diplomatic historian at Columbia University and Director at the Carnegie Endowment of International Peace, to support the work of the Reparations Commission.[84]

From the assessment of the credit and debit of each nation, the Reparations Commission inferred how much debt (including German debt in the form of reparations) could be written off for each nation. For example, the experts determined at the Brussels Conference "that France owes 219 billion prewar francs in loans," mostly borrowed on French capital, and to a small extent (about one-sixth, or 38 billion) on foreign (British and American) creditors.[85] "This amount," Gide continued:

> corresponded exactly to our estimate of the general wealth of France; or if we prefer to measure interest rather than capital, it corresponded to 14 billion francs-gold, to which were added 10 billion francs-gold in pensions to invalids, widows and children (a debt also contracted because of the war), which meant that France had to pay 24 billion francs-gold of interest, e.g. more than 70 per cent of the total yearly income which was not over 35 billion.[86]

The French debt was thus unsustainable if the Germans refused to pay some reparations, which is why international experts computed that Germany would need to pay annual payments of 3 billion gold marks each year for forty-two years – an amount that seemed more reasonable than the initial French government's proposal, which had asked Germany to pay forty-two annual payments of 12 billion gold marks (to reimburse a total Allied need of 200 billion gold marks with France claiming 110 billion gold marks).[87]

The assessment of the credit and debit of each European nation was the preliminary step before the implementation of a general policy of debt cancellation or stabilization of all European moneys (not just the mark): "a legal change in the value of the money, a procedure which we call 'stabilization,' a euphemism" for the reevaluation of the debt, as Gide wrote. The Reparations Commission demanded that all nations (including the French) assess exactly how much debt they could support and how much they would have to write off. For Gide and Oualid, France's creditors, for instance, should not expect to recover the entirety of their wartime loan, as "the taxpayers would have to give away the entirety of their fortunes to pay back the nation's debt to the stockholders (or 70 percent of their yearly income)."[88] As Mauss wrote, it was of paramount importance for the French people to realize that from "creditors of the whole world, the French people have become debtors, whose creditworthiness . . . depended on their ability to retain gold" and to "stabilize the French franc"[89] at its right parity with the gold standard, e.g. at the amount of gold the French central bank possessed inside France and in obligations outside.

In 1921, the Reparations Commission seemed to work relatively well: in anticipation that the Germans would not be able to pay their reparation debt for that year, Germany's creditors engaged in a new round of negotiations on reparations, which ended in London in May 1921 with the London Agreement. The British asked France to honor legality rather than occupy the Ruhr, as the Versailles Treaty stipulated that sanctions should occur after a default of payment, and not in anticipation of a default.[90] With the London Agreement, the German reparation debt was restructured in order to avoid seeing Germany default. The Reparations Commission set a new total at 132 billion (rather than 200 billion) gold marks to be paid in two steps: first the Germans would pay the annual interest and amortization of a loan of 50 billion gold marks used for Allied reconstruction (corresponding to 2 billion gold marks per year, the sum that the Germans had proposed to pay in 1919, plus some 26 percent of the benefits of German exports); second, after German economic recovery, the Germans would pay the interest and amortization on another Allied loan for the remaining 82 billion gold marks.[91] This was a major "haircut" on the public debt owed by Germany to its neighbors, but it wasn't sure it would be enough to solve the problems in the long term.

Unfortunately, the same problems that plagued Germany's currency and Europe's economic recovery in 1921 resurfaced in 1922: the 1921 London Agreement between Allied governments had only postponed the solution to the problem of German reparations, but it had failed to address the institutional weakness of the Reparations Commission, which could only hope that their recommendations would influence macroeconomic policies in France as well as in Germany. But hope and persuasion was all they got, since the German government largely ignored its calls for stabilization, while the French government continued to insist on full payment of the renegotiated sum. In 1921, Germany had failed to pay the annuity because it stumbled upon two ongoing problems: inflation first, and the balance of payment second. Indeed, the German chancellor failed to convince the German financial conglomerates to stop issuing credits, thereby raising the mass of monetary instruments in circulation in Germany, which fueled what Mauss called the "policy of bankruptcy" of the German government, as "the German Republic wished to demonstrate that it could not pay the reparations that the Allied bankers believed it capable of paying."[92] As Loucheur told Léon Blum in July 1922, while the two were elected deputies, Germany should be "sincere and clear about its desire to comply with its international legal obligations," when instead, its monetary policy "encouraged the plunge of the mark," to the discredit of its "standing and its interest," which were intrinsically associated with France's "ability to be repaid."[93]

Furthermore, the payment of reparations heightened Germany's balance-of-payments problems: due to the large decrease of its foreign exports during the war and postwar eras, Germany did not have enough foreign currency to pay reparations with French and Belgian francs and British pounds. As a result, Germany had to sell marks (rather than exported goods) to buy foreign moneys and pay what it owed in reparations, and the speculation against the mark led to further depreciation.[94] The French government then lobbied for the stabilization of the mark[95] and agreed to bypass the German problem of buying foreign currencies with payment in kind, in coal or cession of shares of the industrial coal conglomerates upon which France's steel industries depended.[96] But German industrialists, aided by the British, who opposed the creation of large Franco-German cartels in the coal sector, successfully opposed a tax on capital and only agreed to increased taxation on wage earners to generate new revenues – which could never generate enough cash to pay the reparations.

This is why in 1921, the Reparations Commission proposed to engage a much larger and more comprehensive round of multilateral debt cancellation by the creditors of Germany and France: this idea of multilateral debt cancellation had been first formulated at the very beginning of the work by the two British negotiators in the Reparations Commission, John Maynard Keynes (1883–1946) and Robert Brand (1878–1963), a British colonial administrator in South Africa and a London banker. The world-famous British economist and his colleague had expressed their conviction that "the United Kingdom would benefit more in the long-term from the cancellation of French war debts, and the international prosperity that would result from a parallel settlement of the reparations questions."[97]

Keynes, who later participated in the Brussels Conference during which a first "haircut" of German reparations had been decided, had been one of the first to propose that the British and Americans should make the first gift by cancelling the inter-allied debts that France (and to a lesser extent Belgium and Italy) owed them.[98] Then, so Keynes reasoned, the reparations to be paid by Germany to France could be scaled back to a reasonable level, as France and Italy would not insist on receiving as in-kind reparations the German coal that Austria needed. Besides, for Keynes, the inter-allied debts were "odious debts" as the loans that France had contracted in the United States had not paid for investment in productive economic activities, but had been used to fight a war in which the United States had claimed to act as an ally, not by providing men but weapons.[99] As Brand had said, justifying their proposal, "when everyone adopts egoist tactics, it is human to reject altruism, but if we do not all want to suffer, one must make the first move, and it is within our tradition and character to do just that."[100]

But in 1922, the Reparations Commission had been unable to convince states to move beyond a partial and limited "haircut" granted to Germany. In 1922, there was no longer any talk of partial debt cancellation among French solidarists, including Mauss, as the British government reimbursed all the war debts it owed to the United States after the Cannes Conference, which had failed to generate a consensus on the question of reparations among Germany's creditors. So, there was no longer any hope that the United States would erase the wartime debt that France owed to the New York bankers. Although Mauss had believed that a multilateral partial cancellation of sovereign debts might have been an interesting solution in the early days of the reparations debate, in 1922 this solution no longer appeared acceptable: the British payment of their wartime debt meant that the French should do the same as the British, and reimburse first its inter-allied debt, as "a people gets richer by paying its debts, because … of all the credit it gets from the world."[101]

The priority, then, was for the solidarists to convince the French government to accept some debt rescheduling of the German reparations, by delaying German payments and extending the number of their annuities. It was a legal trick meant to avoid irritating the French nationalist press, which would have balked at the idea of giving Germany another haircut on the sum of reparations it owed to France. But the French government of Raymond Poincaré (1860–1934) conditioned his agreement to reassess the schedule of German reparations to the reevaluation of the war debts that France owed to its own creditors: the British and the American banks (especially J.P. Morgan, which floated loans to the British and the French for almost half a billion dollars in 1915 and 1916).[102] Indeed, after the Cannes Conference, the French government asked for Germany to either pay in full the large sum negotiated at the time of the Versailles Treaty, or for the Allies (the United States in particular), to cancel part (or all) of the debt that the French owed to them as a result of their purchase of war material. This was a tough negotiating position.

For Mauss, when the French asked the United States to write off their debt first, they committed the same mistake as the Soviets when the latter "declared the Russian state bankrupt."[103] As the US bankers and the US government warned the French in July 1922, they may agree to lower the inter-allied debts, but as Mauss wrote, "if French leaders were to wait for this before their own revision of reparation, they shall wait in vain."[104] Prefiguring his reflection in *The Gift*, Mauss observed the reality of the politics of sovereign debt: no nation wanted to be the first to give, as a gift would be perceived as a sign of weakness, and not of strength. This was a misperception that Mauss wanted to change. In *Le Populaire*, Mauss told his fellow socialists that if the French cancelled part of the German debt, then "the British and the Americans could not but do the same, but the British and American taxpayers would never admit that the interests of a debt contracted by France would be cancelled if the French creditors were not first treated in a similar way,"[105] i.e. if France did not devalue the franc (and its national debt to French creditors) by 60 percent (in 1922 Mauss estimated the franc at 40 percent of its prewar value).

Such was the context in which Mauss first wrote about the need for France to make a large gift to the Germans, and to see the circulation of sovereign debts as based on the principles of a gift exchange economy. Mauss proposed that the French should follow the precedent of the British government after their victory over Napoleon: "after victory, the British lent France some money … the gold with which the government of Louis XVIII operated during its first month was British gold which was introduced into France thanks to the Rothschilds,"[106] the ancestors of the Jewish bankers who proposed to stabilize the mark and franc in 1922. In the absence of such a gift, Mauss believed that German default of payment was bound to occur again in 1922. Then, inflationary cycles would continue to destroy Germany's ability to meet its reparations payments. This was unfortunately the most likely outcome, as Mauss was very pessimistic about this possibility. As he wrote in 1922, the French public was misled by:

> the German wish to demonstrate that Germany could not pay the reparations that the Allied bankers believed it capable of paying, and which, for that reason, had let its gold and its credits be exported outside of its soil, with the result that the whole wealth of Germany was now depreciated ... and the German public no longer trusts the mark, but places its faith in foreign currencies instead.[107]

In addition to discussing the necessity for France to extend large gifts to its former neighboring enemy, Mauss's op-eds discussed another available instrument to restore European solidarity: the idea of a moratorium on German reparations, which he believed could be more acceptable to the French public. Indeed, Mauss argued that if "the State stops paying its debts during a certain amount of time [until it proceeds to devaluation], then it can resume its payment, which even if reduced, would again be payment in gold, and with amortization of the debt."[108] The socialists of the SFIO, especially Blum, agreed: Blum insisted, "Germany must meet its obligations, but to do so, we must give her the means to recover economic prosperity."[109]

The temporal sequence advised by Mauss, Hubert and Blum in 1922 looked as follows: first, France and its Allies would make a large gift to Germany by writing off a large amount of the reparations debts; then, Germany would take the time to reorganize its economy and financial system; and, finally, Germany would pay back the original gift by reimbursing its restructured debt. As Mauss underlined, it was important "that 1) the Allies should grant a moratorium long enough to recover its payments on its budget surplus, 2) that they should reduce the German debt to a reasonable level, 3) that the Germans should balance their budgets; 4) that they should stop inflation which meant adopting a higher interest rate."[110] Mauss's position was also shared by the British government, which urged German Foreign Minister Rathenau to apply for a moratorium on payments, rather than accept to default.[111]

Thus, Mauss introduced in his political essays of 1922 an original concern for the temporality of debt repayments, which manifested in his reflections on the inherent asymmetry of interstate relations. The extension of a moratorium was a useful way to avoid deadlock between the French government and its Anglo-American creditors over which nation would make the first gift, or, rather, which nation would be the first to write off part of the debt that the others owed it (and what conditions would be made on that gift), and whether default of payment would be met by sanction.

As Henri Hubert wrote to his former Minister, Albert Thomas, the moratorium – short of solving all the institutional problems affecting Germany's financial health – could be a short-term patch placed on the hemorrhage of German marks, and it was certainly more useful than extending a short-term loan to Germany for them to pay their reparations annuity, or erasing another section of the German debt, which the French adamantly opposed:

> Having the Germans pay 30 billion to the Allies, as this dishonest idiot of Keynes [who was arguing for a major "haircut" in today's parlance, from 132 billion to only 30 billion] is as hard as getting Germany to pay the 132 billion gold marks fixed in London. The real problem is a problem of instrumentation, and the instruments that have been used so far are just ill adapted to the situation ... At the present exchange rate, it is as ridiculous to ask the German government to use marks to pay for the material [industrial equipment, coal, etc.] that it is legally obliged to send to France as reparation-in-kind, as it is to force Germany to buy foreign currencies to pay the few millions it has to pay in cash for reparations. The credit lines that the financial sector may extend to the German government will not help them pay what they owe to us: the money lent will be immediately used to temporarily restore the value of the mark, but as a result of speculative attacks, the amount of the loan will be immediately pocketed by the speculators who bet on the downfall of the mark.[112] Thus, any loan extended to Germany will fail to produce the desired outcome. Here's what our politics should be: We should propose without any delay a complete moratorium on the payment of reparations in cash, and as long as needed for the current system of payments to be reorganized – a period which will last for no less than six months.[113]

But the French public also found the moratorium impossible to accept, as long as the Anglo-American creditors refused to erase the debt that France owed to them. The French nationalists insisted that German reparations were the continuation of war through other means. Helping the Germans recover first economically, before forcing them to pay reparations, smelled of high treason. Mauss and other solidarists had good reason to be worried.

At the end of 1922, the situation indeed seemed hopeless. J.P. Morgan refused to cancel the debt that France owed to the bank: instead, he agreed to float a loan to Germany so that it could avoid a default for 1922, and proposed that, in exchange, France write off some of the amount of reparations.[114] Responding to J.P. Morgan's offer, the government of Poincaré agreed to a partial debt rescheduling but used a subterfuge: in inter-allied negotiations with the British and American governments, Poincaré agreed to write off only part of the 82 billion gold marks that Germany had to pay in the future, not any of the 50 billion gold marks that it had to start reimbursing immediately. This was in line with the program which Raymond Poincaré had promised to implement when he formed his nationalist government in France, after the French right-wing press had called for a policy of sanctions: France could, for instance, seize "collaterals"[115] if Germany failed to honor its reparations debts.

The whole debt renegotiation scheme was thus on the verge of collapsing. For Mauss, the fault was Poincaré's, whose financial solution was a "fake sacrifice since the French would only renounce payments that could not be made, while asking the British and American taxpayers for a large gift,"[116] i.e. the immediate cancellation of inter-allied debts. Confronted with the risk of a German default of payment, André Lazard then encouraged the Lazard Frères of London to extend a long-term credit to the German government so that Germany could meet its financial obligations for 1922 – but he warned his associate in London to proceed with the utmost confidentiality, as any association between the name of Lazard and a credit extended to Germany risked backfiring against the French branch and spur a rise in anti-Semitic attacks against the Lazard Frères as a consequence.[117]

Indeed, on top of the financial instability, anti-Semitism and nationalism were on the rise and showed their ugly faces when a right-wing fanatic assassinated the German Foreign Minister, Walter Rathenau, during the reparations conference of bankers held in June and July 1922. His assassination showed the price that German politicians (especially Jews) would pay for agreeing to negotiate with the Allies, and it ended the negotiations of a moratorium on German payment. The German nationalists, as Mauss had feared, started to associate the payment of reparations with a transnational Jewish plot. Does it seem so extraordinarily strange to us? In a way, it does, and at the same time, we should recall that when Greek Finance Minister Yanis Varoufakis called on the Greek government to abandon any plan of unilateral debt cancellation (if only partial) and negotiate instead a moratorium on payments and a debt rescheduling arrangement with the Troika (the IMF, the European Central Bank (ECB), and the European Commission (EC)) in charge of ensuring the full implementation of the plan imposed by Greece's creditors – a plan very much like the one that Mauss proposed in 1922 to solve Europe's sovereign debt crisis – many Greek nationalists and left-wing radicals saw in his public statement the proof that he was taking his orders from the Jewish billionaire George Soros and thus part of a Jewish conspiracy to destroy the birthplace of Europe's democratic traditions of sovereign autonomy.[118] Sadly, history often repeats itself, as either farce or tragedy.

4 THE GIFT: IN SEARCH OF LEGAL PRECEDENTS FOR THE MORATORIUM ON REPARATION PAYMENTS

The difficult renegotiation of European sovereign debts raised one of Marcel Mauss's central lines of questioning in *The Gift*: How to jump-start a cycle of gift-giving in a noncooperative game? At the same time as Marcel Mauss and Henri Hubert wrote about the necessity for France to make a true gift to Germany by granting it a moratorium on payments, the two friends – but Mauss especially – were thus engaged in the rebirth of *L'Année sociologique*, in which Mauss eventually published *The Gift* among many shorter review essays. As said previously, Mauss finally put together the new *L'Année sociologique* of 1924 thanks to Max Lazard and David David-Weill of Lazard Frères in Paris, the very same family of bankers whose financial policy he lauded in *Le Populaire*.[119] The new volume of *L'Année sociologique* also contained other important essays by Mauss's collaborators, in particular François Simiand,[120] whom Mauss regularly consulted on the question of the stabilization of the franc,[121] although the latter did not agree with Mauss on everything. It was thus not a surprise that the questions raised by the reparations dispute found their way into the sociological volume.

The topic of Mauss's essay was indeed very similar to the one he tackled in his political essays, as Mauss believed that the exchange of gifts in all kinds of societies was akin to the payment of debts, and international debts in particular, by modern nations.[122] Mauss sometimes even used interchangeably the notions of gift and debt, for instance when writing on the potlatch among Northwestern American Indians:

> their economic system is as much based on credit as is the economic system of civilized peoples ... Indians do not have any writing device and therefore, their transaction must be public to be secure. The *potlatch* consists in contracting some debts on the one hand, and in paying some debts on the other hand. This economic system is so developed that the capital possessed by all the individuals associated with the tribe far exceeds the quantity of values at hand [the liquid values, Keynes would say]. In other words, this society shares with our society similar properties: if we desired to pay back all our debts, we would not be able to find enough money to pay them. When every creditor seeks the reimbursement of his loan, it creates a disastrous panic which hurts the community for many years.[123]

As seen in this quote, Mauss distinguished the partial payment of debt called potlatch (paying off one loan and taking out a new one)[124] – which can easily be done by "writing off" the debt of some nations when the economy is based on writing devices – and the total reimbursement of debts, when the debt is completely paid off and the bond between creditor and debtor erased. For Mauss, the potlatch did not erase the debt, nor did it erase the social bond, between creditor and debtor nations. The potlatch just redistributed the debt within a community of nations whose common destiny was made manifest by the acceptance of the redistributed (and consolidated) debt. The "regime of contractual law and system of economic prestations"[125] known as potlatch actually strengthened the bonds between communities as it articulated a set of legal duties, "the duty to give ... the duty to receive ... and the duty to give back."[126] *The Gift* thus detailed the socio-legal conditions which ensured that the partial payment of (national and international) debts would increase (international) solidarity. Indeed, Mauss asked: "What is the legal rule and the incentive which ... forces the gift received to be obligatorily given back?"[127]

Mauss was also very careful to underline that the logic that presided over the exchange of gifts belonged to the realm of sovereignty: it was practiced for and by sovereign powers; and to the extent that Mauss's reflections related to debt issues, they concerned mostly sovereign debt, and not the reimbursement of ordinary loans between private members of a tribe. The logic of the gift was indeed the exact contrary of the utilitarian logic of petty merchants, who did not understand that economic exchanges of gifts were not just economic actions but also political acts of alliance-formation.[128] For Mauss, it was thus essential to distinguish the act of gift-making, which was a political act, from the utilitarian logic of speculation.[129] In rituals of gift-giving, national leaders rejected the petty logic of bargaining as, by giving, they sought to establish the honor of their nations, and even their superiority in the gift-giving contests or "wars of properties."[130] For instance, in the ceremony practiced by the Kwakiutls of the American Northwest, there was no bargaining, but the parody of a declaration of war, in which the gift-giver acted as if he did not give anything, "as if the thing given was ignored … even distrusted … after it has been thrown to its feet by the gift-giver who must affect a fake modesty."[131]

The Gift is an interesting textual hybrid, as it integrates for the first time Mauss's reflections on a series of published ethnographic findings – in particular, from the writings of German-trained but English-speaking ethnographers, like Boas, Thurnwald, and Malinowski – as well as archaeological findings, which he mostly borrowed from his best friend Henri Hubert, who had written with Mauss two of the latter's most important articles on the functions of sacrifice and of magic in *L'Année sociologique* at the beginning of the century.[132]

The lives of the two friends were intrinsically tied at many levels: intellectual, since after their first essay on the nature of sacrifice, Hubert decided to focus on gift exchanges and other contractual forms in ancient European societies (like the Celts and the Germanic tribes),[133] while Mauss decided to study and teach at the EPHE on similar topics in the context of non-European societies (India especially, but not only); financial, as Mauss's mother had lent some money to Hubert to help him buy his home;[134] emotional, as Hubert named his first son "Marcel" in reference to his best friend, whom he considered his son's uncle;[135] and social, as Hubert's circle of friends overlapped in many ways with Mauss's own circle. Indeed, Hubert's other best friend from his student years was Marcel Drouin (1871–1943), who had married the sister of André Gide's wife,[136] and who had cofounded with Gide *La Nouvelle Revue Française*, where the young Blum, André Gide's best high-school friend and Mauss's collaborator in *Le Populaire*, published his early essays.[137]

If anthropologists today are familiar with the worlds of the Trobrianders, those Argonauts of the Pacific, and the Kwakiutls of the American Northwest, I have had more than one anthropologist colleague tell me that she always wondered what role the equally important sections on Germanic tribes played in Mauss's now classical text. Where did these findings on Germanic tribes come from? And what purpose did Mauss seek to achieve by placing them after the description of the kula or potlatch systems? A first answer may be that, by doing so, Mauss drew inspiration from Hubert's work on the Germanic tribes, and that he included archaeological data from Europe's past practices of gift exchange to generalize the observations of ethnographers into a universal theory of solidarity and gift exchange, based on all ethnographic, archaeological, and historical facts known to the *savants* of the time. Fine: that is an important part of the puzzle. There is a second equally plausible answer, which relates to Mauss's methodological preference: that Mauss was primarily a philologist, who liked to reinterpret recorded tales and texts from the whole world, rather than a field ethnographer who liked to conduct primary fieldwork in territories previously unknown to Western scientific teams (archaeologists, ethnographers, biologists, etc.).

There is another (complementary) way to explain why Mauss gave so much space to his description of Germanic gift-making practices, which is more sensitive to the porosity of the boundary between Mauss's political and academic writing: that Mauss sought to back up his political claims that the Germans would understand their legal obligations if part of their debt was written off, or if they were granted a moratorium on payments, by pointing to legal precedents of the potlatch in the Germanic legal tradition. As Mauss insisted, "Germanic societies ... have such a clearly developed system of exchange with gifts, voluntarily and obligatorily given, received and given back, that one would have trouble finding an equivalent"[138] except, perhaps "in the practice of gift-exchange found by Mr. Malinowski in the Trobriand islands."[139] As Mauss wrote, "the gifts play such an important role in the legal culture found among the Germans" and the "persistence of such mores" is so evident that "they must be very solidly grounded on strong roots in the German soul."[140] Indeed, with the exchange of gifts, old Germanic nations (as well as nations in the Pacific and other parts of the world) exchanged the "fundamental proof of the military, legal, economic and religious recognition of the leader of a nation."[141] The two logics of gift exchange and market exchange were inherently antithetical, added Mauss, who wrote that in Germanic society the logic of the gift was so strong that "Germanic civilization was a long time without markets ... and in earlier times, this civilization only developed the potlatch."[142]

Thus, Mauss used his academic writing as a venue to diffuse a solid anthropological justification of the kind of financial policies he and other collaborators of *L'Année*, like Henri Hubert, discussed in their conversations and private letters as well as in their op-eds. The two worlds of politics and science were not so far away in France, or in the countries taking part in the discussions of the Reparations Commission. For instance, in 1924, Mauss had written to that not-so-little economist whom Hubert so passionately disliked, John Maynard Keynes, to ask him whether the Royal Economic Society would be interested in receiving *L'Année*, and sending books to review to its editorial board.[143] Sensing that Mauss may have been animated by, if not carried away by, such political considerations, Hubert wrote to Mauss that his conception of the Germans' sense of obligation was a bit hopeful, and certainly biased by his contemporary preoccupations with Germany's understanding of its legal obligation to pay back reparations:

> The question of whether, and how international trade can modify an economy of the kind of the kula trade, is quite problematic [in your essay]. Let's take what you write about the ancient Germans: you write that Germanic law did not include the possibility of market exchanges. But the Germanic world in the bronze age cannot exist without markets. Indeed, there was not one atom of copper or tin in Germany, and this is still the European country with the highest number of discoveries of bronze objects. Germans have exchanged metal against amber, and there was a market for amber. I can certainly explain the paucity of terms in the Germanic vocabulary to refer to market exchanges. There has been a long eclipse of markets during the Iron Age, but then, the profound influence of the Celts has been felt, with the diffusion of the words *leihen* and *Werth*, and all the system of pledges and confiscations. I have thousands of traces of exchanges with foreigners which followed purely economic logics. It all depended on the specific periods, as the phenomena did not follow direct lines, but rather, they drew cascading patterns ... This is why I expected that you would tell us much more about the evolution of economic logics after the ancient Germans, by describing how Roman law affected the situation ... And what you write about the fact that there is still something of that kind [as the potlatch] in our social fabric is very nice, but contradictory with what you said about the instability of these forms of economic exchange: I can see some stability in the Celtic world, in Ireland or in Gaul, but I do not see such stability in the Germanic society. These are issues which you should study without any consideration for their political and/or moral dimensions.[144]

Hubert's criticism of *The Gift* thus focused on what he knew best and what Mauss knew least: the Germanic culture of gift exchange. For Hubert, the Germanic world was rife with market exchanges as far back as the Bronze Age, for in fact all of the bronze used in Germany came from other countries, traded against amber – and claiming otherwise was disingenuous. Henri Hubert was more a specialist on the Germans and the Celts than Mauss was, as Hubert had taught a yearly class on the ancient Germans in 1924 and 1925 at the School of the Louvre (Paris's major art history school),[145] and he was still working on his book *The Celts*, which Mauss later edited and published after Hubert's death in 1932.[146] Meanwhile Mauss had only published one article on the Thraces, who, like the Celts and the Germanic tribes, lived in the confines of the Greco-Roman world.

In general, Hubert was quite critical of Mauss's essay,[147] which he found at times "quite foggy and imprecise" especially in word choice. In particular Hubert thought the expression "prestations totales" unfortunate, as he wrote that "there's always something that escapes the realm of prestations" (something more sacred for instance), at the origins of group solidarity.[148] But Mauss saw in the exchange of gifts or "prestations" (a word with legal meaning, as it was also found in the Versailles Treaty) the perfect illustration of how old Germanic nations understood the formation of international contractual bonds; it encompassed how "[c]lans with tribes, great extended families within the clans, chiefs and even kings" interacted outside "the closed circles of their own groups" and how they forged "links, alliances and mutual assistance [contracts which] came into being by means of the *gage* (pledge or collateral) . . . and acts of generosity."[149] Thus, Mauss insisted that these exchanges united different collectives and he appeared to stick to his point that all Germanic tribes manifested their sense of total (economic, social, cultural, religious, political) belonging through such ceremonial exchange of goods and services – hence, the use of the term "prestations totales."

If Mauss was guilty of an exaggeration – or rather, an essentialization, according to his friend Hubert – about the rules observed by Germanic tribes in their practices of exchange, Mauss would have agreed it was because of the political goals he sought to accomplish with his essay. The elective affinity between Mauss's academic and political agendas was most visible with his reflections on the temporality of gift-making practices in the Germanic context. Applied to the interwar context, Mauss's analysis of gift exchanges and the origins of international solidarity could not but echo the discussions that Hubert, Blum, Thomas, himself, and many others had on the desirability of granting a moratorium to the Germans. If the readers of *The Gift* followed his argument to its logical end, they would understand that if Germany was granted a moratorium on the servicing of its reparation debts, it would no doubt start reimbursing in full the reparations once hit by economic recovery. The logic of gift exchange required that the Germans start paying back reparation debts only after some time had passed – otherwise, the payment of reparations would look like the extraction of a war bounty by former victors and neutral bystanders.[150] Mauss's reflections on the gift showed that such a moratorium was not an exceptional demand placed upon the French government by unworthy allies, but a universal rule of good global governance, which placed trust and long-term reciprocity over the strict conformity to contractual obligations asked from debtor nations, even in self-defeating cycles, which hurt both debtors and creditors.

In *The Gift*, Mauss indeed found that certain anthropological conditions related to the rituals and temporality of gift-making practices were necessary for the quasi-legal obligation to "give back" after a first gift to be observed. As Mauss told his readers, "Time is necessary to execute any counter-prestation: the idea of a 'term' is always implied" in the exchange of gifts, "when people exchange visits, when they contract marriages or alliances, or when they establish peace."[151] Indeed, said Mauss, citing Simiand, with the exchange of gifts, nations created bonds between past and future.[152] The exchange of gifts always escaped the present, as gifts were not even looked at by the gift-giver and the gift-receiver, and always heralded counter-gifts in the future. In contrast, market exchanges could only occur in the present, without concern for the past and future of the co-contractors: in market exchanges, a complex system of credit allowed economic agents to anticipate, in the present, the future returns of a deal, and to agree on the payment of interests at the moment of the transaction.[153] But that was not how nations manifested their solidarity.

Thus, Mauss found in the anthropological discourse a way to justify his concern for the temporality and asymmetry inherent in the type of negotiations from which a sense of European solidarity could manifest itself through the global management of Europe's financial affairs in the Reparations Commission. Rather than seeing reparations obligations in purely legalistic and economic terms, he looked beyond the question of whether the German state had met its contractual obligation by paying the exact amount in due time, and he introduced the notion that European solidarity could only be constructed on solid ground anthropologically if the exchange of payments and "prestations" followed a certain temporal rhythm – which he feared could not be reduced to the contractual temporality of a simple debt contract, with its highly predictable schedule of payments. For a European sense of solidarity to emerge from the reparation payments, the temporality of their occurrence could not be aligned on the linear sequence envisioned by the French nationalists: payment or default followed by sanctions. As seen in this reading of *The Gift*, the gift that Mauss asked France to make by stabilizing its money, writing off part of the German debt, granting a moratorium on payment, and expecting future debt forgiveness from its Anglo-American allies, was more than a purely monetary policy. Rather, such an act would have represented a fundamental change in France's alliance policy, as well as a fundamental change in how France conceived the temporality of debt exchanges.

5 THE OBLIGATION TO GIVE BACK, AFTER SOME TIME: A CONSERVATIVE POLITICAL AGENDA?

Many readers of *The Gift*, when they understand that Mauss's interpretation of the anthropological "facts" presented therein was more rather than less affected by Mauss's political inclinations, want to know more about the latter. If Mauss was a self-declared socialist, what kind of socialism was he representing? Did his positions evolve during the course of the 1924 run-up to the electoral victory of the SFIO, which led Blum's party to become France's first political party (although one that was unable to govern, for it lacked a majority)? As anthropologists, sociologists, and historians, we are trained to doubt the validity of uncontrolled historical parallels. But the earlier reference to Varoufakis's position in the present-day debate about the management of the Greek debt crisis may be helpful to position Mauss in the range of policy positions debated at the time. In each sovereign debt crisis, both men offered a middle course, or third way, between a radical policy of unilateral sovereign debt cancellation[154] and the harsh implementation of a program of sanctions (or "conditionalities," in modern day IMF parlance) that liberals and neoliberals imposed to the debtor nation to ensure that the servicing of the external debt would follow the schedule of payments decided by its creditors. In so doing, just like Varoufakis has been accused by radical left-wing activists, like Eric Toussaint, and a large section of the Syriza party, for failing to denounce the "odious" (and hence illegitimate and illegal) character of a large part of the debt owed by Greece to its European creditors,[155] Mauss was suspected of having sold his soul to the tycoons of financial capitalism – in particular, the Lazards, whom he counted among his friends – by some of the more radical left-wing intellectuals, like François Simiand, who also wrote on the reparations question.

Before I give voice to the left-wing criticism of Mauss's position in favor of debt rescheduling and moratorium – rather than debt cancellation – it is fair to first present the criticisms that Mauss mounted against the French liberals and right-wing nationalists, which he published in twenty-eight articles in *Le Populaire* (from December 1923 to May 1924): in these articles, he strongly criticized the sanctions that the government of Raymond Poincaré implemented, when it sent the French armies to occupy the Ruhr, after the Germans defaulted on their 1922 reparation obligations.

For Mauss, the French occupation of the richest Western German regions showed to Germans that reparations paid to France were not a token exchanged to place Europe's economies on a path to economic growth and financial stability, but rather, a kind of indemnity that France extracted by force to pay for the costs of war and occupation from a nation which France still treated as an enemy. The reparations that Germany was supposed to pay to France were immediately used to pay the costs for France to maintain occupation forces within and around a defeated Germany. As Mauss wrote, the militarization of the French response to German default meant that France had to bear the "costs of keeping a standing army for three years: these were two billion gold-marks that went to the bailiff rather than to the victim,"[156] i.e. the Belgian and French families whose properties were destroyed.

In the early 1920s, French troops were also dispatched in Syria and Lebanon (former Ottoman provinces which had allied with Germany during the Great War), where they opposed the army of Feisal at a cost which Mauss estimated to be 1 billion francs (half of the yearly German reparations).[157] Furthermore, French troops were maintained in Morocco (where Germany had expressed territorial ambitions until 1905) at an estimated two and a half billion francs over five years;[158] and, most importantly, loans to buy French weapons were extended to Poland and Eastern European states of the *petite entente* for a sum of 2 billion francs (the very sum that the Germans failed to pay in 1922), so that these nations could threaten Germany from the east.[159] It meant that France did not intend to use reparations to restore European financial solidarity but to strengthen its military position vis-à-vis its former enemy. France either prepared for war, or had never really ended the war, in the eyes of many contemporaries.

Furthermore, Mauss bet that France would not prove capable of administering the industries of the Ruhr, and he was soon proven right: French engineers failed to produce the same amount of coal from the Ruhr as the Germans,[160] largely because Berlin adopted a policy of "passive resistance" in the Ruhr by paying workers to stay at home, which forced Paris and Brussels to send French and Belgian engineers and workers to man the trains and mines of the Ruhr.[161] As a result, "whereas the Germans had sent 11 million tons of coal to France in 'reparations in kind,'[162] by invading the Ruhr, the French government spent millions to only produce four million tons and bought from the British their coal to supply the difference."[163] In this light, the occupation of the Ruhr looked like a complete economic fiasco, which no one, not even Louis Loucheur, who acted privately to broker a compromise between the French and German authorities, could salvage.[164] In many ways, the episode conjures the more recent memory of the failed and ineffective policies that the Troika implemented in Greece as part of the "conditionalities" that Greece was forced to accept after the event-which-must-not-be-named: the 2010 Greek "default."[165] In the Greek case, too, the sanctions resulted in a massive economic contraction of the national income.[166]

The French occupation of the Ruhr took the whole German nation hostage, and as Mauss wrote in *The Gift* one year after – maybe with the sad smile of the prescient Cassandra on his face – the "Rhine gold" could also prove "fatal to the conqueror," as many old songs on the "theme of the fateful gift, which turns itself into poison" have warned generations of students of Germanic folklore, which plays on "the double meaning of the word *Gift* as gift and poison."[167] As Mauss wrote in *The Gift*, the idea of holding a collateral, depending on the nature of the collateral, could either be clever or stupid. Indeed, as he wrote in his academic essay, "our word '*gage*'" found its origins in the German legal culture: it comes "from *wadium* (in English, wage)," which refers to "the contractual bond."[168] And as Mauss continued, "[i]n Germanic law, each contract, sale or purchase, loan or deposit, entails a 'gage' or collateral: one partner is given an object, generally something of little value like a glove or a knife, or perhaps – as with the French – a pin or two."[169] But invading the Ruhr to get a grip on the black "gold of the Rhine" (coal) could not be called the exchange of a "gage," as the latter must be "an object of little value." At least, readers of *The Gift* would be able to understand that.

If they didn't read *The Gift*, the readers of *Le Populaire* could get a grip on the wisdom contained in old Germanic tales by merely looking at the economic situation of France and Germany one year after the beginning of the

Ruhr occupation. In Germany, the financial crisis convinced the government to stabilize the mark by creating a devalued new money: the Rentenmark, created on November 15, 1923. As Mauss lamented, "the French army in the Ruhr, which is on a French payroll ... finds its subsistence on location, spends money on location, and exports so many francs that ... the Germans and the little German girls are full of francs, which they now sell,"[170] as they started to trust their new currency. Partly due to the stabilization of the mark, the franc suffered in January 1924, as indeed, the "Germans started to prefer their *renten mark* to the franc, and even to gold. Therefore, they gave away masses of francs."[171] The effects of a lax monetary policy were similar in Germany and in France, although the responses lagged in the short term, as France started to feel the effects just as Germany recovered. The franc, which was exchanged against the British pound at 50 francs for 1 pound at the beginning of 1923, was then exchanged at 75 francs for 1 pound in the summer of 1923, and by the end of the year fell to almost 100 francs for 1 pound. The effects of these sales of francs were combined with the desperate need for France to buy foreign currencies at the end of 1923, when the French government realized, too late, that they needed to buy more coal on foreign markets. This situation led to an increasingly rapid depreciation of the franc, which Mauss, a patriotic socialist, bemoaned.

At last, for Mauss and Blum, the fateful invasion and occupation of the Ruhr marked another important fatal casualty: the spirit of multilateralism, which had animated the Reparations Commission until then. Indeed, after the 1922 German default, the Reparations Commission failed to transform itself from a site from where experts compared national accounts to deduce the amount of debt transfers necessary to ensure the financial stability of the European economic area, into the authority in charge of deciding when a "credit event" (a default in modern parlance) had occurred, and which policies to apply afterwards. The Versailles Treaty had not granted the Reparations Commission the authority to establish penalties and sanctions against the defaulter nor to establish an order of priority among the creditors whose interests were harmed by the default. As a result, after the Commission found Germany in default of its coal payments in January 1923, it could not stop the government of Raymond Poincaré from sending troops to occupy the Ruhr. Charles Gide had hoped that default of payment would be treated otherwise, and lamented that "international public law lagged years behind private law, where the idea that an insolvent debtor should be jailed or dismembered was no longer fashionable."[172] Unlike the Troika today, the main interwar multilateral financial institution was not complicit in the decision of creditor states to send the debtor state in the "debt-prison,"[173] but it was too weak to resist revengeful creditors.

Mauss thus concluded that, in order for France to create a sustainable European (and Western) political order after the Great War, it was essential to buttress the legitimacy of multilateral institutions like the Reparations Commission, and that France should give time to Germany rather than impose harsh measures that would make the German debt unsustainable. That being established, it is still unclear how his position could be criticized from the left. Here's how: for some of the most left-wing French socialists, Mauss's model of the gift, and its application to contemporary financial issues (with its emphasis on the moratorium, to give time to the Germans for them to rebuild their economy), seemed to place the goal of restoring France's financial solidarity above that of speeding up an international revolutionary upheaval. The same arguments that had been used by the Marxists against Mauss's cooperativist endeavors before the war – that they would delay the coming of a Revolution – were expressed against Mauss's notion of gift exchange, and its application to the European sovereign debt crisis.

By calling for the coordinated and simultaneous stabilization of the mark and franc in 1923 and 1924 (at a parity with gold fixed by the Reparations Commission), Mauss wanted to prevent the French middle (working) class from falling into ruin precisely at the time when the German economy recovered. At the time of the heightened risk of hyperinflation of the franc and the rush for foreign currencies, Mauss asked the government to "devaluate the value of the franc at the same time as taxing the gains made on the capital."[174] He rejected the idea that France could, like the United Kingdom, pay its debt and come back to the prewar parity with gold. Rather, the French government should accept to diminish the value of its currency, thus reflecting the new situation, and tax the capital that Frenchmen could be tempted to export abroad in a context of high inflation. In particular, with the latter measure, Mauss targeted "the French bourgeoisie, and even the French petty bourgeoisie, which have been touring the occupied countries like conquerors going for their bounty, in the hope of profiteering from the exchange rate, which disfavored the poor Germans, and which allowed the Frenchmen to live like little princes."[175] For Mauss, the "many Frenchmen … who purchased houses and hotels in the Rhineland, even in Berlin … in enemy territory," and who therefore exchanged francs against marks, committed "crimes against the credit of the State and of the Nation."[176] As he concluded, "it was the French capitalist, cosmopolitan *par excellence*,[177] who got rid of the national currency"[178] in the crisis of late 1923, when the price of the franc spiraled downed.

Other left-wing intellectuals disagreed with Mauss. Of course, if the French government refused to pay inter-allied debts until the Germans paid reparations in full, the franc would continuously depreciate, and this situation would work to the advantage of speculators who could move their capital to foreign lands, buying lands and goods where the currency was more stable.[179] But as Simiand wrote to Mauss, he "found it hard to reconcile his position on monetary questions" with that of Mauss, "as he disagreed with everything" that Mauss wrote on the topic. In particular, "he found it surprising that Mauss supported the ideas of the French central bank," which insisted on fighting the depreciation of the franc above all. Simiand thought this goal was in complete contradiction with the "revolutionary goals" of the socialist party. Indeed, he wrote, "if the monetary depreciation has the revolutionary ability to ruin the middle class, and if this ruin fulfills the socialist goals, why would the socialist party want to save the franc"[180] as Mauss advised?

The difference between Mauss and Simiand can be easily illustrated with how each perceived the outcome of the Ruhr occupation when evaluated according to the goals they assigned to the socialist movement. As the collapse of the mark, which followed the French occupation,[181] deprived the German government of any leverage with respect to economic matters, the French occupying powers renegotiated directly with the German industrialists of the Ruhr to obtain reparations payments in kind or cash. The French administration in Dusseldorf reached an agreement with the German industrialists in September 1923 which worked directly against the interests of German workers:[182] the industrialists ended the policy of "passive resistance" and gave the French 18 percent of the coal produced in exchange for the abolition of the pro-labor laws passed by the Weimar Republic.[183] This situation shocked Mauss, but not François Simiand, who argued that the social situation in Germany was by now explosive, and conducive to a revolutionary upheaval.[184]

To Simiand, Mauss's argument in favor of a comprehensive rescue package, based on the logics of the gift exchange, which would protect the interests of the German and French middle classes, unduly privileged financial responsibility over the transnational revolt of the working class against the German and French industrialists. Simiand was not completely wrong in his assessment that Mauss's views comforted more conservative voices in the world of high finance. Giving priority to the maintenance of a peaceful European financial order over an international revolution clearly put the middle-aged socialists like Blum and Mauss on the side of the conservatives in the socialist party. As Henri Hubert (who was not a socialist himself) wrote to Albert Thomas (taxed for being one of the least revolutionary voices in the old socialist party), in 1923, although he "would not go as far as saying that he had influenced Mauss to the point of turning him into a quasi-reactionary thinker, [he] was surprised to see that Mauss was getting closer to his view as he was writing on politics,"[185] and added, "he sees the France which is not socialist." This viewpoint led Mauss, according to Hubert, to think that the more conservative socialist Albert Thomas should leave the ILO in Geneva and come back to lead the French socialist party, claim victory if the left-wing coalition won the 1924 elections, and break with Blum's policy of "support with no participation" by accepting a Ministerial post in the future coalition[186] – something that Thomas rejected because he believed that he had a better position at the ILO to "keep the sympathy of the working masses."[187]

Simiand was also right when he asserted that Mauss's notion of gift exchange, with its emphasis on long-term and noncontractual reciprocity, as illustrated by the undetermined German moratorium on payments, had become the rallying cry of an unlikely rapprochement between bankers and socialist intellectuals: both were found for instance to be active in the Stable Money League, which had lobbied for the moratorium on German payments of their reparations, followed by the stabilization and devaluation of European moneys since 1921 – rather than the restoration of their prewar levels of parity with gold – and was successively presided over by socialists like Norman Thomas (a leading American socialist and six-time presidential candidate), solidarists like Charles Rist (Charles Gide's coauthor and collaborator at the Reparations Commission), as well as Max Lazard (Albert Thomas's deputy at the ILO), and bankers, like Louis Rothschild (Austria) and Sir Josiah Stamp (from the Lazard bank in London).[188] As Guy de Rougemont shows in his history of the Lazard Frères bank, André Lazard and David David-Weill and some of their key partners like Josiah Stamp had indeed become central figures in the battle to stabilize the franc: they were those who managed to convince the French central bank to stabilize the franc at its past exchange rate after it was attacked in March 1924.

This alliance of pro-stabilization bankers, politicians and public intellectuals finally obtained its most manifest victory when, in early 1924, the managers of Lazard Frères in Paris and New York bet that the quick depreciation of the franc did not follow any economic logic other than pure speculation, and that a coordinated response from the Banque de France and Paris-based and New York-based banks could actually work to stop the depreciation. The restoration of the alliance of Allied bankers identified early on the main causes of the depreciation of the franc on international markets: for them, Italian and Austrian speculators drove the depreciation, as they took very large short-term loans in francs, which they converted immediately into US dollars or British pounds, thus driving further the depreciation of the francs, which allowed them to reimburse their loans with a big profit thanks to a favorable exchange rate.[189] At the beginning of 1924, the administrators of the Banque de France did not agree, but when the value of the franc reached the critical level of 130 francs exchanged for one British pound in March 1924 and the franc couldn't find any buyers in New York, panic seized them, and they finally agreed to follow the Lazard's strategy: in March 1924, J.P. Morgan was tasked with raising more than 100 million dollars to fight the "battle of the franc," while Lazard Frères were asked to raise 4 million pounds in

London. In Paris, David David-Weill and his associates monitored all sales of francs in Amsterdam, Genoa, Frankfurt, Berlin, Vienna, London, New York, and Paris, and used the money loaned to the associated banks to buy them immediately, in order to sustain the rate at which the French currency was exchanged.[190] In five days the "battle of the franc" was won, as the pound went down from 123 francs back under the symbolic bar of 100 francs. The press, even *Le Figaro*, lauded the coordinated action of Lazard Frères and Morgan, and at the end of the month the pound passed under the bar of 80 francs. Their allied victory had the additional advantage of ruining the Austrian and Italian speculators as the latter could no longer reimburse their short-term loans at a profit.[191] The Viennese stock exchange, from where most of the speculative attacks originated, looked like a "devastated battlefield" according to the Viennese *Times* correspondent.[192] Their strategy, combined with a loan that J.P. Morgan floated to Germany, allowed Germany to pay part of the reparations it owed to France, which in turn allowed France to pay back part of its inter-allied debts to the US. The intricate link between the political and economic logics that Mauss assumed to exist in gift exchanges – and sovereign debt swaps that are meant to preserve peace – had resisted the test of reality.

Informed of these high finance strategies by his friends at the Lazard bank, Mauss turned *Le Populaire*, although a socialist journal, into an echo chamber where the international action of Lazard Frères bank was consistently lauded for conforming to the logic of gift exchange. As Mauss wrote in March and April 1924, the franc stopped plunging when "international finance gave for the franc and saved it"[193] by buying francs in order to show that one could trust the French nation to hold its obligations. In all fairness, the Allied bankers behaved like good doctors to bring the franc back to its real value: they started buying francs while the enemies (the Italian and Austrian banks) continued to speculate against it; and as they did so, they made quite a lot of money since they successfully bet that the value of the francs would rise again.

6 FIGHTING FOR CURRENCY STABILIZATION AND AGAINST ANTI-SEMITISM: MAUSS'S PRIORITIES

The relationship between Mauss's conclusions in *The Gift* and the conversation Mauss developed with socialist and solidarist intellectuals on the question of European solidarity, war reparations, and sovereign debt forgiveness has not been properly understood.[194] With the recent exception of Frédéric Ramel,[195] Marcel Fournier, and Jean Terrier,[196] "rare are the commentators who associate Mauss's scientific studies with his normative conclusions,"[197] as Sylvain Dzimira notes – one could add the names of Jane Guyer[198] and Keith

Hart,[199] in the Anglophone world. Even among those who pay attention to that link, scholars have mostly related Mauss's anthropological writings with his political writings on domestic issues, like the creation of a welfare state,[200] or the convergence of his approach with economic sociology.[201] But a joint reading of Marcel Mauss's political writings on reparations and his anthropological writings on the gift economy shows that they both derive from the same matrix: Mauss's desire to identify the conditions for a sustainable and peaceful international order that would prevent another devastating war in Europe. Rather than assuming that the former were only political texts and the latter only scientific texts, they must be seen as a coherent body of work, which shapes the contours of a normative model of multilateral sovereign debt management.

The ambition here is not only to trace the genealogy of the concepts of gift exchange and cooperation in various academic disciplinary discourses, and to associate the latter with the strategies of academic entrepreneurs or the effects of "invisible colleges"[202] and their institutionalization in academic niches,[203] but also to see how academic disciplines have used the discourse of the gift as an epistemic solution to the problem of knowledge and as a normative solution to the problem of order in different times: in particular, in the context of the interwar European debt crisis.

By publishing *The Gift*, Mauss sought to carve a place for anthropology in the range of comparative sciences (like history, sociology, and religious studies), which could be mobilized for the scientific study of reparations, forgiveness, debt, financial solidarity, and other Durkheimian and solidarist notions. By combining normative concerns and scientific explorations of the working of gift exchanges in international financial relations, Mauss reassured himself (and his readers) that the normative model of gift exchange he advocated to create European solidarity after the Great War had a serious anchor in the comparative knowledge of human societies. Anthropological knowledge of gift-making practices helped his contemporaries understand the legal (the evolving conceptions of contractual law and sanctions), political (the anti-imperialist alliance management policies), and anthropological (the ritual and temporality of gift-making practices) dynamics at work in issues of reparations and sovereign debt cancellation, which were so prevalent after the Great War.[204]

With anthropology, Mauss hoped to ground his normative model of the gift on a quasi-universal analysis of societies and their relationship to war and peace. Whereas Gide, Simiand, Blum, and Lazard were lawyers or financiers trained in either economics or law, Mauss mobilized the discourse that anthropology produced on the noncontractual elements of international debt exchanges in order to highlight the role of temporality in the formation of international solidarity through the exchange of debts. As he showed, if the goal of reparations was not just to sanction a state crime committed by Germany during the Great War, but also to create European solidarity, France had to accept that the temporality of debt payments would remain ambiguous rather than follow a clear calendar of payment. France had to recognize the role of uncertainty, asymmetry, and discontinuity in the relations between debtor and creditor nations for obligations deeper than the purely contractual to manifest themselves. Only the extension of a moratorium on the German payment of reparations could introduce a beneficial term between the wartime destruction of properties and the act of giving back. By placing the current sovereign debt crisis and its management in a long line of precedent, which included many instances in Germanic history, Mauss hoped to convince his contemporaries that the multilateral rescheduling of the reparations owed by Germany to the Allies was the only way to build European solidarity.

Mauss's perspective on international economic governance was also attentive to the cultural perceptions of ethnic groups, and how the latter strongly affected the perception of economic solutions. The financial conservativism that Hubert applauded and Simiand denounced in Mauss's reflections on Europe's debt crisis was justified by Mauss's fear that the ruin of the French middle class would not bring a socialist revolution, but the accentuation of nationalist, xenophobic, and anti-Semitic trends in European countries. The French right-wing representation of bankers was characteristic of the implicitly (and sometimes explicitly) anti-Semitic attacks against the "cunning Talmudists,"[205] as Blum would be called by a French deputy when he stepped in as France's prime minister twelve years later, who deceived the good "old Gallo-Roman nation," to enrich themselves. Mauss was very conscious of the "stupidities of *L'Action Française*"[206] and other anti-Dreyfusard journalists who relentlessly attacked "the Jewish and Protestant bankers"[207] who worked to defend the value of the franc. In 1924 Mauss saw the rebirth of anti-Semitism not only in the popular press, but also under the pen of social scientists and historians.[208]

In *The Gift* one can only be surprised by the fact that he made no mention of the practice of Jewish communities giving a tribute to European monarchs to ensure their continued existence within the Christian kingdoms. Silences and omissions are as important as explicit additions and long developments. Such omissions revealed a carefully thought out intellectual and political agenda: in the same way Mauss had fought anti-Semites who attacked Dreyfus, claiming that he defended all men rather than only a Jew, in his scientific essay Mauss avoided attacking the anti-Semitism of those who believed that gift exchanges were not practiced by Jews.[209] He preferred to claim that all peoples practiced gift exchanges, including the Germans: in *The Gift*, he elaborated a universalistic message, according to which all races and ethnicities (in the language of the time) were equally recognizant of the three obligations found in gift exchanges: the duty to give, the duty to receive, and the duty to give back. If gift practices were universal, then, they were therefore practiced by Jews.

In his op-eds in *Le Populaire*, Mauss attacked the anti-Semitism of the anti-stabilization coalition much more explicitly: for instance, he skillfully inversed the stigma placed upon American and Jewish European bankers by the nationalist and xenophobic French press, according to whom the foreign bankers of international finance were the cosmopolitan enemies selling the franc. Mauss fought head-on against this racist stigma by arguing that it was:

> the foreigners who read clearly in our books: the foreign bankers know exactly the value of our gold and our merchandise which cover both the mass of paper-francs in circulation and our loans (both short-term and long-term) . . . and when the franc [was] attacked, we [were] weighted, and our paper money [was] tested, just like the bad gold money of the king was tested by goldsmiths and money-changers, the good bourgeois, the Jews and Lombardi with their cupel and blowlamp.[210]

For him, the episode of the "battle of the franc" illustrated how Jewish and Protestant bankers had become France's true allies: as he wrote, the franc stopped collapsing when "the J.P. Morgan Bank started buying francs, as well as the 'five Big' banks in London that were associated with the Rothschild Bank and the Montagu Bank."[211] French Jewish banks also gave for the franc, in particular, the Lazard Frères Bank of Paris, directed by André Lazard and David David-Weill.[212] The stabilization of the franc proved that investments did not follow a purely utilitarian logic, as the "cosmopolitan" French bourgeoisie and their imperialistic government believed. For Mauss, the conformity to the model of gift exchange proved that "universal peace and inter-allied Entente could not but raise our credit."[213]

Mauss's efforts, in many ways, were vindicated, as his recommendations were partly heard in 1924: after the "battle of the franc" was won, at last, all state parties (including the United States) gathered at a large multilateral conference to make compromises and gifts in the form of organized debt rescheduling.[214] A committee of experts worked on a comprehensive stabilization plan (known as the "Dawes Plan," written under the chairmanship of US Vice President Charles Dawes),[215] based on their review of Germany's capacity to pay reparations and France's capacity to pay inter-allied debts. As the Allied bankers' strategy worked, putting an end to the depreciation of the franc, Louis Loucheur finally succeeded in convincing Raymond Poincaré to move toward the acceptance of the new plan. As Léon Blum wrote in *Le Populaire* in April 1924, at last "the experts, disavowing the policy of Poincaré, declared themselves in favor of a moratorium"[216] along the lines that Blum and Mauss advocated inside the SFIO against its more revolutionary elements: "during the first years, limited contribution of the Germans to the Allied reparations effort by payments in kind" until the Germans could accumulate enough money to start paying back. Poincaré "was forced to change his general policy, and to adopt the principle of increased taxation [on income and profits], reaching budgetary equilibrium, paying back debts rather than inflating the printed money."[217]

The SFIO leadership also managed to cash in on this political victory in electoral terms. Ultimately Mauss's efforts were rewarded when the Cartel des gauches won the election in May 1924, with Blum's SFIO as the first party in the new parliamentary majority. This victory, which left the editing team of *Le Populaire* exhausted, convinced Blum and Mauss to stop the publication of editorials, ending Mauss's series of articles on sovereign debts and gift exchanges. Had he also published all he had to say at the time? Maybe, but also, after the electoral victory of 1924, it was expected that Mauss would distance himself from the old SFIO and the politics of the left, as he had moved closer to the solidarists (like Charles Gide and Charles Rist), "progressive" liberal thinkers (like Max Lazard), "conservative socialists"[218] (like Albert Thomas), and even "neo-socialists" (like Marcel Déat),[219] some of whom invested their energies in expert committees tied to international organizations, like the French Association for Social Progress,[220] whose main agenda was the creation of an international committee to control credit and exchange rates – a function that the IMF would take over during the Bretton Woods era.

Was Mauss right to point at the necessity for social scientists to attack both the rise of anti-Semitism and the speculative logic of markets where exchange rates were priced? When one knows how European history unfolded ten years after, his writings were certainly prescient. Indeed, problems continued to plague the sovereign debt disputes, even after the socialist electoral victory of 1924 and the acceptance of the Dawes Plan. The proposals of reform of the international financial system, which Mauss and Hubert discussed in the aftermath of the "battle of the franc," went well beyond what Dawes and the US financial specialists had made the Europeans accept: for the two friends, the stabilization policies that they had already discussed in spring 1924 could only be a temporary patch placed on the hemorrhage of francs from which France had suffered. In 1924, they were convinced that it was necessary to go beyond and transform the Reparations Commission into a large financial wholesale in charge of administering German finances, as Hubert underlined in a letter to Albert Thomas (in which he reported having discussed the matter with Mauss, and being in agreement with his friend):

> The Reparations Commission is the biggest financial organization in the world. It has 60 million marks in deposits, and it can claim the whole amount of the reparations due by Germany to the Allies: 132 billion marks. Furthermore, it administers the financial aspects of the occupation of the left bank of the Rhine. It's only missing a few agencies and some sizeable autonomy. To strengthen it, it should be shouldered by the League of Nations. That being done, it could then help Germany fight against downward speculation on exchange rates . . . My argument is backed up by the precedent of the inter-allied control of exchange rates, which

> clearly helped stabilize the franc during the war. Thus, we need to find a mechanism that provides foreign currencies to a clearinghouse established by a Consortium of German banks, which could administer all payments for goods imported from Germany. German banks know how to coordinate. The Reparations Commission could supervise the working of this clearinghouse … It would thus play the role of a very big international bank, and the Reparations Commission would then be at the center of payments between Germany and the rest of the world. With all these bonds, these deposits and shares, it would have an immense credit in the whole world. It could even raise taxes on payments, for instance, on customs. In exchange, it could act as lender of last resort, should Germany suddenly need some cash. In this way, the Reparations Commission could administer Germany's whole sovereign debt due to the Allies, until Germany could claim its autonomy back.[221]

Mauss and Hubert's proposal of international technocratic oversight of a nationalized wholesale in charge of a major country's international economic relations hardly resonates with the themes of the current radical European left, which still has to grapple with the fact that a Troika composed of the ECB, the EC, and the IMF, has taken over key administrative roles of the formerly sovereign Greek state. In the 1930s, Mauss's perspective on gift exchanges left little room to the social question of how to improve the welfare of the working class, but it had the merits of addressing the main international issues of the time: Mauss foresaw that the authority of the Reparations Commission would not survive the rise to power of the National Socialist Party, and that with a default, and Germany's active rearmament, war would soon follow.

In general, Mauss criticized the French socialists for failing to take as seriously as he did the rise of Adolph Hitler in Germany: as he wrote to Blum in 1933, Blum's "irresponsible predictions on the short-term fall of Hitler"[222] led him to take his distance from the old SFIO. The divorce between Mauss and the SFIO that Blum completely controlled in the early 1930s, was finalized. As Mauss wrote to his old friend and colleague to explain why he left the old party:

> What are we going to do when, the franc being detached from the value of gold, the gold standard will end? What are we going to do when Hitler will raise his army? These are the two questions that keep me thinking all the time.[223]

In 1933, Germany defaulted on both reparations and foreign debts:[227] out of the 132 billion gold marks the Allies wanted Germany to pay, Germany had paid only 22 billion gold marks in reparations to European nations (including 9.5 billion to France), which left France to pay about seventy percent of the costs of the interwar reconstruction.[228] No one was surprised when Nazi Germany unilaterally cancelled its debt, since its leaders had argued for years that they did not recognize the legitimacy – and even humanity – of its creditors, whom Nazis presented as Jewish bankers who had conspired with French nationalists to make Germany pay for the whole of Europe. The German default of 1933 – which contrasted with the financial responsibility showed by most of the successor states of Eastern Europe that had been "hesitant to interrupt service [of the debt] on the grounds that much of their debt had been arranged under League of Nations auspices"[229] – proved that Nazi Germany rejected the whole philosophy of solidarity in Europe, and its associated system of macro-economic governance. The German state did not see itself responsible for the fate of those whom it considered non-Aryan populations in the interwar era: instead, Hitler claimed that the new Reich had a higher responsibility (beyond that recognized by treaties) to defend and protect the interests of all ethnic Germans, wherever they might be located (especially in new states with large populations of German-speaking minorities), thus challenging the sanctity of territorial boundaries drawn by the postwar treaties. Not long after, war ensued in Europe, and soon after, it engulfed the whole world into its most deadly conflict. Racial hierarchy, anti-Semitism, and war of the races became the dominant principles of European international politics for the next ten years.

4

The Gift as Colonial Ideology

Marcel Mauss and French Colonial Policy before and after the Great War

As Lygia Sigaud has claimed, among interpreters of *The Gift* there is a "general indifference to Mauss's preoccupations with rights and obligations"[1] – despite the fact that Mauss conceived of his essay as part of a broader exploration of the evolution of contractual law, the rules of commerce, and the making of international solidarity, which stems from the globalization of trade and finance. In so doing, Mauss continued his uncle's exploration of the "noncontractual elements of contracts,"[2] but at the same time he displaced his uncle's focus when studying the origins of solidarity. In contrast to Durkheim, who distinguished between a "mechanical solidarity," which he observed in "archaic" societies characterized by the absence of a division of labor in the sphere of production, and an "organic" solidarity, which he observed in societies with a higher level of division and complementarity between the various productive forces,[3] Mauss focused on the sites of exchange of goods and "prestations" to distinguish between various forms of international or intersocietal solidarity. With this move from production to exchange, Mauss no longer postulated that solidarity assumed the existence of a tightly bounded society within which individuals experienced solidarity.

After reading *The Gift*, Mauss's British colleague, Bronislaw Malinowski (1884–1942), had sensed – although he misunderstood it – the radical change of perspective from Durkheim to Mauss, when writing to Mauss in 1925 that:

> I have read your admirable article in AS [*L'Année sociologique*] proofs with great interest. Remarkably enough, I have come to very similar conclusions in working on the problem of law (now in print) ... But as you no doubt realize, both you and I give the *coup de grâce* to Morgan's concept of clan unity – also emphasized by Durkheim. If *reciprocity* is the keynote of primitive sanction, it really relegates *solidarity* at best to the second rank. Your article disposes of 90% of [Durkheim's] *Division du travail social*.[4]

While Mauss would have certainly disagreed with Malinowski that the analysis of solidarity was anything different from the analysis of reciprocity, and that the former should be restricted to the analysis of "in-group solidarity" (as in studies of "clan unity"), it was true that his approach to solidarity (or what I would call "out-group solidarity") was different from Durkheim's perspective. Mauss was primarily interested in understanding an international process – or rather, an "intersocietal" phenomenon, as sociologists like Mauss claimed that not all societies had reached the national level of development – which he characterized as a system of gift exchange.

The idea that sociologists and anthropologists could study intersocietal solidarity, and that the latter could take many forms, not all of which corresponded to how solidarity was understood and experienced by modern nations, was in fact related to another little-known aspect of Mauss's essay, which is the relation between Mauss's reflections on the gift exchange and the changing contours of the new imperial ideologies that French colonial administrators delineated after 1919 when attempting to reform the relations between the French metropolis and its colonies. Until now, commentators of *The Gift* have paid little attention to the colonial context which foregrounded Mauss's reflections on international solidarity.[5] But now that we can read Mauss's manuscript *The Nation*,[6] thanks to the transcription conducted by Jean Terrier and Marcel Fournier, we can better understand how Mauss's reflections on solidarity related to debates about French interwar colonial policy, and the relationship between European solidarity and centrality on the one hand, and the search for global peace and progress on the other hand.

By looking at Mauss's analyses of systems of reciprocal exchanges in the colonial context, this chapter questions whether, and how, Mauss refined his analysis of contemporary international politics when the latter diverged from his (optimistic) normative model of gift exchange. In 1925, Mauss proposed a bold conclusion at the end of *The Gift*: that most systems of reciprocal exchanges of "prestations" lead to the recognition of a duty to give back, and thus increase the sense of solidarity between exchanging partners. But at the time Mauss published *The Gift*, the rise of anti-Semitism, which was associated in Germany with a discourse that targeted the reparations provisions of the Versailles Treaty, indicated that he might have been too optimistic. In this broad context, Mauss took a step back to understand how contemporary politics of international solidarity diverged from his normative model of gift exchange, and what hidden variable could explain the differences between predicted outcomes – that gifts between the exchanging partners are always repaid and that they strengthen international solidarity – and observed reality.

This chapter shows how Mauss reevaluated his normative and theoretical model of the gift to deal with the biggest international issue of the time: the relationship between European and imperial solidarity. In *The Nation*, Mauss provided a general framework for understanding the positive and negative effects of the reciprocal exchange of prestations between sovereign peoples in the context of the French interwar Empire. In many ways, this geographical refocus – or rather, this geographical extension – of Mauss's anthropology of the gift to the whole world led the solidarist thinkers, like Gide, Thomas, Jaurès, Oualid, and the longtime Minister of the Colonies, Albert Sarraut (1872–1962) to tackle one key issue which Mauss had not addressed in his 1925 essay: How do societies understand the contractual obligations stemming from gift exchanges when they present highly disparate levels of development (or in Mauss's terms, of "integration")? Must such contractual obligations be reciprocal, as Mauss claimed in *The Gift*? Or do societies across various levels of integration understand such obligations in different ways? Could the exchange of gifts accelerate the race to war, economic exploitation, and military occupation? Or could it still work as a buffer to prevent war and disintegration from erupting in this context?

By answering these questions, this chapter demonstrates how Mauss's anthropological writings in *The Nation* contributed to nuance his original vision on gift exchange published in *The Gift*. It proceeds as follows. First, it shows how Mauss's writings echoed those of influential interwar colonial reformers like Albert Sarraut and other "progressive" apologists of the French Empire, who sought to reform the Colonial Pact in the interwar period, and it traces the origins of their interwar reflections in the prewar criticisms raised by Albert Thomas, Jean Jaurès, and Charles Gide, among others, against the abuses of colonial subjects by the chartered companies. It centers in particular on the criticisms raised against the chartered companies in Congo which were voiced by the French Committee for the Protection and Defense of Indigenous Populations, in whose activities Mauss participated in the 1900s,[7] and by Mauss's socialist colleagues, like Jean Jaurès and Albert Thomas. Looking at these prewar debates gives an important insight into the socio-historical genesis of key concepts used by Mauss in *The Gift* (like "prestations," "gifts," or "generosity," "contractual gifts") and found in political discourses on colonial reform. It also highlights the continuities between the prewar and interwar struggles between intellectuals and colonial administrators in the colonial field: André Gide's famous 1927 denunciation of the exploitative practices of the chartered companies in the French Congo finds its origins there.

Then, the chapter shows how Mauss's reflections in *The Nation* inspired the doctoral students he gained after the creation of the Paris-based Institute of Ethnology. The preoccupation of Mauss's students for the effects of varying levels of integration on the working of gift exchanges was driven by the French Empire's colonial expansion, and the new reformist mandate that Mauss gave to the ethnologists and colonial administrators who came to work under his supervision. Mauss's students were sent to the colonies and other non-European contexts to assess the validity of his model of gift exchange when exchanges circulated within and across societies characterized by various levels of integration. Looking at the political and administrative battles in which Mauss's students were involved in the colonial field leads to the following conclusion: Mauss's model of gift exchange gave these young reformers a powerful theoretical incentive to treat as an empirical question – whether the French Empire had a positive effect on the integration of colonial societies – what many orthodox colonial administrators considered as a matter of unquestionable principled belief – that, indeed, it did have a positive influence. Mauss's influence led them to question the main assumption under which colonial administration operated, or at least, to doubt its universal validity. But it did not go as far as to encourage them to rebel against the French presence outside of Europe; far from it.

1 SOLIDARIST COLONIALISM: THE INTERWAR DEFENSE OF THE FRENCH EMPIRE

Before the Great War, France's President of the Council Georges Clemenceau had famously claimed that the French dream of colonial expansion was a mirage that distracted from France's military reconstruction and future revenge against Germany. Many intellectuals agreed, like Maurice Barrès (1862–1923) and Déroulède (1846–1914), who lamented that the Republic's colonial project consisted in replacing the "two sisters" of Alsace and Lorraine that France lost after the 1870 defeat with "twenty servants."[8]

But after the experience of the Great War, most French politicians had turned themselves into public apologists for colonialism. The French socialists in particular no longer saw in empire a dangerous terrain of war: this had been a serious concern, especially for Jean Jaurès, after Germany and France had clashed over the occupation of Morocco. But since the defeat of Germany in 1919, they believed that colonial expansion would go hand in hand with a permanent stabilization of national frontiers in Europe.[9] As Raoul Girardet writes, the colonial expansion "had given back on the promises placed in it"[10] during the Great War: not only did 30,000 Berbers fight for France in the Great War, as Maurice Barrès had predicted in 1911,[11] but about 1 million soldiers came from overseas to defend the French trenches against the German advances – and out of these million soldiers, which included the famous "Black force"[12] made up of colonial regiments from Senegal, one-fifth (more than 200,000) were killed in combat.

In the 1920s, among the left-wing parties, only the Communist party was thus clearly opposed to colonialism on principled grounds, and consistently denounced the socialists like Blum as "lackeys of imperialism," when the latter said, for instance, that he refused "to confuse the movement of liberation of oppressed peoples with the proletarian emancipation movement"[13] – a statement Blum made during the 1920 Congress of the SFIO, during which the communists seceded and formed their own party. From the opposite side of the political spectrum, only the most racist fraction among right-wing nationalists, such as Charles Maurras (1868–1952), continued to criticize France's engagement with non-European "races" outside of Europe in the interwar period.[14]

Policymakers and colonial reformers who reorganized the field of colonial practice in the 1920s believed that colonialism was not in itself an evil, but a force for good, especially if it accelerated the national integration of the colonial society and its future integration in a world of interdependent nations. They found much hope and promise in the fact that the Great War had dramatically intensified a sense of imperial solidarity among the metropolitan population and political parties: in particular, trade with the colonies had also dramatically increased after 1919. Where it corresponded to less than 13 percent of general foreign trade in 1913, twenty years later it had doubled, reaching almost 27 percent in 1933.[15]

Among these administrators and public intellectuals who came to dominate the French colonial field, the influential Minister of the Colonies, Albert Sarraut (1872–1962), publicized his views in two widely influential books: one published in 1923, and another in 1931, the year of the International Colonial Exhibition in Paris. Sarraut, who had spent the war as Governor General of Indochina, held the position of Minister of the Colonies from 1920 to 1924 (and from 1932 to 1933), as well as Minister of Interior from 1926 to 1928 (and from 1936 to 1938), during which period he was in charge of domestic affairs in Algeria (as Algeria fell under the Ministry of the Interior). Albert Sarraut and the colonial reformers like Marcel de Coppet (1881–1968), a friend of the Gides (particularly André, the novelist and nephew of Charles), wanted to turn the French Empire into the leader of a new solidarist experiment in colonialism.

As Sarraut wrote in two chapters, titled "The Colonial Obligation of France" and "The French Colonial Doctrine," based on lectures he gave in the mid 1920s before students of the Colonial School,[16] the French people were uniquely positioned to help non-European societies reach what US development theorists like Walt Rostow would later call a more "advanced stage of development."[17] Sarraut asserted that "Frenchmen are altruistic; their genius reflects a taste for the universal; their humanity, their sense of right, fairness and beauty foment the altruistic conceptions which they develop well beyond the national confines to expand to humanity as a whole their dreams of justice, solidarity and fraternal goodness." As he added, "Christian or secular, soldiers for the King or Republic, Frenchmen feel the obligation to give and to give oneself so that they can bring the lights of civilization to races less fortunate than theirs."[18] When Sarraut found evidence of brutal and egoistic exploitation in France's colonial history, it was only due to the "trial-and-error"[19] nature of France's colonial advancement, rather than French official state practice, which, to him, was interspersed with numerous examples of altruistic gifts and counter-gifts on both sides.

Sarraut's apology of French colonialism, which he mixed with calls for a policy of "generosity," explicitly asserted the moral superiority of French colonialism over that of the British and German: for him, what fundamentally distinguished the French national character from the Anglo-Saxon character was the rejection of the ideology of racial purity and superiority held dear by the latter.[20] As he told the students of the Colonial School, the colonial contract should no longer be characterized by an "act of force,"[21] as in the beginning of colonial expansion, but it had to become a "fact of law," almost a "total social fact" in Maussian language.

In contrast to German law scholars like Carl Schmitt who rehabilitated the theory of *terra nullius* to justify why the European powers could claim a right to rule overseas territory,[22] Sarraut slayed the idea that the benefits that France should derive from the colonial relations derived exclusively from a right of first occupation – the act of "taking"[23] recognized at the Berlin Congress of 1885 in which the European great powers divided colonial possessions in the Congo – or that the duration during which that right should be exercised depended upon the commercial benefits that the metropolis could derive from the exploitation of the colony's riches.

Of course, this call for an altruistic form of colonial gift exchange represented a great departure from the French nineteenth-century justification of colonialism, which started with the loss of Haiti in 1825 and the subsequent invasion and pacification of Algeria after 1830, paid for by Haiti,[24] and which King Charles X justified with the necessity for France to extract from Algeria the agricultural products (cacao, sugar, etc.), which France could no longer extract from the lost colony of Saint Domingue. This economic motivation, as well as a military strategy that did not rule out extermination against the Regency of Algiers and the troops of Abd El Kader, had been associated with some problematic episodes in French colonial history, so did Sarraut timidly acknowledge, but this time of ruthless colonialism was over.

With the end of the Great War began a period of "reciprocal gifts" between the French metropolis and the colonies, as Sarraut believed: if the reality of colonial relations still proved the contrary, at least, the idea of a new colonial "contract" was widespread in the discourses of colonial high administrators as well as academics and colonial administrators. One can think of the writings of Hubert Lyautey (1854–1934), the famous General who pacified Northern Madagascar in the 1890s, and then the frontier between Morocco and Algeria in the early 1900s; or those of Georges Hardy (1884–1972), a friend of Lyautey and a former ENS student who defended a PhD thesis in history on the *mise en valeur* of Senegal; or in the public speeches of Hardy's successor as Director of the Colonial School, Robert Delavignette (1897–1976), who also worked with Lyautey and the Museum of Ethnology team on the organization of the 1931 International Colonial Exhibition which celebrated a century of French colonialism in Africa.[25]

For these colonial reformers, progress in the European administration of the colonies could be made if the metropolis adopted a "giving colonialism"[26] truly inspired by the principles of a coherent solidarist doctrine. The gift, conceived in solidarist terms as an implicit contract between two political societies,[27] which were engaged in reciprocal exchange of "prestations," created obligations and duties for both. Applied to the colonial doctrine, the recognition of contractual rights meant that certain acquired colonial rights like property rights or the right of first occupation – those rights based on purely "dogmatic fictions," against which Sarraut opposed "living, positive and productive right"[28] – should be disregarded. Colonial powers had instead the obligation to pursue a "higher utility," as peoples everywhere had "a superior right which is the total right of the human species to live a better life on this planet, a life fuller of material and spiritual riches, which can be best achieved thanks to the solidary collaboration between races."[29] Against that "total right," the right of "first occupation" held no power, as a "right that prevents humanity from benefitting from its right of universal progress is not a right: no race, no people, has the right to egoistically cut itself off from the universal movement of life . . . as the whole of humanity has the right to live off the totality of natural riches dispersed on the globe."[30]

For Sarraut, since 1919, the French state no longer understood the colonial contract as an absolute "right of the most powerful" but as a "right of the most powerful to help the least powerful"[31] to extract the most of a territory's natural and human reserves for the benefit of all, including first and foremost those least powerful, but also other European nations. In fact, Sarraut explicitly related the development of the colonies with the making of a European order based on the Versailles Treaty in which European nations would cooperate with one another for the development of all. As Minister of the Colonies in 1920, he proposed a plan, which was rejected by the Parliament, in which aid to the colonies would be financed by the German reparations payments.[32] Of course, his plan was imperiled by the failure of the Germans to pay reparations in the 1920s, with the effect that grants-in-aid were not extended to the colonies, at least until 1930, when the French Parliament finally let the colonies float loans for a total of 5 billion francs – a decision, which as William Cohen writes, had the unwanted and unanticipated effect that the servicing of colonial debts soon "used up an excessive proportion of their budgets."[33]

Even if the record, in purely financial terms, proved that the French Republic had not been particularly generous with its colonies, as the indebted colonial treasuries (rather than the metropolis) paid a major share of administrative costs in French Africa, and the cost of economic development devolved to the colonies themselves to a greater extent in the French Empire than in the British one,[34] most French colonial administrators and intellectuals with a stake in the colonial field argued the contrary. Mauss was no exception. When he wrote *The Nation*, Mauss was a little bit less disingenuous than Sarraut in his analysis of French colonial history, as he pointed to specific moments when the French had spread racist ideologies, from Napoleon's time in Saint Domingue to the early twentieth-century practices of the French concessionary companies in the Congo,[35] but he remained in general an apologist of the French ability "to give" to its colonial subjects so as to create some form of positive solidarity.

Forever an optimist in his writings, Mauss was not far from agreeing with Sarraut that the French "honor derived from the fact that," against the ideology of racist superiority and the mercantilist inspiration of the Colonial Pact exemplified by the early British colonial enterprise (which doomed those peoples whom Sarraut called the "inferior races"[36] to an everlasting specialization in raw material extraction and agricultural labor), France was the first colonial power to understand the "human value of retarded races and its sacred obligation to respect and develop such human value."[37] The French interwar experiment in colonialism would prove that the "inferior races" could slowly join France in the joint management of all human affairs (not just raw material extraction but also industrial manufacture) without losing their singularity. For Mauss, there was reason to believe that a positive process of development had taken place under the experience of late French colonialism: as he wrote in *The Nation*, "whatever the crimes of imperialist colonization, it pushed away Barbary, war, slavery, and misery in important parts of the globe." He added, "it [is] still better for a Moroccan to be governed by Frenchmen than by warlords, for the Arab to be under the British rather than Ottoman tutelage."[38] But was it, really? It is an understatement to say that contemporary historians strongly disagree with Mauss's assertion.[39]

2 THE NATION: MAUSS'S SCIENTIFIC CONTRIBUTION TO THE DEBATE ABOUT FRANCE'S COLONIAL DESTINY

Mauss's biased perspective on the French Republic's experience with colonialism may be evidence of the association between anthropology and colonial apology – or an attempt to civilize colonialism to ensure its long-lasting presence – which has been condemned by postcolonial scholars like Talal Asad.[40] But before drawing any conclusion, it is worth pausing to try to understand Mauss's singular contribution to the debate about France's colonial destiny.

Reading Mauss's unpublished manuscript *The Nation* in parallel with Sarraut's essays, one cannot but be impressed by the complementarity of views between scholars and politicians involved in the colonial field on the issue of whether French colonialism could be characterized in terms of gift exchange between the metropolis and its colonies, and the related question of whether it had been good for the social, political, and economic development of the colonies. But whereas *The Gift* formulates an unequivocally optimistic view on the ability of gift exchanges to create solidarity between nations, the unpublished work which Marcel Mauss spent most of his time writing in the 1920s – the manuscript of *The Nation* – was much more careful when assessing the relationship between the two. What colonial administrators like Sarraut took as a matter of principled belief – that French colonialism was altruistic and beneficial to the colonies – Mauss considered an empirical question, which could be answered differently depending upon the various contexts in which the French Empire had extended its tentacles.

During the 1920s, as Jean Terrier and Marcel Fournier assert, if "Mauss insisted on the fundamental openness of societies, the porosity of social boundaries, and the circulation of goods and ideas . . . as exchanges express the 'constitutive mix [*mélange*] of all things, values, contracts and men,'"[41] Mauss considered that these exchanges of reciprocal "prestations"[42] between societies could have both negative and positive effects, depending on the types of "borrowings" (*emprunts* in French) that circulated from society to society (whether the latter concerned civilizations, techniques, aesthetics, religions, or legal forms),[43] and the structural elements present in the context of exchange. In *The Nation*, Mauss questioned whether colonialism (whether altruistic or not) had actually created political solidarity and community out of contractual exchanges across and between societies. The answer was unclear to him, or rather, not as clear as he had wanted it to be in *The Gift* – or as Sarraut, Lyautey, and other colonial apologists had claimed.

To answer this question, Mauss first needed a scale, a ranking, an index, or some form of benchmark that would allow him to decide whether colonial societies had moved up or down the ladder of development – or "integration" – as a result of gift exchanges between the French metropolis and themselves. In *The Nation*, Mauss thus proposed a general comparative and historical framework that allowed him (and later his students) to rank societies according to a gradation of neighboring "degrees of *integration*,"[44] so as to identify those systems of gift exchange which helped the exchanging partners move to a tighter degree of integration (a positive outcome, for Mauss), and those which harmed such integration (a negative outcome).

At the lowest level of integration, Mauss found what he called, after Durkheim, "poly-segmentary societies":[45] some of which lacked a permanent organization, and, like Melanesian or aboriginal Australian societies, only gathered as a whole during totemic ceremonies to celebrate rituals; some of which actually did present a slightly higher level of integration, as they benefited from permanent but not centralized political structures that checked the centrifugal forces of clans and extended families, like in the "tribal societies" of the North American or African continents (Sioux, Iroquois, or Bantu).

At the highest level of integration, Mauss placed the "nation," which characterized societies where intermediary bodies no longer buffered relations between individuals and the state, and where a strong sense of territorial boundaries limited the desire for imperial expansion. Such a conception of the nation conceived as a daily plebiscite, in the words of Ernest Renan (1823–1892), was quite in line with the French Republican definition. Not surprisingly, Mauss found that only two Western countries could claim the title of nations: France and the United States. In these two nations, "the two poles in the continuum of social beings, individuals and the society, symbolized by the state, face one another,"[46] and individuals only recognize the authority of the law of their own nation-state. Apart from France and the United States, Mauss asserted that even if "the surface of the globe [had] been vascularized"[47] by an explosion of exchanges between formally equal nations which were all members of the League of Nations, most political societies organizations could not be called nations in the proper sense.[48] In *The Nation*, Mauss "warned his contemporaries that there is a missing echelon in the ladder that the League of

Nations placed upon the wall of history" to reach world peace: that of the "nation, which most societies [had] not yet arrived at."[49]

To these two poles of social organization, Mauss added an intermediary stage: "empires," where the force of integration had deepened (compared to tribal societies) under the increased presence of a central political authority, but not to the point of creating a centralized nation of individuals united by a common national consciousness as well as by their willingness to use the state as a means of political and social reform. Under the category of empires, Mauss listed "societies of Muslim law, Chinese law, Hindu law,"[50] as well as Tsarist Russia, ancient Greece, Egypt, Mexico, Germany, and colonial societies.

With this typology, Mauss thus proposed a vision of colonialism that was completely in line with the interwar version of the French colonial ideology. Indeed, the latter distinguished colonial societies by their different levels of integration. In turn, their level of integration left them more or less close to (national) autonomy, and determined their right to be decolonized or not. As Mauss had already written to the Minister of the Colonies in 1913, self-rule should be postponed to a more or less distant future, depending on the nature of colonial societies: he recognized that "populations in Algeria and the Tonkin could, to some extent, develop and prosper by themselves," but that "those in New Caledonia, the Congo, and elsewhere are completely dependent on our benevolent tutelage."[51] How colonial societies scored on the Maussian Index could thus affect the lives of millions.

But Mauss's typology of levels of integration could also be used to evaluate critically the effect of colonialism on colonial societies: Mauss judged whether the exchange of prestations between a metropolis and its colonies had positive (true gift) or negative (fake gift) effects by observing whether the exchange of prestations moved the colony closer to the model of the nation, in which individuals united around the celebration of a centralized authority within their society, or whether it led to the further fragmentation of societies and economic systems. Those systems of gift exchange which encouraged the formation of a national consciousness and the organization of national conglomerates were, for Mauss, those which had a positive influence on exchanging societies, whereas those that thwarted such process of national unification – including in the economic domain – were those which had a negative influence.

Mauss's implicit assumption was that "intersocietal" exchanges (rather than the organization of labor within closed societies) are the main drivers of history, responsible for how societies with varying degrees of integration co-evolved sometimes in tandem, sometimes in a contrapuntal manner. [52] For instance, Mauss claimed that the potlatch represented the trading practice and the specific understanding of customary contractual obligations by which poly-segmentary tribal societies had moved up to the level of quasi-empires,[53] as in the case of the large Native American empires, which Mauss's student Jacques Soustelle later studied in his doctoral thesis.[54] Thus, Mauss put forward a view of the potlatch radically opposed to that of British colonial administrators who had passed laws in Canada prohibiting Native Americans' exchange practices and defined harsh incarceration charges and fines against those guilty of practicing the potlatch – alleging that when Native Americans practiced the potlatch, they destroyed valuables, and thus violated central Protestant principles of individualistic wealth accumulation and capitalist discipline. What the Protestant missionaries abhorred, Mauss glorified.[55]

Still, Mauss found that systems of reciprocal exchanges did not always move exchanging societies closer to the national model of integration. Before the Great War, Mauss realized profoundly the destructive potentialities of the colonial project: as he had already written in 1902 to the Minister of the Colonies, "in order to be humane, colonial administration needed to respect and use local beliefs and practices so as to avoid a brutal confrontation" in the colonial encounter, "which he believed should only very gradually change the economic and technological regimes in place."[56] Mauss wrote that colonization could be "a hazardous project, costly in time and money, which ends up producing a disaster in civilizations as old as ours, and whose morality is as respectable as ours, and whose artistic forms are sometimes superior to ours."[57] This point is why he believed that the French Republic would fail its colonial subjects if it did not use as many people as possible ("missionaries, doctors, administrators, colonizers and indigenous *savants*")[58] to protect the living memory of these subjects and their culture, by collecting local artifacts to be displayed in museums, for instance.

In the non-European context, Mauss also found that the "privately owned chartered companies, working under the protection of European states, have monopolized the extraction of coal, rubber and oil" and had inhibited the ability of colonial exchanges to move colonies up the ladder of integration, "leading to a great resentment among the smaller nations."[59] These chartered companies did not help colonial societies coalesce around a central legitimate authority with which the local populations (of both European and non-European descent) could identify. On the contrary, Mauss wrote in *The Nation*:

> The Colonial State often appears to acquire the entirety of the product of the soil of the colonies, or the labor of the natives for a very small sum of money, or for nothing, or by raising taxes among the natives . . . The French colonies have long applied this principle to appropriate the means of import and export of the colonies exclusively to the benefit of their own capitalists, thus securing a place under the sun for them. There are some ugly things in the modern world.[60]

Mauss thus initiated in *The Nation* a normative reflection, which was absent from *The Gift*, but which was connected to the denunciation by colonial reformers of the old Colonial Pact between the colonial state and the chartered companies, whose exploitative practices (especially in extraction of raw materials like rubber) could lead to mass extermination or political rebellion if they brutally extracted all the social and natural resources of the French Empire. What we may call the "monopoly colonialism" of the chartered companies was an essential component of the "Colonial Pact," whereby the colonial subjects consumed metropolitan industrial products and extracted raw materials for the benefit of concessionary companies that had been awarded by the metropolis an exclusive monopoly over large portions of the colonies. Mauss found that the latter were thus maintained in a state of economic dependence due to their overspecialization in agriculture or raw material extractive economies.[61] Rather than opening colonial economies to the opportunities of global markets, Mauss criticized the fact that the colonial monopolies that flourished under the French state's authority produced effects that ran contrary to the "mandates" that the League of Nations had endowed to the French and British Empires after the Great War: e.g. to create, through cultural, social, and economic exchanges, the conditions through which colonial subjects could arrive at a developed stage where they could be given the authority to rule themselves in interdependence but also independence from the metropolis.[62]

At last, closer to Europe, Mauss accounted for the breaches in the recognition of reciprocal duties made manifest with the question of German reparations by the various levels of integration reached by different political societies in Europe, the relative newness of the collective experience of national consciousness in Europe, and the "permanence of dynasties of German descent" in German political life, which might still be influenced by "the traditions of the police state that characterized the Austrian or Russian model" of state formation.[63] Mauss found that the "persistence of upsetting elements" within European nations, like Germany, whose territorial boundaries and financial duties had been explicitly written in the Versailles Treaty, could explain why the German state had not benefited from its participation in a network of European neighboring nations to grow an open national consciousness.

In *The Nation*, Mauss thus focused on trade and financial forms of exchange as the main factor responsible for the development or contraction of a national consciousness within various historical – both European and non-European – contexts. This was a fine and ambitious intellectual program, which nonetheless failed to challenge the colonial mindset of the colonial administrators who glorified French colonialism. Indeed, by blaming mostly the chartered companies and the Anglo-Saxon or German imperial experiences, Mauss avoided raising the possibility that the French Republic bore an essential responsibility for the destruction of colonial societies – whether the state had put in place formal structures facilitating the economic exploitation of the colony, the establishment of settlers or the total annexation and assimilation of colonial subjects.[64] Mauss's perspective completely failed to take into consideration whether imperial state structures (and specific forms of constitutional organization) played a role in the maintenance of exclusion and fragmentation within colonial societies; and whether colonial societies should immediately declare their political independence or not. Mauss even wrote that he regretted that many political scientists and legal theorists, like Max Weber (whom he did not hold in high esteem),[65] confused the two notions of state and nation, and that they privileged the study of the former over the latter: for Mauss, the questions which related to political status (the constitutions and treaties through which sovereignty manifested itself) had less importance in asserting the positive or negative effects of colonialism than the question of the contractual ties and social obligations that stemmed from the organization of international economic exchanges between peoples.[66] As Mauss wrote in the introduction to *The Nation*, he did not consider the study of "problems of sovereignty, of the Constitution, of democracy, of the evolution of legislative or administrative powers,"[67] or the historical study of diplomacy and treaty-making practices, with emphasis on "secret, or rather, purely diplomatic and anti-democratic" practices of contracting,[68] to be relevant for the comparative study of various forms of national consciousness.

In this respect, his views strictly belonged to the interwar era, during which it was next to inconceivable that such an apparently robust colonial edifice as the French Empire of 100 million subjects could be destroyed in the near future; or that the decision to grant independence to France's colonies could come either from the colonial subjects themselves or from a quasi-supranational organization like the League of Nations. In fact, the political priority that Mauss assigned to the League of Nations was to bring its member states closer to one another, so that the League could become an association of "*neighboring nations*,"[69] in the scale of integration. Of course, Mauss admitted that there was nothing natural in this convergence: no superior law of history dictated that nations would move closer to each other as a result of increasing exchanges between them. As Mauss wrote in *The Nation*:

> it is clear that modern nations will not be able to reach a sufficient stage of internationalism necessary to guarantee a mutual peace until they succeed in giving one another material proof of relative disinterestedness [*désintéressement relatif*], in exchanging mutual services of all kinds, economic in particular. Perpetual peace, to the extent possible, can only be established among equally good and serviceable (if not idealist) nations, which agree to sacrifice a reasonable portion of their interests for one another.[70]

This was a dream worth pursuing still, and Mauss believed that the French nation could start implementing it with its colonial possessions.[71]

3 MARCEL MAUSS IN THE CONGO: THE LATE NINETEENTH-CENTURY STRUGGLE OF THE INDIGENOUS COMMITTEE AGAINST THE CHARTERED COMPANIES

While the case of Marcel Mauss's relation to colonialism hardly falsifies Tal Asad's claim that the development of anthropology as a comparative science was deeply tied to the colonial mindset, the analysis of Mauss's ideas on the power of chartered companies also complicates it. In *The Nation*, Mauss condemned the chartered companies and their despicable practices of forced labor implemented without any state sanction, their dishonest financial tendencies which consisted in setting any cost they incurred against the budget of local governments, and the moral corruption that they entertained among the Parisian editorialists, politicians, and speculators who united to defend their role in the Colonial Pact. Indeed, Mauss saw in the "private appropriation, under the authority of the great [European] states, of many basic commodities necessary for the life of other nations (coal, oil)"[72] a deeply problematic development associated with modern industrial forms of colonialism. All of these factors led to the destruction of a spirit of national solidarity, both in the colony and in the metropolis.

That Mauss rehabilitated the normative model of gift exchange in modern political thought at the same time as he struggled against the power of the chartered companies may seem paradoxical to historians of political ideas. Indeed, since Harry Liebersohn's *The Return of the Gift*,[73] we now know that the circulation of gifts as the preferred mode of colonial governance was denounced precisely by those late eighteenth- and early nineteenth-century British philosophers who opposed the gift-giving practices of the chartered companies, like the East India Company.[74] Thus, it may appear surprising that the "return of the gift"[75] to theories of good government found its way through the writings of twentieth-century anthropologists who denounced precisely the same chartered companies.

This paradox, however, can be explained by Mauss's prewar involvement in the debate over the French chartered companies operating in the Congo. Their abuses were blatant in the case of the Congo, about which Mauss had collected secondhand information since 1900 in the context of his participation in a small but influential organization called the French Committee for the Protection and Defense of Indigenous Populations (hereafter, the Indigenous Committee), founded in 1892, which had ties with an associate organization, the Franco-Swiss League for the Protection of Indigenous Populations in the Congo, chaired by the novelist Anatole France, whom Mauss consulted on the topic of forced labor.[76] It was Mauss's participation in the Indigenous Committee that led him, maybe for the first time, to work alongside Charles Gide.[77]

In 1906, the Indigenous Committee addressed a letter (co-signed by Mauss) to the Minister of the Colonies, protesting the decision made by the General Government in the Congo "to reduce the productive capacity of the indigenous populations to two-thirds of the productivity of workers in the French concessionary companies."[78] For Mauss and other members of the Indigenous Committee, the decision revealed the complicity of the French administration in the Congo with the repressive policies of chartered companies whose only goal was to force the local population to work for them, whatever the costs for the region. The Indigenous Committee also denounced the French officials' toleration vis-à-vis the worst examples of forced labor and mass killings that were performed by the chartered companies in these regions. Indeed, the companies routinely organized "hostage camps"[79] of women to force their husbands into accepting deforestation labor, which men otherwise refused to perform.[80] This horrible practice, which led to the death of thousands of women due to malnutrition in the camps, was so widespread that it triggered an official investigation, led by the delegate of the Minister in the Congo, Savoyan de Brazza (1850–1905), who documented a wide range of mistreatment of colonial subjects by the chartered companies operating in the Congo. Mauss collected evidence from Brazza's secretary, Félicien Challaye (1875–1967), another ENS student close to Charles Péguy, who published regularly in Péguy's *Cahiers de la Quinzaine* – until the latter distanced himself from Jaurès and Mauss in 1906. Later, in 1911, Challaye continued to investigate and denounce the complicity of the Paris-based editorialists, industrialists, and politicians with the worst exploitative practices of chartered companies in the context of the N'Goko Sangha scandal,[81] providing arguments for the socialist parliamentarians gathered behind Jaurès – as described below.

In fact, their campaign against "chartered companies" and "trusts" operating in the Congo was truly transnational, as it involved many intellectuals and colonial officers across Europe who were revolted by the situation they witnessed on the ground: the British official Roger Casement (1864–1916) may have been the first to denounce officially the exploitation of the Congolese populations by the "trusts," whose only motivation was the appropriation of short-term gains at the expense of a long-term developmental strategy. The report on the Congo he wrote in 1903 contributed to the creation of the Congo Reform Association, which developed branches in the United States (1905), Switzerland (1909), France (1908, created by Challaye), Italy (1908), and Germany (1910).[82]

Thus, even if the association between gift exchange and the positive development of solidarity seemed to be unambiguously positive in *The Gift*, Mauss and some of the solidarist thinkers with whom he was associated in the Indigenous Committee were deeply aware that the exchange of "prestations" could be negative as well as positive, depending on other contextual elements, and specifically the motivations of the chartered companies in charge of developing the concessions.

In fact, the word "prestations," which Mauss used as an anthropological concept in his 1925 essay, was used by that very same Committee to refer to the labor practices that the chartered companies required from colonial subjects: in a letter signed in 1901 on behalf of the Indigenous Committee by Paul Viollet (1840–1914) – a historian of ancient law (from the Gauls' legal system to medieval customary laws) who long served as the librarian of the Paris Law school, where he met many specialists in colonial law – and addressed to the Minister of the Colonies, the Indigenous Committee asked the minister to "formally prohibit that any corporation in charge of public work in the colonies pay workers with another currency than the legal money"; that "any in-kind payment (especially in alcohol) would be strictly prohibited"; that the word "forced labor" [*corvée*], which brought up so many bad things, be replaced by the word "*prestation*" (or in English, "requisition"); and that "women could no longer be requisitioned for digging and earthwork" so as "to limit the number of abuses that have proliferated in Guadeloupe, New Caledonia, Indochina,"[83] and in the French parts of the Congo. In contrast to "forced" labor, the exchange of "prestations" had to have a "voluntary character." This did not mean that it should adopt the exact same contractual form as a "wage," but that its logic should not be purely exploitative – and that some "giving back" should be realized in the broader colonial context. In many ways, we find here the earliest trace of Mauss's famous definition of the "reciprocal prestations" discussed in *The Gift* in which Mauss stressed their "voluntary character, apparently freely given, yet coercive and interested."[84]

In this context, the same socialist thinkers who, a few years before, had stood against the accusers of Alfred Dreyfus, like Jean Jaurès and Albert Thomas (who later tried to use his influence as the first director of the ILO to prohibit forced labor in the early 1930s),[85] expressly related the fight for Dreyfus and the fight against forced labor. As a result, in 1906, the League of Human Rights (Ligue des droits de l'Homme), which they had created during the Dreyfus affair, declared itself to be the "tutor of the rights of the indigenous populations,"[86] and worked to publicize their campaign against chartered companies.

While Charles Gide and Marcel Mauss remained private in their condemnation of the chartered companies from the Indigenous Committee to the Minister of the Colonies, Jaurès and Thomas took a much more public stance, especially during a scandal that involved the N'Goko Sangha Company,[87] which had obtained a concession in the French Congo in 1899. The N'Goko Sangha case exposed the reality of colonial administrative practices, which was all the more unfortunate in the region where Mauss claimed, in a 1913 letter to the Minister of the Colonies, that the colonial subjects needed most a benevolent and enlightened colonial administration: the Congo.[88]

The socialists first rebelled by denouncing the commercial and labor policies of that company on the ground. As the French local administrator in Gabon had written in 1908 to his governor in a letter transmitted to Albert Thomas, the existing system of exchange between chartered companies and local colonial subjects in the Congo did not benefit the latter at all, largely because of its reliance on in-kind payments, which did not follow any useful function. At the time, the company paid its local colonial workers with overpriced "gun powder, which was the main currency used by the *Pahouins* to pay the bride's dowry," and "which was under the exclusive monopoly of the Company":[89] this situation thus allowed the company to fix whatever price (calculated in hours worked for the company) it wanted for that good, whose sale was in fact prohibited by other European chartered companies in the Congo region, as it had the obvious disadvantage of arming local populations – even if it also allowed them to build families.[90] Echoing the demands made by the Indigenous Committee, Thomas proposed that the French state should impose the "obligation for companies to pay indigenous populations in cash and money" rather than in kind.[91]

Mauss's socialist friends in Parliament also criticized the financial montages that the French investors organized in order to make the colonial subjects pay for the oppressive practices which were imposed upon them and from which they suffered. In so doing, they prefigured in part Mauss's distinction between exploitative short-term practices driven by utility-maximizing private agents and the logic of honor found in the exchange of real (as opposed to fake) gifts.[92] Jaurès criticized in Parliament the short-term logics of economic exploitation in the colonies and the financial hypocrisy of the colonial apologists who indebted future generations of colonial subjects by having them pay for these colossal and unwanted projects. As Jaurès said in 1911, France's financial policy with the colonies "consists in hiding the real costs of France's colonial policy by multiplying threefold, sometimes fivefold the taxes levied on local populations, and by accumulating local debt, paid at interest rates which are highly profitable" to the French capitalists, "so as to fund large expenses in big public construction works – the construction of roads and railways which serve no apparent function when much more needed irrigation systems are neglected – whose costs are placed on the accounting books of local governments."[93]

With the N'Goko Sangha Company, the financial scandal took an even more extreme form, as the company obtained a formidable sum of money (to be paid by future generations of colonial subjects) thanks to an arbitration procedure denounced by Thomas, Jaurès and others. Indeed, the company, acting like a modern-day vulture fund – like those which recently sued the country of Argentina in New York courts after the restructuring of the Argentinian debt through an obscure clause known as *pari passu*[94] – asked the general government of French East Africa to pay reparations for its failure to enforce the monopoly over the exploitation of rubber. This monopoly had been extended to the company in the French Congo in 1899. Less than ten years later, the company lawyers claimed that the company had suffered from the exploitation of latex trees by German companies located in the same territory, in violation of its rights of exclusivity,[95] due to the French state's 1908 swap of large territories granted to the company in the Congo and Cameroon with the German state. Indeed, they claimed that, after failing to secure the border between the French and German territories in the Congo and South Cameroon, the French colonial administration had let German factories return on the N'Goko Sangha company's territory after 1905, and that the German companies had proceeded to even greater forest destruction in retaliation for the (undelivered) threat of legal proceedings by the company in Germany.[96] Thus, in 1910, the N'Goko Sangha company requested the formidable sum of 6 million francs in reparations from the French state, including 1.5 million for torts suffered before 1905 and 4.5 million for torts suffered after the swap of lands in Congo and Gabon. The arbitration tribunal, where André Tardieu sat as the company representative and Martial Merlin (1860–1935), Governor General of French East Africa, represented the French state, found a compromise by awarding to the company 2.3 million francs, which were placed on the accounts of the general government of French East Africa.[97]

For the socialists sitting in Parliament, the arbitration case was a grotesque travesty of the reality of the colonial practices on the ground. The fact that such a company could receive reparations from the French government in East Africa meant that the colonial subjects were exploited twice: first by being coerced into almost-unpaid forced labor, and second by forcing their children to reimburse the debt created by the local government's payment of reparations to the company. As Marcel Labordère (1870–1946), an economist, trade cycle specialist, and a friend of Thomas, wrote to the latter, the arbitration of the N'Goko Sangha case was a complete setup from the start. The N'Goko Sangha Company extracted wealth and profit from legal action against the state and from the organization of public campaigns which hid the fact that the company had failed to fulfill its developmental obligations. Indeed, when the French state first gave compensation to the company in 1905 (by giving concessionary rights on millions of hectares in Gabon in exchange for the de facto loss of forests in Congo), the company had the choice to "either [accept] the gift as it was" and knowingly decide to fight the German economic competition in the new Gabonese territory by investing economically, or to use the new territory, where there was a known German presence, as an opportunity to "seek even more profit by means of further legal action against the State."[98] By choosing the latter strategy, the company not only proved to be ungrateful (as it did not consider the economic potential of the millions of hectares on which it had gained concessionary rights), but it also proved to be extremely deceitful, as from the start it had planned to use "an arsenal of legal means which, conveniently deployed by a reserve of friendly forces, could help it make profit in the vast field of reparations claims at the expense of the national interest."[99] This strategy was twofold: first, the company abandoned its claims in German courts,[100] where it lacked the support of powerful voices to pressure the courts to obtain a favorable settlement; second, it moved to the French courts where it counted on "friendly forces"[101] within the Colonial Party. These influential voices included Victor Augagneur (1855–1931), the Governor of Madagascar in 1904 and then Resident-General in Tunisia who has long been a socialist member of Lyon's municipal Council, before turning into the apostle of massive investment in rail and road construction work.[102] It also included legal experts such as Henry Berthélemy (1857–1943), a colleague of Augagneur at the municipal Council of Lyon, who served as legal expert in the N'Goko Sangha arbitration case.[103] It also comprised the powerful voice of André Tardieu, who wrote positively in the press about the arbitration procedure in which he took part to protect the private interests of the company.[104]

For Jaurès, these conflicts of interest, which were characteristic of Tardieu's multipositionality for instance, combined with "the lack of parliamentary control of arbitration procedures," proliferated in "colonial affairs in general."[105] Indeed, before becoming a leading voice in the reparations debate, Tardieu was a parliamentarian and an editorialist at *Le Temps*, as well as representing the company in the arbitration procedure. In the very critical words of Jaurès, he helped chartered companies "earn money by stealing from the State's budget rather than by making profit out of its economic activities."[106] This multipositionality at the intersection between the metropolitan and colonial fields of power – that characterizes the way "*compradores*"[107] operated in Europe as well as in many other countries from the Global South – turned ministers into "the servants of obscure and occult forces" which "organized the hunt for reparations"[108] by predatory companies who lived off colonial taxes (present and future).

The announcement of the award granted by the arbitration tribunal to the N'Goko Sangha Company so much infuriated Albert Thomas, who sat on the Budgetary Commission of the French Parliament, and Maurice Viollette (1870–1960) – a young solidarist from the radical socialist party, whom Mauss had known before the war, and who later served as Governor General of Algeria in the interwar period before he became Léon Blum's Minister of Interior in 1936 – that both Thomas and Viollette asked for the establishment of a commission of inquiry to annul the whole arbitration procedure.[109] For them, the scandal implicated too many French politicians within the Colonial Party, whose practices were reminiscent, at least to Albert Thomas, of the worst manipulations revealed during the Dreyfus affair. Indeed, noticing that "the N'Goko Sangha company had presented secret documents which were not communicated to the State" during the arbitration procedure, Thomas wrote that the "State had been condemned to pay a sum which it didn't owe, based on secret documents, just like in the Dreyfus affair."[110]

These prewar scandals are particularly interesting because they clearly illustrate the stark differences between the singular position that French anthropologists occupied in the metropolitan and colonial fields of power, compared to anthropologists in other European countries. For instance, British anthropologists and colonial administrators who were members of the London Anthropological Society, wore double hats as ethnographers and propagandists of the dubious financial instruments by which concessionary companies were financed to develop far away territories in Asia, Africa, and Latin America.[111] As Marc Flandreau has recently showed, the London-based development of learned societies, which operated in the shadow of the London stock exchange, provided colorful description of distant tribes to future bondholders of concessionary companies in charge of administering these new subjects, and certified the claims of these companies before a gullible public. In this context, British ethnographers and anthropologists found a new social purpose, far from the disinterested pursuit of knowledge in the academic chapels of higher learning: British ethnography and anthropology were then used to certify the financial worth of colonial projects sponsored by London-based learned societies, where stock brokers, investors, and indeed anthropologists met and discussed the worth of various ethnicities for developmental (and thus financial) purposes.[112]

In contrast, French anthropologists who gathered around Mauss remained armchair academics, who didn't claim to know such distant territories as the Congo, but who used the social capital and access to media that they had accumulated during the Dreyfus affair to fight against the avatars of the British anthropologists, propagandists, and financial crooks who operated from Paris. Marcel Mauss and his socialist friends in Parliament fought against the chartered companies who claimed to develop regions when in fact, their only source of revenue was the extortion of French taxpayers under threat of litigation. Even if neither Jaurès, nor Thomas, nor Mauss contested the principle that France had a civilizing mission in the non-European world,[113] and that the exchange of gifts was a priori a useful way to think about the economic development of, and political solidarity between, the metropolis and the colonies, they denounced the reality of colonial practices on the ground that involved a perversion of gift exchanges. Their fight against vulture funds and their sponsors, agents, and other propagandists operating from the national parliament and Paris-based press organs, thus demonstrates an important difference in the way anthropology developed in London and in Paris.

4 THE INTERWAR FIGHT AGAINST THE FRENCH CHARTERED COMPANIES IN THE CONGO

In the pamphlets, addresses and letters written by French socialists before the Great War, these words – "gift" or "prestation" – functioned as positive markers of the French mission in Africa: what these public intellectuals placed in the pillory was the failure by chartered companies to uphold the ideas of honor that had justified why such companies had been granted public powers in the first place. As Thomas explained in the National Assembly in 1911, chartered companies like the N'Goko Sangha Company should lose their concessionary rights when it was blatant that they failed to honor their promise to invest in developing the region – the counter-gift that chartered companies had to give back in exchange for their concession, to live up to the ideals of altruistic colonialism (and the very reason "why the French state granted concessions to these companies in 1899").[114] Indeed, "concessions were meant to encourage chartered companies to effectively administer large territories"[115] in the absence of state and military support. That chartered companies behaved like the worst capitalists showed that they did not understand how gift exchange between solidary societies should be practiced – which may be one reason why Mauss undertook to describe such "ideal" rules of gift exchange in his 1925 essay.

After the Great War, such intrepid proposals actually found their way in Mauss's manuscript *The Nation*. Indeed, anticipating the wave of nationalization of French private companies that followed the Second World War in France – when, as in the case of the car manufacturer Renault, the decision to nationalize the company was a sanction against the collaborationist behavior of the owners and top management – Mauss also advocated the nationalization of chartered companies which did not honor their debt to the metropolitan and colonial societies.[116] He wrote eloquently in favor of the creation of socially and democratically controlled monopolies (wholesales) in charge of the administration of the vast sectors of the economy presently controlled by the chartered companies.[117] Such nationalization could pave the way toward harmonious development if it followed certain rules.

First, the notion of "nationalization" needed to dissociate the "nation" from the "state." The nationalization that Mauss advocated differed from the "state socialism" embodied by the Bolshevik Revolution, as nationalization was not purely state control of capital, but rather the "social" control of capital. Second, "the term nationalization implied that only societies having reached the national stage in the life of societies could logically and practically decide to nationalize something."[118] Third, the term "nationalization is associated with the ideas of organization, justice and legality which are absent from the term of socialism."[119]

Apart from the fact that the last sentence represented quite an extraordinary statement from someone who had claimed to cofound the SFIO, one can remark that Mauss mentioned these ideas of legality and justice, but he did not explicitly discuss the question of whether a just compensation would need to be paid to the private holders of capital at the time of the nationalization. For him, a private chartered company should indeed lose its right to exploit the soil in distant colonies if they failed to exploit to the fullest extent the resources of colonies in an altruistic fashion, as Albert Thomas had claimed was the case of chartered companies that behaved like the N'Goko Sangha Company – e.g. exploiting the French legal system and the colonial subjects, without any regard for the collective good of either the metropolis or the colony.

When the reality defied this utopia, the solidarists, socialists, and other colonial reformers gathered around Sarraut, Mauss, and Blum did not hesitate to denounce the power of "trusts" and other chartered companies after the Great War. As Sarraut was writing his book, *Colonial Grandeur*, and Mauss *The Nation*, the exploitative practices of the chartered companies had not disappeared – far from it. The extractive companies which operated in African colonies – in Senegal, extracting peanuts; in the Ivory Coast, cocoa and coffee; in Eastern Africa, rubber and cotton – requested unrealistically high production quotas, which local French administrators obtained by imposing forced labor and higher taxes as well as harsh sanctions in case of noncompliance. This Stakhanovist system most often led to direct wealth destruction: for instance, in the late 1920s in the Ivory Coast, African colonial subjects went to British-controlled Gold Coast to buy the cotton that they were required to, but could not, produce, so as to avoid being sanctioned.[120] Thus, the battle against private interests still raged among the French colonial reformers interested in jump-starting the economic development of colonies, especially in Africa.

In fact, the same network of solidarists and socialists who had denounced the practices of the N'Goko Sangha Company before the war continued to denounce similar abuses by the chartered companies that continued in the Congo. In the mid 1920s, Charles Gide's nephew, the novelist André Gide, traveled to the Congo with his companion Marc Allégret on invitation by the local governor, Marcel de Coppet, who became the leading advocate against the exploitation of colonial subjects by the large extractive companies: this time, the target was the Compagnie forestière Sangha-Oubangui, whose stocks were ornamented with the orientalist drawing of a young Black Amazon and elephants' ivory tusks, as represented in this book's cover. This was the last French chartered company, whose privilege extended until 1935. If we believe Gide's report, rather than representing the young and proud Congolese girl standing with a spear in her hand, as if ready to defend her territory, a more realistic representation would have showed her back broken by long hours spent collecting and transporting the rubber for the company.

André Gide first published in 1927 his famously critical report on the Congo's French chartered companies, as articles in *Le Populaire*, the journal edited by Léon Blum (Gide's best friend in high school), which by the late 1920s reached more than 100,000 readers, and then as a book – which Blum reviewed extensively in two articles published in *Le Populaire*. Like Mauss and Sarraut, Gide refrained from attacking the principles of human solidarity which, according to them, inspired French colonial policy in the interwar period: he lauded many colonial administrators like de Coppet who advanced French civilization and engaged in honest exchanges with local populations, whose living standards they helped raise by abolishing unpaid prestations in the form of forced labor.[121] He limited his denunciation to the abuses he saw perpetrated against local populations by exploitative capitalistic endeavors (in the form of forced labor, mass repression against the evasion of absurdly high taxes, etc.),[122] and by judicial trials against local populations trying to escape forced labor: in particular, he denounced the chartered company in charge of building the railway, the Compagnie forestière Sangha-Oubangui, for systematically relying on forced labor (imposed on women especially) to generate more profits. Thus, Gide's denunciation, written by a Nobel laureate in literature, was framed in the exact same terms as found in the letters sent by the Indigenous Committee before the war, or in the parliamentary attacks against the N'Goko Sangha Company expressed by Thomas.

Interestingly, Gide also remarked that the conditions of forced labor were disguised in the same language of "prestations"[123] which the Indigenous Committee had advised the Minister of the Colonies to use, and that Mauss used in his essay on *The Gift* to identify gift exchanges. Gide was not the only one to condemn the inflated level of "prestations" that the French administration in the Congo required from the colonial subjects yearly: in 1919, as William Cohen writes, "it was estimated that in order to collect enough rubber to yield the tax money designated as prestation, the inhabitants had to work between sixty and one hundred and twenty days a year, depending on the area in which the rubber was collected."[124] Thus, even if the administration no longer used the word "*corvée*," but had followed the recommendation of the Indigenous Committee to the Minister of the Colonies to use "prestation" instead, the practice had not changed much compared to the 1900s. And although they explored both the negative and positive aspects of reciprocal relations known as "prestations," albeit through different formats, neither Gide nor Mauss were completely unaware that such reciprocal exchanges of gifts and counter-gifts conceived as free prestations could hide the most coercive and exploitative practices.[125] The notions of reciprocity, solidarity and gifts were indeed ambivalent, as Mauss had remarked in *The Gift*.

In response to André Gide's pamphlets, the administrator general of the Compagnie forestière Sangha-Oubangui replied in an open letter, also published in Blum's journal, *Le Populaire*, that his company, having renounced some of the privileges of a chartered company after the Great War, could not be held responsible for the failure to administer justice in the Congo. Those to blame were not the company officials, but the local chieftains and their associates in a corrupt and understaffed administration.[126] To him, decades of understaffing in the French administration, and the continuation of barbaric local mores, which included anthropophagy and the starving of prisoners taken during local feuds, were responsible for the poor state of law and order in the Congo region, his letter alleged.[127]

Still, whatever the Compagnie spokespersons said, Gide had targeted forms of brutality in the French Empire that had long been covered up by the French administration and that remained, at least in the Congo, well entrenched in the colonial field of practices. The arbitrariness and brutality of the administration of justice in the Congo, were not a surprise to colonial reformers. The French administration, in particular under the government of Martial Merlin (Governor General of the French Government of Eastern Africa), "had satisfied itself with the decision to send to this colony all the administrators deemed unfit in other colonies,"[128] according to contemporaries of Mauss and Gide. As William Cohen writes about the Congo, "no matter how inefficient or brutal, most [French] administrators were considered good enough for service in the Congo: that colony was the receptacle for administrators unwanted in other French territories."[129] At the Colonial School, where Mauss started teaching ethnology exactly when Gide published his pamphlet, it was well known that colonial administrators sent to the Congo lacked the basic training in colonial administration, not to mention ethnology.

To be fully understood, Gide's intervention needs to be contextualized in the struggles that divided the colonial field at the time, and the attempts to not only change the training of future administrators, but also the current economic, social, and political direction of the developmental projects undertaken by the colonial administrators in Africa. Gide had decided to visit the Congo and Chad after Marcel de Coppet had encouraged him to expose the continued practices of forced labor of private companies: De Coppet met Gide with Georges-Henri Rivière (Mauss and Paul Rivet's assistant at the Museum of Ethnology), after being introduced by the novelist Roger Martin du Gard (1881–1958), his best friend from military service.[130] He invited Gide to observe (and criticize) the construction of the Congo-Ocean railroad, a project launched by Victor Augagneur in 1921.[131] The two colonial administrators had long expressed many doubts, divergences and outright criticisms about their colonial ambitions. Before the Great War, Marcel de Coppet had worked for Augagneur when the latter was the Governor General of Madagascar. There, he saw that Augagneur's policy of massive investments (paid for by local taxes and debt) obligated local populations into forced labor (generally conceived in terms of a tax), which depleted the local labor markets of a substantial portion of its labor force, thus impeding growth prospects in the colony.[132]

After the Great War, which he spent in Senegal recruiting thousands of Senegalese soldiers whom he sent to the French trenches,[133] de Coppet worked as Sarraut's press manager before returning to Eastern Africa, specifically Chad, where he could again observe the effects of Augagneur's policy (which included the building of a railway), which he publicly criticized for its heavy reliance on forced labor. When, after Blum became Prime Minister in 1936 and named de Coppet Governor General of French Western Africa, it was Marcel de Coppet who ordered his governors to abolish forced labor in the developed regions of their colonies, and to institute instead a tax to finance further public works.[134] De Coppet was one of the few registered socialists, who had long sided with Thomas, Blum and Blum's Minister of the Colonies, Marius Moutet (1876–1968), whom Mauss had met shortly after the Dreyfus affair, when Moutet was a lawyer for the League of Human Rights,[135] active against the power of the chartered companies.

Denunciations of the chartered companies were thus articulated in the 1920s by colonial administrators well endowed with what George Steinmetz calls "colonial capital," which they acquired through experience in the colonial service in Madagascar or West Africa, but also through networks of ties developed with the *écrivains-voyageurs* like André Gide, or editors like Jean Paulhan (1884–1968) at Gallimard (who worked with de Coppet in Madagascar before the Great War, and who succeeded to André Gide as Gallimard's most influential editor in the 1940s and 1950s), as well as politicians like Albert Thomas and Léon Blum. The ideology of "altruistic" colonialism thus distinguished its promoters from the traditional colonial economic elites, who only saw in the colonies an opportunity to obtain raw materials at a cheaper price. As Mauss did in *The Nation*, or as Thomas did in Parliament, Sarraut blamed these speculators and merchants (especially private chartered companies) for their egoistic understanding of commerce: as he wrote, the latter should be made to understand that "the distant possession is no longer a simple enclave [*comptoir*], a reserve of riches, a market opportunity for the conquering nation, which comes to grab spices and sell its merchandises by pressuring the local populace which it exploits without limitation."[136]

This coordinated push against the exploitative practices of French chartered companies thus gained momentum around the time Gide published his essay, and it even found some relays in the Geneva-based international organizations where French socialists had gained an important voice. After Albert Thomas, then Director General of the ILO, read André Gide's first drafts, he wrote to Gide that he would "be happy to help him crush a number of adventurers he had already fought against."[137] After circulating Gide's essay at the ILO, Albert Thomas acknowledged that the section titled "Indigenous Labor" of the ILO read "[Gide's] essay with passion,"[138] and that in publishing it, Gide had done a great service to the cause of indigenous emancipation. He noticed that there was still a widespread belief among students of the Colonial School in Paris that "forced labor serves a pedagogic mission"[139] by socializing indigenous populations in the hardships of industrial labor. Later, Thomas tried to prohibit "forced labor" at the 1930 ILO conference on the topic, but France's opposition prevailed against its complete prohibition. Thus, it was not until Blum was finally elected prime minister in 1936, that forced labor was eventually prohibited in France by the law of June 17, 1937, which was prepared by Blum's Minister of the Colonies, Marius Moutet.

Before concluding on this episode, I can hardly resist mentioning that, with his uncommon sagacity, André Gide also explored the ambivalence of reciprocal bonds known as prestations in his novels – a little-known facet of his literary work, which shows that fights in the colonial field had ramifications in the French literary field as well. Indeed, in his novels, Gide consistently explored the darker sides of reciprocal attachments, the poisonous qualities of gifts that Mauss had also underlined in *The Gift*, and which seem to have fascinated him. For instance, in his novel *The Counterfeiters*, published in 1925, which André Gide dedicated to Roger Martin du Gard (de Coppet's best friend, who later became de Coppet's father-in-law after de Coppet married his best friend's daughter), Gide deployed various intrigues which showed how the solidarity between the characters of his novel (young boys and old men, mostly) could be negative for their morality and overall destiny: such negative solidarity could take the form of a dirty secret, like the secret attraction of an older man for younger boys, or the sudden revelation of an illegitimate ancestry, or the participation in a criminal group like a ring of counterfeiters.[140] It was as if André, the son of a law professor in Paris who died at a relatively young age, subverted the notion of solidarity that his uncle Charles had theorized and made the founding block of his progressive agenda for the Republic.[141]

5 HOW MARCEL MAUSS'S STUDENTS FOUGHT POLITICAL BATTLES IN THE COLONIAL FIELD

But now, back to Mauss, and to his writings on imperial solidarity and gift exchange. One riddle which still remains in need of an explanation is why, despite the fact that Mauss's interwar writings generalized his reflections on the question of gift exchange that he published in his 1925 essay, he didn't seek to publish this manuscript *The Nation*: could he have possibly feared political repercussions?

One possible interpretation of his discretion may be that he did not want to jeopardize the creation of the Institute of Ethnology that he was in the process of establishing at the same time as he published *The Gift*. The year 1926 was not a random date for the creation of the Institute, as it corresponded to the victory of left-wing parties that Mauss had helped win the election thanks to his numerous op-eds on the reparations question in *Le Populaire*.[142] At last Mauss's two-decade-long efforts were rewarded. The creation of the Institute finally gave Mauss an instrument that enabled him to gather facts through his students' primary fieldwork, as well as to train colonial administrators to better appreciate the cultural context in which their actions took place. The Institute of Ethnology, funded thanks to taxes levied in the French Empire, was France's first university training in ethnology, and it directly targeted colonial administrators. As Alice Conklin writes, "this new [ethnological] science was supposed to serve" the empire: according to the Minister of the Colonies, Edouard Daladier, who agreed to fund it, the Institute would improve the "training of colonial administrators from the Colonial School"[143] created in 1889, which had never successfully provided highly skilled administrators for the empire. As Mauss wrote in 1925, when presenting the newly founded Institute, "the Institute serves the French Colonial Governments and Protectorates and provides them with information about (French and foreign) missions, with studies of indigenous races, as well as collects documents, artifacts and thereby contributes to the study of social facts."[144]

Mauss hoped that the creation of his Institute would deeply affect the kinds of methods that he and his students could rely on in their academic writings: for ethnology to be relevant to the administration of colonial subjects, ethnology had to change and become grounded on strong ethnographic field methods. Mauss's prewar essays on sacrifice and the origins of contractual law, which he published with Henri Hubert in *L'Année sociologique*, reflected the poor advancement of ethnographic methods in France. In these essays, the two friends explored "how the sacrifice-gifts first emerged, when offerings to Gods were presented as gifts," and how they changed "when the bloody aspects of the sacrificial rites gave a penal character to the sacrifices, and turned the sacrifice-gifts into expiatory sacrifices."[145] Mauss and Hubert mostly based their findings on their reading of the Bible and the Veda,[146] and on the application of philological methods, which Mauss had studied under the supervision of his PhD adviser, Sylvain Lévi, the famous Indologist. At that point, and up until the mid-1920s, Mauss and Hubert lacked the capability to collect primary documents and stories, which is why they mostly discussed the work of another philologist, the British historian of religion, James Frazer and his comparative history of sacrifice, *The Golden Bough*.[147] The French colonial administrators' lack of interest in the pursuit of ethnological knowledge before the Great War forced Mauss to rely on such philological analysis of ancient texts or on secondhand analysis of ethnographic facts, which he read in the Anglo-American ethnographies which he reviewed in *The Gift*.

The year 1925 thus marked the moment when Mauss secured the centrality of his position in a European space of science (ethnology), situated at the intersection between the logic of colonial administration and the comparative study of gift exchanges. The creation of this Institute in 1925 made it essential for Mauss to publish *The Gift* and to keep *The Nation* unpublished for the time being: in his famous article, Mauss reviewed the scholarly production of the Anglo-American and German ethnologists[148] – such as Franz Boas's work on the Kwakiutls and Richard Thurnwald's study of gift-giving practices in the Solomon Islands[149] – whom he identified as the community of peers with whom he intended the young French doctoral students in his future Institute to converse. Publishing such a comprehensive survey, filled with references from various national ethnographic traditions on gift exchange, had the additional advantage of illustrating the scientific spirit of cosmopolitan solidarity among men of science and claiming a new role for French sociology and ethnology as co-leaders in the field of ethnology with the German and Anglo-American ethnologists.

Through Mauss's work of citation, discussion and debate, which he displayed in *The Gift*, Mauss sought to invite Euro-American ethnologists, whose ties had sometimes been severed by the Great War, to engage in close collaborative enterprises in the advancement of this new research program: the comparative analysis of gift exchanges which he developed in *The Nation* and which provided him with a collective research program that the doctoral students of the newly founded Institute of Ethnology could adopt to conduct single-case ethnographies. His students would ask and provide answers to the following questions: Were colonial practices a positive force for the development of a common political consciousness within the colonies? Did they foster the expression of concrete forms of solidarity between and among groups? Or did they have mostly negative effects on the solidarity within groups and across exchanging parties, mainly, the French metropolitans and the colonial subjects? But when answering these questions, they would have to weigh the benefits of academic discretion over political intervention.

In many ways, the mandate that Mauss had received when obtaining funding from the French government for his diverse endeavors (Institute, Museum, and the Chair of Sociology he obtained in 1931 at the Collège de France), was fulfilled perfectly, as one can see from the careers of some his students in the colonial field. Mauss sought to ground his students in both ethnography and colonial administration in a deeper appreciation of each other's comparative merits. He sought to influence the colonial administrators he advised, by grounding their colonial practice on a more humanistic understanding of the diversity of human experiences, to implement a solidarist colonial policy based on the rejection of the Colonial Pact – which was possible only if his students reached high positions in the ladder of colonial administration.[150]

Bernard Maupoil (1906–44, killed in 1944 in a slave labor camp in Germany) was a good example of how Mauss taught colonial administrators, who either came from the Colonial School, and discovered ethnology thanks to Mauss's seminar, or who used their free time as colonial officers to conduct doctoral research under his supervision. Maupoil was posted in Dahomey in the mid 1930s, where he conducted an ethnographic study of geomancy,[151] thus advancing ethnological research at the same time as he used that research to claim better knowledge (and thus better administration) of the local populations, despite the hurdles placed by the administration to his ethnographic work.[152] After 1936, Maupoil worked as a civil administrator in French West Africa under the orders of the Governor General Marcel de Coppet, whom he lauded for the freedom the latter gave him to conduct fieldwork "to study the 'Fa', the God of destiny in Southern Dahomey."[153]

The careers of the ethnology students that Mauss took under his supervision were thus, not surprisingly, protected by the same colonial administrators who battled since the beginning of the century against the interests of the chartered companies that Mauss denounced in *The Nation*, and that Gide had targeted in his essay. But in order to secure their jobs in the colonial administration, Mauss advised his students to carefully avoid voicing "negative views on colonization, and especially the capitalist form of colonialism,"[154] which, as he cautioned Maupoil in a letter, could only harm the scientific integrity of their findings – as well as their careers in the colonial service and the Institute's reputation. As Mauss added, his words of advice toward some of the criticism expressed by Maupoil against French colonial interests in Western Africa "did not reflect a substantive disagreement," but rather, the necessity to "keep some discretion"[155] over one's political views. This prudence was all the more necessary for Maupoil in that, with the exception of Marcel de Coppet, his superiors in the French administration held the time he spent doing ethnographic research against him. In 1934, for instance, he was re-affected in the bush, far from his original fieldwork, which illustrated the mistrust that the colonial administration still showed toward the officers who conducted ethnographic research.[156]

Mauss gave the same advice to Richard Le Cœur, his favorite student, the son of a colonial family in Morocco whose career spanned academic and colonial fields, and whom Mauss later wanted to appoint as his successor at the EPHE.[157] But unfortunately, Le Cœur, who joined the Free French forces during the Second World War, was killed in 1944 on the battlefield during the campaign of Italy. In fact, Le Cœur was not critical of French colonialism: the last section of his dissertation concluded with a chapter on Lyautey's protectorate policy, which Conklin describes as quite baroque: it included poems and ended with a hagiography of Lyautey's policy of "love" in Morocco,[158] which Mauss claimed was a great accomplishment.[159] Still, Le Cœur's first dissertation draft included some more critical remarks on colonialism, especially as he studied the relation between the evolution of European colonialism in the interwar era and monetary evolutions in Europe (focusing on the difference between the franc and the mark). After reading his student's reflections, Mauss insisted that his thesis should not appear too Marxist in inspiration, and that Le Cœur should also pay attention to the cultural and pragmatic factors associated with the "colonial mentality."[160] As he wrote to his student in 1938, "there are many other things that capital exports in the act of colonization," so Le Cœur should "keep Simiand and take away Marx"[161] from his theoretical tool kit. This shift would also have the advantage of limiting the criticism of French colonialism in his final dissertation. Mauss was consistent: he wanted his students to reform colonialism from within not from outside.

To help a cadre of young French ethnologists to conduct empirical research and investigate the effects of colonial practices on the local peoples (or populations) administered by the French colonial state in West Africa, Mauss also needed the resources to pay for his students' costly ethnographic trips. As head of the Institute, he encouraged Franco-British scientific collaboration, such as that between his student Maurice Leenhardt (1878–1954), for whom he obtained a scholarship from the Rockefeller Foundation (for which he served, along with Charles Rist, as the contact person in France),[162] and Alfred Radcliffe-Brown (1881–1955), to do ethnographic research together in New Caledonia. Maurice Leenhardt, a Protestant pastor stationed in New Caledonia from 1902 to 1921, was a good example of the missionaries who took classes with Mauss: as Conklin writes, Leenhardt had "struggled for years in order to understand Kanak concepts of the sacred in order to render Christian terms into vernacular idiom more truthfully,"[163] and it was thanks to Mauss's dedication that his student's thesis was published after his return to Paris in the late 1920s.

Mauss also used his network of friends among British anthropologists – like Charles Seligman (1873–1940) – to ask, for instance, the British colonial administrators for collaboration and free passage for the French ethnographers who sought to do ethnographic fieldwork in African territories under British control.[164] For instance, Mauss's other student, Bernard Maupoil, not only conducted fieldwork in French West Africa, but also secured from the British colonial administration the right to interview the Yoruba in British-controlled colonies to finish his dissertation.[165] Already in the 1920s, US funding and Anglo-American scientific exchange were key to the development of French social sciences: nothing much has changed since then.

To find resources for his students' ethnographic "voyages," Mauss's entrepreneurial spirit did not stop at the border of the academic world. In large part thanks to the

Museum of Ethnology – later renamed Musée de l'Homme – the students whom Mauss and Rivet trained there also tapped into the economic resources of the art collectors to fund their research trips. The ties that Mauss had developed in the world of high finance were recycled to place these young French ethnologists on Europe's map of art collectors, museums, and ethnologists working in the colonial societies.[166] The conversion of social and economic capital into ethnographic capital was most apparent when Mauss helped his student, Marcel Griaule (1898–1956), a specialist on Abyssinia and Ethiopia who graduated from the Institute of Ethnology in 1927, to raise the funds for a fact-collecting mission that would start in Dakar and end in Djibouti, thus crossing Africa from west to east, and traversing mostly French but also British territories.

Mauss spared no energy for this mission: Griaule was deeply thankful for the "effective but silent" mobilization that Mauss conducted on the side of foundations, as Mauss, with the help of Charles Rist,[167] raised about 300,000 francs from the Rockefeller Foundation in 1931.[168] Mauss also lobbied his socialist friends (Renaudel in particular) to pass a law appropriating funds for the Dakar–Djibouti Mission, which allowed Griaule to leave (with Michel Leiris as secretary) for Dakar in 1931.[169] In these endeavors, Mauss joined forces with David David-Weill of the Lazard Bank, which had become a major shareholder in the car company of André Citroën,[170] which sponsored ethnological missions and other car explorations in unchartered territories.[171] Griaule's enterprise, although criticized by some of Mauss's other PhD students, like Bernard Maupoil, produced an extraordinary amount of data in the form of art, files, photographs and other artifacts: in December 1931, Griaule reported to Mauss that his short trip through the Dogon territory had allowed his mission to send to the Museum of Ethnology 2,000 objects, 1,500 photographs, 695 meters of shot film, 40 recordings and more than 2,400 ethnographic files on the Dogon people alone.[172] As he told Mauss, "this mission is an industrial factory."[173]

A few years later, Mauss told his student Bernard Maupoil that he was proud of Griaule's mission, and that with such a success, "Africa cannot really complain of the task performed by the Institute of Ethnology,"[174] which had allowed Europe's community of ethnologists (and more broadly, the European public of the new Musée de l'Homme created in 1937) to access a wealth of information on Africa's traditions and cultures, and thus to realize how rich those traditions were. Whether the African populations from which these artifacts were taken away agreed or not was another matter. Furthermore, as Maupoil wrote to Mauss, Griaule's mission had made manifest the contradiction between the two goals that the Institute of Ethnology pursued: gaining credibility for ethnography within the ranks of the colonial administration, and attracting the attention of the broader public. As he wrote, "the Griaule mission didn't leave a good impression in Dahomey,"[175] where Maupoil was stationed, and Michel Leiris's *Afrique fantôme*, in which the young secretary of Griaule's mission criticized colonial society, was a disservice to ethnology.[176] Indeed, its critical tone reinforced the prejudice in which ethnological missions were held among colonial administrations – thus making Maupoil's task much more difficult.[177]

The emphasis on European solidarity through colonial expansion, Franco-British ethnological data-collection missions and the display of artifacts in ethnological museums prepared Mauss's students to play a key role in the organization of the 1931 International Colonial Exhibition in Paris (visited by more than eight million people, with more than thirty million tickets sold). The International Colonial Exhibition, which marked the one hundredth anniversary of the French colonization of Algeria, was the apex of this outreach campaign, as it sought to internationalize its audience. The Minister of the Colonies, delivering the opening remarks at the Exhibition, as well as Hubert Lyautey, the organizing force behind the Exhibition, insisted that the colonial ideal marked a profoundly European phenomenon which united nations of Europe and the rest of the world in a common destiny. For the organizers of the Exhibition, the "colonial œuvre" offered European citizens a guarantee against the coming of a new war, both in colonial territories, and in Europe, as the increased trade between the French and British metropolises and their respective colonies decreased the conflicts between European powers. France's colonial project could really be a truly European project, and Mauss's ethnological science a truly cosmopolitan endeavor at the service of a more humane French colonial project. As Lyautey wrote in 1931, "the world now sees with clarity that it is through colonial action that it can realize the notion of human solidarity."[178] Lyautey was a figure admired and loved by Mauss's inner circle, in particular by Max Lazard, who appreciated that Lyautey had been one of the rare Dreyfusards within the ranks of the military: they also appreciated that he had forced peace upon various Moroccan tribal sheiks in 1912 through a policy of repression and "gift" or "love," as expressed in his deceiving language.[179]

As Alice Conklin remarks, the interwar generation trained by Mauss and Rivet at the Institute of Ethnology thus not only "failed to condemn French colonial rule"[180] but actively participated, along with Mauss, Rivet, Lyautey, de Coppet and other colonial administrators in publicizing the French solidarist colonial project. Jacques Soustelle comes to mind as another good example of a doctoral student of Mauss who tried to apply ethnological lessons to the colonial context. Soustelle was also a kind of "heir" endowed with colonial social capital, as, although from a modest family with a Protestant background, early on he married Georgette Fagot, the daughter of a close collaborator of Victor Augagneur at Lyon's municipal Council, before Augagneur left Lyon to become Governor of Madagascar in 1904 and then Resident-General in Tunisia.[181] On a scholarship from the ENS, it was Soustelle's wife who first met Marcel Mauss, who was teaching at the Collège de France and the Institute of Ethnology at the time. Mauss introduced them to Rivet, then head of the Museum of Ethnology, for whom the couple worked until they later moved to Mexico, where Soustelle conducted research on the Lacandons, considered to be long-lost descendants of the Mayas.

Even though Soustelle's work may seem more distant from the realities of colonial administration in West Africa than that of Maupoil and the other Africanists like Le Cœur, as France had no possession in Central America, Soustelle still gave his work some resonance in the field of colonial administration. After the proto-fascist riot in front of the French Parliament that left fifteen dead in February 1934, Mauss, Rivet and Soustelle participated in the creation of the Watchfulness Committee of Antifascist Intellectuals in March 1934. They were among the first signatories, and as such, they negotiated with other signatories, like the philosopher Alain, or the physicist Paul Langevin (Mauss's colleague at the Collège de France), the exact wording of the declaration against "a fascist dictatorship" and "against the power of the banks, trusts, and armament manufacturers who want to subvert the Republic, the true Republic which is embodied by the people, the working, suffering, and thinking people which seeks its emancipation."[182] Jacques Soustelle also participated in the foundational meetings at Langevin's place, where he met numerous communist intellectuals, including some who introduced him to Soviet ethnography – a completely "outdated ethnography"[183] – which convinced him that fascist perils needed to be addressed, but that the communist tool kit was useless in the battle of political ideas.

Soustelle's activism was strongly influenced by Mauss. When Blum was elected prime minister in 1936, Mauss wrote to Blum advising that the government should invest in the creation of "centers of propaganda in Italian and German" so as "to fight against the fascist propaganda" that had, as Durkheim had already noticed during his wartime experience, an incredible and "pathological influence on collective representations,"[184] not only in the metropolis, but also in the colonial field. If Mauss failed to convince the socialist prime minister, his advice resonated with Jacques Soustelle.[185] Soustelle later recalled that the realization that Hitler's Germany was preparing a European war, and that the French intellectuals should do something about it, came to him as he saw an unending line of trains moving heavy armament across Germany while he traveled with Mauss across the Third Reich in 1938, as the professor and his student were on their way to a conference in Copenhagen.[186] One year later, in 1939, Soustelle created a center of counter-propaganda in Mexico, where he remained posted at the onset of the war.

Like Maupoil and others, Soustelle used the comparative framework that Mauss developed in *The Nation* and in his seminars to study how colonial exchanges could lead exchanging societies closer to, or further away from, the highest levels of integration where the imperial nation was supposed to lead its colonies. In 1936, based on his research findings in Mexico, Soustelle argued that the French colonial administrators in Africa should take inspiration from land redistribution plans he observed in Mexico[187] to capitalize on the presence of benevolent socialists in Blum's government during the 1936 Front Populaire and expand the social benefits granted by the metropolis to its colonial subjects. For him, it was important to associate together the struggle against the fascists and the reform of colonial administration.

As these battles of ideas between socialism and fascism took to the colonial context after the mid 1930s, Mauss also used his ties to his doctoral students, some of whom served as colonial administrators, especially in the West African colonial field, to get information from the field and report back to various associations including the League of Human Rights, which he had helped create in the context of the Dreyfus affair. The collection of documentation they gathered included information on the colonial companies' abuses.[188] For instance, Bernard Maupoil, who, by 1935, had taken the presidency of four tribunals in Senegal, denounced in a letter to Mauss the collusion between some fascist elements in the colonial administration and a happy few from both the metropolitan and colonial society, who appropriated large benefits from the exploitation of forced or cheap labor. He decried the impunity of the Governor General in Senegal and his main associate, "a freed and self-enriched slave who exploited the peasants," over the vast portion of land that his mafia controlled, and whom the League of Human Rights left alone, as the "negrophiles"[189] there did not want to admit that exploitation could be performed by local black businessmen as well as metropolitan companies. Maupoil thus urged Mauss to see his friends in the League to denounce these abuses.[190]

In the mid 1930s, as tensions grew between left-wing and right-wing colonial administrators, Maupoil kept Mauss informed of the cabals which divided the field of French colonial administration between socialists (close to Marcel de Coppet, whom Blum elevated to the rank of Governor General of French West Africa when he became Prime Minister) and conservatives and fascists, who followed Jacques Doriot (1898–1945), a former communist who formed a new populist party in 1936.[191] As Maupoil wrote to Mauss in 1937, the fascists had the support of the son of the former Director of the Colonial School, Maurice Delafosse: because of Delafosse *fils*, who worked for the Governor General in Dakar, it was no longer rare to meet "Franco's men" cruising in the streets of the capital of Senegal and agitating against the socialists.[192]

At the time, one of the main issues of contention between socialists and conservative administrators in West Africa was the future of the Office of the Niger, which was in charge of developing the valley of the Niger River thanks to a large public works irrigation program. This Office had been set up by de Coppet, then Governor General of French West Africa (before being sent to Madagascar a year later as Governor General), and in 1928, the Government of French West Africa had already spent 400 million francs for the program, in addition to the 300 million that it had raised in France – creating a debt that continued until 1986. Marius Moutet, Blum's Minister of the Colonies, had strongly supported de Coppet's vision and his preference for irrigation work rather than road construction – the latter had been Augagneur's trademark. But despite great progress on the ground, as Maupoil wrote to Mauss, the Office of the Niger could no longer find capital in the metropolis in 1938.[193]

After 1934, with a sick wife – his former secretary, whom Mauss married in January of that year, at age 60, and who was permanently injured in a failed suicide attempt three weeks after their wedding,[194] – Mauss had less time and energy to participate in these political battles to reform colonial administration, even if he still followed his students' initiatives, and continued to follow the socialist party internal politics from afar.[195] With Blum's electoral defeat in 1938, the incoming conservative government intended to close the Office of the Niger, and to Maupoil's dismay, the metropolitan socialist newspapers – some of which were controlled by the powerful colonial interests in Lyon's municipal council, where Augagneur, who was carded as a socialist, still had a lot of influence – paid little attention to the effort of colonial reformers who wanted their economic policies to benefit their colonial subjects: as he wrote to Mauss, even the socialist press, in particular *Le Populaire*, was no longer interested in reporting the attacks that the "big trusts" organized against the "colonial administrators who risked their career by adhering to the socialist party."[196] Maupoil and Mauss agreed that it was a lost opportunity to show how ethnologists could help colonial administrators succeed in creating the political conditions necessary for the economic take-off of the colonies, but the resistance they encountered in the colonial field, coupled with Mauss's waning forces, was stronger than expected.[197] Little did they know that the beginning of the Second World War would soon shatter their existence and the world in which they had lived, where they (wrongly) assumed that ethnology could be put to the service of an enlightened and human colonial administration in West Africa.

6 A MIXED LEGACY IN THE COLONIAL FIELD IN WEST AFRICA

Both *The Gift* and Mauss's unpublished manuscript *The Nation* aimed at placing the theoretical focus of anthropology on transnational circulation and transfers – or, in Maussian terms, "intersocietal" contacts, a term he preferred, as he emphasized that not all societies (almost none, in fact) had attained the status of "nation." In *The Gift*, Mauss proclaimed unequivocally that the exchange of goods, prestations, and reciprocal services was the safest way to ensure the solidarity between exchanging societies. But *The Nation* started where Mauss's reflection in *The Gift* ended, as Mauss developed further his ideas on the destructive aspects of the colonial encounter. In *The Nation*, Mauss listed the practices that prevented such a reciprocal exchange of prestations from having positive effects on both exchanging parties, especially, but not exclusively, for the colonial subjects. Still, his criticism was limited to the power of the chartered companies operating in Africa to provide colonies with fake rather than true gifts: a lamentable fact which he criticized on behalf of a policy that the philosopher Alexandre Kojève would later call the program of "giving colonialism,"[198] in a lecture delivered at the invitation of Carl Schmitt after the Second World War.

In this unpublished manuscript, Mauss thus paid much more attention to the obstacles that could explain why the exchange of reciprocal prestations could go wrong and fail to bring about the kind of international solidarity Mauss wished to see within Europe and between Europe and the rest of the world. But he focused almost exclusively on the monopolies and concessions granted to chartered companies (especially in the exploitation, trade and administration of raw materials like rubber), in which he saw a transient organizational form that could either morph into national monopolies – and thus avert colonial wars – or could continue to exploit the social and natural resources of the French Empire, leading to rebellion, fragmentation, and violence, and even to the collapse of the Republic, which was not protected from the peril of fascism. Mauss's focus on big trusts and private companies may be where his theory of international relations and international solidarity was limited as well as prescient.

Indeed, Mauss's perspective was limited to the extent it endorsed the French colonial mindset of the interwar era: Mauss almost completely missed the colonial oppression and exploitation organized by the state itself (and the army in particular) when looking for the sources of obstacles to the political development of colonial societies. In the 1930s, Mauss helped his colleagues and students to denounce practices of forced labor or other gross abuses against local populations by forwarding information to the League of Human Rights, but in general, he advised them to remain cautious. In the nebula of public intellectuals, colonial administrators, and policymakers, which included, among others, Léon Blum, Marius Moutet, Albert Thomas, Marcel de Coppet, Charles and André Gide, who lobbied the French government and international organizations like the ILO to ban the existence of forced labor, Mauss was a timid voice. Mauss cannot claim a large part of responsibility for the victory that Léon Blum's government experienced when it finally abolished forced labor, even if his students and colleagues consistently lobbied against it. And the socialists' victory was short-lived, as the fascists and conservatives gained power in the ranks of the administration of Senegal and other colonies of West Africa. Not surprisingly, as the Second World War broke out, it was Félix Eboué (1884–1944), then Governor of Chad, who rallied the government of East Africa to the government in exile of General de Gaulle, whereas the governors of Senegal and West Africa in General pledged allegiance to Vichy and Marshall Pétain, who sided in favor of collaboration with the Nazis – while de Coppet, named Governor of Madagascar, made the tragic mistake of not siding in favor of de Gaulle.

One may thus ask whether Mauss's teachings and writings failed to prepare his students and the colonial administrators under his supervision to support the movements in favor of political independence which emerged during and after the Second World War in the French colonies and in Algeria. This is the key question that the next chapter will explore in further detail, although the evidence must be treated as suggestive rather than conclusive: indeed, many of his students were killed during the war, and one cannot predict how an entire cohort of ethnology students would have reacted to the rise of anti-colonial movements in Indochina or Algeria, had they survived.

But even so, Mauss's anthropological perspective on international economic relations may have been prescient, considering the postcolonial fights for economic independence led by the newly independent states after their political independence. In the 1970s, the themes that Mauss had addressed in *The Nation* seemed to come back at the center of debates on global governance and gift exchange: the last section of *The Nation*, which ignored the question of political independence but called on new states to nationalize chartered companies, promoted the policy that French Algeria would ultimately follow when its governments decided in 1971 to "nationalize" the oil and gas extraction trusts operating in its territory. Could these decisions and the associated calls for a "new international economic order"[199] expressed in the 1970s by Algeria and other Third World nations be then interpreted as the last trace of Mauss's influence in international relations? Chapter 6 will answer this question, by showing how anti-colonial scholars and policymakers in Algeria addressed the question of economic independence, although in a different way than Mauss had anticipated.

5

Marcel Mauss's Disciples in Algeria

The Anthropology of the Gift and the Shock of Decolonization

In September 1959, Jacques Soustelle – by then Minister of Atomic Energy and the Sahara – wrote to French Prime Minister Michel Debré, "the Algerians exist, but there is no such thing as an Algerian people."[1] In so doing, this former graduate of the Paris-based Institute of Ethnology, who had become the world's leading expert in Central American ethnology, opposed the principle of "self-determination," which President de Gaulle had recently advocated when he announced his decision in the summer of 1959 to let Algerians decide their own fate. In fact, Soustelle expressed both a political statement on the legitimacy (or lack thereof) of Algerians' claims to independence, and an epistemological claim: indeed, he affirmed the primacy of ethnological knowledge over the manifestation of a political will through a referendum on the question of Algeria's independence.

For Soustelle, any consultation of the Algerian residents, as decided by de Gaulle, ignored the more important realities discovered by ethnologists and generations of French administrators in Algeria: Algeria was multiple and complex. In fact, Soustelle wrote to Debré, the French government "shall not accept the possibility that the Algerian people could determine, *en bloc*, the destiny of a unified entity conceived as a State" as Algeria lacked the "ethnic and cultural homogeneity which is a necessary condition for the validity of a vote in which the majority can legitimately impose its views on the minority."[2] As he added, the "future consultation of Algerians shall thus be conceived in such a way that it leaves to 'the peoples' who live in Algeria, rather than to an alleged 'Algerian people,' the possibility to express themselves."[3] Deciding otherwise, would, for the Maussian ethnologist turned minister, be equivalent to accepting the "oppression"[4] of the dominant ethnic group over the less populous ethnic groups. Based on his opposition between ethnographic diversity and democratic voice, Soustelle thus motivated his impassioned rejection of de Gaulle's pro-self-determination policy in the hope of convincing Debré, who had been a staunch defender of the pro-French Algeria policy, to resist de Gaulle's choices.

Soustelle's view may, at first sight, appear to depart from Mauss's central claim that the colonization of non-European peoples could only be justified as a means to foster a national consciousness and help create democratically controlled national economic conglomerates. But it also reflected Mauss's attachment to the idea that ethnographic knowledge should be used by colonial policymakers as a guide for action. Soustelle mobilized ethnographic knowledge to answer one of the most important questions of his time: how could European statesmen decide that a colonial people (or group of peoples) had reached a sufficient level of national integration so as to justify granting their national independence? As we have seen, Mauss largely eschewed the question in his interwar writings: he argued that most societies had not yet arrived at that level of national integration,[5] but he also affirmed the principle that colonialism should foster such national integration so that a true inter-nationalism could be built. The prospect of decolonization seemed so distant that he never got bogged down in the practical details of whether national integration would automatically mean national independence – nor the legal conditions of future secessions.

But in the postwar era, characterized by the revolt of the Vietnamese and then Algerians against continued French tutelage, Mauss's disciples could ignore the practical issue no more. They had to take a position as to whether ethnographic knowledge showed that Algerians were now ready for independence; and, further, whether ethnographic knowledge should be the guide on that question, or whether the expression of political will – expressed by guns or votes – would suffice to gain independence. In this chapter, I thus ask: did Mauss's students draw on the anthropology of the gift exchange to decide this issue, especially in the context of the war in Algeria? How did Mauss's analysis of gift exchange help them justify either the continued integration of Algeria within a greater France, or Algerian independence? Which rhetorical resources were deployed by the mobilization of ethnology for either pro-independence or pro-French Algeria claims?

To answer these questions, the chapter first investigates how two of the few students whom Mauss had trained before the Second World War and who also survived the war, Germaine Tillion and Jacques Soustelle, deployed and reframed Mauss's concepts of gift exchange and intersocietal integration in the context of the Algerian War. The first section shows how they adapted their mentor's theory of integration to the postwar era, when the debate concerned whether the French Republic could move toward a post-national political society, with Algeria and the French metropolis tied together; or whether Algeria could be granted independence without risking its implosion. For them, ethnological findings demonstrated that no Algerian national consciousness united its citizens in a common democratic framework, and more broadly, that Algeria lacked the necessary economic and financial resources for its national autonomy. As there was great risk that Algerian independence would mean "de-development" – e.g. a socioeconomic regression with respect to the period of integration within the French constitutional framework – they thus argued in favor of continued French presence in Algeria as well as for a constitutional reform that would further integrate the various components of the societies "France" and "Algeria" into a post-national political body. As Giuseppe di Lampedusa had written in 1958 in *The Leopard*, everything needed to change, so everything could stay the same.

The application of the model of gift exchange to rethink economic relations in the colonial context in general, and the Algerian context in particular, was hardly surprising, since Mauss founded ethnology in France at the nexus of colonial administration and academic theorizing. Furthermore, as the French Empire had shrunk by 1954, and as Algeria was at the center of intellectual and constitutional debates about the future of France itself, it was natural that Mauss's students would apply their master's theory of integration (and reformulate it at the same time) to think through the relations between France and Algeria and their possible integration in a French multicultural, postcolonial, and post-national Republic. At the same time, the theory of integration developed by Mauss's students in the Algerian context represented a radical departure from the creation of a society of independent nations, which had been the League of Nation's objective in the interwar period – and the implicit ideological map onto which Mauss projected the possible futures of colonialism.

Among the younger generation of anthropologists and sociologists whom Mauss had directly or indirectly influenced, not all agreed with Jacques Soustelle and Germaine Tillion. But, more importantly, structural transformations in the postwar French academic field led to the emergence of the French discipline of political science, which, as this chapter demonstrates, called into question the very notion that ethnology had anything to say about international relations in general and the future of Algeria in particular. Combined with the end of the French war in Indochina in 1954, shortly followed by the beginning of the insurrection in Algeria, these structural changes led to the rise of new voices who disputed the legitimacy of the application of the model of gift exchange to the analysis of international relations, and the specific conclusions that Maussian ethnologists drew with regard to Algeria. Paradoxically, it was Mauss's cousin, Raymond Aron, who argued most strongly that ethnology in general, and the model of gift exchange which Mauss had developed in particular, should no longer influence the reasoning of the French government with regard to Algeria. Instead, Aron argued that economics and the new science public administration should ground the judgment of policymakers on this most complex question.

Aron's realist vision of international relations, argued the Maussians, doomed the Algerians, as the latter would never be able to attract enough capital to modernize their economy – not to mention their skepticism about the Front de Libération Nationale's (FLN) ability to let Algerian citizens enjoy democratic rights. But the blow that ethnologists had suffered, so this chapter then argues, eventually led to ethnology's downfall, and its relegation to the sciences of the local. The attack against ethnology in general, and the anthropology of gift exchanges in particular, was all the more fatal that it was relayed by ethnographers themselves, as the chapter goes on to show by focusing on the writings of Pierre Bourdieu in Algeria. To claim that relations between metropolis and colonies could be viewed as gift exchanges was deeply wrong for Bourdieu: remains of gift exchanges could be observed at the local level in Algeria, but not at the international level. With Bourdieu, the idea that the model of the gift could provide a valid heuristic to think through colonial and postcolonial intersocietal relations became anathema, as it smelled too much of the old colonial ideology that marked his elders' political essays. From then on, the chapter concludes, he and younger anthropologists applied the model of the gift solely to talk about socioeconomic exchanges at the local level, thereby closing the historical parenthesis during which the gift had returned as a legitimate discourse about global governance.

1 ALGERIA: A LABORATORY FOR SOUSTELLE'S THEORY OF POST-NATIONAL INTEGRATION

Many debates today, in France as well as in Western Europe, revolve around the notion of "integration." In a context of rising right-wing populism in Europe, fueled by the instrumentalization of women's rights to police the borders of citizenship along the lines of race and religion, we often hear injunctions from politicians that migrants – especially the nationals of former French colonies and Algeria in particular – must better "integrate" into French society.[6] French populist thinkers and politicians demand that migrants and second-generation Muslims from Algeria, Tunisia, or Morocco conform to newly reinterpreted norms of gender equality and secularism, which are reframed in such a way so as to paradoxically make the very "integration" of Muslim migrants and their children more difficult, as these norms ask them to choose between certain understandings of their own religion and the possibility to work or study in France.[7] In many ways, integration, in these academic and political discourses, has come to refer to the relation that each individual within minority groups entertains with the political, cultural, and social mores of the dominant group.

Even if not completely reducible to the concept of "assimilation," the concept of integration today has come to characterize the way individuals relate to, and absorb, social norms. It is a social reality, which can be measured by demographers and sociologists. In the United States, mainstream sociologists of migration have framed their contribution to the policy debate on migration by measuring levels of integration of migrant population of different ethnicities or national origins in their host society and by developing what they call "segmented assimilation theory."[8] This modern use of the term "integration" (used interchangeably with that of "assimilation") is also found in the work of French social scientists who build indexes of "social integration," which they use to compute the relative ease with which individuals of various migrant communities are likely to adopt the dominant social norms and values once they interact with the majority.[9] Integration is thus a loaded term, in a context in which French right-wing pundits have saturated the media with their ranting against the alleged evils of multiculturalism.

Integration in the postwar era was not a purely academic term either, but its meaning encompassed a very different political and legal reality than that which today's social scientists and right-wing politicians associate with the term. The question concerned whether all French citizens (including those adhering to the Muslim code in Algeria) could participate in the political life of the French Republic; and what form such political participation should take. Before the Second World War, Algerian Muslim residents seeking French citizenship were presented with the drastic choice between their religion and customary law on one side, and the benefits of French citizenship on the other side, with the effect that very few had pursued French citizenship before 1946. In some sense, it is sad to notice that French citizens are close to being brought back to this era, as the French Parliament has decided that no one in public office (including, since January 2018, members of parliament) can wear "exterior signs of religion," thus forcing practicing Muslims out of state mandates and curtailing their right to hold public office. But this was not the case in the 1950s. With the end of the Second World War, the constitutional architecture moved from an imperial policy of domination to one of federal "association" within an organic federation of "peoples and nations" working for the "harmonious development of each civilization."[10] In the 1950s, the debate emphasized the political dimension of the concept of integration rather than its sociocultural dimension: French politicians discussed how all Algerian citizens, including Muslims, would participate in the political life of the nation, without asking Muslims to abandon their adherence to their socio-cultural mores. This political integration was pushed further in 1958, when the new Constitution of the Fifth Republic was adopted, as I will explain now.

The heavy emphasis on the political rather than sociocultural dimension of integration came in various stages, starting with the adoption of the new Constitution of the Fourth Republic in 1946, whereby the Republic affirmed the constitutional integration of Algeria within France itself. The preamble of the 1946 Constitution put an end to the empire, and replaced it with a Union based "on the equality of rights and duties, without distinction of race or religion."[11] This meant that all Algerian citizens could be considered part of the same body politic on equal footing with the metropolitan citizens. The distinction between citizens and colonial subjects (who were to be led through the colonial relation to autonomy and independence) was abandoned, and the 1947 Statute of Algeria considerably enlarged the number of rights granted to French nationals in Algeria. In fact, the *loi-cadre* that the various governments of the Fourth Republic debated in the 1950s in order to fix precisely the terms of the political participation of all citizens in France's overseas territories (including Algerian Muslims) allowed for the possibility that non-white populations who had been previously excluded from political participation would be fully integrated, without having to adopt all the social mores of the French Christian majority.

The shift was largely a consequence of the war, after which it was recognized that Algeria had played a key role in the establishment of the French liberating army which had crossed the Mediterranean, and which allowed France to sit with the other three great powers at the table of peace negotiations. The colonial subjects had given to the metropolis: they would be granted political citizenship in return. Integration was thus an essential component of the gift exchange between the metropolis and Algeria. This national myth – a "myth" not because it was completely untrue, but because it fostered national cohesion after the trauma of defeat and collaboration[12] – can be summarized in the words of Raoul Girardet: "during the war, it happened that not only the political initiative, but also the locus and principle of French sovereignty itself, had moved from the metropolis to the Empire, from the continental France to the France from overseas,"[13] and Algeria in particular. This mythical narrative praising the colonies' participation to the Resistance and France's ultimate victory was found for instance in the writings of postwar colonial policy-makers like François Mitterrand, the young minister of "France from overseas" (the new term for the Minister of the Colonies) in 1951 and 1952, and then Minister of the Interior (in charge of Algeria) until 1955, who wrote that "with the exception of the mandate in Syria, the Empire had not suffered from any cracks" during the war. As Mitterrand added, "beyond the surface of personal intrigues and political ambitions, the peoples (those of Algeria and Senegal, Tamatave and Conakry, Fort-Lamy and Saigon) had given what they had been asked each time they were asked: their men, their resources, their trust. The Empire of Asia" he continued, "held the fort on behalf of Vichy; the African Empire remained split, with Western Africa in favor of Pétain, and Equatorial Africa for de Gaulle, and Algeria shifting, but always in resistance"[14] against the Germans.

Although the myth of the colonies' resistance was a greatly simplified reality, it is true that the colonies (and Algeria in particular) participated in the French military effort against the Germans to an extent even greater than during the First World War: already during the German invasion of the metropolis, one-third of the 60,000 French casualties were from colonial armies, which had supplied about 500,000 men on the northern front. After the Allied troops landed in 1942 in the French protectorates of Morocco and Algeria, public authorities in Algiers led an immense effort of mobilization of colonial soldiers to participate in the reconquest of the south of Italy and then France. In 1943, the French colonial battalions (headed by General Giraud and US General Patton)[15] gathered about 170,000 Frenchmen of "European" ethnicity from Algeria and Morocco and 150,000 from the "indigenous" populations of the Maghreb, in addition to 100,000 men from Senegal and other African territories.

This is why French politicians debated the *lois-cadres* which would best acknowledge the wartime African effort in the 1950s. Jacques Soustelle was a leading voice in these postwar debates about the "integration" of Algerian subjects. Political integration for Soustelle was to be inscribed in the Constitution of the Republic, in statutes and laws. The policy of integration that Soustelle promoted was an ambitious attempt to create a new level of integration beyond the national (and inter-national) integration that Mauss had envisioned as the ultimate step for the colonies. His program was premised on the realization that the implementation of the 1947 Statute of Algeria was lacking on the ground, as elections to the newly formed Algerian Assembly were notoriously manipulated, and French citizens who followed Muslim customs were underrepresented in a segregated college of electors. As in the United States, "separate but equal" was a contradictory motto, as the very maintenance of segregation in political life was meant to preserve inequalities between Algerians of European descent and those of Muslim faith. To be truly complete, the logic of the gift exchange thus needed to reach the political and even constitutional affairs of the French Republic.

Soustelle proposed to create a new level of transnational (and postcolonial) integration for both the French metropolis and Algeria: a level of integration that neither Mauss in his writings on *The Nation* nor any apologist of colonialism writing in the interwar period had imagined.[16] Soustelle aimed at creating a collective consciousness in Algeria that would be completely tied to the political institutions in Paris, rather than to those located in Algiers.[17] He did not advocate the creation of an Algerian national consciousness around a new flag, a new people ruling as a an independent sovereign in its territory, and whose relation with an independent French metropolis would be redefined so as to become truly "inter-national." To the contrary, in Soustelle's mind, Algeria was to be fully part of the French Republic until the end of time, and Algerian populations were to be integrated in a post-national "greater France" composed of both the Algerian and metropolitan societies.

Integration in the political language of Soustelle was thus a multi-level concept, which aimed at creating a new economic, social, cultural, legal, and political reality – a total social fact – neither previously experienced, nor desired, by colonial empires. As Soustelle wrote to the members of the Union for the Salvation and Rebirth of French Algeria (or, in French, USRAF) – an organization he created for the purpose of "creating a climate of solidarity between the metropolis and Algeria,"[18] and which included the former general governors of the French Empire and ministers of the colonies (like Maurice Viollette, Roger Leonard, and Marcel-Edmond Naegelen), as well as political elites (like Georges Bidault, Michel Debré, and Georges Pompidou) and many central academic and intellectual figures in the colonial field, some of whom had been closely associated to Mauss's Institute of Ethnology (like Maurice Delavignette, Paul Rivet, or Jean Paulhan)[19] – integration meant in the long term the creation of a "French Algeria in which the Algerian country cannot erect a distinct state, with its distinct diplomacy and army, and in which the French citizen of the metropolis enjoys the full rights of an ipso facto citizenship,"[20] and vice versa. As Soustelle added, integration meant:

> in the economic domain, the suppression of the trade customs between Algeria and France and the abolition of the financial autonomy of Algeria; in the social domain, the implementation of all [metropolitan] social laws to the Algerian territory; in the administrative domain, a vast program of decentralization to the benefit of communes carved around the many tribal boundaries that fractured the Algerian society, and the creation of inter-communal syndicates; in the political domain, the dissolution of the services of the Government General in Algiers, and their reattachment to the various Ministries in Paris, as well as the creation of a Minister of Algeria.[21]

In Soustelle's view, the Minister of Algeria in the future government he called for in the mid 1950s would be in charge of arbitrating conflicts between the various administrative layers of power in Algeria from Paris (rather than from Algiers, which he belittled as a "pseudo-capital of a state").[22]

Soustelle thus proposed in 1956 and 1957 to repatriate all legislative sources of law and power in Algeria to Paris, in order to protect the policymaking process from the pressure of both white settlers in Algeria (who were fiercely conservative as far as the protection of their economic and civic privileges were concerned) and pro-independence Muslim populations. Soustelle's proposal of political integration in a greater post-national France thus went well beyond the *loi-cadre* project which, in the version discussed in 1957, would grant all French colonies of the Union a local parliament with a local government in charge of budgetary decisions.[23] In the 1957 project discussed by the French Parliament, Soustelle found riskiest the proposal that legislative and administrative power should be devolved from Paris to Algiers (either to the governor general or to the Algerian Assembly). Although Soustelle's first decisions as Algeria's governor general in 1955 had been to support the creation of a unique college of electors for the Algerian Assembly (which marked the end of the segregated and unequal system of representation in Algeria's consultative Assembly with two colleges, one for the minority of "Europeans" and one for "Muslims"), as time went by, he saw peril in giving this Assembly more legitimacy, as it could turn into a "constituent assembly."[24]

Translated in political terms, Soustelle's post-national theory of integration meant that the Fourth Republic needed to backtrack the law of September 1947, which gave Algeria a distinct "civil personality, with a special budget, as well as a distinct administrative organization characterized by the regulatory power of the Governor and the monitoring of budgetary matters by the Algerian Assembly."[25] The Algerian Assembly would be kept in its purely consultative role; or be disbanded and replaced by a Coordination Council – a kind of socioeconomic council of Algeria – located in Paris, where the diversity of the Algerian society would be fully represented with select members of civil society as well as representatives of municipal councils in

Algeria. This Council would meet to discuss Algerian issues, but its role would remain purely consultative.[26] Instead of a strengthened local government, Soustelle wanted to institute a unique college charged with the election of Algerian parliamentarians directly in the French Assembly in Paris. It was the only way he found to integrate the Algerian populations (not culturally, but politically and economically) into a French political society whose heart would beat in Paris, far from the veins of the Algerian body politic.

The reform that Soustelle and the members of USRAF wanted to bring forth in the name of integration was thus not only oriented toward Algeria but also toward metropolitan France, as it involved a deep constitutional reform of the Fourth Republic itself. Indeed, the inclusion of all Algerian voters (no longer segregated into various colleges) in the body politic in charge of electing representatives to the Paris Assembly meant technically that the "Algerians would get about fifty parliamentarians in the French Assembly in Paris, including about fifteen Europeans, thanks to a proper division of the electoral map."[27] In 1956, General de Gaulle seemed to agree with him, as, commenting upon Soustelle's ideas, he wrote to him that, although Soustelle did what he could as a governor general in Algeria to solve the problem of Algerian claims to independence, the Algerian rebellion required a "very great policy"[28] – one that was not in the hands of the governor general of Algeria, but in the hands of a constituent assembly that would give both France and Algeria a new constitution. The "regime" of the Fourth Republic had to die for a new constitution to enshrine the post-national level of integration in which he and Soustelle believed: that which eventually established the Fifth Republic.[29]

The need to change the French Constitution explains why Soustelle spent the three years after he left the Governor's residence in Algiers multiplying contacts in the intelligence community to build up momentum in favor of de Gaulle's return to power and the abolition of the Fourth Republic. This rebellion against the regime in Paris climaxed with the street protests of Muslims and Europeans in Algiers, the storming of the palace of the governor general and the creation of civilian–military Comités de Salut Public in May 1958. Shortly after, Soustelle was recognized by the putschists in Algiers as the de facto power in Algeria, in defiance of the French government in Paris. Based upon this assertion of statesmanship, and threatening to send paratroopers to Paris, Soustelle called on the government in Paris to abdicate and to call in de Gaulle to form a new government, which would then propose the planned new constitution written by a new constituent assembly. Of course, Soustelle expected to lead the new government as prime minister, but de Gaulle failed to fully honor his debt:[30] if Soustelle indeed participated in co-writing the Constitution of the Fifth Republic, adopted by referendum in November 1958, he was given a haphazard portfolio including the Ministry of Atomic Energy and the Sahara in the government of Michel Debré.[31]

In many ways, Todd Shepard is right when he sees in the adoption of Soustelle's theory of integration and its constitutional translation in the new Constitution of the

Fifth Republic a radical discontinuity in the French legal tradition, with its clear nationalistic viewpoint.[32] The new Constitution adopted Soustelle's vision of "integration" between Algerian citizens and French metropolitan citizens in post-national institutions. It clarified that Algeria was part of the French Republic, rather than part of the French Union (Articles 3 and 75, according to which the French metropolitan and Algerian territories were "indivisible"), in contrast to all the other colonies whose status had been revised by the *loi-cadre* of 1957. With the adoption of the new Constitution, the Algerian subjects (whatever their civil status) could now vote in parliamentary elections for the national assembly in Paris, leading to the election of sixty-seven Algerian deputies (including fifty-six Muslims) to the Paris Assembly in 1959.

With the new Constitution, Soustelle and the members of USRAF had thus overcome the three main obstacles to their reform. First:

> the fear expressed by the metropolitan citizens to see the political life of the metropolis arbitrated by the hundred or so Algerian deputies sitting in the French Assembly in Paris; second, the opinion voiced by the Algerians of European descent who worry that their interests will be disregarded as a result of the absorption of all electors in a unique college [in Paris rather than Algiers]; third, the fear of the Muslims, that the metropolitan Frenchmen shall not want this reform.[33]

And this indeed brought Muslim deputies to the French Parliament. The Algerians, including the Muslims, who were consulted for the first time on the matter of their organic link to the metropolitan body politic, voted largely in favor of the new Constitution in September 1958. They also voted massively in the 1959 municipal elections – with a participation rate of 61 percent in Algeria – despite the threats of the FLN to murder Algerians who voted. For Soustelle, their participation was a sign of positive adhesion to the new post-national Republic.[34] Little did Soustelle suspect that de Gaulle would soon change his mind on the Algerian question.

In parallel to these administrative–legal endeavors, Soustelle's integration policy pursued another goal, which may at first seem contradictory, but which was in fact perfectly aligned with the previous objective, as both sought to squash the emergence of an Algerian national consciousness. Like Mauss, Soustelle acknowledged that societies did not all have the same level of integration, that the "national" integration of individuals in metropolitan France was quite unique, and that the Algerians did not represent a "nation" in the Maussian sense.[35] But, from this observation, Soustelle drew the conclusion that the French should not help these various Algerian communities coalesce at the national level as a people. Rather, Soustelle and his USRAF followers promoted a multiculturalist understanding of the French state administration in Algeria, which prided itself on the many distinct cultural practices and social groupings that existed within its society (the Arabs, Berbers, Bedouins, etc.), and which gave to each some visible presence, with no need for anybody to abandon their cultural and religious traditions. Each ethnic group was to be attributed quotas within the Algerian administration, which meant that some positive measure of discrimination would be applied to reserve specific places in public administration for various Muslim ethnicities.[36]

In that sense, Soustelle's theory of integration was the exact opposite of that by which French populists from the left and right since the 2000s have come to understand the obligations of migrants to assimilate ("integrate," in today's parlance) the dominant customs, norms, and values of the French white majority. In fact, Soustelle denounced the policy of cultural assimilation that the French socialists in the government of the socialist Guy Mollet promoted until 1956.[37] For Soustelle, the essential feature of the "Algerian personality" was "its diversity,"[38] and the French state had to foster such an ethnic, cultural, political, and administrative diversity at the same time as it had to develop among Algerian subjects a sentiment of political identification with the Paris government. In other words, Soustelle advocated that the French state recognize the Algerians in their ethnological diversity (and indeed distinct personality), at the same time as he denied that they were destined to experience an independent national destiny. As Soustelle wrote to Prime Minister Debré in 1959, "integration and personality were not incompatible terms,"[39] quite the contrary. But the danger came from the fact that, too often, those who used the term "personality" to refer to the Algerian society shifted imperceptibly from an *ethno-cultural* understanding of the concept (characterized by a religious, ethnic, and culturally specific reality), which Soustelle neither denied nor tried to reduce, to a *political* understanding – that of a state, which Soustelle found a "deadly" shift.[40]

Lauding Algeria's ethno-cultural diversity at the same time as upholding the ability of Algerians to integrate (economically rather than culturally) into the modern French economy and political system established by the Fifth Republic served the same goal: to avoid the emergence of an (independent) national level of identification in Algiers around which the various fractions of Algerian society would unite. Consistent with this view, he presented the FLN, which claimed to represent the national political will, as a totalitarian "Islamo-fascist" movement, which "called for the destruction of everything European in the Maghreb and of every Muslim who refuses to submit its will to theirs and which calls for the forced conversion of all the survivors of its extermination policy, as well as to the institution of a theocratic and racist state that will enter into the Arab League."[41] For an ethnologist, that was quite a remarkably unnuanced statement. For a politician, it was not completely off the mark, even though it anticipated the very problematic discourse that burgeoned after September 11 on the perils of "Islamo-Fascism" – a term that Soustelle may have been one of the first public intellectuals to use in reference to the FLN.

2 ETHNOGRAPHIC LESSONS AFTER THE ALGERIAN INSURRECTION: A DISCIPLINE IN SEARCH OF POLITICAL RELEVANCE

The model of post-national integration between citizens in Algeria and in the metropolis that Soustelle – and behind him, the dominant Parisian intellectual and political elites of the USRAF – promoted as part of a broad model of gift exchange between France and Algeria was thus grounded on epistemic claims of knowing a certain ethnographic truth about the intrinsic diversity in Algeria's society, and its incompatibility with the extension of political participation to all citizens in a separate Algerian national polity, independent from France. In general, the articulation between such truth claims and the broader constitutional politics of the postwar era raised the question of the relation that anthropology, ethnology, and French constitutional politics entertained in the 1950s.

Two striking differences distinguished the relationship that the interwar and postwar French anthropologists entertained with the political elites in the field of colonial power. First, Mauss and other interwar ethnological luminaries such as Paul Rivet did not doubt that colonialism would last until Europeans decided to end it – when colonial subjects would have reached sufficient levels of integration. Their purpose was not primarily geared at saving the French Empire, but, rather, at saving the local traditions which were at risk of being destroyed and forgotten as all colonial subjects became further integrated into the French economy. In contrast, after the war, Soustelle and other Maussian anthropologists like Germaine Tillion or Claude Lévi-Strauss doubted that the French state could much longer tame the political will to independence expressed by colonial subjects. The end of the war in May 1945 had been marked by massacres of Algerian subjects carried out by Algerian citizens of European descent, whose criminal action had been covered up by the benevolent silence of the French administration. As a French general, who oversaw the repression against Muslims in May 1945, cynically said to the surviving Muslims in the mosque of Constantine: "I have just given you peace for ten years." In a way, he was right: in 1954, the FLN launched the insurrection.

Second, and even more importantly, Mauss and other solidarists like Charles Gide had discovered and denounced the horrors of colonialism (forced labor, mass killings, natural depredation, etc.) in a colonial context where the exercise of French public law was notoriously inexistent, as the chartered companies had privately organized public affairs, especially in the Congo, where the administration was incredibly weak and embodied by corrupt officials. In contrast, Mauss's students in Algeria were confronted with the evils of colonialism in a context characterized by a dense presence of French public law as well as a thick network of intersocietal and economic exchanges between the metropolitan population and a large minority of European settlers grouped in city centers (1 million out of the 10 million Algerians). Whereas it made no sense for Mauss to envision how the Congolese subjects, almost enslaved by the chartered companies, could be made to participate politically in the life of the Republic, Maussian students were obsessed with finding ways in which the Algerian subjects of Muslim faith could be made to participate more in the decisions of the Republic's government, so as to avoid the FLN winning the hearts and minds of the majority of non-white residents in Algeria.

These differences between the interwar and postwar concerns of Maussian ethnologists can best be illustrated through the evolution of the work produced by one of the two students whom Mauss sent to Algeria in the 1930s, and who returned to Algeria in the 1950s: Germaine Tillion. The daughter of a judge and an amateur archaeologist,[42] Tillion worked at the Museum of Ethnology (later the Musée de l'Homme) until her departure for Algeria in 1934. After taking Louis Massignon's (1883–1962) classes on orientalism and religion at the Collège de France, and graduating from Mauss's Institute of Ethnology in 1932, she continued to attend Mauss's seminar until 1934. Tillion could finally do ethnographic work after Mauss secured two grants to support fieldwork in Algeria: one for Tillion, and one for Thérèse Rivière, the sister of Georges-Henri Rivière (Paul Rivet's assistant at the Museum of Ethnology).[43] Although Tillion lost her dissertation manuscript when she came back to Paris and was deported to Buchenwald as a result of her participation in the early Resistance movement of the Musée de l'Homme, she continued to practice ethnology after the war, as well as teaching at the École Pratique des Hautes Etudes (EPHE) from 1959 to 1970 and writing on the societies of the Maghreb and the Mediterranean in general.

From 1934 to 1940, Tillion conducted various missions in the Aurès, among the Chaouia tribes who lived in a tiny mountainous region in Algeria. Mauss and Tillion had chosen Berber villages – or as Tillion called them, Berber "republics"[44] – precisely because they looked as removed as possible from the French and capitalist civilization, which allowed her to conduct an experimental test of Mauss's ideas about the value of commerce and intersocietal exchange on changes in integration levels: even when scarce contacts existed, she hypothesized, these remote colonial subjects in Algeria's mountainous regions would entertain some exchanges with French civilization and law, and she would be able to test whether these exchanges moved these Berber republics closer to the national level of integration.

Mauss encouraged her to study this problem, as he was interested in having his students learn how practices of gift exchange (here exchanges of services, like the administration of justice, the construction of roads and schools, the collection of taxes) between the French administration and local tribes were affected by the differences between the levels of integration reached by each society (the colonial and the local); and whether, in return, such contacts created a dynamic of integration across societies, or not. Tillion found much evidence of the preservation of a Chaouia tribal public law (e.g. their unwritten system of "customary law," whose "rules are not binding obligations, if it is the opinion of the majority that they should be ignored")[45] as well as of "private law" customs (e.g. their rules of marital exchanges). But she also found some form of accommodation and inclusion of the

French system of rule.[46] The Berbers had very limited interactions with the French administration and colonial settler populations, but they knew perfectly well how to use the French colonial presence as a last resort, for instance, when they had exhausted traditional means of justice and wanted to avoid a bloody settlement of claims.[47]

Tillion's ethnological research in Algeria empirically demonstrated how the dynamic of judicial and cultural pluralism that was created by the colonial encounter worked in a peaceful yet conflict-ridden way. She focused on how local communities practiced law, religion and culture in a pluralist manner, as local populations navigated between various systems of rules. The question of integration that Mauss encouraged his students to raise in the 1930s was unconcerned with whether the Algerian tribesmen and women could be made to participate in the political life of the metropolis through the establishment of a renewed constitutional machinery. To the contrary, Mauss had written in *The Nation* that he wanted his students to move away from the study of constitutions and treaties. In the 1930s, Tillion did not even think about the possibility for an alternative constitutional system in which all the Algerian and metropolitan citizens would equally participate in a common democratic polity.

The purpose of Tillion's postwar ethnographic missions in Algeria was very different,[48] and this difference, in turn, marked how anthropologists in general, and Tillion in particular, used the concept of integration after the Second World War. When she first came back to the Aurès in the 1950s, the local populations had rebelled against the French administration, leading to a massive envoy of military forces to the region. Indeed, immediately upon the insurrection launched in November 1954 by the Algerian FLN, Germaine Tillion was sent to Algeria by the Minister of the Interior, François Mitterrand, under the pressing recommendation of Louis Massignon, her former PhD co-supervisor and Mauss's former colleague at the Collège de France, to study the root causes of the rebellion and to make sure that human rights were respected in Algeria by the police forces responsible for the repression of the FLN insurrection.[49] The possibility of integration for Muslim Berber populations, and the form that such integration would take – in a rebellious pro-independence national movement or in the context of a greater France? – was thus no longer an academic question but a pressing political and constitutional issue. The question of integration was now less concerned with the capacity of intercultural exchanges to move the Algerian peasants further from their tribal sense of solidarity and closer to a national sense of belonging, than with the eminently political question of whether these populations wanted to die for the end of the French presence in Algeria.

Quite characteristically, at this point the question of integration in Tillion's research thus changed from an academic endeavor meant to describe how social solidarity among local tribes and between those tribes and the French administration operated, to a political project, ultimately aimed at finding effective ways to retool Algerian peasants in training centers so as to give them the adequate economic and political skills to fit in with the imperatives of a modern economy whose prosperity would convince newly constituted Algerian voters to remain attached to the French presence in Algeria.[50] Upon returning to these villages whose families she intimately knew – in particular, the tribe of the Ouled Abderrahmane where she had studied about sixty families – Tillion was no longer an ethnographer collecting stories, dreams, tales, customs, and laws, but an agent chosen by the French government who could be used by the Berbers to publicize their views and negotiate rights for their men and women arrested by the police; or, on the contrary, who could betray them and give names to the French military forces. Furthermore, she had been charged by Jacques Soustelle, Governor General in Algeria since February 1955 and whom she had immediately reencountered when she arrived in Algeria, with the responsibility of designing and leading a large social program to integrate the poor Algerian teenagers and youngsters into the modern economic life of Algeria's urban centers – a program which she went on to lead for several years.

As far as the situation in Algeria was concerned, Tillion and Soustelle did not agree on everything, far from it. For instance, they parted ways during the trial of a leading FLN terrorist, Yacef Saadi, as Soustelle was called by the prosecution as a witness, whereas Tillion, with Jean-Paul Sartre (1905–80) and Massignon, appeared as a witness for the defense (which condemned the increasing reliance on torture by the army during the Battle of Algiers).[51] During the winter of 1956–7, Tillion had indeed participated in private negotiations for a truce with Yacef Saadi, who had decided to launch a wave of terrorist attacks against civilians in Algiers in retaliation against Mitterrand's decision to execute the political prisoners sentenced to death by the military tribunals.[52] Tillion had tried to convince the French authorities to de-escalate the conflict by stopping the execution of political prisoners accused of terrorism, in exchange for Saadi's decision to put an end to terrorist bombings in Algiers – but to no avail.[53]

Still, the two former students of Mauss were deeply engaged in a collective effort to position ethnography as a useful instrument of government that could be used to make the political integration of Muslims in a French Algeria possible as well as desirable to everybody concerned. Tillion's approach to ethnography, and how she articulated the lessons of her scientific approach with governmental logics in the Algerian context, was not unique in that respect: although many of Mauss's students (like Bernard Maupoil, Charles LeCoeur or Mauss's assistants at the Musée de l'Homme) were killed during the war, those who survived, like Soustelle and Tillion, moved their ethnographic studies to bear direct lessons to the authorities at the center of the colonial field in Algeria.

This direct and intense political involvement with the Algerian question also characterized the emotional attachment that anthropologists and ethnologists showed toward debates about the future of Algerian and French political societies.

For instance, another ethnologist who had been inspired by Mauss (although not one of his doctoral students), and who organized big public conferences on the topic of Algeria in the 1950s, was Jacques Berque (1910–95).[54] The career of Jacques Berque shows the influence of Mauss on ethnologists and colonial administrators even beyond the Parisian alumni of the Institute of Ethnology. Indeed, Berque studied at the University of Algiers, where he was influenced by the Durkheimian legal anthropologist Louis Gernet (1882–1962), an alumnus of the ENS and a member of Durkheim's close circle of editors of *L'Année sociologique* who specialized in the anthropology of ancient Greece. Berque became a colonial comptroller of local tribunals in Morocco in 1934, from where he published essays in legal ethnography – which he sent to Mauss – [55] and which he saw as being inspired by Mauss's essay on contractual relations, gift exchanges, legal pluralism, and customary legal systems.

After the Second World War, Berque continued publishing on legal pluralism in Morocco, along lines that were not dissimilar to those that Tillion followed in the 1930s. Eventually, the quality of his essays led him to accede to the Collège de France in 1956 to teach on the societies of the Maghreb. He, too, became very involved in debates about the future relation that France should form with Algeria. For Berque, the debate about Algerian independence opposed those who, like Soustelle, defended "a French rule of law in Algeria, at the same time as they acknowledged an Algerian [total social] fact within this system," and those who, like him, wished to "recognize an Algerian rule of law, and within that Algerian legal system, a French [total social] *fact*."[56] As this summary of the main ideological division on the Algerian question shows, Berque concluded that France should first recognize Algerian political independence and legal autonomy and negotiate with the FLN as a prerequisite for the creation of new relations between France and Algeria as two independent nations with interconnected destinies.[57] Berque's understanding of inter-national integration between two independent nation-states thus remained much more faithful to Mauss's reading of the direction of history, whose end point they both defined as a society of independent nations, with each nation moving closer to the ideal-type that Mauss had defined in his writings on the nation.

3 THE CONVERGENCE BETWEEN LIBERAL ADMINISTRATIVE ELITES AND POLITICAL SCIENTISTS ON THE ALGERIAN ISSUE

Ethnographers' strong contribution to Algerian politics in the 1950s led them to hold particularly important positions, not only in the field of colonial administration, but also in the mainstream metropolitan public sphere, where the question of Algeria was ardently debated. In so doing, anthropology clashed with competing disciplinary approaches to the international life of nations, in particular, political economy and political science: two disciplines that started from very different epistemological premises and that arrived at divergent policy solutions when applied to the issue of

Algeria's future relation with France. This disciplinary rearrangement in the metropolitan academic field filtered the anthropological voices engaged in public debates.

In the interwar period, anthropology, archaeology, and ethnography had been articulated with international public law and political economy in the explanations of the origins and operation of European solidarity through the circulation of debts and the solidarity between European colonial societies and their metropolis. The postwar era was different in the sense that the two approaches more often clashed than converged. The shift of international power away from Europe toward the United States and the Soviet Union in postwar international affairs partly explains why Mauss's studies of solidarity between European societies and colonial ethnicities were given less relevance to think about East–West relations outside the colonial context: in the age of nuclear deterrence, formal studies on military and political decision-making as well as sociological studies of mass media, party politics, and administrative elites carried more weight to predict the dynamics of the Cold War than ethnographic studies of local tribes and their religious, cultural, economic, and family practices – maybe wrongly so, as the US military soon discovered in Vietnam.[58]

The divorce between anthropology and political economy was also due to institutional logics related to the creation of a new discipline that stood between the two: political science, which was being institutionalized in the early 1950s in the French academic field by a young guard of public law scholars and political sociologists, who found jobs in law schools outside Paris or in the Instituts d'Etudes Politiques (IEP). These young men, who founded the *Revue Francaise de Science Politique* in 1951, were interested in the study of law, state administrations, budgetary policies, and political economy, which they related to the domestic history of political parties and social movements rather than to the evolution of religious belief systems and legal practices found in ethnographic explorations of the private and public lives of African communities.

Ethnology, and Maussian ethnology especially, was notoriously absent from the mix of academic disciplines that coalesced around the new discipline of political science. As Jean Leca writes, institutional and political reasons explained why Maussian anthropology failed to influence the founders of the new science of politics, and vice versa: for him, "Mauss especially ... but the École des Annales at the École pratique des Hautes Etudes [EPHE, later the EHESS] in general, did not appreciate the Institut d'Etudes Politiques,"[59] and thus did not want to make the effort of proposing classes in these institutions – in contrast with Mauss and his students' efforts to teach at the Colonial School in the interwar period. Reciprocally, political scientists believed that Maussians saw them as too close to economic power, as Sciences-Po and the universities' law schools had long ranked high among the institutions where the French bourgeoisie sent its children.[60] Whereas Mauss's former doctoral students had moved to the center of the field of colonial power, thanks to their mobilization of cultural and colonial capital, the newcomers transformed their economic capital into academic and political capital in the metropolitan academic field.

Ethnography was thus not only increasingly instrumentalized by the colonial authorities in the context of independence wars but also relegated by competing academic disciplines in the metropolis to the study of local communities in colonial contexts, in Algeria and other African countries. Political scientists denied that anthropology had anything to say about international relations, international solidarity (a topic they deemed peripheral to their theoretical endeavor) or relations between states. Most political scientists and public law scholars of this generation shared with the tenants of German-trained "realists" who had migrated to the United States during the war to found the new science of international relations the belief that the realm of international life translated first and foremost the power relations between competing sovereign states, contracting with one another on a limited and temporary basis, and according to their best interests.[61] In France, it was paradoxically Mauss's cousin, Raymond Aron, a former ENS student (where he had met his nemesis Jean-Paul Sartre), who ranked among the main academic movers and shakers who sidelined the Maussian interpretation of international relations in the academic field.

In the early 1930s, Aron had worked at Célestin Bouglé's Centre de documentation sociale, where Mauss and Durkheim's ideas were deeply influential, after which he discovered German (Weberian) sociology during a student exchange in Germany in 1934. This was a revelation for the young man: to Mauss's dismay,[62] Aron then became largely influenced by Max Weber's thought and German sociology in general. After spending the war as the director of a small Free France journal in London, Aron had not only moved to the center of the academic field, as he was elected to a professorship at the Sorbonne, but he also became an editorialist at the right-wing daily *Le Figaro*. At the Sorbonne, he headed the Centre de sociologie européenne, from which he initiated a profound reconfiguration of the social sciences in France, along with political sociologists and public law scholars (including international public law) who wanted to move beyond the confines of comparative administrative law and mix their study of legal and administrative documents with a Weberian perspective on the study of political and administrative elites.

Many among these practitioners of the new discipline of political science, trained in constitutional and administrative law, drew inspiration from the work of Max Weber, partly under Aron's influence, and partly because of the influence the German sociologist also had on Maurice Duverger (1917–2014), who included sociology and political economy in his analyses of state and international dynamics. Compared to Maussian anthropologists who put the concept of international (or intersocietal) "solidarity" at the center of their analysis, these postwar political scientists placed the study of formal state structures and domestic practices of government back at the center of their concern. Among the scholars who applied this post-Weberian approach to the study of contemporary international relations, and to cite just a few, we find Charles Eisenmann (1903–80), a comparativist in constitutional law from a long-standing family of French jurists; François Luchaire (1919–2009), a professor of constitutional law in Paris who participated in the drafting of the 1958 Constitution of the French Republic under the authority of Michel Debré; Marcel Merle (1923–2003), professor of public law who wrote about the creation of international criminal law with the Nuremberg Trials before moving on to found a historical sociology of international relations and decolonization movements; Jean-Louis Quermonne (1927–) a professor of law in Grenoble and a founder of the study of the emerging European Union law; Madeleine Grawitz (1911–2008), a professor of law in Aix and then Paris who taught international public law and international institutions; or Jean-Baptiste Duroselle (1917–94), a historian who specialized in the study of international relations; and, at last, Alfred Sauvy (1898–1990), who coined the term "Third World" to designate the new nations who represented the "Third Estate" in the world society.[63]

The academic competition between political science and anthropology was not without consequences for the public debate about the future of Algeria and the place France should have in the community of Western liberal states. Indeed, in 1957, building on recent economic analyses, Raymond Aron published a small pamphlet that became an immediate bestseller, in which he claimed that the French debt, which continued to grow as a result of France's involvement in the war in Algeria, and the plans of massive investment in Algeria promoted by Soustelle and Tillion, harmed the economic health of the French metropolis.[64] For Aron, the money spent on keeping Algeria in France was wasted, as it was clear that, one day or another, Algeria would become independent and would cut ties with France. For Aron and other realists – the Gaullists in particular[65] – Algeria's independence was not only the natural endpoint of history, but it would also benefit the French economy: the examples of the Netherlands and Germany showed that the amputation of the colonial territories from European empires could lead to a highly profitable integration in global capitalist markets.[66] Aron thus proposed to immediately liquidate all French assets on Algerian territory (including unmovable ones, like properties held by repatriated European elites) and to compensate the European landowners for their loss.

Aron's pamphlet was inspired by new approaches in political economy but it also built on the criticism already articulated in the summer of 1956 by Raymond Cartier (1904–75), a longtime reporter of the Indochina war who published a series of articles in the French popular magazine *Paris Match*, in which he popularized the notion that the preservation of the French Empire cost much more than it benefited the French metropolis – and, more importantly, that the question of the preservation of colonies should be judged from the sole point of view of economic rationality.[67] As the war in Algeria escalated, with the national assembly voting to grant the president of the council emergency powers to restore order in Algeria, Cartier asked his readers to consider whether the estimated 1.4 trillion francs that the

French had invested in the colonies since the nineteenth century would not have had a higher return if invested in the metropolis. As Cartier, and later Aron, argued, metropolitan France should no longer export its capital to Algeria, but rather to the territories of its European or transatlantic Allies.

By publishing such a provocative essay, Aron not only gave voice to those who opposed the continuation of the socialists' program of integration between metropolitan France and Algeria, but he also articulated a criticism of the continued French colonial presence in Algeria that could speak to the concerns of both conservatives and liberals in France. His reasoning was less controversial than François Mauriac's criticism of the atrocities conducted by France on behalf of colonialism (torture, population displacement, arbitrary detention, extrajudicial killings) – a position which Soustelle disparagingly attributed to Catholic sense of "bad consciousness,"[68] which he found both illegitimate and inappropriate as the French army was involved in battling terrorists.

Still, these were polemical proposals. At the time of the publication of Aron's pamphlet, the prime minister, Guy Mollet (1905–75), implemented an "assimilationist" policy, which drew its inspiration from a plan that Blum had prepared in 1936 together with his adviser Maurice Viollette, when they proposed the complete extension to the Algerian workers of the generous social rights that his government adopted for metropolitan workers.[69] Their proposal had been based on the realization that in 1930, Algeria absorbed 40 percent of the metropolitan commodity exports to the colonies and provided about 45 percent of the products that the metropolis imported from its colonies,[70] which meant that some form of socio-economic harmonization should be found between the two countries in order to conduct, in the words of Marius Moutet, when he served as Minister of the Colonies, an "altruistic policy"[71] that demonstrated "human solidarity" and rejected a "policy of egoism."[72] The Blum–Viollette project, revived in another form by Guy Mollet's neo-Fordist colonial policy, thus received the strong support of the deputies from the cotton-producing regions like Lyon, Normandy and the North. With the legal assimilation of Algerian subjects, Mollet thus bet on the long-term economic benefits that metropolitan industries would derive from the rise in salaries in Algeria: the socialists hoped that France would find in the Algerian markets the economic opportunities that its exporting industries (like the cotton and garment industries) needed to continue generating profits.

Even if Aron's views initially represented a minority view in the French media and among the political parties, they found fertile ground among the liberal financial elites within the French public administration who argued that the assimilationist model wronged the French nation, as it could survive only because the French government hid the costs of the subvention to the dying cotton industries in the balance of payments: the costs of buying some industrial commodities produced in the metropolis at a high price were hidden in the budget of the colonies; and the costs of buying some raw materials also produced at a high price in the French colonies were hidden in the budget of the metropolis. Some liberal economists and administrators of colonial banks, like Edmond Giscard d'Estaing, thus lobbied in favor of a more open vision of the empire, in which France and its colonies would both find a role as exporters in the global economy – alongside the British Empire and the United States.[73] For instance, Giscard d'Estaing did not believe that the colonies' economic development should be concentrated in agricultural or extractive activities only, and he pressured the government to open French colonies to foreign investments in order to turn the colonies into exporters of industrial goods, and thus solve France's balance-of-payments problems.[74] For him, the preferential treatment between France and its colonies weighed on the colonies' ability to export their raw materials or industrial products (should they produce any) outside of France, and thus on their ability to accumulate foreign currencies. He also believed it was absurd to decide by decree that "all laws should be applicable to the French metropolis and the colonies,"[75] as Blum's government and then Mollet's government had tried to argue.

Political scientists like Aron and high civil servants like Giscard d'Estaing built on the critical work accumulated for more than twenty years by the liberal economists to criticize the socialist neo-Fordist policy as a misuse of France's scarce capital. Since the mid 1930s, liberal economists argued that exporting industries in the metropolis and in the colonies needed to be competitive worldwide, which meant that French capital should go where labor costs were lower (in Algeria for instance), and that "the Metropolis had to accept immediate sacrifices without guarantees [*sans contreparties*] to the benefit of the Colonies, where, one could hope, but with all the assumed risks, that one day in the distant future, prosperity and industry will blossom."[76] A truly generous policy toward the colonies meant trusting them with the ability to turn capital investment into profitable joint ventures, so that they would generate a foreign demand for francs by selling their products to non-French clients – thus keeping stable the balance of payments. In general, liberal economists argued that an apparently favorable commercial balance with the colonies had no positive impact on France's balance of payments, since the industrial goods that France exported to its colonies (and which it counted as exports on the commercial balance) were all denominated in French francs (or in local currencies only convertible in French francs).[77]

In many ways, Aron's criticism of continued French economic investment in Algeria only hastened an intellectual and political tendency that had grown within the ranks of administrative public elites since the mid 1930s.[78] The trade specialists, financial experts, industry and bank representatives dealing from and in the colonies, who gathered at the Economic conference of Non-metropolitan France from December 1934 to April 1935, were already not far from agreeing with the views that Aron expressed twenty years later.[79] Among them, Israel William Oualid, the Algerian-born lawyer who had worked as Albert Thomas's collaborator at the Ministry of Armament during the war and with Charles Gide when the two assessed the costs of the Great War in the context of the reparations debate, also claimed that the trade specialization imposed by the cotton industries was a state subvention in disguise which, overall, did not provide any financial advantage to France: it did not bring any foreign currency to the French Treasury, since the imports of cotton fabrics from the metropolis to the colonies were denominated in francs.[80] During the Second World War, the economists who opposed Blum's neo-Fordist colonial policy mechanically rose in the ranks of the administration in the Vichy government as the socialists were jailed (like Blum), exiled (like André Philip or Jacques Soustelle), or killed (like Jean Zay, Blum's Minister of Youth) by the Vichy regime. Then, they encouraged massive capital investments in the empire because the Nazis occupied most of metropolitan France, which meant that capital should move from the occupied zone to Algeria. But, for these liberals, this relocation of French industries did not mean that the salary levels in Algeria should rise to the levels reached in metropolitan France. In 1942, when Admiral François Darlan, Minister of the Colonies of the Vichy regime, chaired the Economic African Conference, he followed financial specialists, like Paul Bernard (1892–1960), an inspector of finance (like Giscard d'Estaing), who stated that the French metropolis could not extend all social laws to Algeria if France wanted its economy to remain competitive.[81] Following the same logic, the first postwar five-year plan adopted by Jean Monnet in 1947, which integrated the colonies as essential parts of France's postwar development, had already abandoned the redeployment of French industries from the (formerly occupied) metropolis to the colonies in favor of the reindustrialization of the French metropolis thanks to US support.[82]

The consensus found among these French administrative elites thus reflected the fact that, as Jacques Marseille writes, in the 1950s they had "integrated the problem of the commercial balance in the broader and more complex problem of the balance of payments."[83] In the mid 1950s, they argued that French capital should come back to the European continent and leave Algeria, which was under the threat of a future FLN "occupation": a prudent investment policy demanded that French capitalists anticipate and protect their assets by relocating them in the metropolis. In many ways, the French capitalists had anticipated on their policy recommendations. In the early 1900s, Europe received about two-thirds (21 billion francs) of France's total capital exports (30 billion francs), whereas French colonies received less than one-tenth of the total (between 2 and 3 billion francs), and the situation was not much better after the Great War.[84] This was not much, but as Jacques Marseille shows, compared to the 1900s, by the 1950s France even halved its productive investments (in relative terms) in Algeria: although the total of French investment for the period 1947–58 amounted to 12 billion francs (calculated in 1914 francs), which was equal to the absolute amount of public investments from 1880 to 1945, a much longer period,[85] total colonial investments (of which Algeria received a great part) represented about 7 percent of the French budget from 1900 to 1914, whereas the billions devoted to public investments by France in its colonies from 1950 to 1958 only amounted to 4 percent of France's budget (excluding the costs of war). Most of this spending was directed toward avoiding the collapse of the civilian administration. Jacques Soustelle, when he became governor general in Algeria in 1955, discovered that France's public investments in Algeria only served to provide the local government in Algeria with the minimum amount of cash needed for it to function on an annual basis: the funds coming from France for the budget of Algeria were insufficient to build new schools and hospitals.[86]

In 1957, Aron thus took the conclusions of liberal economists to the next step in his pamphlet: if France had invested so little in the colonies during a half century, now was not the time to do more, but on the contrary, to leave behind the little capital that France had invested in Algeria and invest in Europe and in allied nations instead. Indeed, these were the regions in which the French industries would find the best opportunities to increase their competitiveness. Aron and the economists read in the huge deficit of France's balance of payments a host of problems, but, foundationally, they concluded that the maintenance of the French Empire would be too costly for France in the long term if drastic political changes were not made.

4 THE MAUSSIANS STRIKE BACK: TO GIVE MORE RATHER THAN TO LIQUIDATE

When it was published in 1957, Raymond Aron's defense of Algerian independence and repatriation of French capital and manpower to the metropolis (coupled with French integration in global capitalist markets) spurred an intense public debate which was fueled by Mauss's former doctoral students: for Soustelle and Tillion, stopping the effort, liquidating all French assets, and pulling out would be a demonstration of moral weakness. As good socialists, they argued that Aron's policy of "liquidation" of the empire would be both a failure to honor France's collective responsibility and a prioritization of the petty calculus of financial elites over the French moral grandeur.[87] It ran in direct contradiction with the logic of gift exchange that they had glorified in their anthropological and political essays.

In a famous essay that followed Aron's publication, Tillion lamented that Aron's position encouraged French policymakers to invest less in Algeria, as it was no longer perceived as a safe environment. She wrote that it showed a vulgar petty bourgeois (rather than statesmanlike) conception of economic affairs: if Mauss had long noticed that the economy of gift exchanges was not "natural" to laymen because gifts escape the everyday commercial logic of the market, which only sanctions transactions that have a calculable risk of default, Tillion emphasized that fortunately, "negotiations, exchanges, quarrels, reconciliations, loans and gifts are managed at the level of Ministries rather than by lay people."[88] Thus, she hoped that despite their popularity, Aron's financial arguments would be ignored by the French statesmen who could be expected to respect the logic of honor; and that the French bourgeois and Algerian workers would one day "wake up realizing their nations now form an Entente – like the Entente cordiale [of the interwar period] – from which they will benefit."[89] Soustelle used the same Maussian language to counter the arguments served by the "cohort of liquidators" to the French "moderate bourgeoisie, to whom it is better to speak of pragmatic reasons rather than grand principles."[90]

For Soustelle and Tillion, continued payments and capital investments to Algeria were a question of international – and thus collective – responsibility. Soustelle acknowledged being ashamed at the idea that, as Aron proposed, the French should place limits on the "responsibilities that the [French] Community can acknowledge vis-à-vis a fraction of itself."[91] For Soustelle, this responsibility was either recognized or repudiated (with the loss of honor that such repudiation would entail, as the Berbers of Tillion or the Kwakiutls of Mauss well knew), but it could not be fractioned and negotiated like a merchant negotiating a price on the market.[92] To Tillion, Aron's call to liquidate all French assets held in Algerian territory was offensive for failing to recognize the solidarity that stems from the acknowledgement of a "shared responsibility" (here between the French and Algerians) – a central principle in solidarist thinking. As she wrote about the French responsibility in the "pauperization"[93] of Algerians, "we are both responsible and innocent – as innocent and responsible as those who are the victims of pauperization."[94]

As this debate raged on during 1957 and 1958, economic liberalism and unprotected integration of the French and Algerian economies in the global markets became the two main enemies of the Maussian polemists, who argued in favor of the renewed circulation of gifts between the metropolis and Algeria. Tillion saw the changes engendered by the introduction of global capitalism that Aron and the liberals promoted as the root cause of Algerian pauperization:[95] if they acknowledged that two million Algerians of Muslim faith were internally displaced through force by the *regroupement* law that followed the beginning of the insurrection in 1954 (when the French army rounded up village populations in camps to control and "protect" them from terrorist attacks by the FLN), according to her, an additional almost three million people were displaced "voluntarily" – or rather, driven by market logics due to the pauperization of the village farmers.[96] Thus, for Tillion, it was the process of bringing a capitalist "planetary civilization"[97] to Algerian communities that was responsible for the pauperization of its displaced persons, and thus for their overall revolt. Economic globalization was responsible for Algerians' protests, not French colonialism.

To Tillion and Soustelle, Aron's proposal of immediate independence and unilateral liquidation of French assets was wrong, not only because it ignored the moral dimension of the issue – the duty to respect a sense of honor and solidarity toward the colonial subjects who had to be treated as French citizens – but also because the economic analysis on which it was based was flawed. Soustelle blamed Aron for the ignorance he displayed of Algeria and for the contempt he displayed toward Algerians, both those of "European stock" whom he wanted to repatriate, and Muslims whom he found "not profitable."[98] During the 1958 General Assembly of the USRAF, Soustelle violently criticized the "damage created in the minds of the bourgeoisie by their shameless propaganda, which evoke 800 billion francs or even one trillion francs"[99] that the war in Algeria would cost to French taxpayers – Cartier even wrote off 1.4 trillion francs. Soustelle disputed the decision to include in the total the operating costs of the army, which had been deployed in 1956 by the government of the socialist Guy Mollet to the whole Algerian territory – a decision that Soustelle regretted, as it gave the impression that the rebellion had escalated to a full-blown war.[100] For Soustelle, after careful examination, these 1 trillion francs were "reduced to 100 billion francs if economists only included the *additional* costs engendered by the war, which was justified as the French government would have paid for its army in any case, whether soldiers were located in West Germany or Algeria."[101]

Soustelle went further in his criticism of the economic costs of abandoning Algeria: he found Aron's proposal to repatriate the one million Europeans in French Algeria to the French metropolis and pay them 500 billion francs in reparations (about 400,000 francs for each individual) upon independence of an Algerian Arab state deeply problematic not only from a moral point of view, but also from an economic point of view.[102] Indeed, Soustelle estimated that at least 4 trillion francs (or the total annual expense budget of the French government) would be needed to fairly compensate the Europeans for their losses – double what Tillion proposed to "give" to Algeria (including both Europeans and Muslims) to develop their economy in an integrated framework with France.[103] Instead, Soustelle relayed the views of the Maspétiol Commission, which had found in 1955 that "the French state should invest 1.3 trillion francs in ten years in order to triple Algeria's production,"[104] not only in wine and other products from agriculture, but also in the oil and gas sectors, in order to create a modern economy in Algeria. Translated in administrative terms, Soustelle believed that this policy of gift exchange in which France was the first to give could take the form of a complete integration (fusion) of the Algerian budget within the metropolitan budget. Such a budgetary integration avoided charging future Algerian generations for the money raised to develop the Algerian economy in the next decade: the French metropolitan taxpayers would immediately pay for Algerian development in their present taxes.[105]

Drawing implicit inspiration from Mauss's writings about the necessity for France to be the "first to give" in the context of the German reparations debate, Tillion defended the model of gift exchange as a way to accompany the political integration[106] for which Soustelle called before the constitutional revolution of 1958: as she wrote, "Let's give," in the form of massive investments in training in local industries, "and we shall receive in return."[107] As she further stated, "we have to be the *first* to pay the price."[108] As Tillion recognized, the French government was not going to invest massively if the region did not share the same currency, if it did not belong to the same currency zone and did not share the same budget, and if it did not envision the same political future – as otherwise, it would be in the "national interest to avoid exporting French francs"[109] by spending on expensive oil production technologies and training for a large industrial force in the Sahara when it was cheaper to buy oil on the global market. Only if the two peoples were tied for a long time by the common institutions established by the constitution of the Fifth Republic would French investors and policymakers agree to sustain a massive financial effort.

To make their case even stronger, Mauss's former doctoral students not only attacked the economic diagnosis behind Aron's critique of continued French presence in Algeria, but also Aron's prognosis that Algerian and French economic problems would be solved thanks to the clean political separation between the two. For the Maussians, Algeria's independence was one possible *political* solution to a *political* problem,[110] but it was not likely to solve Algeria's economic, social, and cultural problems – the "total social fact" in the language of Mauss that Tillion named the problem of "de-development" or "pauperization." Siding with Soustelle, Tillion strongly criticized the motivation of Aron and other high civil servants who argued in favor of Algerian independence: as she wrote, "anti-slavery often served as the alibi of colonialism, and one may wonder if anti-colonialism is not the alibi of pauperization,"[111] furthered by the egoistic tendencies of the French bourgeois and their reduction of the colonial issue to a purely economic problem.[112]

For Tillion, with independence, the leaders of the new Arab state would be unable to find the necessary resources to respond to the populations' needs and to honor their debts. A "free contract" between two independent sovereign states created a lesser bond than that needed for the type of gifts that Tillion wanted France to spend on Algeria. If Algeria became a newly independent nation, its population would soon lose French aid, as Tillion cautioned that "the money given to the poor countries by prosperous countries is useless to the former – when it does not aggravate their condition – and, at the same time, the money represents a heavy sacrifice for the latter,"[113] which explained why the latter continuously reduced development aid payments. Neither the United States nor the Soviets would make such a large gift as the 2 trillion francs Tillion estimated were necessary for the immediate retooling of a large section of the Algerian population: "to the contrary," she wrote "independence will not solve this problem … and without our collaboration, these problems cannot be solved, whatever happens"[114] in the political realm. For Tillion and Soustelle, much greater sums of money than those currently spent by capitalist states on development aid to independent new nations were needed.[115]

Tillion argued it would be much worse if the Algerian population was no longer sheltered by protective French trade barriers, which maintained some aspects of the gift logic to the relations between France and Algeria: too few Algerians benefited from social security, modern medical facilities, and high attendance rates in French schools (including by Muslim children), which meant that an independent Algeria risked collapsing.[116] From raw calculations, done simply by extrapolating the budget of one family multiplied by the total number of Algerian families, Tillion concluded that the independence of an Algerian state would increase Algeria's problems of economic poverty, cultural alienation, and political resentment: she predicted that the European economic elite would leave Algerian cities to their fate, when it was precisely in these city centers that the social, cultural, and economic problems were being solved by the programs of economic integration she had helped set up since Soustelle hired her in 1955.[117] As Tillion wrote, if the French were to pull out of Algeria in the near future, "all that we give now, like the devil's gold, will be turned to dry leaves."[118]

In many ways, the return of Soustelle to the government in late 1958 and the adoption of the five-year Constantine Plan (1959–63) gave Soustelle and Tillion hope that the French state could finally work to realize their ideas: the Constantine Plan, an investment plan adopted in 1959, exemplified how a gift exchange economy linking the two countries could work. The Plan called for massive investments in Algeria in order to solve the "problems of industrialization and modernization of the Algerian economy," in large part "thanks to the exploitation of natural gas in Lacq and the exploitation of the Sahara for oil extraction," which led to the decision of the French government "to sell oil and gas at such a cheap price to Algeria that Algeria will be one of the countries where energy is the cheapest in the world."[119] In parallel, back in the government, Soustelle lobbied for the "suppression of the absurd financial autonomy" of the Algerian population, the integration of Algerian expenses into the French budget, and the maintenance of a distinct fiscal policy, as "the Algerians' standard of living being much lower than in the metropolis, the Algerians could not bear the burden of French taxes to the same extent as the metropolitans."[120] This integration of the Algerian and metropolitan budgets meant, de facto, that the Algerian (present and future, if not past) debt would be erased, and that the French metropolis would pay, according to Tillion and Soustelle's plan, to train 400,000 people in Algeria and to develop oil extraction in the Sahara at a cost of 2 trillion francs.

As Minister of the Sahara, Soustelle also put in place the reform of the oil code in November 1958, which was inspired by the "regimes in place in the Middle East and Venezuela, which equally distributed the benefits to the public authorities [granting the concession] and the shareholders of the companies."[121] Soustelle believed the new code would encourage the French (and foreign) oil companies to invest in oil extraction in Algeria and provide cheap energy to Algerians rather than import it at a high price. It was ironic that Mauss's student hailed the modernized system of concessions as a benefactor to the colonial society, when his former mentor and the previous generation of solidarists had spent so much time campaigning against the abuses of chartered companies in the colonies and writing in favor of their nationalization. Soustelle's plan of massive investment in Algeria (shouldered by metropolitan taxpayers) was supposed to open a new phase of post-national political integration in the relations between the two societies, and close the gap between rhetoric and reality.

But the Constantine Plan came too late, and amounted to too little. The uncertainty over de Gaulle's commitment to keeping Algeria in metropolitan France certainly did not help the political elites solve the problem of underinvestment in Algeria. The investments to which France consented as part of the Constantine Plan were largely insufficient to balance the free movement of capital that was observed in 1959 and 1960: as an editorialist noticed, "during its first two years, the Constantine Plan injected 56 billion francs in Algeria, 18.3 billion coming from Algeria, and 38.4 from metropolitan France. But," the journalist added, "each year, Algeria exports about 250 billion francs of capital to the French metropolis, which means that the overall mass of capital in Algeria has decreased."[122] The trend, far from decreasing, accelerated, as the rich Algerians anticipated the possibility of independence and hedged their bets by investing their money in metropolitan France. Thus, the only solution to turn the flow of capital investment upside down was to introduce "capital controls" and strictly restrict the export of capital away from Algeria, on behalf of an "economic patriotism, which translated 'pro-French Algeria' slogans into investments in Algeria."[123]

5 THE GIFT AS DISSIMULATION: PIERRE BOURDIEU AND THE ANTHROPOLOGY OF THE GIFT IN ALGERIA

Tillion and Soustelle's 1957 public interventions provoked many disputes in academic and intellectual circles: they were widely commented upon and criticized by other intellectuals, like historian Pierre Nora (1931–), for deploying a purely rhetorical defense of colonial administration in Algeria, and downplaying the role of the institutionalized racism against Arabs found among European populations in Algeria.[124] The idea that Algeria could remain attached to the French Republic as part of a multicultural and giving post-national society began to look like a mirage. As the decoupling between the rhetoric of the gift and the reality of Franco-Algerian relations grew even wider, a new generation of anthropologists started to question whether the model of gift exchange could be applied to international relations without merely being a form of colonial propaganda.

Within the academic field, the scission between the generation of Soustelle and Tillion and the new generation grew wider as their slogans, and their application of the model of gift exchange to international relations, were increasingly associated with the defense of the French presence in North Africa. Then, it was no longer Berque or Aron who wrote against their use of Mauss's model of the gift, but a doctoral student whose pre-independence writings reshaped the political and anthropological discourse on Algeria and the gift: Pierre Bourdieu. As various historians of sociology like Julian Go and Johan Heilbron have recently demonstrated, the years that Bourdieu spent in Algeria were deeply formative for his later writings.[125] A freshly graduated philosophy student from the ENS, Bourdieu began thinking about the Algerian issue during his military service, for which he worked in the information service of the Minister-resident in Algeria, Robert Lacoste, who had replaced Soustelle in 1956.[126] Bourdieu's job gave him a particularly good vantage point from which to assess the reality of Algerian society as well as the duplicity of colonial propaganda: in the summer of 1957, thanks to his mother's connection with a colonel from his region (the Béarn, in the southwest of France), he participated in the collection of information which rationalized the "psychological action" (aimed at forcing the Algerian masses into compliance with French rule), and he wrote various reports, one of which was designed to support the French position on "the Algeria problem" at the United Nations. Then, from 1957 to 1960, he obtained a lecturing position at the University of Algiers, in an academic context still heavily marked by colonial ethnographic science, which insisted on the "fragmented" ethnic space of Algeria rather than on a unified Algerian "national" society.[127] As such, Bourdieu had a foot in both worlds: the academic one, where he defended unorthodox positions, and the colonial field, where he wrote small essays that could be useful to the French administration.

Still, Bourdieu did not endorse the French official position, and his rejection of Soustelle and Tillion's opinions on Algeria led him to naturally gravitate closer to Aron, whom he met in 1959 when the latter delivered a lecture at the University of Algiers. Bourdieu not only appreciated Aron's expression of support for Algerian independence but also his Weberian sociological orientation (quite different from Soustelle and Sartre). He asked Aron to be his dissertation adviser (as Bourdieu wanted to transform some ethnographic studies he did in Kabylia into a thesis). Although Aron redirected Bourdieu toward another adviser, he did hire him as his teaching assistant in 1960 at the Sorbonne, where Bourdieu also took his class on international relations,[128] and where Bourdieu became associated with Aron's Centre de sociologie européenne (a center whose direction Bourdieu later inherited from Aron).

Thanks to this process of "hybridization" between different positions in the field of ethnology and political science, Bourdieu thus managed to completely distance Mauss's mode of the gift exchange from Soustelle's vision of post-national political integration.[129] Like Berque, Bourdieu argued in his first essay on Algeria (1958, reprinted in 1961) that, in contrast to what Soustelle claimed, a certain unity existed across Algeria: even if some of his books, either published alone or with coauthor Abdelmayek Sayad (1933–98), were articulated around chapters devoted to different ethnicities (Chaouia, Kabylia, Arabs, nomads from the Sahara, etc.),[130] Bourdieu assumed that there was such a thing as an Algerian "rule of law" or customary law, and that the latter was different from the French "fact" which existed alongside (and corrupted, from Bourdieu and Sayad's point of view)[131] the free operation of Algeria's rule of law. For Bourdieu and Sayad, the first step for ethnographers was thus to get to know who the Algerians "really" were and what united them, rather than assume that they could never coalesce as "a nation." In their endeavor, they found in Mauss's anthropological model of the gift a particularly useful heuristics: conformity to this system of customary law known as the gift characterized how the Algerians understood economic exchanges as well as questions of sovereignty and morality, which put them at odds with the Europeans, who clearly departed from (and subverted) this logic of the gift, using it as a rhetorical tool in order to advance their narrow and egoistic goals.

Bourdieu found in Kabylia many examples of "gifts" and "counter-gifts" exchanged between families – in particular, "gifts of brides" through which alliances were sealed between families within the same tribe (commonly) or between tribes (in exceptional cases).[132] To seal these marital alliances no paper was needed, as an exchange of dowries manifested the alliance: the memory of the gifts exchanged was preserved by the community, whose "collective opinion is the law, the tribunal and the agent in charge of implementing sanctions"[133] – the highest possible sanction being exile and the loss of honor it represented.

According to this Algerian customary rule of law, the same logic of the gift that ruled over the obligations between humans also ruled those between humans and the land – even among the nomadic tribes from the Sahara, which Soustelle believed to be a *terra nullius*,[134] but where the boundaries of collective property rights exercised by tribes were in fact fiercely negotiated, and sealed in a network of tacit "contracts, each of which are overcome but latent conflicts."[135] The Algerian gift economy was really a "total social fact" beginning with the seasonal rhythms of nature, which required Algerian peasants to plant seeds in some parts of their fields while leaving other parts unplanted in the expectation of some later higher return. This counter-gift that the fields gave to them in exchange for the collective protection of the soil had its social correlation: among fellows of the same tribe, no exchange was monetized. Bourdieu and Sayad cited Algerian peasants who stressed that the "earth only gives to those who give to her" – and that peasants had progressively fewer and fewer means to follow this prescription of their customary rule of law.[136]

Thus, the Maussian inspiration in Bourdieu's work was direct and clear, as Bourdieu found a common customary basis in Algerians' recognition of the "logic of the gift" (and its three obligations), which for most tribes represented a form of customary law – an observation he shared with Tillion and Soustelle. But compared to Mauss's former doctoral students, Bourdieu redefined the relation between contracting agents (e.g. the relation characterized as a gift exchange, with its specific ordering of time and reciprocity) and the types of contracting agents (whether the latter were individuals or sovereign entities). Whereas Tillion and Soustelle asserted that the logic of the gift applied (or should apply) to the relations between European and non-European communities in Algeria, Bourdieu vehemently denied that this was the case.

If Bourdieu and Sayad found that the logics of honor and gift exchange had ruled most aspects of life in Algeria before French colonization, the colonial encounter between Algerian tribesmen and the French Republic could not be characterized as a "gift exchange" except if by the latter, one meant a deceitful exchange during which one party lost everything. For instance, as Bourdieu and Sayad underlined, colonial legislation, from the Senatus-Consulte of 1865 to the Warnier law of 1873 – sponsored by Auguste Warnier (1810–75), a longtime explorer of Algeria, geographer, politician, and military planner – formalized and redistributed property rights in Algeria so as to facilitate French colonists' access to private property in France's closest and dearest colony.[137] For them, the law of the Senatus-Consulte was the most powerful instrument of economic warfare against the political economy of gift exchange, as it created a system of formal individual property rights over land in a region where most land had been managed under informal property rights exercised collectively by tribes according to a logic of honor and gift. The destruction of the solidarity between tribes and land was applied continuously until it reached an apex with the military rule known as *regroupement* (1954–9),[138] which led to the internal displacement of millions of Algerians – a massive breach of human rights.

For Bourdieu and Sayad, these legal measures were emblematic of the colonial enterprise, which consisted in breaking down collective solidarities between fellows of the same tribe and between a tribe and a territory, relationships which were organized juridically and politically through farming, cultivating, and exchanging the products of the land.[139] As a result of such colonial measures, backed by military force, Bourdieu and Sayad observed the breakdown of the old customary rule of law:

> old contracts of association are replaced with contracts of employment . . . and the old community traditions – loans of service, collective labors, tacit conventions, in-kind exchanges – fall into desuetude and when they do not, they are seen as illegitimate constraints by individuals who have learnt to see in money the universal medium of all human exchanges and in the form of a salary the universal compensation for labor.[140]

For Bourdieu, this revolution in attitudes toward legal/economic obligations was exemplified in the changing perception of migration to the cities (either in Algiers or in the metropolis): whereas their ancestors migrated to help protect the land and thus the tribe which collectively owned the rights to live on it (by providing remittances that were invested in the protection or expansion of the land controlled by the tribe), Algerians in the 1950s saw their migration as a permanent exit from the original land – an exit with no return, as most of the time, they migrated after a default on debt they had contracted with landowners.[141] By the 1950s, migration was thus "no longer the realization of a mission granted by the group but an individual adventure by isolated individuals, forced to confront, with no protection, and no possibility to return, a hostile environment."[142]

Beyond the words of Soustelle and Tillion, which claimed that exporting capital to Algeria and importing Algerian manpower to the metropolis would suffice to maintain the system of gift exchange alive in Algeria, Bourdieu, and Sayad found a much darker reality in Algerian cities: marked by decades of alienation, acculturation, and exploitation, Algerian populations were at risk of no longer being able to practice gift exchanges among themselves and between themselves and others. The corruption of gift exchanges in Algeria was made manifest for instance in the changing relation known as the *khammès*:[143] this system had long been used to project a powerful family's status in the public eye by providing gifts ensuring subsistence for the poorer fellows employed to help farm the land on a seasonal basis. In the 1950s this system continued to exist, but it took a decrepit form, as it transitioned toward a system of written contracts of monetized exchanges between employees and employers. The gift exchange had evolved: when poor farmers failed to honor the contracted debts, they faced a loss of honor and fled to the cities, preferring anonymity to shame, and becoming part of the internally displaced population.[144]

For Bourdieu and Sayad, the socioeconomic and cultural outcomes identified by Tillion – like "pauperization," or the "acculturation" of Algerian peasants – were thus the result of deliberate political and legal mechanisms meant to create poverty and anomy rather than the result of natural market forces led by demographic processes. As they wrote, "only by masquerading the context – e.g. the colonial situation – in which economic exchanges take place can we interpret the present revolutionary changes in Algeria in terms of acculturation"[145] led by the natural forces of capitalism. Generalizing from this example of the *khammès*, Bourdieu thus asserted that in such "pre-capitalist" societies as colonial Algeria, he saw in the logic of circulating gifts and debt the operation of a "symbolic violence," e.g. a "violence that is soft, invisible, unknown as such, chosen as much as suffered, a violence that is full of trust, obligation, personal loyalty, gift and debt, from mutual recognition and piety, and all these notions associated with the morality of honor."[146]

Still, according to Bourdieu and Sayad, the gift exchange economy – based on unwritten but binding rule – continued to exist in Algeria, even if it was limited to local and hidden exchanges within the Muslim population. Its persistence was made manifest with the difficulty with which Algerian Muslims adopted "modern" formally written rules: unlike "market specialists, peasants ignore the market guarantees, the witnesses, and the acts of writ in which market relations are now embedded." As they wrote, some Algerian peasants still ignored "economic calculus, conceived both in terms of accounting techniques and in terms of speculation on the future."[147]

But, for Bourdieu, it would have been a travesty of truth to claim, like Tillion and Soustelle did, that the Europeans (both in Algeria and Paris) partook in such a gift economy: the French administrators and European settlers did not respect the logic of honor, as they consistently violated their promises and sought to exploit the Algerian (Muslim) population for short-term economic gains. For more than a century, they had worked to destroy this native Algerian customary rule of law known as the gift exchange, first, by explicitly denying that it was a "rule of law" as the French considered the Muslims they encountered in Algeria to be "savages"; second, by working to subvert it through a series of laws and policies, like the creation of a capitalist market of property rights that weakened collective Algerian landholding solidarities; and, third, and most perversely, by "mimicking" the discourse of the gift through the colonial appropriation of the terms as Soustelle and Tillion did in their writings.

For Bourdieu, when French administrators like Soustelle used the language of the gift – with their emphasis on "honor," "gift," and "generosity" – to frame their pro-integration projects, they went to new heights of cruelty by capturing the language and concepts of that customary law and attaching new meaning to each term. As Bourdieu and Sayad wrote, "politicians, administrators and military men cannot conceive of a higher generosity as that which consists in granting to Algerians the right to become what they should be [according to French standards], e.g. the right to be like the Europeans, which, in fact, denies them the right to be who they really are."[148] This use of ethnology for propaganda purposes was absolutely illegitimate for Bourdieu.

The act of mimicking – by using the language of the indigenous to frame a proposal whose goal was the exact opposite of the preservation of the customary rule of law – produced particularly tragic results, associated with what Bourdieu later called the lifting of the "*illusio*."[149] Indeed, paradoxically, the Algerian peasants who had developed strong moral notions of rectitude within their customary rule of law were those who became the most cynical about the (European and Algerian) discourses on the gift. As Bourdieu and Sayad wrote, those peasants who still believed in notions of "good faith," "honor," and "tacit obligations" were now seen as "fools" and "idiots"[150] by the younger generations, who no longer saw in these words the logic of honor of the customary law of their ancestors, but a ploy used by the colonial administration to exert its rule over pauperized populations. Thus, while some Algerians still understood social relations and relations with the land as their ancestors had, and continued their practice of farming the land – although in a disillusioned way, no longer believing in the magical link that united the tribe with the land – others who left to the cities saw the Algerian peasants as "fools" or poor fellows trapped in extreme poverty.

By using Maussian concepts of gift exchange to analyze a specific local reality (e.g. the working of a pre-capitalist customary rule of law), Bourdieu could claim to be more Maussian than Tillion and Soustelle – but only by ignoring the "political writings" on sovereign debt crises that Mauss had published in parallel to *The Gift*, whose traces could be found in Tillion and Soustelle's essays. In doing so, Bourdieu managed to reclaim ethnology on the side of the realist political scientists who, like Raymond Aron, had condemned France's sustained involvement in Algeria while keeping his distance from the FLN – in contrast to Aron's former classmate at the ENS, Jean-Paul Sartre, who wrote an apology of terrorism in Algeria in his preface to Frantz Fanon's *Wrenched of the Earth*.[151]

Mauss's analytical model gave Bourdieu a viewpoint from which to not only criticize the rhetoric of Soustelle and Tillion, but also the abstract thinking of revolutionary intellectuals like Sartre and Fanon,[152] who wished to change reality by applying great plans which assumed a liberty and freedom among individuals that, according to Bourdieu, did not exist as such. Indeed, Bourdieu and Sayad believed that one of the main dangers faced by Algeria when the latter became an independent republic was a "petty bourgeoisie of bureaucrats who tend to magically deny the contradictions of [the Algerian] reality, as if they were a shameful ghost of the deceased colonial giant."[153] If they denied the permanence of weakened but still persistent traditional expectations about land and social obligations, the new Algerian rulers risked destroying the social pact that had long served to produce peace between tribes, leading to an increasing tendency to act cynically, like the younger generations who found no wisdom in Algerian customary law of gift exchange. To prevent this tragedy from happening, Bourdieu thus proposed to revivify Maussian concepts, but, this time, and in contrast to Soustelle and Tillion, to apply them to the reality to which they claimed it belonged: at the local level.

6 THE TURN TO THE LOCAL IN THE ETHNOGRAPHY OF GIFT EXCHANGES

Even if President de Gaulle accepted to govern under the framework defined by the 1958 Constitution of the Fifth Republic, which Soustelle's theory of integration had deeply influenced, he soon turned his back on Soustelle's policy of post-national integration of the metropolitan and Algerian societies into one republic. In the summer of 1959, de Gaulle decided to instead give considerable "autonomy" to Algeria, thus paving the way for a referendum on the question of Algerian independence – whose terms he started to secretly negotiate with the FLN after 1960. De Gaulle's reversal signed the demise of Soustelle's conception of integration, whose economic translation would have taken the form of a vast system of gift exchanges between the two sides of the Mediterranean Sea.

After de Gaulle started negotiating with the FLN, his new Algerian policy reaffirmed the assimilationist and nationalist character of the concept of integration: those citizens who chose to remain French after the independence had to decide to live in the French metropolis and share the social and cultural mores of the majority there. The support of the French population for de Gaulle at the end of the war in Algeria, when they voted in April 1962 in favor of the Evian Agreements – signed between the French government and the Provisional Government of the Algerian Republic (GPRA, in French) in March 1962 – left him free to implement his vision of France as a pure nation-state, characterized ethnically as a white Christian majority,[154] and free to apply a simple distinction at the time of independence: the Muslims in Algeria were (except for a few exceptions) to be considered Algerians, and the Europeans in Algeria (most of whom had migrated to the metropolis in the summer of the independence in any case) were to be considered part of the French body politic.[155] There was some Charles Maurras in Charles de Gaulle. Despite the doubts of both Tillion and Soustelle as to the ability of a new Algerian state to constitute a new independent "nation" – as they believed that distinction corresponded to a stage of social and political integration that Algerians had not yet achieved – de Gaulle's views prevailed.

Sensing the swing of pendulum, Soustelle left the government in 1960, and when he failed to publicly condemn the new attempted putsch in 1961 by four retired generals in Algeria asking for de Gaulle's resignation, he was forced into clandestine exile for eight years.[156] His exile did not stop him from denouncing the Evian Agreements between the French government and the GPRA as a clear violation of the constitution of the Fifth Republic, in its letter (as the president had to safeguard the "integrity of the territory" rather than give away three departments in Algeria), in its process (as any change to the Constitution had to be made by a supra-majority vote of the Congress rather than adopted by referendum),[157] and in its outcome (as the result of the Evian negotiation with the FLN led to the stripping of French citizenship of those (Muslim) French citizens who could not emigrate from Algeria to the French metropolis between the summer of 1962 and the end of that year). But he had lost the fight: the secession of Algeria put an end to his dreams of integration of various communities in a post-national and postcolonial Republic.

The demise of Soustelle's model of gift exchange in international (or rather, intersocietal) relations did not mean that Mauss's 1925 essay disappeared from the range of classical studies in anthropology. In 1975, the President of the French Republic, Valéry Giscard d'Estaing – son of Edmond Giscard d'Estaing and a center-right and formerly pro-French Algeria politician – asked Jacques Soustelle, by then deputy of Lyon at the National Assembly, to write a report on the future of French research in anthropology and archaeology. As Soustelle acknowledged at the beginning of his report, Mauss continued to determine the intellectual horizon under which French anthropologists constituted their scientific agenda: "Mauss's essay *The Gift* had left a profound mark on [his] generation of researchers in anthropology," even if the generations which came after Mauss often departed from the comparative and "total anthropology that Mauss ambitioned to create," and conducted in its stead original fieldwork in specific communities: "Paul Rivet in Andean America, Maurice Leenhardt in New Caledonia, Marcel Griaule in Ethiopia and Sudan, Alfred Métraux in Chaco, Claude Lévi-Strauss in Brazil"[158] – he could have, but did not, mention Pierre Bourdieu in Kabylia.

In many ways, Soustelle's 1967 *The Four Suns* – a book he published while in exile, when he was chased away by de Gaulle's hitmen – may have been the last attempt by a French anthropologist to articulate the "total anthropology" that Mauss had in mind: it was a comparative attempt to understand and explain "how civilizations die."[159] As he wrote, "all civilizations died": "some, like the Aztecs, because they were murdered by foreigners; others like the Mayas, because of an inner cancer"; and "there was no reason that our civilization would constitute an exception."[160] It is not too hard to read his essay as an anthropological and political reflection on the breakdown of the French Empire and the demise of the French civilization. And, then, "when civilizations died," Soustelle found, "the ethnic groups which such civilizations had constituted fell back to the level of culture, until their culture would constitute again the primary material that a new civilization would rework, as had happened for the Gallo-Romans and the Germans after the collapse of the Roman Empire."[161] Knowing Soustelle's preoccupation for the fate of Algeria, it is impossible to believe that he did not have in mind the fate of the Algerian ethnic groups, which, after being reorganized by the French civilization for a century or more, would now be integrated into new civilizations, either Muslim, communist, or from a rising Third World.

In this context, what was left for ethnologists to study in the 1970s, Soustelle asked in his report to the French president. If they could no longer study the intersocietal gift exchanges that made the life of a civilization, they could study these cultural practices that were observable within ethnic groups at the local level. Even Soustelle came to legitimate the association between the study of gift exchanges and the local level of action: as he wrote in his 1975 report, future ethnologists should focus on the contemporary evolutions of ethnic groups in the French metropolis rather than restrict ethnography to the study of "archaic societies" – a confusing notion which "rested on the wrong perception that human evolution was linear."[162] Indeed, in the "new context of cooperation with newly independent states, [which accelerated migrations in both ways] French ethnographers should devote more resources to studying their own populations" in their ethnic diversity, as was already being done by a "rich body of ethnographic research which proved that the peasant of the Dordogne and the city dweller of Montpellier constitute as legitimate objects of ethnographic study as the African or the Indian."[163] In particular, Soustelle wrote, echoing the xenophobic ideas of Giscard d'Estaing's government, new generations of ethnologists should observe local processes, be attentive to the local circulation of gifts, and conduct ethnographies of "populations of allogenic workers" from Algeria "whose high density in metropolitan city centers represented a threat to integration,"[164] now conceived in the contemporary sense of "assimilation." Again, many anthropologists who call themselves Maussian should be wary of the explicit political goals that Mauss's students have attached to their master's research program, even after former colonies gained their independence.

The "return of the gift"[165] – to cite Harry Liebersohn – as a political discourse on global or least intersocietal governance, grounded in the new disciplines of anthropology and ethnology, was thus short-lived, at least in the French field of power. The publication of *The Gift* opened this new era; Pierre Bourdieu's writings on gift exchange in Algeria, as well as Raymond Aron's pamphlets, participated in closing the parentheses. Between Mauss and Bourdieu, one generation of ethnologists and colonial administrators had used the anthropology of the gift as a normative model for the economic and financial relationships between the metropolis and the colonies. But after Algerian independence was granted in 1962, the reconfiguration of the colonial field of power, which was disrupted overnight, largely relegated Mauss's influence on international economic exchange to the dustbin of history. Or did it? If the end of the war in Algeria, and the shock waves it sent through the colonial field, relegated the anthropology of the gift to the study of migrants' assimilation at the local level, could it be that the gift exchange had survived as a model of international economic governance, although in another form, and attached to a discipline other than anthropology?

6

Decolonizing *The Gift*

Nationalization and Sovereign Debt Cancellation in North–South Relations

If 1962 put an end to the constitutional debates in France and Algeria, none of the socioeconomic questions about which Mauss had written were solved by Algeria gaining its political independence. With the Evian Agreements signed in March 1962 by the French government and the provisional government of the Algerian Republic, the negotiators organized both the independence of Algeria and the sustained cooperation between Algeria and France. The Evian Agreements represented the template of what the French negotiators had in mind when they proposed international "cooperation" to their former possessions after independence. Formally, the logic of cooperation was inspired by the model of gift exchange: according to the Evian Agreements, cooperation was to be based on the "reciprocity of advantages and interests between the two parties,"[1] which was made manifest by the granting of "in-kind 'prestations,' loans, financial participation, or gifts,"[2] from the old metropolis to the newly independent Algerian state.

The Evian Agreements were premised on the prediction that the one million French citizens of European descent, most of whom had never lived in the metropolis, would remain in Algeria after independence, and that some form of financial, economic, cultural, and political cooperation would need to continue to ensure good relations between the Algerian citizens and these French citizens who remained Algerian residents. For a renewable period of three years, the French government thus agreed to maintain intact its financial obligations in Algeria, in order to avoid the collapse of the newly independent state, which would have resulted from an uncontrolled secession, according to the predictions that Jacques Soustelle and Germaine Tillion expressed at the time.

With the Evian Agreements, the French government believed that France had been faithful to its longstanding generosity toward Algeria. This cooperation was costly for France, as it involved, for instance, paying the salaries of *coopérants* (doctors, teachers, magistrates, etc.) who agreed to give a helping hand to the Algerian people during the transition toward social, economic, and financial autonomy. In the Evian Agreements, the French government went as far as committing to help the Algerian state sustain the financial burden of the future nationalization of land[3] – a decision for which the Algerian Minister of Information, Redha Malek (1931–2017), lauded the "realism" of the French delegation.[4] As Jeffrey Byrne writes about the Algerian revolutionary leaders' economic program, the nationalization of land was "perhaps their one clearly and consistently expressed goal after independence,"[5] so there was little doubt that following Algeria's independence, the new independent government would declare the redistribution and collectivization of land ownership. The only realistic way to prevent land nationalization from being implemented without compensation for the French landowners was for France to cover some of the financial burden with its own operating budget.

In exchange, Algeria's provisional government promised to enforce all acquired private and private/public rights on land and subterranean resources.[6] In the Evian Agreements, the Algerian representatives committed to the principle that all nationalization should be compensated in a "fair and fixed manner,"[7] and that payments should be promptly executed. The future Algerian government not only promised to fairly compensate the large landowners, with the support of the French government, but it also promised not to expropriate the immovable properties (buildings, houses, or apartments) that French citizens owned in Algeria. At last, Algeria guaranteed the integrity of the acquired rights on oil research and extraction,[8] which were defined by the 1958 Oil Code whose preparation had been overseen by Jacques Soustelle when he was the Minister of Atomic Energy and the Sahara in the first government of Michel Debré.

The Evian Agreements were emblematic of many other devolution and independence agreements written by France in the early 1960s, inspired by the philosophy of post-independence "cooperation." If de Gaulle indeed believed that history would naturally bring colonies to their independence, and that it was more economic for France to accept it sooner rather than later,[9] the notion of "cooperation" reintroduced the idea that a transitional period was necessary for postcolonial societies to adapt after the moment of political independence and until the moment of economic independence. The government did not yet speak of "failed states," but, clearly, the metropolis wanted to prevent its former colonies from experiencing economic collapse as a result of achieving independence. During a transitional period, newly independent states that emerged from the ashes of the French Empire would march according to different rhythms, but along the same straight line and with the benevolent support of the former metropolis, which would generously provide expertise, financial support, and political guidance to these new nations as the latter sought ways to organize themselves internally, to find resources on external markets, and to form alliances within the orbit of France's soft hegemony.

Still, the fact that the provisional Algerian government (or GPRA) accepted to sign cooperation agreements that were inspired by this philosophy of cooperation was a surprise – if it wasn't just a temporary concession. Indeed, with the Tripoli Declaration of 1962 in particular, the GPRA had rejected the concept of "cooperation" with French economic interests, in which they saw the gravest danger raised to the revolution by "the seductive guises of liberalism and financial cooperation that only purports to be disinterested."[10] Algerian revolutionaries denounced in the post-independence philosophy of cooperation the same paternalism they saw in the colonial mindset characteristic of the interwar imperial administrators who believed that overseas societies had not reached the highest point of maturity, and thus needed the continued support of the metropolis, even after being granted their independence. Mohammed Bedjaoui, eminent Algerian jurist, who served as a jurisconsult of the GPRA in the Franco-Algerian negotiation,[11] and who became the first secretary general of the government after 1962 – a role similar to that of a prime minister, to the extent that he organized the weekly Cabinet meetings with the Algerian ministers and coordinated the implementation of decisions with the relevant ministries[12] – clearly opposed the Gaullist concept of "cooperation" in which he saw the prolongation of colonial relations of interstate subordination in the post-decolonization era.[13]

Even though the GPRA did sign the Evian Agreements in March 1962, the Algerian diplomatic team fought hard against the general philosophy of bilateral cooperation in other public venues, such as the UN General Assembly (UNGA). Upon becoming Algeria's first president, Ahmed Ben Bella (1918–2012) made it clear that he saw in the French projects of cooperation a neocolonial project aimed at ensuring the prolongation of France's wrongly acquired rights on land expropriated at the time of colonization.[14] The French financial guarantees served the same function as the continued presence of French military forces in the territory of newly independent states: their overall goal was to insure French investors (especially in the oil business) against the threat that their investments might be nationalized with no compensation.[15] Citing the Swedish economist Gunnar Myrdal (1898–1987) and his criticism of the "forced bilateralism" associated with the continued exploitation of the South's natural resources by the Global North, Bedjaoui repeatedly argued that French financial help was far from a disinterested gift: he saw in "cooperation" a guarantee or "collateral" (*contrepartie*) that Algeria would protect "the interests of the French state and the acquired rights of the legal persons on Algerian territory."[16]

In many ways, Bedjaoui implicitly agreed with Bourdieu and Sayad's idea that the language of gift, cooperation, and solidarity that the metropolitan statesmen spoke before, during, and after the independence of former colonies was just a devilish charade aimed at confusing the peoples of newly independent states.[17] As Bedjaoui wrote in 1978, the fake gifts that the North extended to the South under the guise of "cooperation agreements" and "barter conventions signed on the side of aid agreements [between North and South], perpetuate the illusion among the rich countries that they deliver a truly authentic and disinterested aid to the countries of the Third World," when in fact, these "supposedly fair and freely accepted exchange contracts perpetuate the soft exploitation of the latter."[18]

The Algerian statesmen who would later come to be associated with the fight for a New International Economic Order (NIEO) in the 1970s, thus clearly distinguished between the bilateral cooperation between North and South proposed by the French government, and the multilateral South–South and North–South relations they envisioned. Ben Bellah's goal was to make Algeria the exemplary Third World rebellious nation, which meant confronting head-on de Gaulle's project of postcolonial cooperation, and forming new alliances in the South, in particular with Tito's socialist Yugoslavia, in which he found a model for the redistribution of land he announced in March 1963,[19] or with Cuba and other countries of Asia, Africa, and Latin America. Indeed, upon gaining its independence, Algeria became a "Mecca of Revolution,"[20] to use Jeffrey Byrne's title, as Algiers hosted some of the most important conferences where the non-aligned movement came to an agreement on the broad strategy needed to establish the NIEO.

In these debates, Algerian diplomats played a key role: the NIEO was launched in September 1973 during the Algiers conference of heads of state and government of the non-aligned countries, which concluded with a call by Algerian President Houari Boumédiène (1932–78) to the UN Secretary General to convene a special session of the UNGA to study problems of raw materials, sovereign debt, and development.[21] The subsequent UNGA session was organized in May 1974, under the tenure of Abdelaziz Bouteflika (1937–), Boumédiène's longtime Foreign Minister (1963–79) who was also the UNGA's president in 1974: during this session the UNGA adopted the Declaration on the Establishment of the NIEO, complemented by a program of action and the Charter of Economic Rights and Duties of States at the end of 1974. In parallel, Mohammed Bedjaoui also called for states from the Global South to reject neocolonial cooperation with their former metropolis and to engage with the Global North in honest "global negotiations" covering the topics of debt, concession rights and economic development on a multilateral basis, and recognize an inalienable right of all nations over their "wealth, natural resources and economic activities"[22] – an inalienable right which was later referenced in the Convention on the Succession of States in respect to State Property, Archives and Debts that was adopted in 1983 by certain states of the Global South (but which never entered into force). This Treaty was discussed within the group of expert lawyers chaired by Bedjaoui himself, which had been tasked in the mid 1960s by the UNGA to reflect upon economic transitions after independences: the International Law Commission (ILC) and its sub-committee on the questions of nationalization of property and cancellation of sovereign debt in the postcolonial context.[23] With the Evian Agreements, a new sequence was thus opened that led to the expression of the demands that non-aligned nations tabled both at the UNGA (1974–9), with the establishment in May 1974 of a Plenary Committee in charge of initiating the NIEO, and at the ILC, in which legal scholars spent twenty years codifying the legal doctrine on the economic rights of former colonies after independence.

In these different debates, two models of the gift exchange clashed with one another: the philosophy of bilateral cooperation between the former metropolis and its former colonies, which was modeled after the Evian Agreements; and the philosophy of multilateral and "global settlements," which was articulated by eminent jurists and diplomats of the Third World, among whom Algerian diplomats in general, and Mohammed Bedjaoui in particular, figured prominently. As far as Algeria was concerned, the support for the NIEO was premised on the recognition that, with the Evian Agreements, French views had shaped the law on the books, but that it wasn't clear whose views would shape the law in practice in the years ahead. The notion of "acquired rights" safeguarded by the Evian Agreements was immediately rendered meaningless by the unexpected and massive exodus of the French Algerians in the summer of 1962, leaving behind all their possessions.[24] The compromise reached on the transmission of sovereign debt and private rights (of French companies) over natural resources also proved temporary, as the two independent countries started to renegotiate the rights of oil concessions in Algeria after 1965. By then, it was hard to predict whether Algeria would abruptly cut all economic ties with the French economy and French oil concessions, or whether it would leave unchanged the existing French economic interests in Algeria – or whether it would look for a third solution, in between the two extremes. This was the context in which the Algerian statesmen started to develop their own doctrine of North–South relations, which eventually became the NIEO.

Thus, one can hardly say that the gift exchange disappeared as a model of international economic governance with the end of the Algerian War in 1962: rather, with decolonization in general, and the end of the war in Algeria in particular, the gift exchange seems to have been translated into the discourse of international law, and thus suffused with new meanings and novel political connotations. In this chapter, I thus ask: how was the model of gift exchange, which anthropologists quit using to analyze international exchanges around the time of Algeria's independence, recycled in the field of international law to frame the larger governance issues raised by the age of economic independences? Which transformations in the French field of power in general, and those affecting the relations between the French metropolitan and colonial fields in particular, have made this translation of the gift exchange in the language of international law possible? And with which larger geopolitical and economic considerations have these changes been associated?

As Nico Schrijver observes, the promotion of the NIEO in international law pitted the Global South – conceived at the time as encompassing Latin America, Africa, and Asia – in its search of new economic rights, against Western states (the United States and former European empires in particular), who defended the sanctity of contracts securing the economic rights acquired by private companies like oil concessions.[25] But its promoters did not come from just anywhere. Tracing the genealogy of the gift exchange in the Francophone context suggests that some interesting and under-explored intellectual continuities and discontinuities existed between the Algerian intellectuals behind the NIEO and the French solidarists who wrote about international economic relations in the 1930s. Indeed, the intellectual and diplomatic movement in favor of the NIEO has taken to heart the questions that prior generations of socialist policymakers interested in the legal, social, economic, and political underpinnings of colonization and globalization had started to answer in the 1930s, and even before, when they questioned the limits that should be placed on the rights of concessionary companies. But they answered those questions differently, as they drew upon different resources, and spoke from very different positions within the French field of power, at least before 1962.

By focusing on the Francophone context, placed in a global perspective, this chapter prolongs and deepens previous genealogical analyses of the NIEO.[26] In so doing, this chapter operates two intellectual shifts with respect to the current historiography that has been elaborated on the NIEO by historians of ideas, like Balakrishnan Rajagopal, Gilbert Rist, Georges Abi-Saab, Matthew Craven, or Sundhya Pahuja.[27] First, in contrast to previous histories, which are not grounded on sociological analyses of the fields in which the key ideas NIEO concepts were elaborated, this chapter explores the transformations in the Francophone postcolonial context in general, and in the complex relation that existed between French metropolitan and colonial fields of power around the time of Algeria's independence. Second, this chapter operates a geographical shift, as it moves the genealogy of the NIEO from the study of the development discourse produced in the Anglophone and US-centered context (mostly in the disciplines of economics and law)[28] to the analysis of continuities between discourses on colonial and postcolonial solidarity produced in the French field of international law. Therein lies its originality.

To these two shifts, I would add a third, epistemological, repositioning. Indeed, these first two moves require that a French-trained sociolegal anthropologist like myself sit at a different distance from, and with a different attitude toward, the discussed material: no longer from a position of externality, and with a critical tone, but, rather, from a position of reflexivity, nourished by the recognition that my own academic ideas and political heuristics derive in large part from the very same source as the material presently under study. If certain of my predecessors (even at the Graduate Institute, like eminent "post-development" theorist Gilbert Rist), could judge from far above the blinding reductions of the US developmental discourse, and its translation into some of the NIEO doctrines,[29] I shall be much less critical of the dead ends in which the NIEO found itself cornered, as these aporias are in fact similar to those that, in turn, afflicted the sociolegal discourse on international law produced in the wake of the NIEO's demise.

To achieve such "reflexivity" and to understand the genesis of the ideas of the NIEO and their emergence in the French field of international law, this chapter proposes first to quickly expand on the field analysis already provided in Chapter 2, in which I described the objective logics of the French metropolitan and colonial legal fields in the 1950s, at a time of deep intergenerational change. Then, the chapter analyzes the discursive continuity between the solidarist understanding of the notion of gift exchange and key NIEO concepts. Some continuity seems evident: like solidarists, Mohammed Bedjaoui, for instance, articulated a scathing criticism of economic liberalism, which he associated with the egoistic tendencies of *homo economicus*, and against which he counterposed the value of "solidarity."[30] But I also explain how the writings of Bedjaoui about the debt obligations of successor states evolved throughout the 1970s, and how they departed from the solidarist doctrine. By surveying the work of the NIEO thinkers at the United Nations, both in the General Assembly and the ILC, this chapter thus shares Sundhya Pahuja's twofold objective to "show that international law [produced in the postwar era] has both an imperial and anti-imperial dimension and to understand what kind of strategies that engage with law are likely to 'decolonize' international law rather than enhance its imperial quality."[31]

1 ANTI-COLONIAL CAUSE LAWYERING IN THE FRENCH METROPOLITAN AND COLONIAL FIELDS OF LAW

To understand how the model of gift exchange became associated with the defense of decolonization as the use of such a notion traveled from anthropology to international law – precisely when eminent anthropologists of gift exchanges continued to side for an integrated French Algeria –, it is important to explore in further detail the main political divisions found in the French field of law before Algeria won its independence.

The postwar period was marked by the rise of an anti-colonial disposition among international law scholars, which was correlated with the emergence of a more realist and interdisciplinary approach to international law, particularly in the emergent law schools that attracted new talents outside Paris.[32] For the dean of the Grenoble Law School, Claude-Albert Colliard and other international law scholars of his generation, like Suzanne Bastid-Basdevant (1906–95) – Jules Basdevant's daughter, the first woman to become a professor of law at the University of Paris in 1946 (like her father), and the president of the UN Administrative Tribunal from the 1950s to the mid 1970s, who sat on Bedjaoui's doctoral dissertation defense – the lawful actors of international society were indeed states and international organizations; and once statehood was formally recognized de facto and de jure, then, no hierarchy existed between states based on their cultural or civilizational differences.

In the postwar context, Algerian students who came to study in the metropolis, like the young Bedjaoui in Grenoble, could thus get a classical training in constitutional law, administrative law, and international law, and publicly hold anti-colonial positions without suffering any negative consequences from their professors. Bedjaoui's dissertation on the duties, privileges, and guarantees of independence found in international secretariats (with particular emphasis on the League of

Nations, UNESCO, and the ILO)[33] followed the realist and formalist approach to administrative international law, which Colliard had developed in his manual *International Institutions*,[34] and Bastid-Basdevant in her own work on administrative agencies in the League of Nations.[35] None of them defended colonialist positions: quite the contrary, their realist perspective, which focused on the administrative organization of the state and international organizations encouraged them to view all states that had achieved a certain degree of administrative rationalization and political organization through the organization of parties as equal.[36]

In contrast to Maussian ethnologists, who had drawn from Mauss the idea that societies could be ranked according to their degree of integration, these international law scholars were blind to the cultural context in which the states operated. The formalist training in international law a student like Mohammed Bedjaoui received may explain why he never paid any attention to the local customs that were so central to the writings of legal pluralists inspired by Maussian principles. At the same time, as a PhD student in Grenoble, Bedjaoui could organize many anti-colonial meetings with student associations from Algeria and other overseas territories, and political leaders like, for instance the leader of the Tunisian independence movement, Habib Bourguiba (1903–2000), a Tunisian lawyer trained in Paris who was elected Tunisia's first prime minister in 1956 (and then president one year later), after thirty years of anti-colonial fight for his country's independence.[37] With his professor Georges Lavau (1918–90), a native of Guadeloupe who taught classes on constitutional law and political sociology at the Law School of the University of Grenoble, Bedjaoui also organized meetings with radical left parties, like Michel Rocard's (1930–2016) Parti socialiste unifié, in favor of the independence of the French colonies.[38] As Bedjaoui concluded, "we, Algerians, were much better treated in France than Algerians in Algeria: whereas the most minimal expression of pro-independence feeling could cost an Algerian his life in Algeria, we benefited from a great freedom of expression in metropolitan France, in Grenoble, where we organized all these student meetings against colonialism."[39]

In Grenoble, Bedjaoui could dream of upward mobility and benefit from the solidarity between Algerian students, their law professors, and leaders of the anti-colonial struggle. For instance, in 1951, Bedjaoui first took the test to enter the École Nationale d'Administration (ENA), the elite metropolitan school created after the war by Michel Debré to form France's high administration – which he failed because of a bad grade in Arabic, despite having the best grade in the test on general culture, an irony that illustrates the pedagogical and political priorities of French teachers in the Algerian colonial context in which Bedjaoui had been schooled. Ferhat Abbas, an Algerian politician who later joined the FLN, and whom Bedjaoui had met once in Tlemcen, was the one who originally advised Bedjaoui to enter the ENA.[40] As Abbas had made it clear to Bedjaoui, it was important that talented Algerian students get a proper training in administrative law at the ENA to take on responsibilities in a future independent Algerian Republic. Bedjaoui fully trusted

Abbas, as Ferhat Abbas and Ahmed Francis had become famous in 1943 for publishing the *Manifesto of the Algerian People* in which they and twenty-seven other Algerians demanded the formation of a Constituent Assembly in charge of writing a constitution for an independent Algeria. After spending a year in jail after the May 1945 demonstrations in Algeria that were bloodily repressed by the French colonists,[41] Abbas and Francis were both elected to the Algerian Assembly in 1948 and together they created the Democratic Union of the Algerian Manifesto (Union démocratique du manifeste algérien, UDMA), which defended an anti-colonial line close to that defended by Bedjaoui and his law professors.

International law professors from Sciences-Po and from the Law School of the University of Grenoble not only helped create an academic environment where young anti-colonial students could militate, but also helped them when they ran into trouble with the law, or when they suffered undue discrimination. For instance, in 1952, when Bedjaoui tried to pass the ENA exam for the second time, he was denied the right to take the test: specifically, he was sanctioned for having organized pro-independence conferences during his summers in Tlemcen, the city where he had been raised by his mother and maternal uncle after the early death of his father, and where he had taken his pre-university education.[42] The story did not end there, as the ENA authorities also barred a communist from taking the exam: Yves Barel, who was the son of a well-respected French communist parliamentarian. This was enough for the SFIO journals, as well as *L'Humanité*, the journal that Mauss had helped found but which had been under the control of the Communist party since 1920, to turn the political discrimination into a public scandal, which, while not as polarizing as the Dreyfus affair, was denounced in Parliament. In this context, it was Bedjaoui's professor Georges Lavau who wrote Bedjaoui's legal defense *pro bono* and mobilized his lawyer friends who submitted the case before the Conseil d'Etat, which ended up affirming the right of public servants to hold public opinions (including communist and anti-colonialist ones) in the famous "Barel, Bedjaoui and others" case of May 1954.[43] At that point, Bedjaoui could thus have continued with a career in the high civil administration in the French metropolis, despite holding anti-colonial opinions.

But in 1956, the FLN adopted a new strategy in relation to the Algerian students who evolved in the metropolitan academic field, which affected their career prospects as well as the anti-colonial solidarities between students and professors: as the FLN called for a student strike during the annual exams, it forced Algerian university students studying in the metropolis to lose one year of studies (and sometimes end their studies there), or demonstrate lack of loyalty to the Algerian cause. This strategic shift reflected the new diagnosis about the necessity to show a stronger oppositional front, which was decided by the FLN leadership, whose composition had been enlarged to include the leaders of the UDMA, like Francis and Abbas, who had decided to dissolve their own party and join the FLN after reaching Cairo in April 1956.[44] The radicalization of the FLN's strategy forced many young students to become involved more deeply and directly in the fight for Algeria's independence. Bedjaoui no longer considered a career as a French legal scholar or high civil servant. Instead, in March 1956, he tried to reach out to Ahmed Francis, Ferhat Abbas, and to the FLN's representatives in Paris – Salah Louanchi (1923–90) and Bélaïd Abdessalam (1928–), who would later become Houari Boumédiène's powerful minister of energy from 1965 to 1977, and Algeria's prime minister in the early 1990s – asking them if they had any use for a doctor in law, something they had not yet considered at that time.[45]

In January 1957, as Bedjaoui had not yet heard from the FLN leadership, he joined the General Union of Algerian Muslim Students (Union Générale des Etudiants Musulmans Algériens, UGEMA), created in 1955, which sent him to the UN special session on Algeria in New York, where he delivered to the UN Secretary General Dag Hammarskjöld (1905–61), the UGEMA's declaration of support to the FLN – in which the UGEMA declared the FLN to be the only competent and representative authority in Algeria. The main goal of the UGEMA was to prove, against Soustelle's argument at the time, that there was an Algerian nation, and that its political consciousness was expressed through the voice of the FLN. In front of him, Bedjaoui faced the French government, which paraded some notable Algerian Muslim nationals, like a handful of presidents of local bar associations in Algeria, who praised the "generosity" of the French government in Algeria and its "non-colonial" character – some of whom were later assassinated by the FLN for having done so[46] – and who denied that the Algerian nation, if it existed, had pledged allegiance to the FLN.

The divorce between the few Algerian lawyers who had played the rules of the colonial game in order to access the legal profession in Algeria and the metropolitan academic international lawyer whom Bedjaoui had become could thus not have been greater in 1957, when the "battle of Algiers" was raging on the ground and on the diplomatic scene. Even if Bedjaoui's anti-colonial activities were known to the French authorities, Bedjaoui continued to spend most of his time in Grenoble organizing events against the French presence in Algeria. In March 1957, for instance, when Jacques Soustelle visited the University of Grenoble to present his views on the necessity to further integrate Algeria in the French Republic, Bedjaoui publicly criticized the former governor-general in Algeria for failing to engage in a debate with the students, and he was sued in court for threatening the "security of the state."[47] Once, again, being a trained lawyer helped him find the means to defend himself, as it was his former professor of criminal law, François Givord, who wrote his (successful) defense and kept him out of French jails.[48]

2 THE IRONY OF HISTORY: NEUTRALIZING AND RECLAIMING THE JUS PUBLICUM EUROPAEUM FOR ALGERIA'S INDEPENDENCE

In 1958, after a year spent publicly combating Soustelle, Mollet and their postcolonial ambitions for an integrated French Algeria, Bedjaoui was finally recruited as a jurisconsult by the GPRA, newly created in September 1958, with Ferhat Abbas as its first president. Among other things, Ahmed Francis, named Minister of Economic and Financial Affairs in the GPRA, tasked him with actively seeking international legal recognition for the Algerian government in exile. This was the most pressing issue for the Algerian leadership as de Gaulle's return to power in May 1958 and the organization of a referendum on the Constitution of the Fifth Republic in both the French metropolis and Algeria raised a clear danger for the Algerian leaders. The GPRA was created one week before the referendum, and the massive vote in favor of the French Constitution of 1958 was interpreted in Algeria as a demonstration of allegiance to a French Algeria. Indeed, the vote was all the more dangerous for the FLN and the GPRA in that Muslim voters had been included in the consultation: thus, for Soustelle, French Muslims who had participated in the vote, and who had answered positively to the question asked, had rejected the GPRA's claims to national representation one week after its creation.[49] Bedjaoui's first task as jurisconsult for the GPRA was therefore to help the Algerian government regain its credibility outside Algeria, by convincing foreign chancelleries that the Algerian territories under FLN control were in fact under the civilian authority of a government in exile, which claimed international legal sovereignty.

Drawing from the legal capital he had accumulated in the French metropolitan field of law – and from the research resources offered by the UN library in Geneva, where he had spent long hours working on his dissertation – Bedjaoui started writing a book, titled *La Révolution algérienne et le droit*, in which he justified Algeria's claims to independence on international legal principles. The book was published in 1961 by the Association Internationale des Juristes Démocrates (AIJD) – an international association located in Brussels that published essays by lawyers close to the Communist party and the Soviet Union – thanks to the mediation of Pierre Cot (1895–1977), a native of Grenoble, a doctor in law from that same university from which Bedjaoui graduated thirty-six years after him, and who had met Bedjaoui at Sciences-Po Grenoble where Cot had delivered a lecture titled "Political Parties and the State." Cot had held various Cabinet positions in the interwar period in various left-wing coalitions (including as Blum's Minister of Air, where he sold airplanes to the Spanish Republicans during the civil war), after which he participated in the Resistance from Washington and Algiers, and later represented the departments of Savoie and then Rhone at the French Parliament in the postwar era.[50] It was Cot who, as the President of AIJD, agreed to publish and write the preface for Bedjaoui's 1961 book, as well as to brief the GPRA and Francis's team in Geneva when the negotiation with de Gaulle's government started.[51]

With his book, Bedjaoui demonstrated that the GPRA qualified for international recognition as the de jure government of Algeria,[52] despite the opposition of Soustelle. Not only had the GPRA already been granted de facto international recognition by an expanding list of states in the communist bloc and non-aligned countries, but, for Bedjaoui, it qualified for *de jure* recognition as it had the formal structures of a state, effective control over large portions of a territory, and it behaved, as far as the conduct of the war was concerned, like a modern state adhering to the Geneva Conventions – a claim that was largely overstated, considering the exactions against Algerian civilians that the FLN committed. As Bedjaoui wrote, he could have chosen to ground the Algerian claims for independence and economic autonomy on the "new law of decolonization" emerging in the principle of "equal rights and self-determination of peoples" in the UN Charter (article 55) or in Resolution 1514 passed by the UNGA in 1960, which proclaimed the need to end colonialism "with no pre-condition."[53] Instead, he showed how the GPRA respected international public law while the French government violated these same commitments, by conducting torture on a systematic and massive scale.

To accomplish his demonstration that the GPRA deserved the formal recognition of statehood, Bedjaoui referenced only classical notions of statehood found in European international public law. He thus hoped to convince American states (the United States, for instance) as well as the French officials from the Quai d'Orsay with whom the GPRA had started to engage in negotiations, to recognize the legality of Algeria's claim to independence and self-governance by translating these demands into their language.[54] For instance, he offered a scholarly review of the legal instruments from which France had (wrongfully) concluded that Algerian sovereignty had been extinguished (and replaced by France's sovereignty) with the 1830 conquest.[55] He demonstrated how, in view of the four criteria used in international public law to prove such transfer of sovereignty (the end of a public authority, independent from any other state, and recognized by a group of people, with effective management over a territory), the Algerian state had never been extinguished despite the French occupation of some of the Algerian territory since Charles X's conquest.[56] Neither were the Algerian state structures extinguished, nor was the Algerian nationality suppressed at the time of the conquest: it was only in 1865 that the Algerian nationality was unilaterally suppressed by an act of the Senatus-Consulte, which unilaterally declared the Muslim indigenous to be French – but without any real effect on Algerians' disposition toward acquiring French nationality.[57]

Through Bedjaoui's book, the GPRA's defense of Algeria's independence thus shared the same goal as those of Aron and Bourdieu, even though each of them (a legal scholar, a political scientist, and a sociologist, respectively) used very different disciplinary tools, further consolidating the split between ethnology and international public law. Since 1957, Aron had argued that the changing political economy of Western Europe required that the French Republic let go of its less developed colonies to accentuate commercial and financial integration with the leading Western power, the United States.[58] In 1960 and 1961, Aron's teaching assistant, Pierre Bourdieu, denied that Soustelle's plan of massive French investments in Algeria could solidify a postcolonial Franco-Algerian Republic and that Mauss's model of gift exchange had any validity in the realm of modern international relations.[59] Bedjaoui's anti-colonial charge thus ran parallel, but used a very different language, as he argued that the new Algerian government in exile, whose constitutional structure was well thought out, behaved just as classical public international law required, even before being granted independence. Algerians had demonstrated that they deserved independence not because their legal system (customary rule of law) was different and irreconcilable with modern public law, but precisely because Algeria's behavior as a state represented by the GPRA was in total conformity with classical notions found in the *jus publicum europeaum*, against the belief of ethnologists and colonialists who had long professed that the Algerian nation was incapable of forming and adhering to the formal structures of a classical nation-state.

When he analyzed the distribution of powers between the Algerian executive and legislative branches and how the two were articulated within and around the FLN as the single political party, Bedjaoui worked as if he were still a student writing an essay in a constitutional law class of Georges Lavau.[60] But when he articulated his arguments in the context of multilateral UNGA discussion, he gave them a performative effect that revealed the power of international and constitutional legal knowledge as a force for progress and decolonization: the mere fact that an Algerian legal scholar, speaking on behalf of the UGEMA, claimed that the Algerian deep state represented by the FLN, and its government, the GPRA, obeyed the very classical rules of statehood that had been used by colonial international law scholars in the interwar period to deny Algerians the right to statehood, was a very effective way to neutralize the French arguments in favor of France's continued tutelage.

Still, some of Bedjaoui's early critics deemed it an irony of history that Algerian diplomats like Bedjaoui referred only to (European) international public law, or to French law (in order to justify why the Sahara should be considered an integral part of Algeria, for instance), when at the same time, they recognized that the *jus publicum europeaum* and French administrative law had long been the main legal sources of exploitation of the colonial subjects. Remarking on the absence of any reference to precolonial Muslim law in Bedjaoui's writings, and the plurality of sources of law in any colonial society, some political sociologists who mixed Weberian studies with ethnological studies of local societies reviewed his book critically.[61]

Postcolonial theorists inspired by Franz Fanon and Albert Memmi may find in this paradox the classical position of the colonized subject vis-à-vis the knowledge of the colonizer: the former comes to read his own experience of a divided self through the eye of the colonizer, for whom no knowledge coming from the colony is legitimate.[62] But prior training and intellectual trajectory, shaped by the evolutions in the French academic field of in the 1950s, and the split between the metropolitan and colonial fields, can also account for this paradox.[63] Indeed, as the metropolitan field of law, where no classes were offered on Muslim or Kabylian law, was the only place where a young Algerian of Muslim descent could study international law in relative freedom, it was natural that Bedjaoui would mostly justify Algerian independence in reference to key concepts of European international public law. Furthermore, the mobilization of such knowledge by Algerian diplomats achieved essential practical goals: to neutralize international law, and even turn it against the imperialistic designs that it had long helped achieve in the interwar era.

More broadly, the neutralization of international law by anti-colonial legal scholars who used the legal categories once used against them to their own advantage was the preferred discursive strategy of the non-aligned movement. Until the mid 1960s, the agenda of the Non-Aligned Movement gradually taking shape since the Bandung Conference, and the Afro-Asian Peoples' Solidarity Organization, had not yet moved beyond classical notions of international public law when it defended the political independence of new nations from Africa and Asia.[64] At Bandung, the leaders of the non-aligned world had asked for political rights according to a classical and universal conception of international law, as found for instance in the UN Charter: new nations demanded the respect for fundamental human rights, the respect for the sovereignty and territorial integrity of all nations, the recognition of the equality of all races and of the equality of all nations, the settlement of all international disputes by peaceful means, etc.[65] They wanted a place at the table, rather than to rock the table. Likewise, Bedjaoui managed to register the FLN as a member to the four Geneva Conventions in 1960 – a legal success that was never matched by any other decolonizing movement.[66] In so doing, he helped the GPRA assert its authority through international de facto recognition; this, in turn, helped de Gaulle consider the GPRA as the only negotiating partner as he moved toward a realist policy of first, autonomization and, second, acceptance of Algerian independence.

3 THE EVIAN AGREEMENTS AND THE QUESTION OF ACQUIRED RIGHTS: A TEMPORARY DEFEAT FOR ALGERIAN NATIONALISTS?

Until the mid 1960s, and the creation of a multilateral arena in the UN architecture – with the establishment of the UN Conference on Trade and Development (UNCTAD), which was created in 1964 under the impetus of Latin American heterodox neo-Marxist economist Raúl Prébish (1901–86), who theorized the notion of "dependence" through trade specialization – the non-aligned nations that would create the Group of 77 in 1964 had not yet formed a consensus on the best way to prolong political independence with economic independence. Nor had the officials of the GPRA argued for the reform of international economic relations when they tried to obtain the de jure and de facto recognition of Algeria's independence from foreign powers.

Discussions of the economic rights of the future Algerian nation, which concerned the rights of the concessions, the protection of privately acquired rights in

Algeria and the recognition of Algeria's sovereign debt, were only discussed in the highly secret context of bilateral talks between the French government and the GPRA. It was in this context that Bedjaoui turned his attention away from classical administrative and international public law – topics he addressed in his 1961 book – to more immediate questions related to the economic and financial obligations of successor states.

In 1958, Bedjaoui had found in Ahmed Francis a powerful political mentor who could put the young law doctor's vast erudition, sharp analytical mind, and hard-to-match work ethic to good practical use. The experienced Minister of Economic and Financial Affairs of the GPRA overshadowed other political figures who worked from Geneva, Cairo, and Tunis to advance the cause of a free and independent Algeria. Even before his nomination as minister, in the spring of 1958, Francis sent Bedjaoui to Morocco and Tunisia on a first mission to inquire about the positions of nationalist leaders in exile: on the Constantine Plan launched by Soustelle, then Minister of Atomic Energy and the Sahara; on the future of nationality and migration requirements in a post-independence Algeria; and on many other economic topics that the future negotiation of the Evian Agreements would later explore.[67] Then, Francis asked Bedjaoui to settle in Geneva and help him plan future negotiations between the Algerian revolutionaries and the French government, as he was sure that such a moment would arrive eventually.[68] For Bedjaoui, the connection to Ahmed Francis became a key marker of his path to a political career first as jurisconsult, and then as minister in an independent Algeria – even more so that, in 1962, Bedjaoui married the adopted daughter of Ahmed Francis, who was in fact the natural daughter of Abdel Khader Francis and thus Ahmed's niece.[69]

The bilateral negotiations between the GPRA and the French government started after Soustelle was replaced as minister in charge of Algerian affairs by Louis Joxe (1901–91), a career diplomat who had spent the Second World War in Algiers. At the beginning of the negotiations, it appeared clear to both delegations that one of the main obstacles on the road toward Algerian independence was the issue of Algeria's claim of sovereignty over the Sahara and its oil resources, and the challenge that such claims mounted against the acquired rights of French oil concessions. The French government's emissaries initially argued that independence would be granted to the northern departments of Algeria but not to the Sahara, which was considered French according to the theory of *terra nullius*, which had been promoted, among others, by Soustelle, as Minister of the Sahara until 1960.[70] If the French government kept a military stronghold in the Sahara, it hoped that it could reassure the one million *pieds noirs* in Algeria and make sure that their rights would be guaranteed by the independent Algerian Republic. Furthermore, in May 1961, during the first meeting between the two delegations in Evian, the French argued that France had spent 512 billion francs for oil extraction in the Sahara and 60 billion for roads and telecommunications, and therefore the Oil Code could not be reformed unilaterally by the future Algerian state. Instead, a future independent

Algeria should guarantee the "acquired rights" that such lavish spending had secured for France, and recognize the continued sovereignty of the French Republic over the Sahara.

In contrast, in May 1961, the Algerian delegation not only insisted that the Sahara would fall under Algerian sovereignty, but it also envisioned a reform of the "acquired rights": those rights acquired by the French population of European descent on Algerian lands, which were threatened by the GPRA's willingness to reform land ownership and property rights, but also the rights of research and exploitation granted by the French state to its national oil company in the Sahara.[71] The Algerian delegation wanted to reform the Oil Code of 1958 in order to decrease the price of oil for internal consumption, and renegotiate contracts of exploitation and research – claims that de Gaulle's emissaries did not want to hear. The two delegations fiercely argued over the matter of "acquired rights," especially in the meetings of Lugrin (in July 1961), until a compromise was eventually introduced by Louis Joxe's aide, Yves Roland-Billecart (1936–): provided that the Algerian people voted in favor of independence, France agreed to recognize the Sahara and its oil fields as part of Algeria, and in exchange, an independent Algeria would guarantee the acquired rights that France had obtained for the exploitation of 700,000 square kilometers in the Sahara, and a joint organization controlled by the Algerians and the French would take over all matters relating to technical cooperation in the oil sector, according to the post-independence model of post-colonial cooperation that de Gaulle wanted to extend to all of France's former colonies.[72]

The negotiation took more time as a further complication emerged: when Algeria's neighbors Morocco and Tunisia, both claimed a right to oil extraction in the Sahara – claims that meant that territorial boundaries might need to be redrawn through regional negotiations after the end of the war.[73] Security concerns were added to this economic negotiation when Tunisia staked a claim on the prized territory. Indeed, after the secret negotiations of Lugrin in July 1961, the negotiation was put on hold for a few months to quash the anger of President Bourguiba of Tunisia, who had not been informed by the French or the Algerian government of the ongoing negotiation, and who was furious that neither had consulted him on the question of the Algeria–Tunisia borders in the Sahara. Bourguiba made it known to President de Gaulle that Tunisia wanted its share of the Sahara's subterranean resources,[74] and after de Gaulle snubbed him, the Tunisian leader mounted a military operation against Fort Saint in the Sahara, close to the border between Tunisia and Algeria and still occupied by French forces, which ended in a bloodbath after the French opened fire to defend themselves. The Algerian diplomats refused to start negotiations anew to appease the Tunisian leader, but they did not change their position on the question of the Sahara.[75] Neither did the French diplomats, who did not want to compromise the French ability to play guardian of the regional security order in the Maghreb.

But the French projects of bilateral cooperation in the business of oil extraction, coupled with the French government's insistence on maintaining intact the French laws on oil concessions after Algeria's independence, struck at the heart of the Algerian delegation's claim of independence for Algeria. How could Algeria declare itself independent if its future sovereignty was limited by French laws that preexisted its declaration of independence? This, as the members of the Algerian delegation argued, was the mark of a neocolonial project aimed at ensuring the prolongation of France's wrongly acquired rights on land expropriated at the time of colonization.[76] The GPRA claimed that the Algerian people had an "imprescriptible" right to self-determination and "permanent sovereignty over [their] natural resources," which, as Redha Malek, Algeria's Minister of Information, noted, sometimes led the negotiation to take an "academic turn."[77]

On this issue of acquired rights, Bedjaoui presented some of the most radical (if sometimes contradictory) arguments in favor of Algeria's absolute (rather than limited) sovereignty over the Sahara and its natural resources. For instance, Bedjaoui argued on the one hand that France's decision to include the Sahara in French Algeria made it impossible to deny the unification of the northern and southern parts of Algeria now: Algerian boundaries were recognized by French law, so it was hard for the French delegation to now declare that the Sahara was not part of Algeria. On the other hand, Bedjaoui claimed that there could be no law (in particular, the 1958 Oil Code) imposed by French occupiers over Algerian territories that would continue to bind how an independent Algeria would use its natural resources.[78] For Bedjaoui, the philosophy of postcolonial bilateral cooperation only relayed in the post-independence age the claims that colonial lawmakers like Albert Sarraut had made about the sources of imperial solidarity.[79] In place of the recognition of acquired rights, he wanted to guarantee only French "legitimately acquired rights"[80] in the future independent Algeria.

Ultimately, the Evian Agreements of March 1962 did not endorse Bedjaoui's thesis that an independent Algeria should be completely free to decide all economic matters concerning the repartition of debts, concessions, and public properties claimed by France and Algeria, including those that concerned the rights acquired by the metropolitan oil companies over the former colonies' natural resources. The solution initially proposed by Yves Roland-Billecart eventually found its way into the final text: the French government agreed to recognize the integrity of the Algerian territory, which included the Sahara; in exchange, the GPRA agreed to recognize and guarantee the validity of "acquired rights" by also mentioning explicitly that "no one will be deprived of its acquired rights without an indemnization determined in advance."[81] Furthermore, France's "independence agreements were followed by various protocols concerning property, under which the independent state did not succeed to the whole property appertaining to sovereignty," meaning that "in exchange for French cooperation, a limited transfer of property was agreed upon,"[82] and some property (military bases for instance) was ceded to the French.[83]

At last, the Algerian delegation accepted to create a Franco-Algerian cooperative in the oil sector operating in the whole Saharan desert. In exchange, they received the promise from the French government that it would extend some "financial help … in the form of either in-kind '*prestations*,' loans, financial participation or gifts,"[84] to Algeria's projects of public investment in the oil sector, and in Algeria's efforts to integrate the hundreds of thousands workers among the "regrouped populations" back into the economy. The promoters of the philosophy of bilateral and postcolonial cooperation had stroked a first victory.

The Evian Agreements thus settled the matter of economic international relations in the post-independence age in a way that was less progressive than what the Algerian delegation had hoped for, based on other contemporary developments in the international scene. In the debate over international obligations in a post-independence Algeria, it was not so much the legitimacy of nationalizations of either land ownership or concessions that distinguished the interwar solidarists, or the Gaullist advocates of bilateral cooperation, from the thinkers from the Global South, but the question of how to deal with debts associated with the nationalization of concessionary companies or other forms of acquired rights. Should the latter be reimbursed and should concessionary companies be compensated for the costs of exploration and their investments in extraction technologies? Who would decide on the amount of the reparation? And who would pay such indemnity: the former metropolis or the newly independent state? As far as they were concerned, the Gaullists were adamant that all acquired rights should be honored in the independent Algeria, and that, should nationalization occur, the companies should be compensated so that they could meet the debt obligations they had contracted to develop oil extraction.

The Evian Agreements aligned with the Western dominant conception, by repeatedly guaranteeing throughout the text that all acquired rights would be honored in an independent Algeria. If international law had proved to exert a powerful performative function when used by Algerian diplomats to claim political independence in the multilateral scene, the developments of international law in the economic field were too embryonic to compensate for the weakness of Algeria's position in the bilateral negotiation over economic matters. Indeed, as far as the nationalization of oil concessions was concerned, the claim that economically weak nation-states had a right to nationalize extractive concessionary companies was only introduced in the international arena ten years before Algeria's independence: in 1952, when Chile introduced a resolution at the Human Rights Commission, and Uruguay at the UNGA, at the same time as the Iranians were discussing the decision to nationalize the British oil trusts.[85] But against the resolution proposed by Uruguay in November 1952, which asserted the essential link between "complete independence" and "the right of each country to nationalize and freely exploit its natural wealth," and declared the permanent sovereignty of states over their natural resources,[86] the United States and Western European states had claimed that the right for nation-states to decide nationalizations when vital necessities were at stake did not erase their obligations to disburse "prompt, adequate and effective compensation" to the aggrieved private parties,[87] especially if the latter were foreign multinationals. This lesson was not forgotten by the Algerian delegation, which decided to mount a formidable diplomatic fight to change the international economic law of decolonization.

4 THE QUESTION OF COLONIAL DEBTS IN THE ILC

In the context of Algeria's independence, and, more broadly, the expansion of the number of newly independent states represented in the UNGA, the UNGA passed Resolution 1686 in December 1961 to put the ILC in charge of exploring the legal issues associated with the economic problems affecting newly independent nations. To study the topic of the succession of states and governments in view of the phenomenon of decolonization, the ILC formed a subcommittee in 1962, which divided the work into three topics: succession with respect to treaties, succession with respect to matters other than treaties, and succession of governments (not states) with respect to membership in international organizations.[88] The ILC had initially nominated Manfred Lachs (1914–93), a Polish jurist, to serve as special rapporteur of the subcommittee in charge of succession of states with respect to matters other than treaties, but after the latter was elected to the ICJ, not much work was achieved until the Yugoslav representative, Milan Bartos (1901–74), proposed the name of Bedjaoui for special rapporteur. As Algeria's Minister of Justice, and a promising scholar previously trained in the French field of international law, Bedjaoui's name gathered the support of the representatives of non-aligned, Western and communist nations. Even Paul Reuter (1911–90), a specialist in French law in overseas territory, said of Bedjaoui that, "as the French representative at the ILC, he would not be able to vote for Bedjaoui, but that he was personally in favor of his nomination."[89]

After his nomination at the ILC, Mohammed Bedjaoui wrote twelve reports – one per year[90] – in which he gradually derived principles that should guide the establishment of more equitable international economic relations. In so doing, Bedjaoui, and with him, the ILC tried to finally redress the situation that the interwar legal scholar, Alexander Sack had found wanting. Indeed, Sack had deplored the anarchic nature of state successions, which were essentially left to be determined through political compromises,[91] in the absence of "universal rules that could be recognized by all *civilized states* to govern matters related with the *public credit*."[92] As Sack had added, without a clear doctrine to guide the obligations of each state in the case of decolonization, secession, or merger of sovereignties, the "non-repartition of old debts and the sustainability of ties of solidarity and joint responsibilities [*responsabilités solidaires*] between the predecessor and successor states cannot be said to represent a right for the creditors, and not an obligation for the successor states."[93]

To remediate this situation, Sack had surveyed many treaties and conventions in which the question of repartition of public and private debts and assets between predecessor and successor was addressed, at a time when the Allied victors had just dismantled the three long-lasting empires: the German Second Reich (with the Versailles Treaty, 1919), the Austro-Hungarian Empire (Treaties of Saint-Germain and Trianon, 1920), and the Ottoman Empire (Treaty of Lausanne, 1923). But he had conducted the effort of codification with no mandate from any international organization (like the League of Nations) and from a purely academic perspective, and his theory of when, how, and why debts should be cancelled and acquired rights ignored, was far from well respected, when it was known at all.

As far as Bedjaoui and other members of the ILC from the non-aligned world were concerned – and in contrast to the Western jurists in the ILC, in particular, Stephen Schwebel (1929–), from the United States[94] – the work of ILC was also supposed to neutralize the power of international economic law, which, so far, had been eminently conservative, to the extent that it had been based on the recognition of acquired rights of former powers, except in exceptional circumstances. Indeed, the "folk legal theory"[95] that Sack had identified in the texts that the Allied powers had imposed on Germany and its wartime allies, and that he rationalized, was that those inherited debts should be "odious" (and thus cancelled) when three conditions were found: lack of consent of the people when the debt was contracted in the first place, lack of benefit for the people, and creditor awareness of the two first conditions (although the latter condition, which concerned the lenders' responsibility) was not always required.[96]

For instance, the Versailles Treaty had assumed that "the colonies should not bear any portion of the German debt, nor remain under any obligation to refund to Germany the expenses incurred by the Imperial administration of the protectorate," especially if the debt incurred had been contracted for the "purpose of enslaving indigenous populations or for the purpose of helping its own nationals colonize the lands."[97] In fact, Sack had added "it would have been unjust to burden the natives with expenditure which appears to have been incurred in Germany's own interest, and that it have would been no less unjust to make this responsibility rest upon the Mandatory Powers which, in so far as they may be appointed trustees by the League of Nations, will derive no benefit from such trusteeship."[98] In the interwar settlement, this folk theory found its legal concretization in article 254 of the Versailles Treaty, which left to the Reparations Commission the duty to measure the amount of debt that the German and Prussian governments had contracted to help German nationals colonize Polish lands, and to decide under which conditions colonial debts had been contracted, before declaring some of them odious or not. Still, for Sack, the Reparations Commission should not have cancelled the Polish debts to the Germans: before the Great War, the Germans had bought the lands they colonized from Poles at a very high price, and the Germans did not fund these land purchases with loans, but on the Prussian budget, which meant that German taxpayers had already paid for these purchases.[99] The fact the debts were cancelled was a departure from the solidarist principles implicit in Sack's doctrine of "odious debt," which were held dear to the French-speaking international law scholars, most of whom, like Mauss himself, believed in the sanctity of contracts except when the latter blatantly violated rules of fairness.

In fact, the African debts contracted by the German colonial governments were also cancelled after 1919, although Sack had found that it was not clear why they could be called "odious" according to his own doctrine: indeed, Sack believed, some of the debts incurred in Africa by the Germans had been used for the purpose of developing railroads and other infrastructures, and should have been placed on the debit of the local governments that succeeded to Germany's colonial governments. He thus wondered why the Versailles Treaty (article 257, 1) did not create any obligations for the German colonies in Africa and elsewhere – or for the mandate powers designated to administer their development – to repay the debts left by the German state and which had been used for their development, despite express German demands to the mandate powers.

If Sack criticized the Versailles Treaty for applying criteria for sovereign debt cancellation that was too loose, the special rapporteur of the sub-committee of the ILC in charge of codifying the doctrine on such issues, believed the Versailles Treaty had not gone far enough to serve as a model for the new age of decolonization.[100] Revisiting the history of interwar sovereign debt controversies, Bedjaoui arrived at a position more radical than that of Sack and Mauss, as he strongly justified the decision made by the Bolsheviks to unilaterally cancel their sovereign debt upon taking power.[101] For Bedjaoui, the Soviet debt cancellation "gave its letters of nobility to the notion of express agreement," which accompanied "the progressive elaboration of a *voluntary* international law,"[102] with which the anti-colonial lawyers like himself were associated. He went even further, as for him, there was no temporal limit to the period during which a new state could exert a "right of inventory"[103] and decide which legal obligations it would keep and which it would reject. The newly independent states did not have to cancel illegitimate debt immediately after independence: there was no "*délai de dénonciation*"[104] (time limit for denunciation) in the case of decolonizing states, especially as the latter were under too much stress to focus on canceling any debt at the time of independence.

As far as the topic of debt transmission from metropolitan states to newly independent states was concerned, Bedjaoui's position at the ILC was as uncompromising as it had been during the negotiation of the Evian Agreements; but this time, he had more room to maneuver and obtain support (if not consensus) from his colleagues. Even if Bedjaoui praised the previous work of legal scholars, and especially that of Alexander Sack, he was clearly opposed to Sack's attempt to limit the applicability of the concept of "odious debt."[105] For Bedjaoui, the criteria of intended use (for development rather than war or expropriation of natives by colonizers) that Sack had introduced to limit the applicability of the doctrine of "odious debt" to the most extreme cases were not useful guides to determine which colonial debts contracted by the metropolitan state should pass on to the newly independent states. Bedjaoui illustrated his point with the case of Algeria: during the seven and a half years of war between France and the FLN, the administering power had, for political reasons, been "overgenerous in pledging Algeria's backing for numerous loans."[106] These debts contracted to fund the great developmental plans, like, in the case of France and Algeria, Soustelle's 1959 Constantine Plan, had in fact had the effect of "seriously compromising the Algerian Treasury" after independence,[107] to the point that he wondered if such generosity had not hidden darker intentions: that of leaving a nation almost bankrupt at the time of its birth.[108] For Bedjaoui, those debts that the metropolitan states had contracted at the end of the colonial era, even for developmental purposes, were not to be transmitted to the newly independent states: they were thus just one example of the "poisonous gifts"[109] which Mauss had written about, and which Bedjaoui suspected to have caused the "increasingly insupportable debt problem" among newly independent states in the 1970s.[110]

In the ILC discussions, Bedjaoui explicitly cited Algeria as a precedent, which showed that even debts contracted for developmental purposes by a former colonial state could be cancelled. At Evian, the Algerian delegation had fought to include in the Evian Agreements a proposal for France to erase the totality of the external debt that Algerian communities had contracted toward France, in compensation for all the profits that France presumably had made during more than a century of occupation, and for France to inherit part of the Algerian internal debt; but to no avail.[111] As Bedjaoui wrote, the Algerian delegation to the Evian negotiation had argued: "that the [developmental] projects had been undertaken in a particular political and military context, in order to advance the interests of the French settlers and of the French presence in general, and that they were part of France's overall economic strategy, since virtually the whole of France's investment in Algeria had been complementary in nature."[112] The Gaullists had imposed their will during the negotiation of the Evian Agreements, as Algeria's negotiating position was weak at that time. But Bedjaoui remarked that, even though the Evian Agreements did not plan debt cancellation, Algeria rightfully "refused to assume debts representing loans contracted by France for the purpose of carrying out economic projects in Algeria during the war of independence."[113] This had been the situation as far as the law-in-the-books was concerned. But Ahmed Francis, upon his arrival as Minister of the Economy and Finance in Algiers, discovered that the partisans of a French Algeria who rejected the Evian Agreements (the Organisation armée secrète or OAS) had emptied the Bank of Algeria of its gold, cash, and foreign reserves, and had absconded with it to Spain and Latin America.[114] Algeria was completely "bankrupt," which led Francis and Bedjaoui to go to Paris (as Algeria was still in the "zone franc") and obtain Treasury-to-Treasury cooperation to give Algeria some emergency relief and agree on debt cancellation solutions.[115] Then, in December 1966, when Algeria and France settled debt issues after three years of negotiations, Bedjaoui underlined that "Algeria does not seem to have succeeded to the state debts of the predecessor state by making the payment of 40 billion old francs (400 million new francs)"[116] to France. Rather, Algeria and France had engaged in a broad political negotiation, in which the payment was part of a broader economic bargain, including a commitment by France to import certain goods that Algeria had in surplus (oil and, most importantly at the time, wine).

As Bedjaoui argued in the ILC, in principle, all of the state debts owed to the former metropolis should thus be disregarded, and debts owed to private citizens of the former metropolis should be left for the metropolitan state to reimburse. In other terms, in the case of decolonization, "the general principle of non-transferability of the debts of the administering power, to which exceptions may be allowed . . . places the burden of proof on the predecessor state rather than on the newly independent state."[117] This conclusion derived from the general premise that, as far as territories (as well as public properties) and sovereign debts were concerned, the idea that elapsed time would turn wrongs committed during conquest and occupation into contractual rights was not grounded in international public law. Even if more than one hundred years had passed since the occupation had started, the revolution from which a newly independent state emerged meant that the new state was free to act *as if* history had started anew, as if no contractual development occurring after the occupation had any legal basis. In this way, Bedjaoui's discourse on the right of conquest fell in the tradition – beautifully analyzed by Michel Foucault – of the English revolutionaries of the seventeenth century, who argued against Hobbes that the law imposed by the Normans on local landlords after William the Conqueror's invasion (in the eleventh century) had never been legitimate.[118] Closer still, Bedjaoui cited the precedent of Poland, whose sovereignty was "resurrected"[119] in 1919 and until the Russo-German invasion of 1939, after more than a century of joint occupation by the Germans and Russians – a time lapse comparable with the French denial of Algerian sovereignty.[120]

This was a contentious idea: the French jurist Maurice Flory, who wrote his dissertation under the supervision of Hersch Lauterpacht (1897–1960) and Charles Rousseau (1902–93) – himself a former student of Jules Basdevant – argued that this legal fiction according to which the revolutions of the decolonization era would be in fact a series of restorations was nonsensical: for Flory and other French jurisconsults, the legal fiction according to which the Algerian independent state could have survived intact despite a century of absence was unfounded.[121] Even ILC members from the Third World remarked that Bedjaoui's analysis on that matter appeared to "deal extensively with French colonial practice" but much less with Dutch or British colonial practice, which, to a much larger extent than the French, had left the ability to raise taxes or loans to dependent but still "separate administrative units that were largely fiscally autonomous."[122] To these arguments, which contradicted the notion that colonialism had created no obligation for newly independent states,[123] Bedjaoui contended that, even if Algeria was a separate case, as its administration had been integrated into the government of the metropolis, whereas most colonies had remained somehow separate, the lessons he drew from the Algerian experience were valid elsewhere. As he wrote, "even though these colonial debts had formally been contracted 'freely' by separate administrative authorities, all colonial era debts could be held in suspicion (until metropolitan states demonstrated otherwise), since the loans were guaranteed by the colonial power" – whose intentions were rarely generous, despite their rhetoric invoking purity of intention and generosity – and since "the 'organs of the colony' which have contracted the loan in the name of the territory only belong to that colony by a legal fiction: they are in reality, the representatives of the colonial power in the territory."[124]

Due to his prominent involvement in the domestic situation in Algeria, it was not surprising if Bedjaoui drew close analogies between the specific economic claims that Algeria had made before and after the Evian Agreements, with regard to the issues of nationalization, cooperation, and debt cancellation, and the general recommendations he formulated at the ILC. Still, his arguments and those of his critics reached a higher level of generality, which still has some relevance today. Indeed, the wrong notion that developmental projects in the colonies were paid for by the metropolis by taxpayer money, rather than out of the budget of local colonial administrators, and then transferred as debts on the debit of new states at the time of their independence, continues to dominate many popular narratives about colonization, which still use the tropes of "generosity" that Soustelle and other colonial administrators used to justify their hegemonic designs outside Europe. Today, we still hear the notion expressed by nostalgics of the Empire in France or in the United Kingdom that colonialism produced many good things for which colonial subjects should be grateful, in particular, the railroads and hospitals that colonial powers had developed initially for themselves, but which ended up in the hands of newly independent states: in February 2005, the French Parliament went as far as making it mandatory for French history programs at the pre-university level to "emphasize the positive aspects of the French presence overseas, including in North Africa"[125] (a sentence that was deleted one year later). With his reports to the ILC, Bedjaoui thus tried to crush these notions, by placing the developmental objectives that European powers entertained outside Europe in the context of sustained warfare and occupation.

In general, the ILC members from the non-aligned world (Algeria, Yugoslavia, Nigeria, India) supported the conclusions of the special rapporteur: they agreed with Bedjaoui that "even in the case of loans granted to the administering power for the development of the dependent territory (criterion of intended use and allocation), the colonial context in which the development of the territory may take place thanks to these loans disqualifies the undertaking."[126] They followed Bedjaoui when he said that "in these circumstances, it would be unjust to make the newly independent state assume the corresponding debt even if that state retained some 'trace' of the investment, in the form, for example, of public works infrastructures."[127] In so doing, Bedjaoui and other non-aligned scholars in the ILC acknowledged that the principle of intransmissibility of state debts to newly independent states[128] that they wanted to enshrine in the future convention represented less a "codification" of established practice – as "the practice of the newly independent states of Asia and Africa is far from uniform" – than a new principle of international public law which conformed with the general principles of the NIEO.[129]

Methodologically, this conclusion meant to break with accepted principles recognized by professional international law scholars. From the start, Bedjaoui argued that codifying obsolete rules or devolution agreements that had been largely imposed by former metropolises – as had been the case with the Evian Agreements – would have been completely useless, or even counter-productive: diplomatic arrangements found in decolonization cases "had to be interpreted with caution, since some of them had been imposed by metropolitan states on new and weak states and might lead the Committee astray if taken as typical examples" to form a customary law.[130] Even if Bedjaoui acknowledged that it was not the job of the ILC to "create new law under the guise of progressive development,"[131] it was also its duty to analyze emerging "norms known and accepted by most [newly independent] states to a greater extent than traditional law, in whose formulation most existing states [which had come into being through decolonization wars] took no part." For instance, Bedjaoui noticed that the term "succession,"[132] as in the "law of state succession" which the ILC was in charge of codifying, was not neutral, but inherently conservative: the law of state succession was based on the "as if"[133] assumption that private law could be extended to public law matters, and that sovereigns had limited powers to change the order of private property; and that, if they did, they should proceed diligently to compensate private victims of property changes with fair indemnities.[134] To Bedjaoui, such limits placed on the sovereignty of newly independent states by international law prolonged the colonialist conception of limited sovereignty expressed in the interwar period by the Versailles, Lausanne, and Trianon treaties.[135] Thus, international law scholars had to switch methodologies, if they didn't want to remain captive to the colonial biases of their discipline.

Instead of codification, Bedjaoui thus engaged the ILC in an effort of "progressive development" of international law by basing his work "on legal constructions embodying to the maximum extent possible the present trends of international law, the principles of the Charter, the right to self-determination, sovereign equality, ownership of natural resources, etc."[136] In contrast to what he did for his 1961 book on Algeria and international law, which used the language of classical European international law to claim a place at the table for Algeria, without changing the doctrine, Bedjaoui claimed that with the age of political independences now almost over, now had come the time to change legal doctrines, and to evaluate all prior treaties and agreements by examining whether they represented new "progressive developments" in the emerging law of decolonization.[137] Otherwise, international law in general, and the work of the ILC in particular, would remain intrinsically conservative and colonialist in spirit. Apart from some isolated voices, like that of Shabtai Rosenne, a legal scholar from Israel who had initially "favored the formulation of general principles," the ILC members thus decided to prepare "terse and brief articles of the type usually included in a convention,"[138] in order to flesh out which rights would fall to the economic North and South.

5 RISING DEMANDS FOR A NEW INTERNATIONAL ECONOMIC ORDER IN THE CONTEXT OF OIL NATIONALIZATIONS

At the turn of the 1960s and 1970s, the Algerian diplomats at the UNGA and the ILC pursued a similar objective, which consisted in redistributing national debts and assets between North and South in a broad and comprehensive manner. To do so, they used different means: whereas the former tried to engage the North in a political negotiation, the latter tried to obtain from the North the recognition of a new legal doctrine, enshrined in a convention – although Bedjaoui still refrained from explicitly calling it a doctrine of "odious debt," not wanting to shock his Western legal colleagues.[139] Both opposed the attempts by French Gaullists to organize a series of gift exchanges between North and South on a bilateral basis, as they wanted to unite the South first, before engaging in global negotiations with the North.

The Algerian diplomatic offensive started in October 1967, a few months after Bedjaoui issued his first report to the ILC, when Algeria hosted an important conference in Algiers, where non-aligned nations issued the Charter of Algiers, by which they stressed the necessity of increasing the prices of raw materials through revised trade conventions.[140] Among many other actions aimed at rebalancing the financial situation between the Global North and South, the conference of heads of state and government of the non-aligned countries which took place in September 1973 in Algiers was a key landmark during which the leaders of the Global South concluded with a call to the UN General Assembly to agree upon a program of action for the establishment of the NIEO, which recommended "debt renegotiation on a case-by-case basis with a view to concluding agreements on debt cancellation, moratorium, rescheduling or interest subsidization" (section II, article 2.g), starting with the "the least developed, land-locked and island developing countries and to the countries most seriously affected by economic crises and natural calamities" (section II, article 2.i).[141] As President Houari Boumédiène said at the conference of Non-Aligned Countries in Algiers in 1973, the newly independent countries were suffocated by the debt they inherited from the colonial past and the low prices of raw materials such as oil, which made their economic models unsustainable. Bedjaoui had similar claims: citing the Pearson Commission on International Development, Bedjaoui underlined that "debt service alone, namely annual amortization and interest payments, would exceed the total amount of new loans by 20 percent in Africa and by 30 percent in Latin America,"[142] which meant that the level of state indebtedness inherited by newly independent states from metropolitan states left them crippled at birth.

As Nicole Grimaud writes, in the early 1970s, the Algerian oil diplomats became not only the main defenders of the idea of debt cancellation for newly independent nations, but also "the champions of the thesis of national sovereignty over natural resources" on the world scene, which allowed the newly independent states to nationalize oil concessions without inheriting the debts that such concessions had contracted in the past to develop their activities.[143] In particular, the UNGA Plenary Committee affirmed the "permanent sovereignty of every State over its natural resources and all economic activities."[144] The Plenary Committee, which was charged by the UNGA to formalize concrete actions for the NIEO, planned to integrate debt cancellation and debt renegotiation into the broader framework of North–South negotiations for a:

> just and equitable relationship between the prices of raw materials [oil in particular], primary commodities, manufactured and semi-manufactured goods exported by developing countries and the prices of raw materials, primary commodities, food, manufactured and semi-manufactured goods and capital equipment imported by them, and to work for a link between the prices of exports of developing countries and the prices of their imports from developed countries.[145] (section 1, article 1.d)

This Algerian diplomatic offensive, even if it didn't always go as far as the NIEO promoters wished, strengthened the latter's position. In particular, the UNGA Plenary Committee's affirmation of permanent sovereignty over natural resources echoed the May 1974 Declaration in favor of the NIEO, which entitled "each State to exercise effective control over their [natural] resources and their exploitation with means suitable to its own situation, including the right to nationalization or transfer of ownership to its nationals, this right being an expression of the full permanent sovereignty of the State." It complemented this right to nationalize with a "right of all States under . . . colonial domination to restitution and full compensation for the exploitation . . . and damages to, the[se] natural resources" as well as a right to "supervise the activities of transnational corporations by taking measures in the interest of the national economies of the countries."[146]

In so doing, the UNGA rejected the position of the United States and West European states, which conditioned the right to nationalize to the "duty to conform with international obligations."[147] Still, nine months later, when the rights of newly independent states were further defined in the Charter of the Economic and Social Rights of States adopted by the UNGA in December 1974, the absoluteness of the right to nationalize multinational companies (without obligation to impose an immediate and fair indemnization), claimed by new oil-rich nations, was diluted under the pressures of the United States and its European allies: the Charter declared that such indemnization was no longer a decision under the control of the nationalizing state, but a decision that needed to conform to rules enshrined in international law.[148] The change showed the intensity of the fight taking place at the UNGA and the ILC on the questions of debt cancellation, oil nationalizations, and the right to fair compensation.

These resolutions were not merely discourse, but were associated with extremely controversial economic decisions and actions undertaken by newly independent states in the 1970s, especially those who were members of the Organization of Petroleum Exporting Countries (OPEC), which was founded in 1960, but had remained dormant until the late 1960s. The economic program that some of these OPEC member states wished to implement in the 1970s had converged toward the kind of socialist utopias that Mauss had dreamed about: public national companies and land cooperatives would take over the properties of a few colonial magnates and extractive conglomerates, which controlled vast swaths of land and their subterranean resources. Algeria seemed a case in point: Algerian nationalists declared the nationalization of land in 1963, soon after the 1962 exodus of around one million *pieds noirs* who chose French nationality and emigration to the French metropolis. A few years later, in 1971, the government of Algerian President Houari Boumédiène was one of the first Arab League and OPEC countries to declare the nationalization of gas and oil concessions – quickly followed by Qaddafi's Libya, which nationalized British Petroleum's assets in 1971, and then by Saddam Hussein's Iraq and Saudi Arabia, in retaliation against Western support for Israel in the 1973 war.[149] Indeed, in February of that year, the Algerian government decided to claim 51 percent of the property rights of French oil companies operating in Algeria (and 100 percent of the gas sector and the pipelines). This decision was a unilateral cancellation of the 1965 bilateral treaty by which the Algerian government had agreed to respect France's acquired rights[150] regarding the exploration and exploitation of Algerian oil in the Sahara, provided that the French would reinvest half of its oil revenues in Algeria.[151] The 1965 Treaty, in line with the Gaullist philosophy of bilateral "cooperation" found in the Evian Agreements, had indeed created a "Franco-Algerian cooperative association for the exploration and exploitation of oil" in a vast region of the Sahara, with the French contributing 400 million francs each year to the industrialization of Algeria (with 40 million as gifts, 160 as governmental loans, and 200 as private debts guaranteed by a French financial establishment).[152] The Franco-Algerian Treaty also planned that the French would reinvest a large part of their profits in exploring the Sahara, but in 1970, the Algerians raised the bar of French companies' reinvestment of their profits in Algeria from 50 percent to 90 percent. The Algerians knew that this bar was unacceptable to the French, but claimed that it respected the preamble of the 1965 bilateral agreement, which sought to develop Algeria's oil extractive capacities in the "framework of Algerian sovereignty."[153] They thus claimed that Algerian sovereign decisions trumped the technical clauses agreed upon in the treaty itself, along lines that reflected the legal doctrine that Bedjaoui pushed at the ILC.[154] They forced the crisis to justify the nationalization that they had long planned.

Bedjaoui knew very well the file on the nationalization of oil concessions, as President Boumédiène had requested Bedjaoui be "sent to the front line,"[155] by nominating him in 1970 to serve as Algeria's ambassador in Paris, at the very time when he was engaged, together with Foreign Minister Bouteflika, Energy Minister Abdessalam, in the struggle against the French government and the French oil and gas concessions. After Algeria's 1971 decision regarding the oil concessions, Bedjaoui, established as the new Algerian ambassador in Paris, soon received a letter of protestation from the French government, followed by a memorandum transmitted in March 1971 by French Prime Minister Jacques Chaban-Delmas that listed all the French claims against the unilateral nationalization of the oil sector.[156] In this memo, the prime minister recognized "Algeria's right to nationalize," but not without preliminary and fair compensation for the nationalized assets (according to what the Evian Agreements had planned), and he threatened to ask French companies to immediately stop production in the Sahara if a committee charged with determining such compensation was not set up – a demand that the Algerian government rejected, first through the voice of Bedjaoui, on March 15, 1971, and then through the voice of President Boumédiène, when the latter abolished all the concessions in April 1971. Eventually, some agreement was found, in large part thanks to the massive support that Algeria's decision found in the OPEC, and Algeria's active diplomacy, which emphasized that Algeria had showed good will before, when they agreed to destroy 400,000 hectares of vineyards that produced the "red gold" that Algeria had exported to France and which de Gaulle's Minister of the Economy, Valéry Giscard d'Estaing, had unilaterally prohibited from entering the French territory in 1963 and 1964.[157]

The Franco-Algerian oil crisis of 1971 thus put an effective end to the idea of bilateral cooperation between former metropolis and a newly independent state conceived as a "total fact" – in which the private interests of oil concessions are indistinguishable from the public interests of independent states – which Denise Grimaud claims may have been for the better. Indeed, when new decisions clashed with the philosophy of bilateral cooperation that had inspired the Evian Agreements, economic disputes between Algeria and France were immediately turned into state affairs that involved logics of honor and radicalization.[158] With this decision, Algeria sought to signal that it no longer accepted to shape its economic relations with the former metropolis according to the logic of bilateral gift exchange, when the exchange of prestations, gifts, and loans was supposed to follow the logic of reciprocity between two otherwise unequal partners. For Bedjaoui, the rights and obligations of newly independent states and former metropolises could not be symmetrical, or reciprocal. For Bedjaoui and other French legal scholars who accompanied the advances of the NIEO, like Charles Chaumont (1913–2001), the "most favored" clauses and other boilerplates by which the French metropolis had created some fake sense of reciprocity with its colonies just hid the continued exploitation of the South by the North thanks to legalistic artifacts.[159] To institute real (as opposed to fake) reciprocity between the two kinds of states, some time needed to be given to the newly independent states to grow economically, and become prosperous enough, before they could finally give back.

At the same time as Algeria decided to nationalize oil concessions, the ILC addressed the question of debt in the context of the nationalization of private property, especially the oil concessions granted by the former colonial powers to private interests. In 1963, it had appeared that the ILC (despite its mandate that was mostly limited to the codification of international public law) would extend its study to cover how state succession affected the rights of private individuals,[160] especially those of "nationals of foreign states,"[161] as these issues were at the center of negotiations in the case of newly independent states – as illustrated by the Franco-Algerian negotiation. But the issue had been swept under the carpet at the ILC, as it appeared the most contentious ever since the former colonies had gained their political independence. Realizing in 1970 that "the topic of acquired rights was extremely controversial and that its study, at a premature stage, could only delay the Commission's work on the topic as a whole, most members had been of the opinion that the codification of the rules should not begin with the preparation of draft articles on acquired rights."[162] In order to minimize disputes with the ILC subcommittee, Bedjaoui originally restricted the mandate of the ILC to study only issues of transmission of state property – or rather "public property appertaining to sovereignty"[163] – and excluded the thorny issue of the private acquired rights of foreign nationals and multinational (oil) companies.

Still, in 1971, the question of "acquired rights" returned to the ILC discussion, as the definition of the "state property" which Bedjaoui proposed to include in the future convention, and which "devolved automatically and without compensation from the predecessor to the successor state," was no longer restricted to "public property" in the restrictive sense meant by the former metropolises (public buildings, etc.), but encompassed also the oil concessions and all the other items that a newly independent state might declare to be "necessary for the exercise of sovereignty."[164] The ambiguity of this criterion meant that it could more or less include any property that the newly independent state wanted to nationalize if it could claim it was necessary for the exercise of sovereignty. As Bedjaoui remarked, after reviewing the vast body of precedents, he had found "no precise answers in international contemporary law to the two following key questions: (1) what property is required for the exercise of sovereignty? (2) what authority has the power to determine such property?"[165] The two questions were in fact intrinsically related. If ambiguities remained as to which property could be called "state property," then, the main question was whether the law of the metropolitan state or that of the successor state would serve as the source for the definition. Bedjaoui found in the precedents – decisions made by the Reparations Commissions – that no international body had been "in a position to carry out the task [of defining which properties belonged to the sovereignty of the state] without reference to the municipal law of the predecessor state."[166] But he didn't find that the Permanent Court of Justice, or the ICJ, had recognized this principle as part of customary international law.[167]

To the contrary, Bedjaoui claimed that when the law of the predecessor state differentiated between the "public" and "private" property of the state – like in Italy, but also and most importantly, in France – based on the distinction between property rights that were "necessary to the sovereignty" of the state and those that came from commercial activities of the state and which were deemed to belong to the "private" domain of state property, then, countries like France could not ask for compensation from the successor state if the latter nationalized such "private" properties that were in fact, "essential to the exercise of the sovereignty" of the successor state.[168] Whether oil concessions could be considered one or the other was thus ambiguous. The colonial history of the French Empire showed that France had considered that natural resources in its colonies had been so "essential for the exercise of its sovereignty" that it had invaded overseas territories to conquer such resources. And even if France refused to acknowledge it now, Algeria believed oil resources were "essential for the exercise of its sovereignty." As a consequence, Bedjaoui weakened the general rule according to which "public property should be made by reference to the municipal law which governed the territory concerned" by adding the following exception: "save in the event of a serious conflict with the public policy of the successor state."[169] This was an important and broad exception, as it was not completely clear who would decide the "seriousness" of the conflict of law and thus, the ability of the successor state to impose its legal definition.[170]

This general exception found its most manifest illustration in the conflict of law regarding the right to grant oil concessions. As Bedjaoui noted in his 1973 report to the ILC, "it is quite inappropriate to consider the successor state as 'subrogated' to the rights of the predecessor state, or as 'succeeding' the latter regarding the right in respect to the authority to grant concessions."[171] Citing the French jurist Lyon-Caen, for whom a concession is the "juxtaposition of a contract and an act of sovereignty," Bedjaoui reintroduced the issue by leaving aside the "*contractual* aspect of the concession," in order to "deal exclusively with *the act of sovereignty*."[172] As far as this public law aspect was concerned he "considered that the successor state exercises its own rights as a new conceding authority, which replaces the former conceding authority," meaning that it could freely decide to grant or withdraw "by virtue of its sovereignty, the title of owner of the soil and subsoil of the transferred territory."[173] As Bedjaoui continued to work in 1971 and 1972 on these conflicts of law between predecessor and successor states, he made it clear that "the fact that the successor state 'receives' the internal juridical order of its predecessor state should not automatically imply that the concessionary regime is thereby renewed."[174]

After the Algerian decision to nationalize oil concessions in 1971, it was natural that Mohammed Bedjaoui had turned again his attention to the limits that newly independent states could impose on the rights of private companies like oil concessions when he delivered his reports to the ILC.[175] Even if Bedjaoui knew that his reflections on the superiority of the newly independent states' sovereign "vital interests" over the private (and even sometimes moral) rights of citizens and foreign nationals (and the superiority of public law over private law) divided the ILC's subcommittee, the 1971 Algerian decision proved that the ILC could no longer escape addressing the issue, for otherwise, it risked becoming completely irrelevant.[176] In his ILC reports, Bedjaoui made it clear that decolonizing states could and should ignore "devolution agreements"[177] (for instance, those decreed by France for Algeria) and acquired rights of oil concessions when concessions had been obtained during colonial times: then, they were inherently tainted by the colonists' lack of respect for the acquired rights of the colonial subjects (as the colonists, like Soustelle, often used the *terra nullius* doctrine to appropriate natural resources). Against the position that the French delegation had expressed during the negotiations at Evian, Bedjaoui claimed that it was precisely when the newly independent states were incapable of paying "just" reparations that the state needed to expropriate large private interests. Newly independent states could not accept the principle that all rights of foreign nationals should be compensated, as the "lands, the buildings, the transport, the industry, the trade companies, etc., belonged to private interests" during colonial administration, and thus, "compensating them for the loss of their property in case of nationalization would mean that the new state would have to buy its whole country back"[178] which would be economically impossible. In this case "the state would indebt itself in perpetuity, and even [if] the debt was distributed over a very long period, no budget could service such a debt." For Bedjaoui, newly independent states, whose *raison d'être* was the protection of the "vital interests of the nation"[179] (a very Gaullist notion found under Bedjaoui's pen), had the right to reject the sanctity of public treaties when the latter protected illegitimate private rights.[180] Otherwise, the situation would look very much like that of slaves "buying back their freedom."[181] The notion extended the kind of expropriation beyond the question of "unjust enrichment"[182]: with the notion of "vital interests," there was no longer any need for the nationalizing state to prove illegitimate acquisition, but just a need to prove the absolute economic need of such nationalization. In that sense, his program did not focus on the notion of "odious debt," which implied a notion of immorality, but extended to concern all kinds of unsustainable debts incurred by newly independent states: the criteria used to cancel sovereign debt were to be purely economic and political.

6 A WAY OUT OF THE DEADLOCK BETWEEN THE GLOBAL SOUTH AND NORTH? THE NOTION OF "GLOBAL SETTLEMENTS"

At the ILC, Bedjaoui's perspective was far from consensual, and the countries of the Global North strongly objected to the redistribution of property and debt between the Global North and the Global South, and from private companies to publicly owned national champions, that the NIEO entailed. The NIEO promoters' response to the North's objections was that if newly independent states were ready to consider compensating private concessions for the loss of their right to extract oil or gas or minerals, the discussion of the value of that compensation had to take place in the framework of what Bedjaoui called a "global settlement."[183] The latter was based on a comprehensive assessment of the value of nationalized properties at the time of the expropriation by the decolonizing nation, but also on the calculus of past benefits realized by private interests and chartered companies in the colonies, which were not reemployed for the good of the colonial subjects from whom profit was extracted. Thus, only if reparations were to be calculated based on a long-term view of the historical relations between metropolis and colonial territories was Bedjaoui in favor of entertaining compensations and reparations for the expropriation.

Turning the tables, Bedjaoui went even further as he cited the 1961 Declaration by the non-aligned states in Belgrade, which stated quite clearly that the decolonized states were in fact "creditor states" rather than "debtor states" toward the old metropolises.[184] As he asserted that colonial economies were largely extractive and exploitative, as the industrial development of the metropolises had depended upon the ability of colonial private interests to funnel profits toward the metropolis and to cut the local colonial populations off from the benefits of growth, the metropolis had "contracted a debt" with its colonies, such that the nationalization of private interests could be seen as a reparation paid by the metropolis to its colony. If the debtor state was the metropolis, private individuals who sought compensation should turn to their own state rather than to the new independent state.[185]

In the ILC, Bedjaoui's proposition to refer to such global settlements was favorably received among the other non-aligned members, who agreed to inscribe within the article on state succession in respect to property for newly independent states a clause on global settlements. Such clause introduced "the concept of the contribution of the dependent territory to the creation of certain movable property of the predecessor state ... so that such property should pass to the successor state in proportion to the contribution made by the dependent territory."[186] This principle meant for instance that, if Algeria was to settle claims by companies like French oil companies, French companies should also be accountable to claims by Algerian interests.

As the 1979 oil crisis further hit the global economy, consensus between the Global South and Global North became harder to reach on questions of international economic governance. In 1975, Mohammed Bedjaoui had worked on the project of a North–South conference to be organized in Paris when, as Algeria's Ambassador in Paris, he was in charge of organizing the official state visit of French President Valéry Giscard d'Estaing to Algeria; but this idea was abandoned after President Giscard d'Estaing's disappointing official visit, to later be taken up by Mexican President Lopez Portillo and Austrian Chancellor Bruno Kreisky. The North–South Summit which gathered the heads of state of twenty-two nations in Cancun in October 1981 – including President François Mitterrand, who had ruled Algeria as Minister of Interior in the 1950s – showed to the G77 representatives that the newly elected Anglo-American leaders, especially President Reagan, were not interested in talking about the reform of international economic governance, except when reform meant the implementation of neoliberal ideas, and the use of international financial institutions as vehicles for imposing budget cuts and austerity measures to the Global South as conditionalities to new loans. In Cancun, the representatives of the G77 were flabbergasted when they heard President Reagan tell them that he was the real revolutionary because he was in favor of market deregulation.[187] The irony of seeing a former movie star talk about economic revolution was not lost to the Algerian revolutionaries who had suffered from the French repression during their revolution. Thirty-five years later, it would be Emmanuel Macron, a former high civil servant who briefly worked for Bank Rothschild, who cut the ground from under the socialists' feet by launching his presidential campaign with a book titled *Revolution*: it seems that not only US but also French neoliberals like to fancy themselves as "revolutionaries."

Within the ILC, controversies lingered until Bedjaoui released his last report to the UN General Assembly, which decided in December 1981 to convene an international conference of plenipotentiaries to consider the draft articles of the international convention on succession of states in respect to state property, archives, and debts. The conference assigned to the Committee of the Whole the consideration of the draft articles adopted by the ILC. Mohammed Bedjaoui had a very important role in the debates as the special Rapporteur to the ILC on state succession.[188] Unsurprisingly, representatives of the Western states at the 1983 Vienna Conference, called to adopt (or reject) the resulting convention emerging from twenty years of ILC work, heavily criticized the legal doctrine of the NIEO, and more specifically, the principle of intransmissibility of state debts in the context of newly independent states. Western legal scholars and diplomats in the Committee of the Whole did not see how newly independent states could ground the principle of intransmissibility of debts on established practice, except in extreme circumstances. Furthermore, they questioned the link that Bedjaoui made between the cancellation of debts and the nationalization of public assets by newly independent states.

When the text of the final convention was debated in 1983, the former imperial states, led by the British and the French, expressed strong objections to clauses on "global settlements" that could open up reparation debates. The British delegate objected to the statement that newly independent states should inherit property outside their territory (in the territory of the metropolis) "in proportion to the contribution of the dependent territory" as the determination of such property would "require mathematical calculations that were practically impossible to carry out,"[189] thus leading to intractable controversies about reparations – a position which the Indian delegate criticized, but which the French delegate endorsed, as the latter also claimed that "the term 'contribution' lacked precision."[190]

The French delegate even proposed deleting the article on newly independent states, where delegates of the G77 had placed the only exception to the general principle that debts should be transmitted to successor states: the French representatives argued that it created exceptional rules for a category of states defined according to a "political" rather than "legal" criterion. He added that as the decolonization process was almost over, it had lost its relevance for dealing with future cases of state succession – a point which was rejected by the Algerian delegate and the other representatives of the Group of 77.[191] In so doing, the British and French delegates wanted to prevent the imperial history of their states from being open to scrutiny.

Already during the plenary conference the main lines of division appeared between the liberal doctrine of the Western states, which refused to sign, and the communist bloc and the non-aligned states (or Group of 77), which were in favor.[192] The US representative, for instance, justified his opposition due to "the extent and scale of the special treatment given to newly independent states and the unnecessary vagueness of the formulation of a number of provisions,"[193] on the question of debts. The British delegate clearly rejected the view that "the principle of permanent sovereignty over wealth and natural resources and certain so-called rights had the force of *jus cogens*."[194] To take one example that best represents the liberal doctrine on behalf of which the Western states mounted their opposition against the notions of the NIEO embodied in this Convention, it suffices to quote the interventions of the West German representative during the conference. Anticipating the rigid defense of the sanctity of private contracts that the German Finance Minister Wolfgang Schäuble would later express during the Greek debt crisis, the German delegate at the Vienna conference objected that a "conference like the present one, which attempted to formulate existing rules of customary international law and to reach agreements about rules of contractual international law [two different tasks] could not be fulfilled if it did not take into consideration the views of a substantial minority of states."[195] For him, the articles that related to the treatment of debts for newly independent states (article 38) – which affirmed that no "state debt of the predecessor state shall pass to the newly independent state, unless an agreement between them provides otherwise" (article 38.1), and that the "agreement referred to in paragraph 1 shall not infringe the principle of permanent sovereignty of every people over its wealth and natural resources, nor shall its implementation endanger the fundamental equilibria of the newly independent state" (article 38.2) – were particularly inacceptable, a position shared by the representatives of all Western states.

Among the articles on state property, the liberal West strongly objected to the reference to the inalienability of natural resources in newly independent states and the "principle of the permanent sovereignty of every people over its wealth and natural resources,"[196] as the latter represented the gravest threat to the sanctity of private contracts. As the US delegate remarked, he did not believe that article 15 was "an accurate statement of existing law and that its provisions should be accepted as progressive development of international law" – a position echoed by the Dutch delegate, according to whom the term "permanent sovereignty" was not a legal but a "moral" notion.[197] As the Canadian delegate said, the "value of a treaty that did not codify customary law but purported to create new rules, as was unquestionably the case with that convention, depended upon the degree of support it could command among states with different interests on the matter," and as the French delegate regretted, the method of work, which had consisted in voting on articles rather than seeking consensus had imperiled the whole work of the conference, by departing from the jurisprudence of international courts, like the International Center for the Settlement of Investment Disputes (ICSID), created in 1962 at the World Bank, which protected the interests of foreign investors' concerns against the risk of nationalization with no compensation.[198] For the Western representatives, the adoption of the Convention could have created a precedent that ICSID would have had to consider as it based its decisions on international standards rather than on existing national laws.[199]

The Algerian delegate tried to counterattack by arguing that the "principle of permanent sovereignty was already embodied in the 1978 Vienna Convention on Succession of States in Respect to Treaties"[200] and that the principles of "equitable compensation" were well-recognized principles of international law, and that it was only fair to take a broad view of compensation if the global negotiations were open; but from the discussion, no consensus emerged. As a last attempt to salvage the twenty years of work at the ILC, the Committee of the Whole tried to suggest that the Convention did not affect the private rights of oil concessions and other foreign companies operating in newly independent states. As Mohammed Bedjaoui remarked before delegates of the Committee of the Whole, "many speakers had expressed the fear that a successor state might seize property other than that which belonged to the predecessor state, for example, property of a third state or of private persons," but these (mostly Western) delegates should be reassured by the strict definition of *state* property enshrined in article 8, defined in accordance "with the internal law of the predecessor state."[201] The Convention explicitly recognized that "a succession of States does not as such affect the rights and obligations of creditors" (article 36), and as Bedjaoui remarked before the Committee of the Whole, the articles on state debt only concerned debts that "were governed by international *public* law and therefore excluded debts owed by the predecessor state to private creditors."[202] Furthermore, Bedjaoui added that the ILC was of the opinion that "transnational corporations [including oil corporations] were not subjects of international law" and were thus not concerned by the articles on the intransmissibility of debts from metropolitan states to newly independent states.[203] But Bedjaoui's demonstration was not sufficient to assuage the fears of Western delegates: the US delegate, for instance, doubted the validity of the argument that the

Convention protected private creditors, as by restricting itself to the succession of state-to-state financial obligations, it left private creditors with no other choice than to "resort to the general rules of customary international law, and those rules were highly intricate, complicated, often ambiguous and unclear."[204] Others argued that the historical context of the 1970s had suggested that nationalizations could take place with no fair and quick indemnity. [205]

On April 7, 1983, led by the states of the G77, the conference adopted the Vienna Convention on Succession of States in respect of State Property, Archives and Debts consisting of a preamble, fifty-one articles, and an annex. The Convention was opened for signature from April 7 until December 31, 1983, but it has not yet entered into force as it is missing the signature of key UN member states. In particular, the articles that concerned the succession of rights on property and debts in the case of "newly independent states" for which exceptional rules applied (articles 15 and 38, respectively) continued to be the most controversial, as can be seen from a brief survey of the objections of Western states to the Convention.[206] The Algerian delegate could only regret that Western states' "negative attitudes to an instrument which was fully in conformity with trends in the international community paralleled the uncooperative approach which had led to difficulties in the negotiations of the new international economic order,"[207] which by the time the 1983 Convention was open to signature, had lost all relevance since the election of President Reagan and Prime Minister Thatcher.

7 CONCLUSION

Until now, most historians of the NIEO have failed to relate the key concepts of the NIEO with the Gaullist conception of bilateral cooperation between postcolonial nation-states, especially, between France and its former oil-producing former colonies and overseas territories. Writing about Mohammed Bedjaoui in particular, Balakrishnan Rajagopal underlines, for instance, that he had, like "no international lawyer from the Third World, taken aim at the very nature of development and its linearity and progressivism,"[208] which may be right, but not precise enough to capture the key contribution of the NIEO.[209] It is true that Bedjaoui was characteristic of the NIEO scholars from the Third World who stopped viewing history's progress as gradual, linear and oriented toward the end goal of socioeconomic liberalism and democratic modernity. But Bedjaoui's main target was not the "modernization theory,"[210] which was elaborated by MIT political economist Walt Rostow (1916–2003) in his *Non-Communist Manifesto*[211] – whose influence in shaping the linear notion of "development" in the Anglophone world has indeed been crucial but almost inexistent in the French field of law; rather, it was the kind of forced bilateralism which he saw embodied in the Evian Agreements, and which imposed limits to the economic sovereignty of Algeria after it was granted its independence.

Still, while rejecting the notion of postcolonial bilateral cooperation, NIEO thinkers from Algeria didn't intend throwing out the concept of "cooperation" and gift exchange with the murky water of forced bilateralism between former metropolis and colonies. This is the reason why it is difficult to conclude that the NIEO thinkers were responsible for the downfall of the model of the gift in international law, which solidarists like Albert Sarraut, writing mostly on colonial law, had made fashionable in the interwar period. In many ways, the NIEO thinkers promoted an organization of the international system that was not unlike the one promoted in theory (but rarely achieved in practice) by solidarist thinkers who lauded the model of gift exchange as a method to organize relations between European nations or between colonies and their metropolis in the interwar era – the difference being that NIEO thinkers substituted the latter with the relations between independent states in the Global North and the Global South. This chapter thus confirms the conclusion of eminent international law scholars, who coined the "Third World Approach to International Law," like Anthony Anghie, Bhupinder Chimni, and Obiora Chinedu Okafor,[212] or next-generation scholars like Sundhya Pahuja, for whom the NIEO reformulation of sovereignty in "international law was neither still imperial nor newly liberatory – it was both."[213]

This chapter, thus, rehabilitates the attempt of NIEO thinkers to decolonize international law, or at least, end its alliance with colonial prospects. The NIEO thinkers not only defined a broad and ambitious new program for the Global South but also decolonized the solidarist thinking of interwar law scholars, by reformulating international economic relations on the basis of peoples' long-term needs, international trust, and gift exchanges, rather than on the short-term speculative logic of deregulated financial markets.[214] They revived the idea that gift exchanges work to create international solidarity, not only between sovereign parties but also between peoples and private actors: they proposed that newly independent states cement new contractual relationships with the Global North which would redefine long-term exchanges between commodity and industrial products, as well as engage in comprehensive sovereign debt renegotiation which NIEO thinkers coined as "global settlements."[215]

In fact, NIEO thinkers proposed that new international economic relations be grounded on real rather than fake gift exchanges;[216] that is, on long-term international relations based on trust between sovereign nations practicing reciprocal exchanges, rather than on contractual obligations between short-term-oriented profit-seeking private actors (metropolitan oil concessions), or on "cooperation agreements" by which former metropolises imposed a sustained cultural and economic domination upon their former colonial subjects.[217] The reciprocity the NIEO thinkers had in mind also involved some time lapse between the gift and the counter-gift: the Global North would be asked to give first by cancelling debts from their former colonies, in exchange for the gift of peace, stability, and sustainable development in the South, which would eventually benefit the North, as the

South would gain from the initial gift and then buy more goods from the North.[218] For these reasons, NIEO thinkers also promoted the wave of unilateral nationalization of oil companies carried out by Arab states, the cartelization of the oil trade with the creation of OPEC, and the rise in oil prices that would force the North to pay more for oil but that would also allow OPEC to redistribute part of their profits to the least developed countries through an OPEC fund.[219]

In the NIEO historiography, the importance of gift exchange as a model – when used to argue against neoliberalism – and counter-model – when the circulation of gifts was used to justify the bilateral cooperation that the Gaullist had in mind – is rarely underlined,[220] partly because its recycling in the field of international law by the postwar generation of realist scholars made the continuities with anthropological discourses on gift exchange hard to recognize. As this chapter demonstrated, these discontinuities were entrenched in the different trajectories followed by the metropolitan and colonial fields of international law before and after the Second World War, with the former taking off and the latter coming to an abrupt end after Algeria's independence in 1962. The shift from gradualism and pluralism (as found in the writings of Maussian legal anthropologists) to an association between the notion of gifts and an anti-colonial and realist conception of international relations reflected an original attempt to decolonize the model of gift exchange pioneered by international public law scholars who were taught in the metropolitan (rather than colonial) French field of law after the Second World War.

In so doing, this chapter offers a rebuke to hasty readings by post-development thinkers like Gilbert Rist, for whom "the NIEO did no more than reinforce the existing order of things."[221] Judging the NIEO from the surface, Rist indeed believes for instance that its promoters mainly reinforced the US-led discourse in which economic growth, expanding international trade and increased foreign aid to the Global South formed the three main objectives of the US policy toward the South since the famous publicization of the "Truman Doctrine" in 1947. For that reason, Rist concludes, "it is therefore fortunate that the NIEO was stillborn, everything having begun and ended on the same day, May 1, 1974,"[222] when the UNGA issued its Declaration. As a result of this misreading of the NIEO's main claims, it is not surprising to read under Rist's pen that, "far from closing the gap between center and periphery" as it proposed to do, "[the NIEO] actually widened it."[223] If the NIEO only had to offer a defense of rising prices of oil and other raw materials thanks to revised trade agreements, it would be fair to say that it indeed accentuated not only the division between Western states and developing states, but also the division between oil-producing countries and the least developed countries. But NIEO thinkers did not just want to strengthen the power of the oil-producing or rare-minerals-extracting countries, but to take the business of extractive industries outside of the realm of geopolitical conflicts and economic speculation, and turn it into an opportunity to arrive at a stable and peacefully negotiated compromise between creditor and lender states, complementing the overall scheme with special funds that would redistribute some of the profits generated to the least developed nations.[224]

Still, even if it had succeeded in establishing the 1983 Convention on Succession of States in respect of State Property, Archives and Debts, it is worth acknowledging conceptual limitations in Bedjaoui's work at the ILC and the associated NIEO program. In particular, some members of the ILC rightfully regretted that "the definition of the term 'newly independent state' ... [which was] restricted to cases in which the territory of the state had been a dependent territory immediately before the date of the succession of states" seemed to eliminate cases which there was no reason to exclude, such as the "emergence of a new state as a consequence of the separation of part of an existing state or from the uniting of two or more existing states."[225] In many ways, by creating rigid boundaries between different types of succession gathered into two broad groups (transfer, union, separation, and dissolution on one side, and newly independent states from Asia and Africa on the other side), and creating two opposite sets of rules for each group (as far as the issue of state debt was concerned), Bedjaoui restricted the principles of the NIEO to the newly independent states of Asia and Africa – most of which had already been through the process of independence at the time.[226] In doing so, he assumed implicitly that those state debts that could be deemed "odious" were those that exclusively fell on the shoulders of the "newly independent states" (since those were the intransmissible debts) and vice versa, so there was no need to add a separate discussion of the doctrine of odious debt as related to the other categories of state succession (transfer, union, separation, or dissolution) in other non-African and non-Asian contexts. NIEO scholars thus excluded the possibility of applying the principles they agreed upon for "newly independent states" to other states in the future, for instance, those that would secede, for instance, from the Soviet "Empire," first in Eastern Europe and then in the Balkans,[227] or from new currency zones like the Eurozone, when the case of Grexit began to be discussed in 2015. That may well have been a big mistake, which explains why his theory remains little used in the present-day debates about the sustainability and cancellability of the debts held by Cyprus, Greece, or other countries that have long suffered from a colonial or neocolonial domination.

With these limitations in mind, it is not surprising if direct references to the work of the ILC on state succession in matters of state debts and assets and to the NIEO more generally have largely been absent from more recent debates about the sovereign debts of developing nations from South Asia and Latin America, or in the case of the recent sovereign debt crisis in Greece. This is unfortunate, as Bedjaoui's contribution to the NIEO (with notions of "global settlement," "permanent sovereignty over natural resources" or the "principle of non-transmissibility of debts" in a postcolonial context) would prove much more useful to contemporary debt cancellation activists to defend their claims than Sack's doctrine.[228] We can thus only regret that Bedjaoui failed to associate his name with a new (and more progressive) doctrine of "odious debt": as some ILC members regretted, "although the question of odious debts had been discussed by the Commission ... and the Special Rapporteur's earlier proposals [were] quite interesting, no provisions relating to it had been included in the draft articles."[229] In fact, Bedjaoui's definition of "cancellable" debts emphasized the notion of their unsustainability, as he proposed to assess whether former debts should be cancelled or not based on economic and political rather than moral criteria.

Whether one believes that it is unfortunate that neoliberal prescriptions imposed themselves as the solution to the sovereign debt crises of the Global South in the 1980s or not, it is true that the combination of both dealt the NIEO a fatal blow. Still, calling it an utter failure would be wrong: indeed, the rise of the NIEO participated in disentangling the newly independent states from former imperial economic interests, and thus helped the former denounce the devolution agreements which, like the Evian Agreements in the case of Algeria, had organized the prolonged economic submission of former colonies to the power of colonial concessions. In so doing, it showed how international law could be used as a force for progress and revolution rather than as a conservative endeavor, whose main methodological precepts serve the purpose of ensuring continuity in the interpretation of international agreements, and thus, continued recognition of the debtor states' legal obligations that have been inscribed by European great powers in generations of international agreements since the colonial times.

In the history of ideas about global governance, the global mobilization of neoliberal intellectuals in favor of the deregulation of financial markets and the strengthened protection of the rights of private investors[230] has often taken all the attention, relegating the NIEO story to the dustbin of history.[231] The sovereign debt crises that have erupted since the 1980s certainly empowered the international financial institutions of Bretton Woods (the IMF and World Bank) and their Western state backers to impose neoliberal policies and stringent tools of monitoring and control upon the domestic policies of borrowing nations, especially in Africa, Asia, Latin America but now also in Europe.[232] As Sundhya Pahuja writes, it is true that the rise of the NIEO on the international stage in the 1970s was related to an "economic boom in the North, a concomitant rise in commodity prices, a brief moment of Third World unity brought on by the oil crisis, and finally a consequent sense of vulnerability of the North,"[233] followed by a quick downfall when the solidarity between oil producers and non-oil producers in the Global South dissolved as a result of the debt crises of the early 1980s, starting with the Mexican debt crisis of 1982. Except for Balakrishnan Rajagopal, who sees in the NIEO a story of relative institutional success,[234] the observed failure of the NIEO movement to stop the rise of such neoliberal ideas of global governance is indeed presented as the ineluctable result of a convergence between adverse external (economic and political) conditions rather than from inner intellectual flaws and contradictions, whose content is thus often left in the background.[235] Winners always get historians' attention, except when the odd genealogist attempts to recover the history of losers. But beyond the questions of whether the NIEO was successful or not, or why it was not, the progressive ambition that the NIEO thinkers have ascribed to international law certainly warrants that we pay more attention to its genesis in the Francophone context from which it arose.

7

International Solidarity and Gift Exchange in the Eurozone

Throughout the many iterations of this text, the full story told here has slowly emerged as I genuinely attempted to connect the many pieces of this complex transnational puzzle in the most objective manner. Writing such a transnational history requires that, like Penelope, we social science history scholars – or historical sociologists – no longer tell the story of Algeria and France as independent national histories of state formation, and that we unravel in the night the lines that we weave into our tapestry during the day. That being true, readers can understand why I find it enjoyable that the time has come to close, finish the weave, tie off the warp ends and hang the tapestry on a bookshelf.

But not so soon. It would be nice if my job as a historian would be over,[1] but readers should not conclude too quickly that the story of gift exchange as a model of global governance has ended with the failed attempt by Third World scholars to decolonize its ideological premises and concrete applications. The story of the gift exchange as a model of global governance did not end in the 1980s with the rise of neoliberalism and the worldwide liberalization of capital markets. It is true that in the 1980s creditor states massively exported neo-liberal economic policies through international financial institutions to the now-called "emerging world" with the zeal of non-practicing gurus – austerity in the service of debt repayment has always been better for the debtor states than for creditors, according to the creditor states. But before we leave the founding fathers of anthropology to rest, we can gain some last insights with a comparison between Mauss's reflections and the considerations about international economic governance expressed by contemporary French policymakers and economists who claim a filiation to Mauss and *The Gift*, and who have in fact criticized neoliberal theses both from a theoretical and political perspective.

The existence of such a filiation today may seem surprising, considering what I've said about the demise of the gift exchange as an epistemic model used in ethnology for the analysis of intersocietal exchanges with Pierre Bourdieu's successful bid to relocate the gift exchange to the local level. Indeed, the ethnologists who followed Pierre Bourdieu, and others who argued against him – like Jacques Godbout and

Alain Caillé and their Mouvement Anti-Utilitariste en sciences sociales (or MAUSS) – pay particular attention to forms of gift-making organized at the local level between individuals, and praise them for their generous motives when they engage in non-utilitarian forms of exchange.[2] I will not survey here the immense and often very interesting production related to the MAUSS, as I purposefully have limited my analysis to the history of the gift exchange conceived as a model of global or at least international governance.

But Mauss's essay seems, like a phoenix, to always rise from its ashes and appear in the most unlikely places. Mauss's latest influence on French ideologies of international governance emerged from an improbable terrain: the political debate about European financial governance in the post-Bretton Woods era and the related theoretical debate among French economists about the hypothesis of market efficiency. This debate opposed those "neoliberal" economists – broadly speaking – who welcomed the liberalization of capital markets because "free markets are efficient" and thus investors find the best productive niches when left unregulated; and those indeed "neo-Maussian" economists who argued that, on the contrary, financial markets only produce speculative bubbles built on thin air when the flow of capital and money is left free to move without concern for national borders. After the French ethnologists' turn to the local, it was thus the turn of these heterodox French economists to claim Mauss's analysis of gift exchange as one of the main inspirations for their interventions in debates on international and European financial governance.

Until now, I have tried to limit myself from multiplying excursions into contemporary politics, even though they could have made the story more appetizing. But now has come the time to analyze more explicitly how one could apply some of Mauss's reflections on gift exchange to contemporary debates about global and European economic governance. I will thus use the space of this conclusion to review, even if briefly, some of these so-called "Maussian" interventions, which I claim could in fact be better qualified as "neo-Soustellian" – even though these scholars do not draw direct inspiration from Soustelle – as these contemporary economists study constitutional and institutional mechanisms to contractualize gift exchanges into hard law. In this chapter, I will highlight similarities and differences between the recommendations of these French economic thinkers in the debate about eurozone governance and what Mauss may have articulated, should he have witnessed the sovereign debt crisis that not only affected Greece after 2009, but also the whole eurozone – which is still struggling to find a pathway leading Greece out of its sovereign debt impediment. In the following pages, I will claim that, just like the jurists of the NIEO tried to decolonize the model of the gift and requalify how it could be applied to shape North–South relations, the neo-Maussian model of European financial and budgetary integration that French economists have articulated in the debate on the eurozone governance should also be examined with a critical and decolonial perspective. If there is much value in the critical perspective that the notion of gift exchange offers to stem the spread of neoliberal ideas, we should also pay attention to the relations of domination that are obfuscated by the simple application of notions of budgetary, fiscal, or financial integration to the eurozone.

1 FRENCH SOCIALISM AND THE NEW FOUNDATION OF THE EUROPEAN UNION

The year for the beginning of this epilogue is 1993. This was the year when a heteroclite group of scholars based in Paris started meeting to discuss the anthropological and economic roles served by money, and the perspectives that could be developed out of a comprehensive and multidisciplinary analysis of money, especially in political societies where the bond between the nation-state and the issuance of currency is relaxed. These French scholars accepted the invitation extended by Michel Aglietta (1938–), André Orléan (1950–) and Jean-Marie Thiveaud (1947–2002), to meet every Friday afternoon, from 1993 to 1998, to discuss the anthropological, historical, and financial aspects of money, trust, and gift exchange – discussions which resulted in the collective volume *La monnaie souveraine*, edited by Aglietta and Orléan.[3] Aglietta and Orléan were two brilliant economists and former students of École Polytechnique and the French École Nationale de la Statistique et de l'Administration Economique (ENSAE) – two institutions that trained many high-level public servants working in the French Planning Commission, the Ministry of Economy and Finance, or the Banque de France[4] – and were fellow travelers of the socialist party. Their five-year long seminar was made possible by a generous grant of the Caisse des Dépôts et Consignations (CDC) – an independent state institution in charge of financing public investments – extended by Jean-Marie Thiveaud, who worked there as archivist and historical adviser of the director of the CDC, Robert Lion (1934–), a high public servant who had served for two years as the prime minister's economic adviser in the first socialist government of the Fifth Republic, which was constituted in 1981 after the election of François Mitterrand to the French presidency.[5]

It is not surprising that the book that resulted from these interdisciplinary conversations not only nurtured deeply theoretical ambitions, but also addressed issues very close to the preoccupations of the socialist government at the time. The date when these conversations started was not a coincidence: 1993 was one year after the Maastricht Treaty was signed. This treaty had momentous importance for European political societies, as it imposed strict limits on Europe's sovereign debt ceilings and annual budgetary deficits – respectively reduced to 60 percent and 3 percent of each country's gross domestic product (GDP). It also required all European states to renounce the right to devalue their currency and asked them to adopt fixed exchange rates – with all European currencies pegged on the mark of the reunified Germany. The mid-term goal was the formation of a common currency in Europe – what became the new currency known as the "euro," which every eurozone citizen started using in their daily transactions ten years later.

The Maastricht Treaty represented the last attempt by the socialist French President François Mitterrand to reign over international politics and decide the course of European history in the post-Cold War context.[6] According to Jacques Attali (1943–), who served as President Mitterrand's adviser for ten years, the Maastricht Treaty crystallized the bargain that the French president had put to Chancellor Kohl in 1989: the French Republic would agree to support the West German chancellor's efforts to accelerate the reunification of the two Germanies, but it insisted, first, that the reborn German nation-state would forever forego the production and possession of nuclear weapons and recognize the sacred character of the 1945 territorial frontiers – conditions that were agreed upon in the 1990 Treaty of Moscow – and, second, that Germany would relinquish its financial sovereignty and help France give to the European continent its first modern currency: the euro.[7] With the creation of the euro, Mitterrand and Kohl changed the rules of financial solidarity and political sovereignty in Europe.

The Maastricht Treaty thus represented a new foundation for the European Union: it initiated changes in the realms of finance and politics that were as profound and unexpected as those brought by the 1957 Rome Treaties to trade relations in Europe. Accepted by referendum in France, it tied the new German giant deeply to the European Union as well as hardened the rules of financial responsibility that all future eurozone countries were asked to respect. But the Maastricht Treaty was also the latest development in a decade of progressive elaboration of common financial rules for the European Union. It was supposed to tie up the loose ends of the European Monetary System (EMS), which had been introduced by Chancellor Helmut Schmidt and Valéry Giscard d'Estaing in 1978, in the context of the fluctuating exchange rates that followed President Nixon's 1971 decision to let the dollar float. Since 1979, the EMS imposed limits on how much the value of European currencies could vary, as it set up fixed but adjustable (within the small margin of plus or minus 2.25 percent) exchange rates among European countries. After the shock of rising oil prices in 1979, which convinced Giscard d'Estaing to adopt the EMS, and the speculative attacks that followed the election of a socialist president in France in 1981, President Mitterrand could have decided to leave the EMS. But instead, he devalued the franc three times during his first presidency, from 1981 to 1986, in order to remain within the authorized limits of the European framework.[8] His political and financial decisions remained steadily driven by his desire to conserve and strengthen the nascent European monetary order in order to isolate the European currencies from the speculative uncertainty of the post-Bretton Woods era. The Maastricht Treaty indeed was a large step on the road toward financial and political integration of Europe, as it not only fixed exchange rates, but also planned the creation of a common currency and imposed by treaty law some budgetary restrictions on all the future eurozone member states.

Its elaboration thus confirmed the pro-European orientation that President Mitterrand had maintained throughout his two terms.

This pro-European orientation of the French government in the 1980s and 1990s could have appeared surprising for the political commentators who did not remember the long political career of François Mitterrand, and who only saw in his ascent the result of skilled and pragmatic craftsmanship which led the French socialist party back to power – the party which Mitterrand had resuscitated in the late 1960s after the slow death of the old SFIO following the end of the Algerian War. Mitterrand's election, which was made possible by a temporary alliance between the French Communist and Socialist parties, closed the fifty-year parenthesis opened when Blum and Mauss took over the old SFIO in 1920 against the Communists who seceded. This party alliance could have meant that France, under Mitterrand's presidency, could be expected to be more neutral – in the sense of not wanting to heighten military tensions between the Soviet Union and the United States on the European continent, and not advancing on the road toward European integration, as the Soviet Union had always seen in the European Union project a program aimed at pushing economic liberalism and keeping Russia out of the affairs of the European continent.[9]

When he was elected president in 1981, Mitterrand was far from a newcomer in French politics: his election occurred after more than twenty years spent in political opposition, during which time he deleted most of the historical traces that associated his name with the Algerian history of colonial repression in the 1950s,[10] or with his collaboration with the government of Vichy, which favored Franco-German collaboration during the Second World War,[11] as well as his prewar involvement in rightwing proto-fascist movements. With the dissolution of the colonial field after 1962, which was accelerated with the rise of the ideology of the NIEO among former French and non-French colonies, Mitterrand managed to present himself as the wise old man who would lead the ideas of May 1968 to power, in a French metropolis that was more curious about its European neighbors than about its past overseas possessions. But this superficial facelift did not determine his actions as president: his direct experience of the Second World War, combined with his robust anti-Communism, drove his sturdy determination to accentuate pressure on the Soviet Union until the latter would eventually collapse, and led him to consistently side with the United States in all the major military confrontations between the East and West, from the Euro-missile crisis to the Iran–Iraq War and the first Gulf War. The events of 1989 gave Mitterrand the unlikely opportunity to prepare the conditions for what he foresaw as a new century of Franco-German peace sustained by tight financial cooperation between, and integration of, European central banks and finance ministries on the European continent. He saw it as his generation's duty to close the chapter that the Allied victory in the Second World War had opened in European history and to bring forth the reunification of Europe, in which a reunified Germany was no longer a threat but France's strongest economic, financial, and political partner.[12]

This necessity was well understood by a group of young left-wing technocrats who worked around Mitterrand, or around one of his closest advisers, Jacques Attali. Attali, before he became known for having chaperoned future President Emmanuel Macron when the latter entered politics in the 2000s, was one of the central forces in Mitterrand's presidential cabinets from 1981 to 1991, after which he became the founder and first Director of the European Bank for Reconstruction and Development – the only post-1989 international organization that included Russia in a club of European member states – and then a consultant, prolific author, and promoter of microfinance initiatives worldwide. Like many other high public servants, Attali graduated from Polytechnique – but also from the ENA – and quickly accessed Mitterrand's inner circle in the 1970s, after he expressed his admiration for Mitterrand, the only man he saw as capable of pushing de Gaulle out of power: Attali's distaste for the Gaullists came from the shock he had experienced of having to flee Algiers, where he had spent the first part of his life as the privileged son of a rich Jewish perfume merchant, who managed to relocate to Paris before 1962.[13] Attali was only one of the young and brilliant intellectuals in the future president's inner circle, along with Jean-Pierre Cot (1937–), the son of Pierre Cot, who had obtained a PhD in international law under the supervision of Suzanne Bastid-Basdevant – who helped Mitterrand run for president both in 1974 and in 1981. Cot became one of the youngest ministers of the Fifth Republic in 1981, as Minister of Cooperation and Development – a position he kept for only a year, during which he prepared Mitterrand's participation for the Cancun conference of 1981,[14] until he resigned when realizing that Mitterrand was intent on maintaining intact the neocolonial relations between France and its former possessions in Africa. Conversely, Attali never accepted to become a minister. Instead, he remained in the Elysée Palace where he worked as President Mitterrand's powerful adviser, in charge of international economic and military affairs, especially in Europe and North America.

During the entire decade from 1981 to 1991, Attali consistently argued before President Mitterrand and against some of the ministers that France should remain within the EMS rather than let the franc float like the dollar, despite the social sacrifices that such a pro-European policy entailed at the time, especially when the franc was the object of various speculative attacks. After 1985, the French President also had a key ally in the European Commission (EC) when it came to negotiations within the French government about European and financial policies. Indeed, despite the fact that it was the turn for a German official to occupy the post, Mitterrand obtained the nomination of Jacques Delors (1925–) to the presidency of the EC in 1985 – a post Delors kept until 1995. A Christian democrat, Delors had been Mitterrand's Finance Minister from 1981 to 1985, after having served as a high civil servant in the French Planning Commission[15] and a member of the Governing Board of the Banque de France in the 1970s.

These men's pro-European orientation may look surprising for an observer of French socialist history, who certainly remembers the opposition of the old SFIO against the Atlanticist and liberal orientations of the European integration projects pushed by Jean Monnet and some of his associates, like René Pleven, who had (unsuccessfully) presented the European Defense Community Treaty to the French Parliament in 1954, where it was killed by the French socialists.[16] Since the beginning, the old SFIO nourished skepticism toward the European Community project, which it saw as the creation of industrialists, bankers, and liberal statesmen, who were more inspired by liberal and Christian democratic values than by left-wing ideals. But, in the 1950s, neither Mitterrand, nor Attali (who was too young to have a political opinion), nor Delors were members of the SFIO: Mitterrand had been the president of the Union démocratique et socialiste de la Résistance (UDSR), a small center-right party that he and Pleven had created; Delors went to work at the Planning Commission for most of the 1960s, where Monnet's ideas and framework of action were being put into action. If these men represented the socialist governmental coalition in the 1980s, their socialism had different roots than the old SFIO cardholders who had defended the Fordist model of high wages for workers, and its extension to Algeria, against the integration of the French economy into competitive European markets.

Still, these men considered themselves to represent voices from the left, and Attali especially, who was more an intellectual than a statesman, embedded their political ideas in the socialist intellectual past, marked by the stellar figures of Jaurès and Blum. In the 1970s, while teaching at Polytechnique and working to prepare Mitterrand's presidential campaigns, Attali wrote various essays with his colleague Marc Guillaume in which the two young economists criticized the misplaced simplicity and the unrealistic assumptions of neoclassical economics, which they blamed for the rise of the "monetarist" perspective – according to which states should intervene in the economy only to make the mass of money created predictable to unregulated financial markets – in the United States, leading to the demise of the Bretton Woods system with the end of gold–dollar fixed convertibility, the push for the deregulation of capital markets and the unraveling of welfare state spending.[17] Although Attali and Guillaume's language, which was inspired by systems theory and a few anthropological references, minimally influenced Mitterrand – who told Attali that his books were hardly readable[18] – their essays gave a wide public audience to academic writings that chastised the utilitarian logics of the neoliberal ideas of the Chicago School of economics whose monetarist views were being experimented in Latin America, after the US-backed coup of General Pinochet in Chile.[19]

2 FROM GIRARD TO MAUSS: WHEN ECONOMISTS REINTERPRET THE NOTIONS OF "RECIPROCITY" AND "GIFT EXCHANGE"

Among the young "socialist" intellectuals who criticized the rise of deregulated financial markets and the monetarist ideas associated with neoliberalism, Jacques Attali was certainly one of the most well-known public figures, but Michel Aglietta was one of most respected voices in this complex nebula, whose reach extended far beyond the strict confines of the French socialist region and well into the French pro-European movement at the French Planning Commission and the Banque de France. While leading a brilliant academic career as a professor of economics at the University Paris-Nanterre, he maintained important positions first in the French Planning Commission in the 1960s, and later in the most important French think tank specialized in international economic relations – the Centre d'Etudes Prospectives et d'Informations Internationales (CEPII). At the CEPII, which was created in 1978 to renew the French long-term economic thinking, Aglietta worked on various forecasts that anticipated the effects of a globalized economy on the French economy, and the advent of the euro on European economies – in parallel, he served as an adviser to the Banque de France.[20] Like Attali, Aglietta tried to renew the interdisciplinary discussion by extending it in the direction of anthropology, where he found new ideas to intervene in policy discussions on European financial governance after 1993.

The French academic scene is sometimes a village, and it will not come as a surprise that some of the men who were gathered by Michel Aglietta from 1993 to 1998 to develop a genuinely interdisciplinary perspective on currency formation, and on the relations between financial solidarity and political sovereignty, were related to some of the characters with whom readers are now familiar. Indeed, the group not only included economists, of course, but also philologists, financial historians, and a few anthropologists. Among the anthropologists, we find for instance Marcel de Coppet's son, Daniel (1933–2002), who was raised in Madagascar where his father was named governor general just before the Second World War: Daniel de Coppet later worked under Claude Lévi-Strauss on a dissertation on gift exchanges in Melanesian islands, before continuing his career as an anthropologist at the EHESS.[21] The philologist in the group was Charles Malamoud (1926), whose family had fled to France from Romania in the 1930s, and who married Léon Blum's granddaughter, Catherine Blum (1928–96), before working under the supervision of Emile Benveniste (1902–76) and becoming the holder of the chair of Indian philological studies at the EPHE, following in the footsteps of Mauss's PhD adviser, Sylvain Lévi.[22]

Jean-Michel Servet, my former colleague at the Graduate Institute, who brought his knowledge of post-independence African financial history to the group of neo-Maussian economic thinkers,[23] makes a clear distinction between the participants who came from anthropology or philology and who entertained a long and deep relationship with Mauss's essay *The Gift* – in which group he included himself, as he discovered Mauss's text thanks to his mentor in Lyon, Jean Marie Auzias (1927–2004), and then continued to discuss notions of gifts and sharing in the context of activities organized by the Cultural Center Thomas More in Lyon[24] – and the more technocratic elites like Michel Aglietta, André Orléan, and Bruno Théret – an engineer from École Centrale, who worked for fifteen years at the Ministry of Finance before becoming a renowned economic historian – who were less interested in Marcel Mauss's sometimes-confusing anthropological writings.[25] In fact, the economists who organized these meetings with anthropologists in the post-Maastricht context were less interested in Mauss's ideas than in the model of antagonistic mimetism developed by René Girard (1923–2005), a Catholic literary theorist and anthropologist. For Servet, Mauss's long historical footnotes bored the young economists who preferred the elegance of Girard's stylized model, which emphasized the essentially antagonistic nature of mimetic desire.[26]

Thus, to understand how Mauss's model of the gift was reappropriated by economists in the post-Maastricht debates on financial European governance, one needs to know more about the philosophy that René Girard developed on the mimetic nature of man's desire, which he discovered by commenting, first, French canonical novels,[27] and then the Bible and biblical commentary.[28] Indeed, from Mauss, French economists took only the notion that some exchanges, which Mauss called "gift exchanges," are particularly "antagonistic," as in Mauss's explanation of the potlatch.[29] But for Aglietta and Orléan, the reason why these specific exchanges were antagonistic had less to do with the politics of war and peace between sovereign communities and political societies – as in *The Gift* – than with particularly individual psychological features that emerge in specific forms of market exchanges: in particular, in financial markets. Here was the psychological reason for the violent antagonism between exchanging partners on speculative markets: when sellers of a specific commodity (or currency) can also act as buyers of the same commodity, as Girard explains well, "the annihilation of rivals is then the product of this confusion between twins." Indeed, so Aglietta and Orléan added, "anyone who seeks in the Other her model can only meet an obstacle, who in reflection, sends him back the image of his own desire."[30] This is the case when financial speculators manipulate the mimetic desires of other market agents, who can both sell and buy goods (gold or diamond, paper or now crypto currencies, real estate, or artistic goods, etc.), and who then turn these goods into fetishes whose price is no longer fixed by their use value for the customers who are likely to buy them, but by the expected profit that buyers hope to make once they resell them for money, especially during bubbles or panics.

To understand the origins of the desire to obtain the goods owned by someone else, even despite a lack of strong use value, Aglietta and Orléan used René Girard's notions of "antagonistic mimetism" and "mimetic desire."[31] Indeed, they wrote "antagonistic mimetism" or "reciprocal violence lets the desire of exchange participants float without fixing itself on a specific object."[32] The intellectual debt that these French economists owed to Girard was already apparent in the first book, titled *La violence de la monnaie*, that Aglietta and Orléan published together in 1982, as well as in the collection that Jacques Attali edited, and for which Attali wrote a laudatory preface in which he praised his colleagues for their efforts to move beyond Marx's and Walras's theories of value, and to ground economic thinking on a more complex anthropological theory of desires.[33] Focusing on antagonistic mimetism and speculative logics led Aglietta and Orléan to break away not only from Marx's theory of value but also from the kind of Walrasian "neoclassical" subjective view of value,[34] which postulates that exchange participants are always rational, in the sense that they pay for merchandise at the price that is commensurate with the subjective utility they would derive from the consumption of equally useful goods.[35]

Their indirect reading of Mauss through the philosophy of Girard thus completely changed the interpretation that French scholars have given to the notion of gift exchange until then, as the latter was no longer a solution to the problem of international order – or a solution to the disorders created by globalized financial markets – but now part of the problem to be solved: these extraordinary forms of exchange that were premised on an antagonism between exchanging partners, like gift exchanges, were precisely what these French economists feared would grow in the neoliberal era, with the deregulation of financial markets. To them, these antagonistic and mimetic processes that proliferated in unregulated financial markets were precisely the kind of processes that could only be tamed thanks to re-regulation, as the Maastricht Treaty ambitioned to do by creating a common currency zone.

Based on the distinction between rational desires and mimetic desires, Aglietta and Orléan introduced the idea that there are in fact two kinds of market exchanges. First, there are those market exchanges in which market participants are clearly distinguished, with sellers on one side and buyers on the other, and where speculative logics are indeed limited, as buyers settle on prices according to the logics of neoclassical Walrasian economics. Then, market relations are pretty harmonious: unhappy buyers can walk away from greedy sellers, who are punished by immediate market sanctions (loss of gains or reputation). In these ordinary markets, money then serves its role as a unit of commensuration and as a transparent intermediary for merchandise exchanges.[36] Second, there are those market exchanges in which participants have "reciprocal" positions – a Maussian term, but here understood in a non-Maussian manner – in the sense that they are both buyers and sellers at the same time.[37] When buyers and sellers occupy "reciprocal" (in the sense of interchangeable) positions,[38] their situation vis-à-vis one another is intrinsically antagonistic. They can only make profit if the others lose money, either because they have sold too quickly during a bubble, or too late during a panic. This situation is typically what happens in financial markets, which started to grow tremendously in the 1970s and 1980s as a result of the deregulation of capital movements, and where the opportunities to act both as seller and buyer of the same financial instrument – e.g. recycled debts – became a great source of instability.[39] In these markets, as Aglietta and Orléan write, "everything conspires to re-create rivalries between twins, the convergence of desires on the same object and the symmetry between subject and rival."[40]

The opposition between ordinary and financial markets, in some sense, could map onto the opposition that one finds in *The Gift*, between ordinary exchanges and gift exchanges – where the sovereignty of the parties of the exchange is at stake, as a refusal to partake in the exchange of debts and accept gifts can be interpreted as a decision to go to war.[41] The rise of speculative market logics, which dominated after the collapse of the Bretton Woods rules, explains why French economists believed it was urgent to develop a new intellectual framework to explain bubbles and panics in financial markets. From 1981 to 1983, and then again in 1992, speculative attacks repeatedly tested the resistance of the new European system of pegged currencies (the nascent EMS), forcing devaluations of the franc and creating tensions within governments – including the French, but also the Italian government, in which various positions on the EMS coexisted – as well as panics among small investors. To explain these deleterious dynamics,[42] Aglietta and Orléan found that Girard's anthropological reflections on antagonistic mimetism – and Mauss's notion of gift exchange, to the extent that it could be related to the latter – could bring important complementary insights to neoclassical economics.

Published fifteen years after their 1982 book, Aglietta and Orléan's second volume, titled *La monnaie souveraine*, which resulted from their conversation with anthropologists and philologists, gave an even more visible presence to Mauss's model of gift exchange, even if their theories of "antagonistic mimetism" did not profoundly change as a result of these discussions. The reference to Mauss's model of antagonistic gift exchange, which they reinterpreted in largely unorthodox (and Girardian) ways, presented two advantages. First, the little attention Mauss paid to relations of domination in the sphere of production, combined with his exclusive focus on the rules of trade and gift exchange, and the fact that Mauss was a canonical reference of the non-Communist left because of his involvement in the French socialist party of Jaurès, allowed Aglietta and Orléan to remain at a safe distance from the Marxist tradition, which, after the collapse of the Soviet Union, was not the most attractive influence to claim. Still, and second, while not being tainted by any Communist appropriation, the reference to Mauss anchored their research closer to the left, whereas René Girard, a French Catholic philosopher expatriated at Stanford, was far from being a recognized trademark in French left-wing circles. Thus, using Mauss's name to refer to a Girardian notion of "mimetic antagonism" offered many political advantages in the French academic and political fields.

But Aglietta and Orléan introduced a subtle but profound change of meaning to the Maussian notion of gift exchange. The distance between Mauss and Girard was obliterated by Aglietta and Orléan when they put the two authors in the same theoretical boat. It was as far a reading of Mauss as one could possibly imagine, and not a small paradox, to claim that Mauss's notion of antagonistic exchanges could be used precisely to define the operations of speculative markets between "twins." Mauss insisted, especially in his writings in *The Nation*, that the notion of gift exchange serves to understand heterogeneous systems of international trade and finance in which contracting parties are characterized by very different forms of political sovereignty (from tribes to empires and nation-states). Furthermore, remember that Mauss had originally developed his model to provide a paradigm of international financial relations that could isolate Europe's political economies from the speculative attacks waged against European currencies, and through which European trade centers could build sustainable and mutually advantageous relations with their non-European Others in the colonies. It is hard to see how Mauss's prescription that states should follow the logic of the gift when exchanging debt obligations and other services known as "prestations" could have been applied to describe operations of unregulated markets in a world in which currencies were free to float at a value fixed by the rational or whimsical – but always speculative – expectations of private capital market actors. But so do circulating references travel across disciplines: sometimes, they produce both misinterpretations as well as interesting new meanings when they are used by to intervene in distant disciplinary debates.

3 THE EUROZONE AT RISK: A GREEK TRAGEDY IN MAASTRICHT

Even if their reading of Mauss proved hugely paradoxical, Aglietta and Orléan proposed solutions that seemed to converge with the political recommendations that Mauss and Blum had expressed in the 1920s, when they wrote about the speculative attacks against the franc and the mark in the 1990s, and the need for European financial cooperation against the international contagion of fears. In 1924, when massive speculation was waged against sovereign currencies, Mauss lauded the renewal of old alliances through noncontractual forms of gift exchange, which took the form of joint action by the Banque de France and the Lazard Frères bank to buy up francs on Austrian and Italian financial markets where speculators attacked the French currency. In central banks, we trust! That could be the motto of all Maussian theorists.

In 1982, as the election of President Mitterrand was followed by waves of speculative attacks, Aglietta and Orléan similarly insisted on the necessity to strengthen the role of central banks as lenders of last resort. In case of panics, the value of a currency cannot be guaranteed against the value of collaterals held by private citizens and public authorities in the vaults of their banks.[43] Indeed, during panics, financial intermediaries face a choice between two alternatives: they can either accentuate the turbulence by selling quickly what they anticipate to be increasingly "bad debts," which entails the risk that they devalue further the capital of their debtors, as the latter include the same bad debts in their accounting books; or they can seek help from a lender of last instance (e.g. the central bank) to refinance their bank by monetizing, or mutualizing, their losses.[44] As Aglietta and Orléan insisted in all of their writings, central banks are needed not only to calculate the right amount of monetary creation during normal times (in a counter-cyclical manner), but also, and especially, during international panics, to restore trust in the ability of nations to honor their debts.[45] Only a central bank acting as a lender of last resort can monetize the unsolvable debts of a community, ensure the loyalty of creditors, and save the financial system from a crisis of confidence.[46] If no lender of last resort exists to back a currency in times of crisis, then nations lose their "monetary sovereignty"[47] and their power to stop financial panics from degenerating into all-out destruction of wealth.

Based on this core idea, which runs through all their work, these economists expressed their ambivalence toward the new governance structure planned for the eurozone by the 1993 Maastricht Treaty, as well as subsequent treaties like the 2007 Treaty on the Functioning of the European Union (TFEU), later integrated into the 2007 Lisbon Treaty. For Michel Aglietta, financial integration offered a welcome response to the general deregulation of capital flows in Europe, but it also created at least two major vulnerabilities for Europe's financial stability.

First, the Maastricht Treaty increased financial cooperation, but it did not turn the European Union into a real European federal compact, with mastery over the issuance of its debt and the control of its budget.[48] Marcel Mauss never addressed the topic of budgetary integration in his writings on international financial cooperation, but in 1958, Jacques Soustelle had already warned French policymakers and economists that if the French metropolis did not integrate in a common budget the expenses that the French Republic planned to spend to develop the Algerian economy, there was no point in fighting to keep Algeria in a common currency zone with metropolitan France, and in the integrated French Republic he wished to defend. Half a century later, it seemed that this lesson, applied to European integration, had been forgotten by the eurozone's architects. Indeed, it was the committee that elaborated the drafts of the Maastricht Treaty, set up by EC President Jacques Delors, which called on European member states to address the problems of a single market of financial services in February 1986 (in the Single Act), by adopting a common currency, without a fiscal compact. For the "Delors committee" members, the decade-long experience of the EMS, which worked relatively well when the value of the deutsche mark – and thus of the other European moneys, which were pegged on the mark – was low, seemed to suggest that a quasi-monetary zone could function without common budgetary policy.[49] By abandoning the objective of true budgetary integration, the EC had aligned its views with the dominant monetarist ideology, and departed from recommendations in its own previous reports.[50] This decision was viewed as a tragic mistake by Aglietta, who believed that the eurozone thence condemned its most vulnerable parts, which would sink if capital started to massively move from Europe's periphery to its German core (as ultimately happened, beginning in the 1990s). Looking back on the Maastricht Treaty after the 2009 financial crisis in the eurozone, Aglietta concluded in 2013 that if presidents Delors and Mitterrand could be lauded for having engineered a "great strategic success" at Maastricht, they could also be blamed for having created a flawed architecture which "led to the European tragedy twenty years later."[51]

Second, and equally important, it was planned in the post-Maastricht deliberations that the future European Central Bank (ECB) of the eurozone was not supposed to serve the function of lender of last resort. Whereas national central banks could issue more paper money and thus monetize public debts in the 1980s, with the advent of the euro, these national central banks relinquished their power to act as lenders of last resort, as no one planned for the ECB to buy at low rates the public debt issued by its member states. For instance, in 2010, based on this reading of the ECB statutes, the first ECB President, Jean-Claude Trichet, refused to buy sovereign bonds that Greece needed to issue to refinance, when financial markets were convinced that Greece would eventually default on its debt and when private actors no longer bought Greek bonds, except at usurious rates.[52] Not surprisingly, the constrain imposed this legal restriction was later released in 2012 by the second ECB President, Mario Draghi; when the continuing Greek crisis threatened to extend from Greece and Portugal to Italy and France, President Draghi announced a policy called "quantitative easing," which allowed the ECB over the next four years to inject more than €1 trillion in the eurozone, which helped keep the sovereign bonds issued by eurozone member states (with the notorious exception of Greece)[53] at interest rates close to zero or even negative.

The creation of the euro on such feeble foundations thus seemed a tragedy to neo-Maussian economists, as the European zealots were immediately warned that the architecture of the new European Union founded in 1993 was deficient.[54] Indeed, the Maastricht Treaty architects justified their decision to create a disempowered ECB based on the alleged success of the EMS in the mid-1980s, precisely at the time when financial speculation proved that an EMS-like model of governance failed to protect European economies during financial panics. When, before Maastricht, Chancellor Kohl decided to convert East German marks at parity with West German marks – a very political decision that did not reflect the dire economic differences in the former two Germanies[55] – he allowed German citizens from the East to consume otherwise inaccessible West German products, but he increased inflation and unemployment in the Eastern parts of the reunified Germany. To end unemployment in Eastern Germany, the German Central Bank unilaterally increased interest rates, which attracted capital into Germany and out of countries like Spain (initially with high interest rates), Italy (with huge budget deficits and rising interest rates which only aggravated such deficits), and the United Kingdom (hit by a severe real estate crisis), thereby aggravating economic crises elsewhere in Europe. Predicting a drop in the value of the pound and Italian lira, the financial speculation against the pound started by George Soros revealed the lack of monetary cooperation between the German and British central banks: the speculation forced the pound and the lira to leave the EMS in the fall of 1992. When the attacks then moved to the franc, its fixed parity with the mark was first defended by Franco-German initiatives in late 1992. But when speculation started again in July 1993, the French Central Bank could no longer defend the franc due to its lack of foreign reserves, leading to the decision that currencies would fluctuate within margins of plus or minus 15 percent within the EMS.[56] Thus, the EMS imploded because of the "incompatibility between free capital movements, fixed exchange rates and the absence of cooperative economic policies."[57] The lesson was clear, but its validity was denied, or forgotten, by the Euro-zealots who campaigned for the adoption of the Maastricht Treaty.

As Aglietta and Brand write, it is fascinating to see that the speculative attacks against Greece, Ireland, or Italy, which occurred when markets started asking much higher rates for the purchase of their sovereign bonds, mimicked the 1990s attacks against the British pound, the Italian lira, and the French franc.[58] In 2009, in the wake of the disastrous financial crisis that hit the United States first and then the rest of the world, the financial markets succeeded in provoking a major panic, bringing Greece to its knees before moving on to Ireland, Portugal, and Spain. The analogy between the 1992–1993 crisis and the 2008–10 crisis is almost perfect; one must only change the names of the four countries to reveal the same sequence of events: 2009 Greece played the role of 1992 Italy; and 2009 Ireland, Portugal, and Spain that of the 1992 United Kingdom.[59] But whereas in 1992–3, the EMS allowed states under attack to leave the common framework, leading to its implosion, after the creation of the eurozone, such temporary "exit" strategies were no longer an option – although certain country creditors, like Germany, and its Finance Minister Wolfgang Schäuble, may have wished such options existed.[60] This legal rigidity, combined with the fact that Greece's ability to reimburse its debt was not adequately assessed, neither by European institutions nor by credit rating agencies,[61] meant that markets did not see the eurozone as providing any credible solution to the Greek financial problems until a comprehensive (but still insufficient) institutional reform was adopted, which reinforced the principle of financial solidarity among eurozone member states.

Fifteen years after the Maastricht Treaty, the institutional architecture that was supposed to ensure European financial solidarity in times of crisis proved too fragile to protect the weakest eurozone member states from the new wave of speculative attacks. In 2009, the panic started when it was revealed that Greece had vastly underestimated its budgetary deficit and debt-to-GDP ratio (capped at 3 percent and 60 percent), thus clearly violating the golden rules of the Maastricht Treaty. Found in noncompliance with eurozone treaty rules, financial markets panicked when the ECB President, Jean-Claude Trichet, claimed that, contrary to what they had expected, he was unable to help Greece by buying Greek debt on primary markets – as that would allow Greece, which was seen as a delinquent state by the German Finance Minister, to force the ECB to create money. Faced with this disastrous announcement, in early 2010, the other eurozone member states reluctantly agreed to extend new loans to buy back (in proportion to their GDP) Greek debt on a state-to-state basis, although at high interest rates (close to 5 percent) and with short maturities – at a time when countries like Germany or France borrowed at rates close to zero, and could thus make some profit out of this program, if Greece did not default, of course. This Securities Markets Programme (SMP) left France and Germany more exposed than other eurozone member states, which was only fair, as the coordinated rescue program allowed the two countries enough time for French and German systemic banks, which owned massive amounts of "junk" Greek bonds, to sell the latter on the secondary market, and thus avoid bankruptcy and forced nationalization – as had happened in the United States when the Obama administration was forced to buy the financial giant AIG for about $180 billion (approximately the level of Greek public debt at the time of writing, ten years after the crisis). From 2010 to 2012, the SMP gave these Franco-German banks time to reduce their exposure to Greek debt, after which the eurozone governments forced the remaining private creditors in possession of Greek bonds to accept a €37 billion haircut on the value of the bonds.[62] While this package represented a small cut for the private sector, considering that Greece's ability to repay the €110 billion that European creditors extended to Greece in 2011 was very much dubious at the time, public authorities were signaling to the markets that they were not ready to see European banks collapse as a result of too optimistic – if not aggressive – lending practices.[63]

Still, as Greece went into a deep economic and humanitarian crisis, which contributed to the 2015 election of the left-wing party Syriza, the ECB pushed the lack of solidarity to its limits: eurozone finance ministers and ECB President Mario Draghi did not accept any haircut on the SMP bonds bought on the secondary market, even though the Greek payments generated more than €7 billion of profit for the eurozone central banks over the 2015–18 period. After the election of Syriza, the ECB president refused to give these profits back to Greece to pay other loans, in violation of the initial promise made by the eurozone finance ministers to the negotiators of the "haircut" accepted by private creditors. As Eric Toussaint writes, the eurozone member states indeed did not show much solidarity with the Greek people.[64]

The European reaction to the Greek crisis revealed the extent to which the Maastricht Treaty architects had failed to plan for the mere possibility that a eurozone member state could, one day, find itself insolvent. As a result of their lack of foresight, when the financial crisis hit Greece, the proper structure of incentives to induce eurozone cooperation with the insolvent member of the

European family was lacking. The blindness of the Maastricht Treaty founders came in large part from their legalistic culture. Indeed, from a purely legal point of view, the Maastricht Treaty seemed self-sufficient. As it imposed the golden ceilings of 3 percent budgetary deficit and 60 percent debt-to-GDP ratio, no treaty signatory should ever default on its debts, as long as it respected the conservative spending treaty terms, which meant there was no need to add to the common currency a common European lender of last resort. Planning for the latter would have meant that the Maastricht Treaty architects planned that countries could be found in noncompliance of their treaty commitment – heresy for a lawyer.[65] Thus, in the midst of the Greek crisis, the eurozone leaders realized that the finance ministers in the Eurogroup and the ECB president lacked the necessary instruments to fight the crisis, which is why heads of state sitting in the European Council then agreed to create, by treaty, various structures that would complement the Lisbon Treaty.

The institutional response to the Greek crisis was driven by the notion that the crisis had purely financial origins, which did not require eurozone member states to adopt a common budget in order to fight the increasing economic divergence in the eurozone. A new structure known as the European Stability Mechanism (ESM) was created, which in 2012 replaced the European Financial Stability Mechanism that had been created in the midst of the crisis, to which eurozone member states committed up to a limit of €500 billion in order to fend off future solvency issues in the eurozone. After its creation, and as the Greek crisis worsened – in large part because of the austerity measures which the "Troika" of international financial institutions (the ECB, the EC, and the IMF) had imposed on Greece since 2010 – the ESM started lending to Greece at a rate much more beneficial for Greece than the creditor states who participated in the SMP, and with much longer maturities, which meant that the operation of the ESM offered a semblance of financial solidarity in the eurozone.

In addition to the ESM, the Greek crisis, followed by the Cypriot crisis, convinced the eurozone states to form a Banking Union, as banks started to reevaluate the value of their collaterals (usually comprising government bonds, such as Greek bonds), as well as those of other banks in the midst of the crisis. Due to banks' reluctance to assess the devaluation of their own assets suffered as a result of the Greek crisis, the EC ordered eurozone member states to ensure full transparency on the value of the assets held by European banks. The exercise was largely aimed at creating a self-reassuring image of the European banking sector, as "stress tests" organized in 2011 did not even plan for the possibility of a Greek default.[66] With these tests, the EU aimed at avoiding the transformation of the solvency crisis in Greece into a liquidity crisis: if banks stopped trusting each other's capacity to meet payments, then the whole interbank system of credit could have suddenly ceased to function, provoking a huge liquidity crisis. A few years later, in 2014, collective reflection led to the adoption of another European treaty which created the Single Resolution Mechanism (SRM), by which eurozone regulators sought to steer an orderly restructuring of private banks – some of which had nearly gone bankrupt as a result of the Greek sovereign debt crisis – should they be affected by another crisis of solvency in the European Union. European banks were also asked to diversify the kinds of sovereign debt obligations in their portfolio and raise capital requirements.

Adding the ESM as a (limited) lender of last resort for countries with solvency issues, helping those economies that were underperforming but were still largely solvent with the ECB program of quantitative easing,[67] and creating a Banking Union with the SRM to restructure possibly bankrupted private financial institutions represented three complementary aspects of the coordinated response given by the eurozone creditor states to the Greek crisis. In many ways, their creation worked to tame the financial speculation on the downfall of Portugal, Spain, and Ireland: the latter did not suffer as much as Greece as they benefitted from stronger protections offered by the new mechanisms. In many ways, the case of Greece stands out as a particularly bad example of mismanagement by the eurozone authorities, for reasons that were as much institutional as political. First, Greece was indeed, the first to suffer, and as the eurozone gained experience in crisis management with this case, it learnt from its mistakes and was better able to channel solidarity efforts to help Portugal, Spain, and Ireland recover from the crisis. Second, political reasons also explained the continuation of the human disaster in Greece, as the conservative governments of the eurozone wished to make an example out of Greece, by punishing a people who had dared to elect a radical left-wing party with harsh austerity measures that were doomed to fail.[68]

Still, for Maussian French economists, even if the new structures may have temporarily halted the toxic progress of financial panics, none of the eurozone responses addressed the economic roots of the problem: the divergence between the economic performance in the center and periphery of the European Union, which was spurred by the free flow of capital in a eurozone that lacked budgetary integration. It was not a surprise if, even after the passing of austerity packages, the Greek disaster continued to worsen: rather than coming back to Greece to invest resources, capital market actors anticipated that austerity packages alone – without redistribution from the richer to the poorer regions of Europe – would fail to restore Greece's ability to reimburse its debts, and that deflation would continue to aggravate budgetary deficits.[69] The eurozone countries (like Greece) which would have benefitted from a devaluation of currency (but no longer could, since the advent of the euro) were no longer able to attract capital, whereas robust exporting states (like Germany) presented a greater attractiveness for capital. This vicious spiral then aggravated deficits in the periphery, leading to more capital flight to the center, and more crises in the weaker states of the Union.[70]

Nowhere better than in Greece can this self-defeating mechanism be found. As the arm-wrestling competition between finance ministers in the Eurogroup heightened in 2015, and the scenario of "Grexit" became a real possibility – as the German Finance Minister Wolfgang Schäuble and his pro-austerity allies in the

Eurogroup believed that the eurozone could weather such a shock and that the expulsion of Greece would actually cleanse the eurozone of its least respectable member – foreign investors fled the country. Then, Greece was not only unable to attract investors to buy the prized properties which the Greek state had to privatize to obey the commands of the Troika, but it also faced a banking crisis spurred by rich Greek citizens who transferred their deposits from Greek to German, Swiss, or French banks, in anticipation of bank defaults and the imposition of capital controls and quantitative restrictions placed on private deposits.[71] The panic was so dramatic that private actors and international financial institutions (including IMF Director Christine Lagarde) were not sure that the German finance minister's strategy would not lead to the death of the currency zone. There was no end in sight to capital flight if the budgetary capacities of the eurozone did not massively increase to allow redistribution to Greece.

4 DECOLONIZING "GENEROUS" PROPOSALS TO SOLVE THE EUROZONE CRISIS

For Aglietta and Brand, the maintenance of all countries within the eurozone means that there must be a "European social contract," which necessitates the existence of a "common consciousness" and a "sense of belonging to the same community of destiny."[72] They argue that a European Budgetary Union should be formed to complement the European Monetary Union, whose central institution could decide to mutualize all member states' debts.[73] This would be a similar gesture to that made by Alexander Hamilton when the US federal government was given the power to raise taxes: as Aglietta and Brand write, "union is created by the mutualization of budgets and public debts and not by a reliance on market exchanges."[74] This was also the solution that Soustelle had proposed in 1958: to integrate the budgets of metropolitan France and Algeria, to make their communities of destiny manifest. Today, if no budgetary union is created in Europe, and if the European Monetary Union remains a simple intergovernmental treaty, governed by the ECB, which artificially sets its monetary policy for "a country that does not exist" (e.g. the average eurozone country),[75] the eurozone is bound to replicate the same mistake that the Europeans made in the interwar period, when they tried to maintain the creed that moneys were pegged on the gold standard by artificially placing some reparation debt on the debit of Germany and the credit of France and its Allies – a creed that was shattered by the failure of the Reparations Conference of 1933 and the German default on Reparations.[76]

Their Eurofederalist approach leads them, as well as other economists like Thomas Piketty and his coauthors, Stéphanie Hennette and Antoine Vauchez – two constitutional and European law scholars[77] – to elaborate complex proposals which would give flesh to their dreams of a complete European Budgetary Union.[78] In their view, a European budget, larger than the current amount administered by the entire EU – and not just the eurozone –, which is limited to 1 percent of the GDP of all member countries, should be negotiated not only by the Eurogroup, but also approved by a new eurozone Parliament, composed in its majority of elected members of national parliaments and a minority of members of the European Parliament (EP).[79] The main argument made in favor of the eurozone Parliament is that the adoption of the euro – and the subsequent eurozone crises – have created a giant leap forward in terms of financial and political integration, which has not yet led to the creation of a democratic structure at the level of the eurozone. Indeed, the eurozone decision-makers are mostly finance ministers acting, with the president of the ECB, in the Eurogroup: they largely evade accounting for their decisions before their own national parliaments when their decision concerns another EU member state (for instance, Greece); or before the EP, which lacks the prerogative to question the Eurogroup on its decisions (as the latter is not mentioned in the EU treaties).

While their proposal has received a lot of attention – and a lot of skepticism[80] – especially after the endorsement of the French Green-Socialist candidate to the 2017 presidential elections, its intellectual genesis and content structure conjures the memory of Jacques Soustelle's proposals to democratize the management of the Franco-Algerian economic zone, which he did by transforming (for four years) the French Parliament into a parliament of the Franco-Algerian zone. Like Soustelle, who claimed generous redistributive and democratic ambitions and who lambasted the greed and irrationality of financial markets, Piketty and his coauthors now claim that their proposal is the only way to end the drastic austerity measures of the Troika in Greece, and improve the democratic character of the decision-making process in the Union. But its structure is criticized as a setback for the Union, as its proposed indirect mode of election would bring the EU back to the early days of the Common Market Community and would make the only body directly representing European citizens (e.g. the EP) largely irrelevant in the management of the eurozone economic, fiscal and social matters.[81] A new eurozone Parliament also runs the risk of complicating the European policymaking structure, making it even more incomprehensible than it is today to most European citizens. At last, in focusing the attention away from the Eurogroup, it fails to tackle the most important reform today, which is the reform of the Council of the EU, and the broader cultural battle to fight racist prejudices against Europeans from the South.[82] Like Soustelle's proposals, which largely ignored the ideological and social context in which the new political structures of representation were supposed to operate – an Algerian society that had been marked by years of political oppression and that demanded political independence before economic support – the proposal for a eurozone Parliament does not seem grounded on a realistic analysis of the present ideological landscape in Europe.

Proposals to solve the problem of economic divergence in the eurozone with budgetary integration may appear both adequate and generous. But as we have learned from surveying the history of the gift exchange in international economic relations, "generosity" has long been associated with the paternalism inherent to colonial and neocolonial modes of thinking. There is no guarantee that, without a direct intellectual and political confrontation of the neoliberal precepts that most eurozone governments take at face value, an institutional innovation such as the creation of a eurozone parliament will upset the austerity measures in Greece. Far from it. With more budgetary integration will come more demands for fiscal conservatism and disciplinary oversight of the most economically vulnerable democracies by the stronger economic powers. More budgetary integration in a context where neoliberal ideas reign will mean more control exercised by the European center on its peripheries. The battle is first and foremost ideological and cultural rather than purely institutional.

In European peripheries, economic policy decisions have often been under the control of Troika-like structures rather than made in complete independence, as was the case in former colonies and semi-independent states of Africa – such as Egypt or Tunisia. As Eric Toussaint writes, since the collapse of Napoleon's empire and its replacement by the British Empire, the economic administration of the southeastern parts of Europe – Greece and Cyprus especially – has long fallen under the control of British, French, German, or other core powers, particularly when these semi-sovereign states failed to reimburse the usurious loans extended to them by private and public financial actors.[83] To this extent, European citizens need to reappropriate the story of debt formation, to understand which interests debt accumulation has served, and to fight against the neoliberal command that all debts should be honored, based on the solidarist principle that illegitimate debts – those that served mostly the short-term interests of financial speculators – can be forgiven if their cancellation works to increase the intersocietal cooperation between European citizens or if the initial loans which resulted in accumulated debts were poisonous gifts in the first place.

This legal, cultural, and ideological battle needs to take place before any institutional reform of the eurozone can be launched. In the Greek debt crisis, the numerous assertions by European policymakers that the "Greeks were different," that they did not know how to administer themselves, that they lacked the modern cultural ethos that would make them compatible with the demands of eurozone conditionalities and capitalistic societies, betray the strength of racial prejudices and sustained hierarchies upon which colonial and neocolonial thinking has long flourished in the south of Europe. Thus, while Mauss's thinking or Soustelle's institutional reflections may be applied to rethink international economic relations between North and South, both within Europe and outside Europe, we should be wary of imposing their lessons on the present context, as the discursive context in which European economic policy in Greece is being discussed has not been cleansed of the many racial and cultural stereotypes that have long isolated a European core from the rest of the world.

If Mauss's model of the gift exchange may still represent a source of inspiration in the context of the eurozone reform, it may be because of Mauss's adamant defense of the humanist creed according to which all societies – however differently organized – are capable of honoring legal obligations, when the latter are formed through genuine manifestations of gift exchange. Equally important, Mauss emphasized in his political and anthropological writing the necessity for gift-givers to give time to the gift-debtors: whether such time needs to be contracted in the form of an agreed-upon moratorium on the payments of either interest or principal (or both), or left implicit, Mauss demonstrated that values of trust, patience and wisdom are key qualities that sovereign rulers must demonstrate to defend the causes of peace and solidarity in international economic relations. This emphasis on trust in para-contractual informality and long-term thinking may constitute Mauss's most important lessons, which should continue to inspire future generations of intellectuals interested in changing the rules of global governance for the better. In some sense, it already has: in his "Modest proposal" for the eurozone crisis, future Greek Finance Minister Yanis Varoufakis proposed a plan that was quite aligned with Maussian principles, as he proposed to extend maturities of Greek loans permanently, which had the advantage of avoiding a Greek default while releasing the fiscal burden from Greek shoulders.[84] Unfortunately, his proposal failed to grasp the attention of eurozone creditors.

To "decolonize" the proposals presently extended for the governance of the eurozone, one may also turn to the attempts by NIEO thinkers to ground the operation of international economic relations after decolonization on new principles of international law. Those who, after David Graeber or Eric Toussaint,[85] wish to decolonize the relation between Greece and its European creditors would do better to turn to the international law precepts formulated by Mohammed Bedjaoui, in his attempt to decolonize the vision of international law promoted by the advocates of French postcolonial "cooperation," rather than to the solidarist doctrine that Mauss espoused in the interwar period. Even if present-day anthropologists like Graeber claim to be inspired by Mauss when they argue, for instance, in favor of unilateral debt cancellation, readers will now know that Mauss wrote in the interwar period on the sacred duty of all nations to honor their debt and respect the obligation to give back, provided that they were the recipients of true gifts – something that could be, and is, disputed in the case of Greece. Decolonizing the principles of financial responsibility in the case of Greece would mean not only reviving Bedjaoui's thinking on sovereign debt legacies in neocolonial contexts, but also extending it beyond the African and Asian territories where it has remained circumscribed. This is indeed an ambitious task; to which, I hope, this book may contribute.

Notes

1 The History of a Political Idea

1. *L'Année sociologique* was not published between 1913 and 1925. Although it is only an article, I place the title of that long essay in italics in the remainder of the book.
2. Karsenti 1994.
3. Lévi-Strauss 1950.
4. Bourdieu 1994: 174–5.
5. Derrida 1991.
6. Sigaud 2002.
7. Sigaud 2002: 335.
8. Zelizer 1994.
9. Taussig 1980.
10. From Bourdieu (1994) to the Mouvement Anti-Utilitariste en sciences sociales (MAUSS).
11. Sigaud 2002: 336.
12. Liebersohn 2011.
13. Foucault 2010.
14. Rist 1996; Teubner 1996; Gilman 2003; Rajagopal; Mazower 2010; Pahuja 2011, 2012.
15. Foucault 2010.
16. Koskenniemi (2001), and Cohen and Vauchez (2007) focus mostly on the interwar periods; Judt (1998) on the Cold War; Shepard (2008) on early decolonization. Kennedy (2006), Mazower (2010, 2012) and Mallard and Sgard (2016) provide attempts to catch at least a hundred years of evolution.
17. Bedjaoui 1978a.
18. Liebersohn 2011.
19. Cohn 1996.
20. Liebersohn 2011: 25.
21. Liebersohn 2011: 25.
22. Weber 1978 [1922].
23. Flandreau 2016: 5.

24. Flandreau 2016.
25. Liebersohn 2011: 161.
26. Shapin and Shaffer 1989.
27. Terrier and Fournier 2013.
28. Mallard 2011.
29. It is indeed Liebersohn's (2011: 123) thesis that these three anthropologists of gift-making practices all shared a deep intellectual link with the German-speaking world and were all "indebted to the same Imperial German learning," although all three were outsiders in German academic circles: "if Malinowski was a Polish Catholic who passed through the German university on his way to England, Boas was a Jew [from Westphalia] who migrated to the United States, while Thurnwald, the only one of the three to make his career in Germany, was by birth an Austrian Catholic who converted to Protestantism and migrated to Berlin."
30. Asad 1973; Cohn 1996; Flandreau 2016. For the German-speaking world of anthropology, the most complete history is Steinmetz (2013).
31. de L'estoile, Neiburg and Sigaud 2005; de L'estoile 2007; Singaravélou 2011; Conklin 2013.
32. Research is based on the consultation of the private archives of Marcel Mauss and Henri Hubert held at the Collège de France, and those of Albert Thomas and Léon Blum held at the French National Archives. For the later generation, I have consulted the papers of Jacques Soustelle, and read most of the published work of some of Soustelle's colleagues, like Germaine Tillion, as well as those who debated their positions – such as Raymond Aron for instance.
33. Prochasson 1993; Candar and Rébérioux 1994; Birnbaum 1988; Topalov 1999.
34. Graeber 2000.
35. The analysis of the "économie solidaire" pioneered by Jean-Louis Laville (2007) is another French school of thought that took inspiration from Mauss's ideas to study local circuits of gift exchange, which I did not review in this book, as my focus concentrates on international forms of exchange.
36. Caillé 1989; Godbout 2000.
37. In many ways, these French scholars from Pierre Bourdieu to Jacques Godbout and Alain Caillé – injected Mauss's normative propositions into an economic debate that pitted tenets of self-interestedness and apologists of disinterestedness against one another in the 1970s; see Bourdieu 1994: 180, 184; Caillé 1989, 2005.
38. Akerloff 1982: 549.
39. Schulte-Tenckhoff 2001: 177.
40. Graeber 2000, 2011.
41. Mauss 1925a.
42. Charle 1980, 1990; Bourdieu 1990.
43. Steinmetz 2013.
44. Mauss 2013.
45. Rajagopal 2003.
46. Rist 1996; Gilman 2003; Rajagopal; Pahuja 2011; Mazower 2012.

47. Just as Mauss praised Emile Durkheim at the same time as he hinted at the failings of his uncle's theorization when he campaigned to obtain a chair at the Collège de France in the late 1920s, Lévi-Strauss – followed by Bourdieu some thirty years after – later used Mauss's name when campaigning to obtain a similar chair at the Collège, but claimed that Mauss had failed to fully understand the role of gift exchanges; see Sigaud 2002: 345.
48. Aglietta and Orléan 1982.

2 The Cast

1. Steinmetz 2013.
2. Bourdieu 1990.
3. Durkheim 1998: 52.
4. Tarot 1999.
5. Hubert and Mauss 1899.
6. Frazer 1890.
7. Frazer (1898, 1902) thanked Mauss for publishing a review of his book in *L'Année*, as well as proposing to review its translation in French.
8. Mauss 1979.
9. Fournier 1994.
10. When he came back to Paris from Oxford, Mauss became a central figure of the Librairie Bellais, where he met all the Dreyfusards and in particular its creator, Charles Péguy (1873–1914), a young philosophy student at the ENS. Durkheim participated in the creation of the Ligue des droits de l'Homme in Bordeaux.
11. In 1904, sixteen out of the twenty-two contributors of *L'Année* were from the ENS (Besnard 1979: 16).
12. Mauss 1997 [1928]: 741.
13. Mauss 1997 [1935]: 756.
14. Berstein 2006: 71.
15. Bert 2012.
16. Durkheim 1998: 136.
17. Durkheim did not see the hegemonic situation of Durkheimians in the Ministry of Armament with very favorable eyes, as he (1998: 473) wrote that the "immensity of their responsibilities" was coupled with the "incompetence of those responsible."
18. Besnard 1979: 13.
19. A. Becker 2003.
20. Halbwachs 1925.
21. In doing so, Halbwachs followed the influence of his old mentors Durkheim and Bergson, but also that of his former colleague at the ENS, Robert Hertz, whose posthumous 1922 book (edited by Mauss) asked how can societies forgive and forget. Still, Halbwachs could not stand Mauss's claim of leadership among the Durkheimian school (Hertz 1922; A. Becker 2003: 395).
22. Blaszkiewicz-Maison 2015: 76.

23. Berstein 2006: 72.
24. Pénin 1997: 136, 160. For instance, in June 1905, Mauss was the French envoy sent by the Bourse Coopérative to a British congress of more than 1,700 delegates of the Wholesale movement, where Mauss was influenced by the ideas of Béatrice and Sydney Webb and the Fabians (Mauss 1997 [1905]: 177, 1997 [1920]).
25. Mallard 2011.
26. Cited in Fournier 1994: 206.
27. Durkheim 1998. It is not clear whether Mauss had an affair with a married woman working at *L'Humanité*, but, in any case, Durkheim obtained from Mauss the promise that he would no longer see this person, whom both his uncle and mother disliked – a promise Mauss broke many times, judging from Durkheim's many letters of condemnation.
28. Jaurès was initially skeptical about the usefulness of fighting for Dreyfus, when the labor movement required all of his attention.
29. Before the Dreyfus affair, Blum was under the tutelage of Barrès rather than Jaurès, but the affair was a turning point in his life. It was Herr who convinced Blum to get involved in the fight for Dreyfus (Mauss 1997 [1928]: 741).
30. Durkheim 1998: 363.
31. Mauss 1997 [1928]: 744.
32. Winock 1992; Prochasson 1993; Candar and Rébérioux 1994; Topalov 1999.
33. Berstein 2006: 26. It is amusing to note that André Gide's platonic marriage with his cousin was the inspiration for Léon Blum's decision to get married in an effort to gain respectability (Berstein 2006).
34. Mauss and Hertz shared an anglophile curiosity at a time when German social sciences were prominent: after passing his *agrégation* in 1895, Mauss traveled for a year in Oxford in 1898, to complement his learning in the emerging social sciences, just as Hertz did a few years later. Mauss's anglophilia not only affected his political leanings but also infused his research, as he went on to write introductions for all the ethnographers working in the British tradition, from Evans-Pritchard to Bronislaw Malinowski – whose works he would later review at length in *The Gift*.
35. Hertz 1922: 15. Hertz's (1922: 37) book titled *Le Péché et l'expiation dans les sociétés primitives* ("Guilt and expiation in primitive societies"), on the reparative power of religions and funerary rituals, was published posthumously by Mauss in 1922 (Hertz 1902). Later on, as he came back from a trip to London, Hertz (1908) acknowledged to Mauss his interest in the Fabians' philosophy. Then, the two developed collaborations, as Mauss served as a benevolent older brother guiding Hertz's initiatives, such as when he advised Hertz to spend a year in London to become acquainted with the English school of anthropology, or when Mauss edited Hertz's book on rituals of purification after Hertz's death during the war (Hertz 1922).
36. Blais 2007. Although Gide knew and cited Durkheim's thesis on the transition from "mechanical" to "organic" solidarity (the latter being the product of the division of labor), Gide did not define solidarity in sociological terms, but

rather in natural terms, which he reconciled with his Protestantism: atoms were "*solidaire*," in the sense of having reciprocal effects on each other, in the same way that all men were "*solidaire*," in the sense of sharing the same destiny as outcasts from paradise as a consequence of man's first sin (C. Gide 1932).

37. Blais 2007: 210.
38. Prélot 1939: 186.
39. Blaszkiewicz-Maison 2015: 92.
40. Groupe Parlementaire de l'Arbitrage 1913.
41. Malinowski 1922.
42. Or Victor Augagneur (1855–1931), the Governor of Madagascar in 1904 and then Resident-General in Tunisia (Augagneur 2010).
43. Blais 2007: 39.
44. As captured by Célestin Bouglé, another Durkheimian sociologist working at the library of the ENS, this notion of the quasi-contract "shares with other conceptions of contractual law . . . the care to 'protect social equality,' in the sense that it seeks to correct the present organization of society so that its members could live as if they had debated the social contract in all freedom, and as if they had debated these conditions with the same amount of freedom" (Bouglé 1924: 84). Bourgeois also said that the quasi-contract was "*le contrat rétroactivement consenti*" (cited in C. Gide 1932: 127).
45. Bouglé 1924: 84.
46. Renaudel 1910; Mauss 1938.
47. Pénin 1997: 103.
48. Pénin 1997: 105.
49. Berstein 2006: 227.
50. Mauss 1997 [1924a]: 539.
51. A pro bono job, since he paid his secretaries' salaries out of his own pocket (Soustelle 1986: 18).
52. These ties were all the more important since David David-Weill was also a member of the committee of French museums which overlooked the Museum of Ethnology.
53. Mauss 1925a: 2.
54. Still, Mauss (1939) did not like Thérèse Rivière, calling her "crazy."
55. Griaule 1931b.
56. Charle 1980, 1990; Bourdieu 1990. It is developed at the international level by Dezalay and Garth 2002, 2010, 2016.
57. Bourdieu 2013.
58. Birnbaum 1988: 73. In opposition to the "Jews of the Court," the traditional role of Jewish bankers at the court of the Austrian Empire.
59. Judt 1998: 41.
60. Berstein 2006.
61. *L'Année sociologique* 1924: 2.
62. de Rougemont 2010: 239.
63. Soustelle 1986: 3.
64. Tillion 2009: 318.

65. Soustelle 1986: 83.
66. Fournier 1994. Mauss helped Déat clear the debt of the journal *La vie socialiste*, which the "neo-socialists" then used to publicize their ideas (see Mauss 1935). During the war, Déat protected French assimilated Jews like Mauss and Bergson while he did not hesitate to send the German Jews in exile in France to German concentration camps (Burrin 1986).
67. Mauss 1925b: 373.
68. Mauss 2016 [1925].
69. Mauss 1925c: 372.
70. Heilbron 1995.
71. Dezalay and Garth 2010.
72. Steinmetz 2013: 4.
73. Furthermore, until 1914, when the ethnographer Van Gennep was recruited by the University of Neuchâtel, the latter attracted more attention than Mauss among governmental circles (Sibeud 2004: 108).
74. William Cohen calculated that less than 20 percent of the colonial administrators had formal training before 1914 (Cohen 1971: 30).
75. Cohen 1971: 41.
76. Cohen 1971: 34.
77. Cited in Cohen 1971: 45.
78. Saada 2003: 14.
79. Cohen 1971: 49.
80. Cohen 1971: 40.
81. Cited in Cohen 1971: 127.
82. Dedieu 2004.
83. Kralfa 2016: 257.
84. Kralfa 2016: 279.
85. Elbaz 2003: 72.
86. Dedieu 2004: 215.
87. It was the Senatus-Consulte of 1865 which declared for the first time who was a citizen and who was not among French nationals in Algeria (Blévis 2014).
88. Dedieu 2004: 216.
89. In 1934, they obtained the restriction that naturalized lawyers be barred from practicing law for a period of ten years after their naturalization – a condition that applied to Algerian naturalized citizens as well (Noiriel 1988: 285).
90. Mauss 1907: 4.
91. Mauss 1907: 22.
92. Mauss 1907: 4.
93. Mauss 1913: 4.
94. Mauss 1907: 8.
95. Mauss 1907: 19.
96. Mauss 1907: 10.
97. de L'estoile, Neiburg, Sigaud 2005; Conklin 2013.
98. Mauss 1913: 2. Thus, as his distinction between ethnology and folklore made clear, Mauss would have liked to lead the science of ethnology in France, while

his best friend Hubert led the science of folklore, thanks to his teaching post at the School of the Louvre and his job as curator of the French Museum of Saint Germain en Laye.

99. Guyer 2016.
100. Mauss 1913b: 2.
101. Mauss 1913b: 1; Mauss 1913a: 2.
102. Mauss 1902: 1.
103. Mauss 1907: 22.
104. Conklin 2013: 240.
105. Hardy 1927.
106. Cohen 1971: 128.
107. Cohen 1971: 87.
108. Steinmetz 2013: 4.
109. Steinmetz 2008.
110. Francioli 2015: 46.
111. In contrast to some of his colleagues among Mauss's group of doctoral students, like Claude Lévi-Strauss, who remained purely in academic positions during and after the war – with the exception of a short stint for the US Information Office.
112. After his return in 1968, Soustelle was elected to the municipal council in Lyon, and he continued publishing in ethnology, his field of specialization still being Central America.
113. Cohn 1996.
114. Kojève 2001: 121.
115. Giscard d'Estaing (1937) knew and appreciated Mauss, if judged from the fact that he congratulated Mauss for his promotion as Officer of the Légion d'honneur.
116. Marseille 1984: 63.
117. Koskenniemi 2001: 314.
118. Mazower 2010.
119. Koskenniemi 2001: 314.
120. Manceron 2003: 148.
121. Before the age of globalization in the 1970s, international law remained quite an academic discipline, considering the paucity of arbitration cases or cases before regional courts, which, like the European Court of Justice (ECJ) had very few cases to review in the 1960s (Vauchez 2013).
122. Koskenniemi 2001: 313.
123. Manceron 2003: 148.
124. For instance, Joseph Gallieni, the commander who led the French campaigns in Indochina, Sudan, and Madagascar, had a similar view of international law (Manceron 2003: 148).
125. Bedjaoui 2016: 9.
126. Bedjaoui 1984: 53. Colliard also wrote on the law of international rivers, nuclear law, law of technological transfers, and other matters that influenced Bedjaoui's writings on maritime law and deep-sea law for instance.

127. *Le Monde diplomatique* 1954.
128. Rajagopal 2003.
129. Rajagopal 2003: 90.
130. Article 2, United Nations General Assembly 1974c.
131. The ILC focuses only on international *public* law, whereas other institutions, like the Rome Institute or the UN Commission on International Trade Law (UNCITRAL), devote their attention to the codification of international *private* law (see Halliday and Block-Lieb 2016).
132. Bedjaoui 1978b.
133. Rajagopal 2003: 89–94.
134. Halliday, Karpik, and Feeley 2007.
135. Halliday, Karpik, and Feeley 2012.
136. De 2012: 62.
137. Kralfa 2016.
138. Thénault 2001.
139. Thénault 2012.
140. Vergès 1968.
141. Thénault 2001.
142. Malye and Stora 2012: 205, 246, 258. Halimi was warned of the danger, and immediately evacuated to Paris, by her colleague, Paul Teitgen (1919–91), then Secretary General at the Prefecture of Algiers. Teitgen resigned in 1957, in protest against torture and targeted assassination.
143. Bedjaoui 2017: 8.
144. Bedjaoui 2017: 8.
145. But as Minister of Justice in the independent Republic, Bedjaoui found the idea of judicial cooperation particularly shocking: when every legislation or rule published in the independent Algeria stated that colonial law no longer applied, how could French judges remain in charge of litigating cases in Algerian courts – especially when most of them would have directly come from the pre-independence colonial field of power? To underline the recovered sovereignty over the Algerian legal system, Bedjaoui also refused to place Egyptian law graduates, whom President Nasser agreed to send – a solution that Algeria's first President, Ahmed Ben Bella, proposed to Bedjaoui (Bedjaoui 2017: 3).
146. In parallel, Bedjaoui teamed up with Ahmed Medeghri (1934–74), Interior Minister from 1962 until 1974 (when he was allegedly assassinated by Boumédiène's security forces after denouncing the lack of a democratically elaborated Constitution), to create the École Nationale d'Administration d'Algerie (ENAA), and thus push aside the phantom of the French colonial presence in Algeria's field of law (Bedjaoui 2017: 7).

3 *The Gift* and European Solidarity

1. Marks 2013.
2. Koskenniemi 2001: 292.

3. Torpey 2003: 4. For many authors, reparations in the Versailles Treaty defined a form of *indemnity* that was very different from our modern sense of reparations, which emerged in response to the Holocaust, as in the German–Israeli Treaty (1952) (Torpey 2003: 43; Colonomos and Armstrong 2006).
4. Binkley and Mahr 1926; Binkley 1929; Craig and Gilbert 1963: 142.
5. Schmitt 2003 [1950]: 266.
6. Maier 2003: 297.
7. Mauss 1997 [1922a]: 478.
8. Toussaint 2017a.
9. Blum 1972 [1923a]: 273.
10. Blum 1972 [1923a]: 273.
11. Mauss 1997 [1924h]: 617.
12. Or in French: *un système de prestations totales*, an expression that he would use again in *The Gift* to characterize societies which abide by the quasi-legal obligation to give each other a bit of everything (Mauss 1921: 389).
13. Durkheim 1893.
14. C. Gide 1932.
15. A. Thomas 1919.
16. A. Thomas 1919.
17. Durkheim 1998: 473.
18. Halbwachs 1917; Simiand 1917.
19. Blaszkiewicz-Maison 2015: 75. On his experience at the Ministry of Armament, see Oualid and Picquenard (1928).
20. Cointepas 2008.
21. Blaszkiewicz-Maison 2015: 29.
22. A. Thomas 1920.
23. de Rougemont 2010: 239.
24. M. Lazard 1908.
25. M. Lazard 1927a.
26. M. Lazard undated.
27. Mauss 2013: 244.
28. de Rougemont 2010: 345.
29. de Rougemont 2010: 178.
30. Cited in de Rougemont 2010: 180.
31. de Rougemont 2010: 185.
32. Cited in de Rougemont 2010: 180.
33. Cited in de Rougemont 2010: 181.
34. de Rougemont 2010: 353.
35. de Rougemont 2010: 361.
36. Cited in de Rougemont 2010: 360.
37. A. Thomas 1925. The ILO also communicated to Mauss that it was interested in his ideas on the international division of labor and the creation of wholesales in nations which specialized in food production (butter, fruits, corn, etc.) (Colombain 1932).
38. Berstein 2006: 227.

39. Pauly 1996.
40. Torpey 2003: 4.
41. The same section also declared "the right . . . to bring before military tribunals persons accused of having committed acts in violation of the laws and customs of war" (article 228), and asked for the surrender of those accused to the Allies. Both the prosecution of a sovereign and the formation of international tribunals to try war crimes were unprecedented.
42. Durkheim and Denis 1915.
43. Durkheim 1998: 424.
44. Durkheim [1991] 1915.
45. Durkheim 1998: 326.
46. Belfort remained French after 1870 because it was never occupied, thanks to the heroic resistance of Denfert-Rochereau, the "lion" of Belfort.
47. The Commission Report claimed that the crime of aggression against Belgium was intrinsically linked with future war crimes conducted in France (like the use of chemical agents) (cited in Laniol 2012: 53).
48. Barthélemy 1917: 62. In Larnaude's organicist vocabulary, reparations were just the product of a "state's reflex" to heal the productive forces after the major injury inflicted by the war (1917: 188).
49. Despite the lack of precedent, they argued that the creation of an international criminal court was in line with the spirit of the new international law embodied in President Wilson's vision – and in fact, Léon Bourgeois's internationalist conceptions of a legal order constructed by courts (Larnaude and de Lapradelle 1918: 20).
50. Commission on the Responsibility of the Authors of the War and on Enforcement of Penalties 1920: 116.
51. Larnaude and Tardieu pushed aggressively for the prosecution of Kaiser Wilhelm against the opposition of Americans James Brown Scott and Robert Lansing, who argued that responsibility for the prosecution of war crimes was best left to the military authority of individual states. Commission on the Responsibility of the Authors of the War 1920: ch. IV, conclusion. For a detailed account of the different legal options that were considered by France, Great Britain, and the United States, see Foltz (1978).
52. Burnett 1965.
53. Still, the French nationalists failed to prosecute Kaiser Wilhelm, and the international prosecution of war crimes did not fare much better: the Germans refused to extradite soldiers and commanding officers accused of war crimes and instead offered to try offenses in the Reichsgericht, Leipzig (then the location of the highest German court). For a detailed discussion of the Leipzig Tribunals, see Willis (1982).
54. The British government at first insisted on a formidable tribute from Germany – although, as observed by the French negotiator on financial aspects, Louis Loucheur, the British prime minister completely changed position in March 1919 on the issue of reparations. In the Committee of Four, they insisted that France could not have suffered more than 30 billion francs-gold in

losses, about the same sum as what the US had loaned to it. To counter the abrupt British policy change, Loucheur presented greatly reduced figures (as compared to Klotz's prior estimations) of the damage suffered by France during the war – e.g. 80 billion francs rather than 160 billion – see Loucheur (1962: 73–4).

55. George 1939: 55; Foltz 1978: 38–40.
56. In preparation for the peace conference, Larnaude and de Lapradelle (1918) had been commissioned by Clemenceau to study the possible legal foundations for holding the German emperor responsible before a criminal court.
57. Indeed, if the Treaty of Versailles presents the illusion of a unified document – negotiated among a group of politicians, diplomats, and lawyers – the reality was much more complicated, incorporating a piecemeal approach of various committees, commissions, and backroom consultations, which all understood the concept of responsibility differently.
58. And, in general, all damage as defined in Annex I of the Versailles Treaty.
59. The Reparations Commission could change the deadline of payment (article 234).
60. Demographically, the results of the war for France were bleak. Out of a population of 40 million people, France lost about 1.6 million men – one-tenth of its active population – while more than 4 million were wounded, about 300,000 of which were heavily crippled. That makes almost 15 percent of the population who directly suffered from the war – many more if we include the resulting deficit of births, which is estimated at about 3 million for France alone. Furthermore, the war and the resulting weaknesses provoked by the conflict facilitated the spread of the Spanish flu, which caused about 400,000 French casualties immediately after the war.
61. C. Gide 1932: 22.
62. C. Gide 1932: 22.
63. Loucheur 1962: 89.
64. Bourgeois 1919: 82. The exception is Belgium, which required that Germany pay its inter-allied war debts.
65. Trachtenberg 1979: 29.
66. Initially, the French were less adamant about the Germans paying high reparation and war costs than the British, as the French minister of commerce hoped to reapportion inter-allied debts and to maintain Allied control of raw materials (coal), a position that he shared with his young adviser, Jean Monnet, who went on to create the European Coal and Steel Community after the Second World War. Even though President Wilson initially opposed the inclusion of pensions, they were eventually introduced in the bill after British lobbying (Trachtenberg 1979: 45).
67. Bourgeois 1919: 92. For instance, Germany accepted that its population would be taxed as heavily as the highest taxed population in Europe.
68. Sack 1927: 163. The burden of proving that debt contracts or reparations obligations were odious was quite high, much higher than present-day calls

for the cancellation of the debt of Third World nations as expressed by the Jubilee network of legal activists (Gulati and Ludington 2008).

69. And even on that point Sack believed that the Versailles Treaty drafters had been too generous in letting the Poles reject that debt (1927: 159).
70. C. Gide 1932.
71. Mauss 1997 [1924a]: 539.
72. Mauss 1997 [1924a]: 539.
73. M. Lazard 1924.
74. Mauss 1997 [1924a]: 539.
75. Toussaint 2017a.
76. Mauss 1997 [1924c]: 572. Mauss's (1997 [1913]: 201) attacks on Klotz predated the war, when Klotz raised the price of establishing a wholesale cooperative in France.
77. Mauss 1997 [1924e]: 608.
78. de Rougemont 2010: 388.
79. Mauss 1997 [1924i]: 628.
80. The sovereign obligations contracted by new Central European states were administered under the auspices of the League of Nations.
81. The British assessment was led by William Beveridge and John Maynard Keynes.
82. Gide and Oualid 1931: 3–4.
83. Mauss 1997 [1922b]: 481.
84. Charles Gide was commissioned by the Carnegie Endowment of International Peace to participate in this study to independently assess a "reasonable estimate of the credit and debit of each warring party" (Gide and Oualid 1931). Andrew Carnegie had already asked Gide in 1911 to chair the Carnegie Foundation section on economics because he admired the journal that Gide had created in 1893: *La paix par le droit* (Pénin 1997: 65, 160).
85. Mauss (1997 [1922d]: 492) used the same numbers.
86. C. Gide 1932: 5.
87. Maier 1988: 237. Even though the Germans claimed that 3 billion was excessive and offered in return only 2 billion annually, in Brussels the British brokered a compromise with the French, setting the amount of yearly payment to 6 billion gold marks for forty-two years (and 12 percent of German benefits on their exports), as well as the cancellation of the 20 billion gold marks that Germany was supposed to pay in 1919 (article 235 of the Versailles Treaty), which the Germans refused to pay.
88. Gide and Oualid 1931: 4.
89. Mauss 1997 [1922e]: 482.
90. In July 1921, Loucheur noted that if France had made it clear that a German default on its reparations obligation would be sanctioned, France had not yet defined the nature of sanctions, and that other sanctions than the occupation of the Ruhr could be decided (Loucheur 1962: 93).
91. Maier 1988: 241. Critics of the Versailles Treaty like John Maynard Keynes welcomed the approval by the Allies of the London Agreement.

92. Mauss 1997 [1922c]: 484–5.
93. Loucheur 1962: 100. The German chancellor tried to find alternative modes of solving the question of reparations other than just paying the money due: he proposed to form large international companies, like a Société des Wagons Lits in civil aviation, or the development of chartered companies tasked with the development of specific domains in Russia (Loucheur 1962: 93, 104).
94. Maier 1988: 244.
95. Mauss 1997 [1922e]: 496.
96. Maier 1988: 251.
97. de Rougemont 2010: 392.
98. Carabelli and Cedrini 2010: 306.
99. Cited in Carabelli and Cedrini 2010: 317; Cedrini 2010.
100. de Rougemont 2010: 392.
101. Mauss 1997 [1922a]: 478.
102. Already in 1918, Gide had written that, at some point, inter-allied debts needed to be cancelled; or that, if their total was renegotiated, a lesser amount could be reimbursed, for instance by the creation of a pan-European loan, "*un grand emprunt international solidaire*" (cited in Pénin 1997: 185).
103. Mauss 1997 [1922g]: 504.
104. Cited in Maier 1988: 289.
105. Mauss 1997 [1922g]: 501.
106. Mauss 1997 [1922f]: 499.
107. Mauss 1997 [1922e]: 484–5.
108. Mauss 1997 [1922d]: 494.
109. Blum 1972 [1923a]: 281.
110. Mauss 1997 [1922g]: 502.
111. Maier 1988: 267.
112. Hubert (1922b) added that Germany's problem was too much freedom, as it fueled speculation against the mark on the international markets; France suffered from the obverse problem.
113. Hubert 1922a: 2, 3.
114. Maier 1988: 287.
115. André Lazard, cited in de Rougemont 2010: 392.
116. Mauss 1997 [1922f]: 499.
117. de Rougemont 2010: 390.
118. Varoufakis 2017.
119. Mauss actually had the authorization to use their names (David-Weill 1925).
120. Simiand 1925: 780.
121. Fournier 1994: 451.
122. Mauss repeated that the system of gifts exchanged or potlatch was a legal rule (a "*règle de droit*") and not just a social norm (1950 [1925]: 193). W. D. Halls translates this term as "rule of legality," but I prefer to use the term "legal rule." I will refer to the translation by Halls in the American edition of *The Gift* (1990 [1925]) where we agree on the wording.
123. Mauss 1990 [1925]: 198.

124. The similarity between the act of contracting a debt and that of paying it was illustrated by the fact that these societies did not have the "distinctions between concepts [of sale or credit] as these antithetical operations were named by the same word," e.g. the gift, which served the same function (Mauss 1950 [1925]: 193; see also 198). In technical legal terms, Mauss referred to the kind of legal rule as one that existed in the absence of a clear system of written law, or when the law was "poorly written" (Mauss 1950 [1925]: 197).
125. Mauss 1950 [1925]: 195.
126. Mauss 1950 [1925]: 161.
127. Mauss 1950 [1925]: 153.
128. Mauss noticed that today, "fortunately, everything is not categorized in [the bourgeois] terms of buying and selling ... and we possess more than a tradesman morality," by which he meant, "there still remain some people and classes that keep to the morality of former times" (1990 [1925]: 65).
129. Mauss 1950 [1925]: 148; 1990 [1925]: 65.
130. Mauss 1950 [1925]: 200, 203.
131. Mauss 1950 [1925]: 177, or 1990 [1925]: 22.
132. Hubert and Mauss 1899, 1903.
133. At the time, there was a strong association between the Celts and the Frenchmen on one side, and the Germanic tribes and the Germans on the other: as Halbwachs wrote in 1917, "war between us was inevitable: this race has hated us at least since the ancient Germans tried to crush the Celts" (cited in A. Becker 2003: 145).
134. R. Mauss 1918.
135. Hubert 1911.
136. Although, in the case of Gide, the wedding remained largely platonic.
137. Drouin 1897.
138. Mauss 1950 [1925]: 251–2.
139. Mauss 1950 [1925]: 185.
140. Mauss 1950 [1925]: 253–4.
141. Mauss 1950 [1925]: 210.
142. Mauss 1950 [1925]: 251–2.
143. Mauss 1924a.
144. Hubert 1925. As Hubert added, "by the way, your paragraph on the 'human rock' on which you base the development of social insurance is also quite nice, but problematic, and there, it seems that you were thinking more about your book on *The Nation* than the topic of this essay."
145. Hubert 1952.
146. Hubert 1932.
147. As Hubert (1925) added in his letter to Mauss: "Overall, your chapter on Germanic law seems absolutely insufficient. Indeed, you should have discussed the role of feudal law and its relation with Roman law. Indeed, it would have been interesting to add paragraphs on the example of social regress characterized by the constitution of client-patron relations in German

societies; at the same time, it consisted in a clear progress compared to the Germanic forms of structuration."

148. Hubert 1925.
149. Mauss 1950 [1925]: 251–2.
150. Similar reflections were later extended to post-war cases of reparations (Minow 1998: 102; Colonomos and Armstrong 2006: 406).
151. Mauss 1950 [1925]: 199.
152. This bond had only diminished in recent times because "of a process which brought together temporalities that were disjoined before" (Mauss 1950 [1925]: 199). Mauss's conception of the gift differs from that of Derrida (1991: 27), for whom the temporality of the gift is consumed in a present "outside temporal chains."
153. Mauss 1950 [1925]: 199. In that sense, the utilitarian logic of loans and credit systems allowed the transaction to be encapsulated in the present.
154. For instance, the legal scholar Carl Schmitt (1888–1985) encouraged the German government to default on the payment of reparations; Schmitt 2003 [1950]: 268.
155. Toussaint 2017b.
156. Mauss 1997 [1924d]: 580.
157. Mauss 1997 [1924d]: 579.
158. Mauss 1997 [1924b]: 569.
159. Mauss 1997 [1924b]: 569.
160. Mauss 1997 [1922a]: 479.
161. Maier 1988: 357.
162. What Mauss called the "*prestations en nature*," using the same term "*prestation*" that he later used in *The Gift* to qualify the gifts exchanged (1997 [1924i]: 631).
163. Mauss 1997 [1924d]: 581.
164. After France imposed sanctions and occupied the Ruhr, it looked impossible to de-escalate the conflict between German workers and French administration of the occupied territories: despite the best efforts of some of the members of the Reparations Commission, who, like John Foster Dulles, tried to find an agreement in July 1923, Chancellor Cuno did not agree to a stabilization plan for the German currency and flipped sides as soon as pressured by nationalist members of his government (Loucheur 1962: 131).
165. An event that was not named as such, as calling the failure of Greece to honor its debt obligations a "default" would have made it impossible for the ECB to activate some of its rescue instruments.
166. In the case of interwar Germany, not all segments of German society suffered the same, however. As Charles Maier (1988: 362) writes, German speculators with access to foreign currencies turned the crisis to their advantage, while "pensioners, retailers and those who had patriotically held government bonds were the silent victims" of hyperinflation.
167. Mauss 1990 [1925]: 63.
168. Mauss 1950 [1925]: 253.

169. Mauss 1990 [1925]: 61.
170. Mauss 1997 [1924d]: 580.
171. Mauss 1997 [1924e]: 585.
172. Cited in Pénin 1997: 214.
173. Varoufakis 2017.
174. Mauss 1997 [1922e]: 496. Income taxation was a relatively new procedure, long called for by Bourgeois, which France only instituted in 1916.
175. Mauss 1997 [1924c]: 575.
176. Mauss 1997 [1924c]: 577.
177. Interestingly, Mauss reversed the stigma of being "cosmopolitan," by which the right-wing press, after Barrès, meant "uprooted" or "*déracinés*."
178. Mauss 1997 [1924c]: 578.
179. Mauss 1997 [1922c]: 485.
180. Simiand 1924.
181. Indeed, the French occupation made it even harder for Germany to obtain foreign currencies, as Germans could no longer export manufactured goods and had to exchange marks against foreign currencies to pay the reparations. This exchange problem accelerated the rampant inflation: between August and November 1923, prices increased a millionfold as the mark was depreciated.
182. Blum 1972 [1924]: 315–18.
183. Maier 1988: 369, 392.
184. Simiand 1924.
185. Hubert 1923.
186. Hubert 1923.
187. A. Thomas 1924. But he still expressed the desire to see both Mauss and Hubert consider the option.
188. In parallel, Albert Thomas, by then president of the ILO, created a joint committee on economic crisis, whose 1923 report denounced inflation and which in 1928 endorsed a report by Max Lazard calling for price level stabilization (Rothbard 1963: 175, 179).
189. de Rougemont 2010: 410.
190. de Rougemont 2010: 415.
191. At the beginning of 1923, neither Prime Minister Poincaré nor the council members of the Banque de France (in particular, Edouard de Rothschild and François de Wendel) were convinced that the French central bank should buy currencies on international markets in order to sustain the exchange rate – which would have meant mortgaging as much as two thirds of its gold to fight the "battle of the franc."
192. de Rougemont 2010: 420.
193. Mauss 1997 [1924j]: 638.
194. This chapter develops an argument first published in Mallard 2011.
195. Ramel 2004.
196. Terrier and Fournier 2013.
197. Dzimira 2007: 27. All translations from the French are mine.

198. Guyer 2016.
199. Hart 2007.
200. Dzimira 2007.
201. Steiner 2005: 209, 225.
202. H. Becker 1982; Heilbron 1995.
203. Abbott 1988; Fourcade-Gourinchas 2009.
204. Torpey 2006: 149.
205. In the words of Xavier Vallat. In 1936, Blum escaped the same fate as Rathenau by a short margin, when he was dragged from his car and almost killed by right-wing fanatics.
206. Mauss 1997 [1924k]: 639.
207. Mauss 1997 [1924n]: 691. The Great War temporarily healed the division between Jews and Catholics opened by the Dreyfus affair (Birnbaum 1988: 158), but the reparations question reopened it.
208. Mauss 1925b: 372.
209. Mauss 1925a: 264.
210. Mauss 1997 [1924f]: 599. Mauss 1997 [1924m]: 652. What these Anglo-American foreigners, Mauss added, these "modern Jews and Lombardi, realized," warned Mauss, was that the franc "might have been a bit less than 40 percent of its parity with gold in 1922, and now it was close to 23 percent" (1997 [1924f]: 599).
211. Mauss 1997 [1924j]: 637, 1997 [1924l]: 647.
212. Mauss 1997 [1924j]: 638.
213. Mauss 1997 [1924k]: 640.
214. Mauss 1997 [1924l]: 649. Putting an end to the Ruhr crisis, the three main points of the Dawes plan of August 1924 were: the end of the French occupation, the immediate payment of one billion marks to France, and the Allied supervision of the Reichsbank (Maier 1988: 418).
215. Loucheur 1962: 174.
216. Blum 1972 [1924].
217. Mauss 1997 [1924m]: 652.
218. Blaszkiewicz-Maison 2015.
219. Mauss 1935. To some extent, Mauss was not far from assuming that class struggles could be overcome in capitalist societies themselves, thanks to the joint action of patriotic workers, industrialists, and indeed financial elites, who would unite to defend the worth of their national treasures – as the wartime experiment of Albert Thomas's Ministry of Armament had illustrated – and that the rise of Nazism required a renewed call for national unity above class conflicts. This emphasis on the need to build national solidarity as a first step before achieving a real inter-nationalism brought him closer to the "neo-socialists" lead by the younger Marcel Déat.
220. M. Lazard 1927b.
221. Hubert 1922a: 5–7.
222. Mauss 1933.

223. Mauss 1933.
224. This leads Stephen Schuker (1988) to claim that the Weimar Republic paid almost no reparations at all, since it largely paid the interest on its reparations debts with US loans.
225. Loucheur 1962: 174.
226. Eichengreen and Portes 1987: 29.

4 *The Gift* as Colonial Ideology

1. Sigaud 2002: 335.
2. Durkheim 1893.
3. Durkheim 1893.
4. Malinowski 1925. This letter proves that Malinowski had read Mauss's *The Gift* as he was writing his book on *Crime and Customs in Savage Society*, something for which Sigaud (2002) claimed to have found no proof in Malinowski's writings.
5. With the exception of Sibeud (2009) Conklin (2013), and Mallard (2018). This chapter greatly expands the latter's argument.
6. Mauss 2013.
7. The Committee was small, and gathered only forty members, out of whom ten were really active (Sibeud 2009: 60).
8. Girardet 1972: 58, 63, 66, 98–9.
9. Girardet 1972: 130.
10. Girardet 1972: 118.
11. Girardet 1972: 100.
12. To use the words of Colonel Mangin (Girardet 1972: 98–9).
13. Girardet 1972: 145.
14. M. Thomas 2005.
15. Girardet 1972: 121.
16. Sarraut 1931: 104.
17. Rostow 1960.
18. Sarraut 1931: 79.
19. Sarraut 1931: 103. When surveying France's colonial history, Sarraut consistently exonerated the French state from past crimes: even when recognizing that Louis XIV's Minister, Colbert, wrote the "Black code" which applied and made possible the Atlantic slave trade and a capitalist system of production based on slavery, he did not blame his predecessor for a lack of humanity or generosity, but rather, for the misguided mercantilist (and almost British) inspiration of his colonial philosophy. Sarraut euphemized the Atlantic slave trade by calling it "imported labor" rather than slavery, a term that almost never appears under his pen (Sarraut 1931: 89).
20. Manceron 2003: 135.
21. Sarraut 1931: 104.
22. Schmitt 2003 [1950]: 228.
23. Schmitt 2003 [1950]: 228.

24. France used the indemnity of 150 million francs-gold that it forced Haiti to disburse (until 1915) to pay for the military costs of France's military campaigns in Africa (Manceron 2003: 71).
25. Girardet 1972: 188.
26. Heins, Unrau, and Avram (2018).
27. It was also very similar to that of Alfred Fouillée (himself an advocate of the French colonial oeuvre) (Manceron 2003: 215).
28. Sarraut 1931: 118.
29. Sarraut 1931: 109.
30. Sarraut 1931: 111.
31. Sarraut 1931: 111.
32. Cohen 1971: 110.
33. In 1937, it was 29.7 percent of the year's budget of the French Western Africa, 40.6 percent for the French Eastern Africa, 17.1 percent for Madagascar (Cohen 1971: 110).
34. The British guaranteed colonial loans thanks to the Colonial Development Fund established in 1929, and according to Cohen, provided more aid than the French to their overseas territories (1971: 113).
35. Manceron 2003: 71.
36. Sarraut 1931: 113.
37. Sarraut 1931: 115.
38. Mauss 2013: 189.
39. Manceron 2003: 83, 160.
40. Asad 1973; see also Steinmetz 2013.
41. Terrier and Fournier 2013: 18; citation from Mauss 1925a: 113.
42. Mauss 2013: 125.
43. If indeed history and the "development of public law in any society" – and the movement of societies from one stage of "integration" to another – "is intrinsically linked to how economic relations function in such society, and reciprocally," it cannot be reduced to it (Mauss 2013: 92).
44. Mauss 2013: 79.
45. Mauss 2013: 77.
46. Terrier and Fournier 2013: 25, 26.
47. Mauss 2013: 158.
48. Mauss 2013: 176.
49. Mauss 2013: 176.
50. Mauss 2013: 82.
51. Mauss 1913a.
52. For Mauss, the circulation of goods and prestations grew in correlation with the multiplication of maritime routes and gigantic harbors, the deletion of spatial distances by the invention of telephony, and the expansion of new trading classes which had come to occupy the traditional niche of Jewish and Dutch peoples (Mauss 2013: 162).
53. Mauss 2013: 178.

54. Soustelle 1967. The (incomplete) transformation of an empire into a nation, as in the case of the German Zollverein of the nineteenth century, also took place thanks to a process of accelerated intersocietal trade that was associated with a qualitative change in the nature of intersocietal contractual obligations.
55. Schulte-Tenckhoff 2001: 167.
56. Mauss 1902: 1.
57. Mauss 1902: 1.
58. Mauss 1902: 3.
59. Mauss 2013: 242.
60. Mauss 2013: 188.
61. Mauss 2013: 252.
62. Mauss 2013: 188.
63. Mauss 2013: 90.
64. Mauss 2013: 184.
65. Mauss 1936b.
66. Mauss 2013: 71.
67. Mauss 2013: 55.
68. Mauss 2013: 56.
69. Mauss 2013: 182.
70. Mauss 2013: 241.
71. That of a cosmopolitan integration (or quasi-federal integration at the world level), which Mauss characterized by "the idea of limited national sovereignty, whose limit is placed by the superior right of all nations, which participate in the making and execution of contracts and which understand peace in good faith" (2013: 176).
72. Mauss 2013: 242.
73. Liebersohn 2011.
74. Liebersohn 2011: 25.
75. Liebersohn 2011.
76. Ligue française et ligue suisse pour la défense des indigènes dans le bassin conventionnel du Congo 1910.
77. Charles Gide, like most economists, opposed the 1885 war in the Tonkin launched by Jules Ferry. Indeed, economists believed the liberal denunciation of colonialism found in the often-reedited *Economic Treatise* of Jean-Baptist Say: in his 1826 essay, Say claimed that the military and civil costs of colonial occupation weighed on the budget of a colonial power, which procured a great advantage to its competitors in a system of global trade openness (Girardet 1972: 7; Manceron 2003: 219).
78. Indigenous Committee 1906: 1.
79. Indigenous Committee 1906.
80. Indigenous Committee 1906.
81. Challaye 1911.
82. Ribi-Forclaz 2015: 55.
83. Indigenous Committee 1901.
84. Sigaud 2002: 336.

85. Blaszkiewicz-Maison 2015.
86. Sibeud 2009: 58.
87. A. Thomas 1911b.
88. Mauss 1913.
89. Leroux 1908.
90. The author noticed that by playing the free rider and authorizing the circulation of munitions and weapons, the N'Goko Sangha Company hoped to attract local workers from French- and foreign-controlled zones where foreign chartered companies did not allow the sale of weapons. But even with this bias, the company failed to do so, as the locals "had no trust in the wealth of the N'Goko Sangha Company and the word of the whites in the administration" (Leroux 1908).
91. A. Thomas 1911a.
92. Mauss 1950 [1925]: 148.
93. Journal Officiel 1911: 1778.
94. Panizza, Sturzenegger, and Zettelmeyer 2009; Nelson 2016.
95. Leroux 1908. The company claimed in 1905 that the Germans had stolen more than 1,500 tons of rubber and had devastated vast forest zones, which is why it first filed suits against German companies in German courts (Hamburg and Bremen). But in 1905, it ended all legal proceedings after receiving from the French state new lands to exploit in Gabon, as well as a promise of indemnity (Tardieu 1910).
96. Tardieu 1910.
97. Tardieu 1910.
98. Labordère 1911a.
99. Labordère 1911a.
100. Leroux 1908.
101. Labordère 1911b.
102. Augagneur 2010.
103. Berthélemy 1910.
104. Journal Officiel 1911: 1773.
105. Journal Officiel 1911: 1773.
106. A. Thomas 1911b.
107. Dezalay and Garth 2002.
108. Journal Officiel 1911: 1773.
109. A. Thomas 1911b, 1911d.
110. A. Thomas 1911d.
111. Flandreau 2016.
112. This stage in the development of anthropology corresponds to what Flandreau (2016: 6) calls the "stock market modality" of anthropology.
113. In the mid 1880s, as a young deputy, Jaurès clearly sided with Ferry against those who criticized France's colonial adventures in the Tonkin (see Manceron 2003: 225). In fact, Jaurès came from a military family and had uncles and cousins, as well as his younger brother, who all fought in Algeria.
114. A. Thomas 1911c.

115. Leroux 1908.
116. Nationalization was a socioeconomic concept and politico-legal reality that has been the subject of intense political debate throughout the twentieth century. In the European context, its defense long pitted economic liberals against socialists and other planning enthusiasts (Amadae 2003; Mallard 2006). It was not a coincidence if socialists also advocated nationalizations in the colonial context.
117. Mauss 2013: 243.
118. Mauss 2013: 252.
119. Mauss 2013: 252.
120. Cohen 1971: 112.
121. Couturier 2006: 96.
122. A. Gide 1927.
123. A. Gide 1927.
124. Cohen 1971: 70.
125. Manceron 2003: 209.
126. Weber [2007] 1927.
127. Weber [2007] 1927.
128. Bordage 1911.
129. Cohen 1971: 81.
130. At the same time, Martin du Gard met Louis Massignon, the famous Orientalist (Couturier 2006: 46).
131. Couturier 2006: 85, 93.
132. Couturier 2006: 29.
133. Couturier 2006: 77.
134. Cohen 1971: 118.
135. At that time Moutet (1909) had also given Mauss some documents on colonial abuses in Indochina that he wanted to publish in the journal *L'Humanité* (on whose board Mauss represented the SFIO).
136. Sarraut 1931: 89.
137. A. Thomas 1926.
138. A. Thomas 1928.
139. A. Thomas 1929.
140. A. Gide [1958] 1925.
141. It is also worth noting that, in his other masterpiece, *The Vatican Cellars*, published in 1914, the novel ends with the famous completely "disinterested action" – which Gide's main character defined in a Maussian way as "a luxury, a need for over-spending" – which consists in the hero throwing to his death an anonymous figure whom he met in a train. And where was this anonymous man supposed to go? The poor victim was en route to a congress of sociologists in Rome! What a cruel fate for a disinterested scholar to be killed for no reason other than the disinterested overspending of energy (A. Gide [1958] 1914: 816).
142. Sibeud 2004: 119.
143. Conklin 2013: 3, 194.
144. Mauss 1925a: 2.

145. Hubert and Mauss 1899: 7.
146. As Hubert and Mauss (1899: 84) emphasized, in the Bible, there were very few sacrifices that did not involve "the idea of buying back" one's debt, which is why they used the term "sacrifice-contract" to refer to this contractual dimension in the sacrifice.
147. Frazer 1890. Frazer (1898, 1902) thanked Mauss for publishing a review of his book in *L'Année*, as well as proposing to review its translation in French. As Marcel Fournier (1994) has emphasized, Mauss's encounter with Frazer in Oxford in 1898 had only reinforced Mauss's philological orientation, and the two men (and Frazer's wife, who was French) formed a friendship which not only extended for more than twenty years, but which also nourished Mauss's institutional-building efforts at the Institute of Ethnology. For instance, Frazer proposed to consider a partnership between his Folklore Society and Mauss's Institute of Ethnology after the creation of the latter (Frazer 1929).
148. Liebersohn 2011.
149. Which Mauss discussed in his study of contractual practices among the Thraces (1921: 1). Thurnwald in particular was an Austrian-born ethnologist who spent his career half in Berlin and half in the United States.
150. For a similar point on the development and institutionalization of ethnology in Germany before the First World War, see Steinmetz (2008).
151. Conklin 2013: 263.
152. Maupoil 1934a, 1934b.
153. Maupoil 1934b.
154. Mauss 1937c.
155. Mauss 1937c.
156. Maupoil 1934a.
157. Mauss 1937a. Le Cœur (1942) preferred to take over Mauss's chair rather than Leenhardt's chair on comparative religions.
158. Conklin 2013: 273.
159. Mauss 1938.
160. Mauss 1938.
161. Mauss 1938.
162. Mauss 1928.
163. Conklin 2013: 266.
164. Seligman 1938. For instance, Mauss (1937d) asked Seligman to seek authorization for a student of Louis Massignon, his colleague at the Collège de France, to conduct fieldwork in Sudan.
165. Maupoil 1934b.
166. Griaule 1930.
167. C. Rist 1930; Rockefeller Foundation 1930.
168. Rivière 1930; Griaule 1931b.
169. Griaule 1931a.
170. de Rougemont 2010.
171. Griaule 1928a, 1928b.
172. Griaule 1931c.

173. Griaule 1931d.
174. Mauss 1937c. Later, Mauss accepted to write letters of recommendation for Griaule, who took over Soustelle's job at the Museum of Ethnology; see Conklin (2013) for a detailed analysis of the postwar controversy over Griaule's wartime opportunism, which led him to accept many responsibilities in the field of ethnology which Mauss and Rivet lost as a result of the Vichy laws.
175. Maupoil 1934a.
176. Maupoil 1934a, 1934b.
177. Maupoil 1934b.
178. Girardet 1972: 132.
179. Maurois 1931; D. Lazard 1990.
180. Conklin 2013: 191.
181. Manceron 2003: 189.
182. Alain, Langevin and Rivet 1934.
183. Soustelle 1986: 47.
184. Mauss 1933.
185. Soustelle 1986: 58.
186. Soustelle 1986: 25.
187. Conklin 2013: 232.
188. Maupoil 1935c.
189. Maupoil 1935c.
190. Maupoil 1935c.
191. Maupoil 1938b.
192. Maupoil 1937a.
193. Maupoil 1938a.
194. Fournier 1994.
195. Mauss instead supported Déat and his run against Blum in the SFIO. As Mauss wrote to Blum in 1933, he was closer to Renaudel and he would have even considered himself a "neo-socialist" (like Déat) if the latter "did not confuse their Jacobinism with socialist utopias" (Mauss 1935).
196. Maupoil 1938c.
197. Maupoil 1938b.
198. Kojève 2001 [1956]: 123.
199. Bedjaoui 1978a.

5 Marcel Mauss's Disciples in Algeria

1. Soustelle 1959e: 3.
2. Soustelle 1959e: 4.
3. Soustelle 1959e: 5.
4. Soustelle 1959e: 4.
5. Mauss 2013: 176.
6. Lépinard 2015.
7. Bouyahia and Sanna 2013; Lépinard 2015; Mazouz 2017.
8. Portes and Min Zou 1993.

9. Lagrange 2010.
10. Girardet 1972: 199.
11. Girardet 1972: 199.
12. Olick and Robbins 1998.
13. Girardet 1972: 195.
14. Mitterrand 1957: 3–4.
15. Girardet 1972: 195.
16. Before the Second World War, Mauss introduced the concept of "integration" in *The Nation* to point out differences between nations, characterized by different levels of integration (from "tribal" to "national" levels), and different developments in national public law (the "inter-national" between two independent true nations being the ultimate stage of development). In contrast, Jacques Soustelle understood the notion of "integration" in a way typical of the postwar political narrative, which stressed the need to further the *political* integration of overseas and metropolitan territories under a shared constitutional Republican framework, which ensured equal political participation to all citizens, whatever their race, legal status, or religion.
17. Soustelle 1956a.
18. Soustelle 1956a.
19. Soustelle 1957a.
20. Soustelle 1957a: 1.
21. Soustelle 1957a: 6.
22. Soustelle 1957a: 6.
23. Cohen 1971: 185.
24. Soustelle 1957a: 6.
25. Soustelle 1956b.
26. Soustelle 1957c: 5.
27. Soustelle 1957a: 8.
28. de Gaulle 1956.
29. de Gaulle 1956.
30. Soustelle 1962.
31. Lacouture 2011: 272; Francioli 2015: 196.
32. Shepard 2008: 67–9.
33. Auriol 1956.
34. Soustelle 1967.
35. Soustelle 1959e: 3.
36. Shepard 2008.
37. Soustelle 1967: 186.
38. Soustelle 1957c.
39. Soustelle 1959d.
40. Soustelle 1959d.
41. Soustelle 1955.
42. Tillion 2009: 351.
43. Soustelle 1986: 18.
44. Sacriste 2011: 46.

45. Tillion 1937.
46. Tillion 1939.
47. Tillion 2015.
48. Tillion 2015.
49. Massignon was persuaded that Mitterrand could not refuse Tillion's mission, as the Association France-Maghreb, which Massignon had founded with François Mauriac and of which Mitterrand was a member, had convinced Mitterrand to resign from his post as minister in the previous government. One year later, Mitterrand was rewarded for his resignation by Prime Minister Mendès France, who named him Minister of the Interior; Lacouture 2011: 235.
50. Francioli 2015: 134.
51. Soustelle believed one should not negotiate with the FLN, especially after August 1955 when the FLN carried out a bloodbath in Philippeville – in retaliation against Algerian Muslims, Europeans killed more than a thousand victims (Tillion 2009: 318).
52. Mitterrand, as Minister of the Interior, adopted this tough execution policy – which violated developing laws of war (as political prisoners could be granted amnesty if peace could be reached) – as he wanted to appear "harder" on terrorists than the Minister of Defense, with whom he was competing to become the next president of the council (Malye and Stora 2012: 196–7).
53. Tillion 2009: 318.
54. Sacriste 2011: 288.
55. Sacriste 2011: 122, 129.
56. Cited in Sacriste 2011: 156.
57. Sacriste 2011: 163.
58. Aron 1959, 1963, 1976.
59. Leca 2001: 7.
60. Bourdieu 1990.
61. Guilhot 2011.
62. A. Becker 2003: 315.
63. Leca 2001.
64. Aron 1957.
65. Shepard 2008.
66. Aron 1957.
67. Marseille 1984: 11.
68. Soustelle 1957b: 46.
69. Manceron 2003: 226.
70. When French capital exports to Algeria had represented in 1914 three-fourths of the total capital exports to the colonies (3 out of 4 billion francs) (Marseille 1984: 68).
71. Cited in Marseille 1984: 337.
72. Cited in Marseille 1984: 323.
73. On this issue, Mauss saw eye to eye with Sarraut and d'Estaing, as he wrote in *The Nation* that the problem of Europe's procurement in raw materials was a collective problem that should not be addressed in isolated terms,

neither conceptually, nor financially, nor commercially: in his unpublished manuscript, he wondered whether it would not be possible to facilitate the import of raw materials in Europe from the colonies, either by the issuance of international subscriptions for national reconstruction projects, or by the creation of an international currency (2013: 245).

74. Marseille 1984: 36.
75. Sarraut 1931: 211.
76. Cited in Marseille 1984: 223.
77. Marseille 1984: 223.
78. Marseille 1984: 63, 76.
79. Marseille 1984: 196, 265.
80. Marseille 1984: 354.
81. Girardet 1972: 25.
82. Marseille 1984: 274, 347, 351.
83. Marseille 1984: 65.
84. Freymond 1951: 89. Thus, in contrast to what early analysts of French imperialism write, before the Great War, the territorial expansion that ensued from Jules Ferry's call for France's colonial destiny was not matched by a similar interest among the financial milieu. As Marseille (1984: 262) sums it up, colonial imperialism of the years 1880–1938 was not the "supreme stage of capitalism," as Lenin once wrote, but rather, the "supreme stage of mercantilism" (1984: 94).
85. Marseille 1984: 104.
86. Marseille 1984: 143.
87. Tillion 1960 [1957]: 56.
88. Tillion 1960 [1957]: 82.
89. Tillion 1960 [1957]: 82.
90. Soustelle 1957b: 5.
91. Aron 1957: 33.
92. Soustelle 1957b: 35.
93. In French, "clochardisation," a neologism she coined. As Tillion wrote, "the black trade and slavery were the biggest crimes of the eighteenth century, colonialism that of the nineteenth century, and the crime of our time was the phenomenon of 'pauperization,' of which the phenomenon of the concentration camp was its extreme rationalized manifestation – an attempt to make the most financial profit out of it" (1960 [1957]: 55).
94. Tillion 1960 [1957]: 82.
95. Tillion 1960 [1957]: 46, 55.
96. The result of both medical progress leading to decreased infant mortality rates in large families and the introduction of imported industrial products in local markets, leaving rural families with no hope of maintaining their economy of subsistence.
97. Tillion 1960 [1957]: 82.
98. Soustelle 1957b: 28.
99. Soustelle 1958.

100. Soustelle 1986: 256. Among the reasons for the escalation in the Algerian War, Soustelle also cited Mollet's decision to disband the Algerian Assembly without creating at the same time a coordinating council which would have met in Paris: as he said, after this decision, the Oulemas, who had representation in the Assembly, went back to their villages and thus joined the revolution of the FLN (1986: 253).
101. Soustelle 1958.
102. Soustelle 1957b: 23–4. Still, Soustelle had not been opposed to population displacement in the case of the Algerian "camps de regroupement."
103. Soustelle 1957b: 28.
104. Chaussade 1958.
105. Soustelle 1957c.
106. Tillion 1960 [1957]: 130.
107. Tillion 1960 [1957]: 110.
108. Tillion 1960 [1957]: 110–11.
109. Tillion 1960 [1957]: 101.
110. Soustelle 1957a: 8.
111. Tillion 1960 [1957]: 56.
112. Tillion considered that the problem of pauperization concerned all rural populations displaced by modern wars and global markets.
113. Tillion 1960 [1957]: 77.
114. Tillion 1960 [1957]: 57.
115. She gave as an example the ridiculous number of 408 out of 500,000 Palestinian teenagers who benefited from professional training under the auspices of the United Nations (Tillion 1960 [1957]: 76).
116. Only those families with a member (generally a young man) working in the metropolis – there were 400,000 Algerian workers in the metropolis at the time – benefited from some monetized income in the form of remittances. The others – the majority – had not seen their living conditions improve as a result of the encounter with the capitalist economy (in its French version) and the French administration.
117. Tillion 1960 [1957]: 91–2.
118. Tillion 1960 [1957]: 67.
119. Soustelle 1959b.
120. Soustelle 1959e.
121. Soustelle 1959a.
122. Laffont 1960.
123. Laffont 1960.
124. Nora 1961.
125. Heilbron 2011; Go 2013.
126. Sacriste 2011: 286.
127. Sacriste 2011: 291.
128. Sacriste 2011: 328.

129. A posture he generalized in his epistemological writings, which endorsed Bachelard's epistemology of the total "rupture" between science and politics (Bourdieu, Chamboredon, and Passeron 1968).
130. Even if Bourdieu (1958) was sometimes guilty of reproducing clichés on the difference between Berbers and Arabs (Sacriste 2011: 292), his main ambition was to identify an Algerian rule of law outside the "civilized" French system imposed from Paris.
131. Bourdieu and Sayad 1964.
132. Hence, Bourdieu agreed that Lévi-Strauss' analysis of gift-exchanges and matrimonial systems still applied to some parts of Algeria (Bourdieu and Sayad 1964: 13).
133. Bourdieu and Sayad 1964: 21.
134. Soustelle 1958.
135. Bourdieu and Sayad 1964: 70
136. Bourdieu and Sayad 1964: 87.
137. In fact, many of the colonists (about 10,000) who benefited the most from the Warnier law were in fact Republicans sent into exile by the coup of 1851, by which Napoléon III ended the Second Republic of 1848 (Manceron 2003).
138. Under which 2,157,000 Algerian Muslims were forcibly moved out of their villages and into camps built and controlled by the French army, in addition to the 3 million peasants who were driven by poverty to move to the city outskirts (Bourdieu and Sayad 1964: 13).
139. From 1880 to 1895, the French colonial possessions in Africa multiplied tenfold (Girardet 1972: 45).
140. Bourdieu and Sayad 1964: 93.
141. Bourdieu 1961: 15.
142. Bourdieu and Sayad 1964: 32.
143. Bourdieu 1961: 71.
144. From this observation, it is not surprising that, in the controversy that Lévi-Strauss (1950) started with his old master Marcel Mauss when latter's writings were collected in a book-length format just after his death, Bourdieu (1980: 167) sided with Mauss, who, according to Lévi-Strauss, was guilty of placing the discussion of gifts at the phenomenological level of individuals' perception of obligations, rather than at the systemic level of the overall circulation of gifts. Like Mauss, Bourdieu was very much aware that binding obligations organized by the exchange of gifts were sometimes violated, leading to losses of honor, as well as anticipations of defaults, which inserted uncertainty into the heart of the system – an uncertainty that Lévi-Strauss failed to acknowledge.
145. Bourdieu and Sayad 1964: 33.
146. Bourdieu 1980: 219.
147. Bourdieu and Sayad 1964: 87.
148. Bourdieu and Sayad 1964: 25.
149. Bourdieu 1980.
150. Bourdieu and Sayad 1964: 90.

151. Fanon 1961.
152. When he entered the ENS in 1948 as a young philosophy student, Bourdieu had admired Jean-Paul Sartre (Sacriste 2011: 281).
153. Bourdieu and Sayad 1964: 169.
154. According to what de Gaulle told his ministers (Peyrefitte 1994).
155. Shepard 2008: 163.
156. Indeed, after the failed coup, Soustelle was told by his friends in the government that he had become a target for assassination by de Gaulle's secret services (Francioli 2015).
157. Soustelle 1963: 84, 163. The Conseil d'Etat declared in a confidential advisory opinion that the referendum of April 8, 1962 was "anticonstitutional, illegal and illegitimate" (Shepard 2008: 150).
158. Soustelle 1975: 11, 13.
159. Soustelle 1967: 106.
160. Soustelle 1967: 106.
161. Soustelle 1967: 106.
162. Soustelle 1975: 11. Soustelle (1967: 107) also reaffirmed Mauss's intuition: that "human history does not follow a gradual and ascending line, but appears to be like an ocean where waves infinitely rise up, rage and fall upon."
163. Soustelle 1975: 13, 15.
164. Soustelle 1975: 18.
165. Liebersohn 2011.

6 Decolonizing *The Gift*

1. Chapter 2, part B, Second Part, Evian Agreements, 1962. For the full text of the Evian Agreements, see Malek 1995: 313–65.
2. Article 2 of Title I, Third Part, Evian Agreements, 1962.
3. Article 13 of Title IV, Third Part, Evian Agreements, 1962.
4. Malek 1995: 200.
5. Byrne 2016: 123.
6. Title II of the Second Part, Evian Agreements 1962.
7. Article 12 of Title IV, Third Part, Evian Agreements 1962.
8. Article 14 of the Title IV, Third Part, Evian Agreements 1962.
9. In contrast, Soustelle believed that there was nothing natural in the organization of the international society as a society of independent states (Shepard 2008).
10. Cited in Byrne 2016: 125.
11. Bedjaoui participated in the meetings in Lugrin (July 1961); in Evian (May–July 1961), during which Bedjaoui remained, with the other experts, on the Swiss side, in the villa of a Qatari prince; and in the Signal de Bougy (December 1961), although by this time Bedjaoui, Ahmed Francis, and Ferhat Abbas were no longer part of the government as a result of a cabal which occurred in the middle of the negotiations, and which distanced the three men

from the active negotiating team (Bedjaoui 2016: 36). See also Malek 1995: 198; Ouguergouz and Bownedra 1999: 5.

12. Bedjaoui 2017: 3.
13. Bedjaoui 1970a: 486.
14. Byrne 2016: 128.
15. Bedjaoui 1970a: 498–9, also 1970b.
16. Bedjaoui 1970a: 500.
17. Bourdieu and Sayad 1964.
18. Bedjaoui 1978a: 94.
19. Bedjaoui 1970a: 469.
20. Byrne 2016.
21. At that conference, Boumédiène succeeded in obtaining an unlikely consensus from Arab leaders and the Shah of Iran, as well as Mexican President Luis Echeverría Alvarez and Manuel Pérez Guerrero, a Venezuelan economist who served as the Secretary General of the UN Conference on Trade and Development (UNCTAD) from 1969 to 1974 (Cox 1979).
22. Bedjaoui 1976: 89.
23. Bedjaoui 1981.
24. Malek 1995: 269.
25. Schrijver 1997: 116.
26. See e.g. Cox 1979; G. Rist 1996; Pahuja 2011.
27. Abi-Saab 1991; G. Rist 2002; Rajagopal 2003; Craven 2007; Pahuja 2011.
28. See e.g. the work of G. Rist 2002. Even if it may appear arbitrary or partial to the specialist of decolonization in the Anglophone or Lusophone worlds to anchor the intellectual and political evolution of the ideas of the NIEO in the context of the Algerian War of Independence, the focus on Algerian jurists and diplomats and their relation to the NIEO can be justified by the leading role of Algeria for the evolution of ideas of global governance in the Global South in general.
29. Which Rist brilliantly deconstructs in his analysis of the developmental discourse produced by UN developmental organizations (G. Rist 2002).
30. Bedjaoui 1978a: 98.
31. Pahuja 2011: 80.
32. Dupuy 1990.
33. Bedjaoui 1958.
34. Colliard 1956. The manual was highly influential in French law schools, after a 1954 reform of the law school curriculum made a class on international institutions mandatory in metropolitan universities.
35. Before the war, she served as the chief of staff for her husband, Paul Bastid (1892–1974), a professor of public law, when the latter became minister of trade in the Blum government.
36. Throughout the years, Bastid-Basdevant continued to review positively Bedjaoui's work and published a very laudatory comment on his 1978 manifesto for the NIEO (Bastid-Basdevant 1979).

37. In Grenoble, Bedjaoui also militated for the protection of the rights of Algerian migrants (as a practicing lawyer registered in the metropolis), by protesting against the especially harsh taxation by the French government to finance the building of collective residences for them (Bedjaoui 2016: 18).
38. Bedjaoui 2016: 11.
39. Bedjaoui 2016: 15.
40. Bedjaoui 2016: 15.
41. During which Algerians demonstrated for the liberation of imprisoned nationalist leader Messali Hadj (1898–1975), parading with Algerian flags on the day of the Allied victory, and were consequently fired on by the police, sparking an outbreak of violence and an even greater French repression – numbers of the massacred are still debated, as estimates of the victims of the indiscriminate executions by the French range from 5,000 to 45,000 victims (the latter being the number officially recognized by the Algerian government). Setif was one of the places where the French repression was the most horrible.
42. Bedjaoui 2016: 15.
43. Ouguergouz and Bownedra 1999: 5.
44. In the interim, Francis had served as the editor of UDMA's journal, originally titled *Equality*, and then after 1954, *Equality, the Algerian Republic*.
45. Bedjaoui 2016: 6.
46. Bedjaoui 2016: 28.
47. Bedjaoui 2016: 24.
48. Bedjaoui 2016: 25.
49. Soustelle 1962: 66.
50. Bedjaoui 2016: 39.
51. "Cot told us where the weaknesses of our positions were," and, as Bedjaoui added, "some may call it high treason, as he advised a government against his government, but it showed instead his high intelligence and his intellectual integrity" (Bedjaoui 2016: 40).
52. Bedjaoui 1961: 114.
53. Bedjaoui 1961: 12.
54. Bedjaoui 1961: 13.
55. Bedjaoui 1961: 18–19.
56. Bedjaoui (1961: 22–5) found recognition of the presence of an active Algerian state by the French government in all the documents cited by French colonialists: the 1830 Convention of Algiers, the 1835 Oran Convention, and the 1837 Treaty of Tafna which recognized the authority of the Emir Abd-el-Qader.
57. Bedjaoui 1961: 31. Even if French Muslims were offered French citizenship after 1919, in fact less than a few thousand Algerian Muslims out of a total of nine million petitioned to obtain this citizenship (Bedjaoui 1961: 29).
58. Aron 1957.
59. Bourdieu 1958.
60. Bedjaoui 1961: 88–112.
61. Flory 1961: 1058.
62. Fanon 1952; Memmi 1957.

63. This explanation seems more precise than the statement made by Rajagopal that Bedjaoui did not wish "to do away with [a classically realist view of] international law at all," an emblematic contradictory position often found in the writings of the "postcolonial lawyer who identifies himself with building his nation" (Rajagopal 2003: 93). See also Anghie, Chimni, Mickelson, and Okafor 2003.
64. Bedjaoui 1978a: 92.
65. Although the Algerian FLN sent a representative to Bandung, the Egyptian leader Gamal Abdel Nasser (1918–70), Yugoslav President Josip Tito (1892–1980), and Indian President Jawaharlal Nehru (1889–1964) led the fight of the non-aligned nations until the Belgrade 1961 conference – where finally a Latin American country, Bolivia, was invited.
66. Bedjaoui 1961.
67. Bedjaoui 2016: 35.
68. Bedjaoui 2016.
69. Bedjaoui 2016.
70. Malek 1995: 137.
71. Malek 1995: 113.
72. Malek 1995: 162. On this complex matter, the GPRA received the help of Claude Cixous on the economic side and Mohammed Bedjaoui on the legal side (Malek 1995: 198).
73. Malek 1995: 148.
74. Bedjaoui 2017: 2.
75. Bedjaoui 2017: 2.
76. Byrne 2016: 128.
77. Malek 1995: 138.
78. Bedjaoui 1961: 33.
79. Malek 1995: 126. As for Sarraut, colonial solidarity derived from the supreme right of the most efficient organization (here, the French oil companies) to claim natural resources, which they exploited for the good of humanity (defined in the ability of oil concessions to provide optimal quantities of oil for the markets and at a competitive price), rather than for the good of the nation where the natural resources were found.
80. Malek 1995: 200.
81. Article 12 of Title IV, Third Part, Evian Agreements, 1962.
82. Bedjaoui 1970b: 147.
83. Bedjaoui (1970: 148) found this principle outdated – and exemplary of the interwar imperial concept of limited sovereignty – and he cited in support of his thesis the opinion of Charles Rousseau (1902–93), a professor of international public law at the University of Paris and jurisconsult for the Ministry of Foreign Affairs from the 1950s to the 1970s. Shabtai Rosenne, an Israeli scholar sitting on the ILC subcommittee chaired by Bedjaoui, had been Rousseau's student.
84. Article 2 of Title I, Third Part, Evian Agreements, 1962.

85. Something Iran did a year later, triggering the downfall of the democratically elected government and the restoration of a regime friendly to Anglo-American oil interests, which was to last until the 1979 Revolution.
86. Abi-Saab 1991: 602.
87. Pahuja 2011: 118.
88. Members included, among others: Sir Humphrey Waldock (UK and Northern Ireland); Mr. Roberto Ago (Italy); Mr. Milan Bartos (Yugoslavia); Mr. Mohammed Bedjaoui (Algeria); Mr. Jorge Castañeda (Mexico); Mr. Erik Castrén (Finland); Mr. Abdullah El-Erian (United Arab Republic); Mr. Taslim O. Elias (Nigeria); Mr. Nagendra Singh (India); Mr. Alfred Ramangasoavina (Madagascar); Mr. Paul Reuter (France); Mr. Shabtai Rosenne (Israel); Mr. Abdul Hakim Tabibi (Afghanistan).
89. Bedjaoui 2017: 20.
90. International Law Commission 1967: 368.
91. Sack 1927: 88.
92. The notion of "public debt" had been discussed by Jèze (1922) – later cited by Bedjaoui in his report – who had been known for taking on the legal defense of Ethiopian Emperor Haile Selassie in 1936 – and, as such, Jèze's classes were blocked by young colonialist students in Paris including future president François Mitterrand (Manceron 2003: 261) – and it was different from the notion of "sovereign debt" which is now widely used in the academic literature, as those public debts which fell upon the shoulders of colonial governments did not imply any recognition of sovereignty.
93. Sack 1927: xiv.
94. Stephen Schwebel was a former State Department jurist who later joined Bedjaoui at the ICJ (and who succeeded Bedjaoui as ICJ president), to whom Bedjaoui once said in an ILC session that "he was for sharing the world [between great powers] when he [Bedjaoui] was for a world of sharing" (Bedjaoui 2017: 21).
95. A concept I draw from Halliday 2018.
96. Although, as some commentators have shown, the first and third criteria may not always be required, even by Sack (Ludington, Gulati, Brophy, 2010; Toussaint 2017a). Still, in general, Sack participated in the global emergence of the norm according to which state debts should be repaid, as his theory was rather conservative (Lienau 2014).
97. Sack 1927: 158.
98. Cited in Sack 1927: 161–2.
99. Sack (1927: 164) estimated that these *Schutzgebietsanleihen* amounted to 183.75 million marks.
100. Bedjaoui 1977: 103.
101. Bedjaoui 1970a: 477.
102. Bedjaoui 1970a: 477.
103. Bedjaoui 1970a: 518
104. Bedjaoui 1970a: 524.
105. Bedjaoui 1977: 57.

106. Bedjaoui 1977: 99.
107. Bedjaoui 1977: 99.
108. In fact, during the negotiation of the Evian Agreements, Algeria's denunciation of French debts contracted for costs related to the Algerian territory had not been limited to the "war debts that France had [initially] charged to Algeria" like "payment of compensation to the victims of 'Algerian terrorism' or expenditures associated with establishment and maintenance of the *harki* force [composed of Algerian men enrolled by the French military forces to fight against the FLN]" – e.g. those debts that even Alexander Sack would have considered "odious" – but they also extended to debts which had been contracted to pay for useful developmental projects. Bedjaoui 1977: 100.
109. Mauss 1925a.
110. Bedjaoui 1977: 100.
111. Malek 1995: 201.
112. Bedjaoui 1977: 99.
113. Bedjaoui 1977: 99.
114. Bedjaoui 2017: 5.
115. Bedjaoui 2017: 5.
116. As Bedjaoui remarked, if it was considered "inherited debt," then "Algeria would have paid the money, not to the predecessor state, but to any third parties to which France owed money in connection with its previous activities in Algeria" (Bedjaoui 1977: 99).
117. Bedjaoui 1977: 103.
118. Foucault 2003.
119. Bedjaoui 1961: 16.
120. Flory 1961: 1060–1.
121. Flory wrote his dissertation on the issues of legality and legitimacy of the acts of governments in exile in London during the Second World War (Flory 1961: 1060–1).
122. Bedjaoui 1981: 28.
123. Bedjaoui 1981: 27.
124. Bedjaoui 1981: 29.
125. Law 2005–158 of February 23, 2005, French Parliament.
126. Bedjaoui 1977: 103.
127. Bedjaoui 1977: 103.
128. Both "debts contracted by the predecessor state for and on behalf of a dependent territory, and debts contracted by the dependent territory prior to independence, but with the guarantee of the administering power" (Bedjaoui 1977: 94).
129. As far as the Evian Agreements (1962) were concerned, Bedjaoui recognized that even if article 18 admitted the principle of succession of both France's rights *and obligations*, it was silent on whether such "obligations" included public debts contracted either by the metropolitan state or by the governor-general, which left room to maneuver (1977: 92).
130. Lachs 1963: 286, 265.

131. Bedjaoui 1968: 97.
132. Bedjaoui 1970a: 463.
133. Riles 2011.
134. Bedjaoui 1970a: 483.
135. Bedjaoui 1970a: 465.
136. Bedjaoui 1968: 97, 99.
137. Bedjaoui 1968: 96.
138. Lachs 1963: 286, 265.
139. Bedjaoui 2017: 8.
140. Group of 77 1967.
141. UNGA 1974b.
142. Bedjaoui 1970a: 518
143. Grimaud 1972: 1298.
144. UNGA 1974a.
145. UNGA 1974b.
146. UNGA 1974a.
147. Bedjaoui 1978a: 177.
148. Indeed, the Charter affirmed a right for each state to "regulate and exercise authority over foreign investment within its national jurisdiction," a right to "regulate and supervise the activities of transnational corporations, and a right to nationalize, expropriate or transfer ownership of foreign property," in which case "appropriate compensation" should be paid by the state adopting such measures, "taking into account its relevant laws and regulations and all circumstances that the State considers pertinent" (article 2, UNGA 1974c).
149. Colson 1972.
150. Rights that were given to the oil companies by the French sovereign state as well as in recognition of the 6.5 billion francs invested in the extraction of oil in the Algerian Sahara (Grimaud 1972: 1280).
151. Grimaud 1972.
152. Grimaud 1972: 1283.
153. Grimaud 1972: 192.
154. They also claimed that from 1965 to 1970, the French oil companies made 7 billion francs profit from Algerian oil exploitation while the French claimed only 1.4 billion francs, leading to disputes about the amount that the French should have reinvested in Algeria per the 1965 bilateral deal (Grimaud 1972: 1285).
155. Bedjaoui 2017: 15.
156. Grimaud 1972: 1300.
157. In retaliation, the French companies initially halted the production and commercialization of Saharan oil by sending letters to all possible commercial partners of Sonatrach (Algeria's national oil company) threatening them with litigation if they traded Algerian oil. The crisis had reached a climax (Bedjaoui 2017: 47).
158. Grimaud 1972: 1307.
159. Chaumont 1970: 350; Bedjaoui 1978a: 63.

160. Already in 1927, Alexander Sack had recognized that the theory of state succession did not purely belong to international public law but represented a legal doctrine *sui generis*, as it organized the relationships between a successor state (or successor states in case of partition) and the creditors (both public and private) of the predecessor state (Sack 1927: 84).
161. Rosenne, cited in Lachs 1963: 287.
162. ILC 1970: 300.
163. Bedjaoui 1971: 177.
164. Bedjaoui 1972: 67. Before, Bedjaoui had claimed that concessions had to be read as contractual obligations with *private* persons – as the ICJ had established in its 1952 ruling on *Anglo-Iranian Oil* v. *Iran* – and not as *public* law documents benefiting from the sanctity attributed to treaties (1969; 1970: 535).
165. Bedjaoui 1972: 67.
166. Bedjaoui 1971: 176.
167. Bedjaoui 1970a: 536. Looking back at the jurisprudence of the Permanent Court of Justice, Bedjaoui found a ruling that concerned the protection of the acquired rights of German nationals expropriated from their lands by the new Polish state, but here, he found that it was a specific treaty obligation (and not a reference to *jus cogens*), which grounded the decision of the Court to ask Poland to compensate the German victims (Bedjaoui 1970a: 555).
168. Bedjaoui 1970a: 146. Bedjaoui (1972: 62) confirmed that he wanted to avoid that "distinction, which, indeed, is unknown to some national laws" and thus proposed the concept of "property appertaining to sovereignty" (1971: 179).
169. Bedjaoui 1972: 62.
170. Bedjaoui 1972: 67.
171. Bedjaoui 1973: 26
172. Bedjaoui 1973: 25.
173. Bedjaoui 1973: 256–7.
174. Bedjaoui 1973: 27.
175. They extended beyond the strict confines of international *public* law, as it was concerned with the "economic and financial acquired rights" of both public and private individuals (Bedjaoui 1970a).
176. Bedjaoui 1976: 82.
177. Bedjaoui 1969.
178. Bedjaoui 1970a: 545.
179. Bedjaoui 1970a: 528.
180. Bedjaoui 1970a: 533. Bedjaoui (1970: 531) cited Léon Duguit (1859–1928) in order to justify expropriation of private property by the state and international debt settlement. Duguit defended the decrees of the Third Republic expropriating the Church's property in 1880 against Maurice Hauriou (1956–29) (Bancaud 2002: 187).
181. Bedjaoui 1970a: 545.
182. Bedjaoui 1970a: 485.
183. Bedjaoui 1970a: 552, 559.
184. Bedjaoui 1970a: 550.

185. Bedjaoui 1970a: 556.
186. Bedjaoui 1978b: 31.
187. Bedjaoui 2017: 34.
188. UN Conference 1983a.
189. UN Conference 1983b: 94.
190. UN Conference 1983b: 98.
191. UN Conference 1983b: 227; UN Conference 1983b: 100.
192. The delegates in the plenary conference who voted against represented Belgium, Canada, France, Germany, Israel, Italy, Luxembourg, Netherlands, Switzerland, the UK, and the US (UN Conference 1983a: 31).
193. UN Conference 1983a: 31.
194. UN Conference 1983a: 34.
195. UN Conference 1983a: 27.
196. Articles 14 and 15, UN Conference 1983b: 62.
197. UN Conference 1983b: 93, 109.
198. Waibel 2011.
199. Dezalay and Garth 1996, 2016.
200. UN Conference 1983b: 96.
201. UN Conference 1983b: 70. As Bedjaoui added, newly independent states like Algeria had objected to article 12, as immediately after a succession there was a risk that the predecessor state would pass its property to a third state in order to protect it from being appropriated by the successor state – as in cases of "fraudulent bankruptcy" – but he did not "believe that on the eve of succession, a third state would risk acquiring property title which might well be contested by the successor state" (UN Conference 1983b: 59).
202. UN Conference 1983b: 193.
203. UN Conference 1983b: 196.
204. UN Conference 1983b: 199.
205. UN Conference 1983b: 194.
206. In the Convention, after six introductory articles, seven articles concerned the issue of "transfers" of *state property* – or, rather, the "substitution of sovereignty" to which "property" was attached, as the articles talked about the "extinction" and "arising" of rights (article 9) in order to stress discontinuity rather than continuity in the process – five articles (14–18) concerned the issue of territorial swaps, thirteen articles (19–31) concerned the issue of the transfer of state archives, ten articles (32–41) codified the issue of state debt in cases of state succession (UN Conference 1983b: 48).
207. UN Conference 1983a: 27.
208. Rajagopal 2003: 90.
209. Rajagopal 2003: 89.
210. Rist 1996; Gilman 2003; Pahuja 2011.
211. In his book, Rostow distinguished between five stages of development – i.e. "traditional," "pre-take-off," "take-off," "post-take-off stabilization" and "high consumerist" (Rostow 1960).
212. Anghie, Chimni, Mickelson, and Okafor 2003.

213. Pahuja 2011: 4.
214. Bedjaoui 1978a: 93–7.
215. Bedjaoui 1984.
216. Ozsu 2015.
217. Bedjaoui 1978a: 95.
218. Bedjaoui 1978a: 97.
219. Bedjaoui 1978a.
220. A notable exception is Ozsu 2015.
221. G. Rist 1996: 149.
222. G. Rist 1996: 153.
223. G. Rist 1996: 152.
224. UNGA 1979.
225. Bedjaoui 1981: 6.
226. Bedjaoui 1981: 14.
227. Craven 2007.
228. Gulati and Ludington 2008.
229. Bedjaoui 1981: 19.
230. Indeed, the norm of sovereign immunity started to disappear in the 1980s, as states increasingly faced court proceedings when defaulting on sovereign bonds (Panizza, Sturzenegger, and Zettelmeyer 2009).
231. None of the main histories of neoliberal ideas mention the contribution of the NIEO to the economic debate (Dezalay and Garth 2002; Best 2005; Ferguson 2005; Krippner 2005; Blyth 2013). In Zettelmeyer and Rogoff (2002: 472), the proposal to set up a debtor-friendly debt commission, inspired by the NIEO and the Plenary Committee, receives scant attention, the focus being on proposals of debt bankruptcy reform initiated and discussed by IMF experts.
232. Florès-Zendejas 2016; Shaffer and Waibel 2016.
233. Pahuja 2011: 95.
234. Rajagopal 2003: 90; see also Anghie 2015.
235. One notable exception being Rist (1996), who criticizes the NIEO for its internal contradictions.

7 International Solidarity and Gift Exchange in the Eurozone

1. That is quite egoistic to say, of course, as the end of the NIEO and the rise of neoliberalism – which I define here broadly as the deregulation of capital markets and large cuts in state spending – brought financial instability and massive unemployment to many parts of the world.
2. Godbout 2000.
3. Aglietta and Orléan 1998.
4. Fourcade Gourinchas 2009.
5. Servet 2016.
6. Attali 2016 [1986]: 324.
7. Attali 2016 [1986]: 321, 338; on the long history of the European negotiations that led to the denuclearization of Germany, see Mallard (2014).

8. Attali 2016 [1986]: 146–59.
9. Mallard 2014.
10. Malye and Stora 2012.
11. Attali 2016 [1986]: 408.
12. This was more easily said than done. With the breaking down of the Berlin Wall in 1989, and the collapse of the Soviet Empire, the Republic of Yugoslavia melted: civil war and ethnic cleansing in Serbia, Croatia, Bosnia, and Kosovo demonstrated the fragility of the new international European order and the necessity to maintain strong Franco-German relations to avoid the escalation of local conflicts into pan-European all-out war.
13. Attali 2016 [1986]: 14, 408.
14. Attali 2016 [1986]: 277.
15. Andersson and Prat 2015: 12.
16. On this episode and its consequences in French political history, see Mallard (2014), especially chs. 4 and 5.
17. Attali and Guillaume 1975.
18. Attali 2016 [1986]: 28.
19. Dezalay and Garth 2002.
20. Moatti 2008.
21. De Coppet 1998.
22. Malamoud 1998.
23. Servet 1998. Servet's expertise in financial history was much larger, as it ranged from postcolonial currencies in Africa to the origins of antique moneys, which he studied in his dissertation (Servet 1984).
24. Servet 1980.
25. They also turned their back on Lévi-Strauss, whose structural perspective did not allow them to analyze endogenous contradictions within systems of exchanges (Aglietta and Orléan 1982: 26).
26. Servet 2016.
27. Girard 1961.
28. Girard 1999.
29. Aglietta and Orléan cited Mauss and Gernet, the Durkheimians who most importantly wrote about debt, but did not give as much of a place to Mauss as they would later do (Aglietta and Orléan 1982: 149, 150).
30. Aglietta and Orléan 1982: 38.
31. Aglietta and Orléan 1982: 27.
32. Aglietta and Orléan 1982: 35.
33. Attali 1982: 21.
34. Whereas Marx relied on the outdated theory of value promoted by David Ricardo – which was premised on the notion that there was a relation between the value of a merchandise and the amount of work that went into its production – and whereas Marx focused on the contradiction between the use-value of a good and the amount of work incorporated in the merchandise itself, and thus on the appropriation of the surplus value by capitalists/merchants at the expense of workers, Aglietta and Orléan focused on the discrepancies between the

(Walrasian) subjective use value of merchandises and their market value, especially when the latter bubbled in speculative markets. Still, Orléan (2011) continued to claim a Marxist filiation.

35. Aglietta and Orléan 1982: 37.
36. Aglietta and Orléan 1982: 47.
37. Aglietta and Orléan 1982: 33.
38. Aglietta and Orléan 1982: 33.
39. Dezalay and Garth 2002; Best 2005.
40. Aglietta and Orléan 1982: 48.
41. In modern times, the decision to sell sovereign currencies and bet on their downfall during panics could be interpreted as the continuation of war by other means, as happened during the currency wars of the interwar period, which Mauss chronicled in his political writings of 1924.
42. These two kinds of market logics are not without any relation. When debts, bonds, or obligations are desired for themselves – for the gains that people hope to obtain from their circulation – panics can result in "the destruction of the means of production," because of a process of auto-validation of self-fulfilling prophecies (Aglietta and Orléan 1982: 76).
43. Aglietta and Orléan 1982: 46. As they write, the only guarantee of the value of money, and beyond, of the value of goods, is the "shared belief by private parties that the institution [in charge of issuing] money is transcendental" rather than purely contractual, and that this authority is somehow immune from the folly of market agents (Aglietta and Orléan 1982: 42).
44. Aglietta and Orléan 1982: 92.
45. Aglietta and Orléan 1982: 84.
46. Aglietta and Orléan 1982: 98.
47. Aglietta and Orléan 1982: 33.
48. Aglietta and Brand 2013: 177.
49. Aglietta and Brand 2013: 42.
50. In particular, the reports presented by Raymond Barre, the Vice-President of the EC, in February 1969, followed by the 1970 report of Pierre Werner, Prime Minister of Luxembourg, called for both budgetary and monetary integration (Aglietta and Brand 2013: 37).
51. Aglietta and Brand 2013: 37.
52. Pénet and Mallard 2014.
53. CNBC 2017. In this period, the ECB bought anywhere from €90 billion eurozone bonds per month to €30 billion per month as the program neared completion in 2018. When justifying its decision to not include Greece in its QE program, the ECB argued that its statutes required that the three main credit rating agencies should first issue statements about the sustainability of the Greek debt, which they did not (Pénet and Mallard 2014).
54. For instance, see Feldstein (1997).
55. Attali 2016 [1986]: 338.
56. Aglietta and Brand 2013: 47.
57. Aglietta and Brand 2013: 45.

58. Aglietta and Brand 2013: 76.
59. Aglietta and Brand 2013: 78.
60. Varoufakis 2017.
61. Pénet and Mallard 2014.
62. Aglietta and Brand 2013: 147.
63. Aglietta and Brand 2013: 147.
64. Toussaint 2017c.
65. Aglietta and Brand 2013: 83.
66. Aglietta and Brand 2013: 148.
67. In contrast to the 1930s, in the 2000s, the European governments and their central banks substituted themselves for private banks when the latter no longer extended any loans to each other: they were then able to reverse the climate of generalized suspicion that reigned at the time, mostly by adopting a policy of quantitative easing, which consisted in expanding the amount of currency available to buy bonds and other liquidities exchanged on financial markets (Aglietta and Brand 2013: 117).
68. Varoufakis 2017.
69. Aglietta and Brand 2013: 79.
70. Aglietta and Brand 2013: 43.
71. Varoufakis 2017.
72. Aglietta and Brand 2013: 169.
73. Aglietta and Brand 2013: 147.
74. Aglietta and Brand 2013: 181.
75. Aglietta and Brand 2013: 175.
76. Aglietta and Brand 2013: 178.
77. Vauchez 2014; Hennette, Piketty, Sacriste, and Vauchez 2017;.
78. Habermas 2009.
79. Hennette, Piketty, Sacriste, and Vauchez 2017.
80. Cohen, A. 2017.
81. Cohen, A. 2017.
82. If citizens indirectly elected parliamentarians of the Eurozone Parliament through national elections, these parliamentarians would mechanically represent the same parties as the ministers sitting in the Council of the EU, thus resulting in a high risk of collusion and lack of accountability at the European level (Mallard 2017).
83. Toussaint 2017a.
84. Varoufakis 2017.
85. Toussaint 2017a.

Bibliography

All URLs and websites were last accessed in February 2018.

Abbott, Andrew. 1988. *The System of Professions: An Essay on the Division of Expert Labor*. Chicago: University of Chicago Press.

Abi-Saab, Georges. 1991. "Permanent Sovereignty Over Natural Resources and Economic Activities," pp. 597–617 in *International Law: Achievements and Prospects*, edited by Mohammed Bedjaoui. Dordrecht: Martinus Nijhoff.

Aglietta, Michel and André Orléan. 1982. *La violence de la monnaie*. Paris: Presses universitaires de France.

(ed.). 1998. *La monnaie souveraine*. Paris: Odile Jacob.

Aglietta, Michel and Thomas Brand. 2013. *Un New Deal pour l'Europe*. Paris: Odile Jacob.

Akerloff, George. 1982. "Labor Contracts as Partial Gift Exchanges." *Quarterly Journal of Economics*. 97(4): 543–69.

Alain, Paul Langevin and Paul Rivet. 1934. "Letter to Mauss, March 7." Paris: Collège de France (Fonds Mauss: 57 CDF 88–23).

Amadae, S. M. 2003. *Rationalizing Capitalist Democracy: The Cold War Origins of Rational Choice Liberalism*. Chicago: University of Chicago Press.

Andersson, Jenny and Pauline Prat. 2015. "Gouverner le 'long terme': La prospective et la production bureaucratique des futurs en France." *Gouvernement et action publique*. 3 (3): 9–29.

Anghie, Antony. 2005. *Imperialism, Sovereignty and the Making of International Law*. Cambridge: Cambridge University Press.

2015. "Legal Aspects of the New International Economic Order." *Humanity: An International Journal of Human Rights, Humanitarianism, and Development* 6(1): 145–58.

Anghie, Anthony, Bhupinder Chimni, Karin Mickelson, and Obiora Chinedu Okafor, eds. 2003. *The Third World and International Order: Law, Politics and Globalization*. Leiden: Martinus Nijhoff.

L'Année sociologique, Comité de Rédaction. 1924. "Avant-Propos," 2–5.

Aron, Raymond. 1957. *La tragédie algérienne*. Paris: Plon.

1959. *La société industrielle et la guerre*. Paris: Plon.

1963. *Le grand débat: Initiation à la stratégie atomique*. Paris: Calmann-Lévy.

1976. *Penser la guerre: Clausewitz*. Paris: Gallimard.

Asad, Talal (ed.) 1973. *Anthropology and the Colonial Encounter*. Ithaca, NY: Ithaca Press.

Attali, Jacques. 1982. "Introduction," pp. 7–22, in *La violence de la monnaie*, by Aglietta, Michel and Michel Orléan. Paris: Presses universitaires de France.

2016 [1986]. *C'était François Mitterrand*. Paris: Fayard.

Attali, Jacques and Marc Guillaume. 1975. *L'anti-économique*. Paris: Presses universitaires de France.

Augagneur, Victor. 2010. *Erreurs et brutalités coloniales*. Paris: Les nuits rouges.

Auriol, Marc. 1956. "Letter to Jacques Soustelle, Oct." (Fonds Soustelle, 112AJ/32).

Bancaud, Alain. 2002. *Une exception ordinaire. La magistrature en France (1930–1950)*. Paris: Gallimard.

Barthélemy, Joseph. 1917. "L'application de la responsabilité de l'Etat aux dommages de guerre." In *La réparation des dommages de guerre*, edited by H. Berthélemy. Paris: Alcan.

Bastid, Suzanne. 1979. "Mohammed Bedjaoui. Pour un nouvel ordre économique international. Nouveaux défis au droit international." *Politique étrangère*. 44(1): 147–8.

Becker, Annette. 2003. *Maurice Halbwachs. Un intellectuel en guerres mondiales, 1914–1945*. Paris: Agnès Viénot.

Becker, Howard. 1982. *Art Worlds*. Berkeley, CA: University of California Press.

Bedjaoui, Mohammed. 1956. "Jurisprudence comparée des tribunaux administratifs internationaux en matière d'excès de pouvoir." *Annuaire français de droit international*, 482–96.

1958. "Fonction publique internationale et influences nationales." *Dotation Carnegie pour la paix internationale*. London: Stevens; New York: Praeger; Paris: Pedone.

1961. *La Révolution algérienne et le droit*. Brussels: L'Association internationale des juristes democrats.

1968. *First Report on Succession of States in Respect of Rights and Duties Resulting from Sources Other Than Treaties*. International Law Commission. http://legal.un.org/docs/?path=./ilc/documentation/english/a_cn4_204.pdf&lang=EFS

1969. *Second Report on Succession of States in Respect of Matters Other Than Treaties*. International Law Commission. http://legal.un.org/docs/?path=./ilc/documentation/english/a_cn4_216.pdf&lang=EFS

1970a. "Problèmes récents de succession d'Etats dans les Etats nouveaux." *Recueil des cours de l'Académie de droit international*. 130: 453–585.

1970b. *Third Report on Succession of States in Respect of Matters Other Than Treaties*. International Law Commission. http://legal.un.org/docs/?path=./ilc/publications/yearbooks/english/ilc_1970_v2.pdf&lang=EFS

1971. *Fourth Report on Succession of States in Respect of Matters Other Than Treaties*. International Law Commission. http://legal.un.org/docs/?path=./ilc/documentation/english/a_cn4_247.pdf&lang=EFS

1972. *Fifth Report on Succession of States in Respect of Matters Other Than Treaties*. International Law Commission. http://legal.un.org/ilc/documentation/english/a_cn4_259.pdf

1973. *Sixth Report on Succession of States in Respect of Matters Other Than Treaties*. International Law Commission. http://legal.un.org/docs/?path=./ilc/publications/yearbooks/english/ilc_1973_v2.pdf&lang=EFSR

1974. *Seventh Report on Succession of States in Respect of Matters Other Than Treaties*. International Law Commission. http://legal.un.org/docs/?path=./ilc/documentation/english/a_cn4_282.pdf&lang=EF

1976. *Eighth Report on Succession of States in Respect of Matters Other Than Treaties*. International Law Commission. http://legal.un.org/docs/?path=./ilc/documentation/english/a_cn4_292.pdf&lang=EFS

1977. *Ninth Report on Succession of States in Respect of Matters Other Than Treaties*. International Law Commission. http://legal.un.org/docs/?path=./ilc/publications/yearbooks/english/ilc_1977_v2_p1.pdf&lang=EFS

1978a. *Pour un nouvel ordre économique international*. Paris: UNESCO.

1978b. *Tenth Report on Succession of States in Respect of Matters Other Than Treaties. Yearbook of the International Law Commission*, vol. II. doc. A/CN. 4/292.

1979. *Eleventh Report on Succession of States in Respect of Matters Other Than Treaties*. International Law Commission. http://legal.un.org/docs/?path=./ilc/documentation/english/a_cn4_322.pdf&lang=EFS

1981. *Thirteenth Report on Succession of States in Respect of Matters Other Than Treaties*. International Law Commission. http://legal.un.org/docs/?path=./ilc/documentation/english/a_cn4_345.pdf&lang=EFS

1984. "*Les Négociations globales*," pp. 45–62 in *Droits et libertés à la fin du xxe siècle: influence des données économiques et technologiques. Etudes offertes à Claude-Albert Colliard*. Paris: Pedone.

2016. "Interview with the author, November 19." Neuilly, France.

2017. "Interview with the author, January 21." Neuilly, France.

Bernardini, Bruno. 2007. *Le principe d'obligation*. Paris: Vrin.

Berthélemy, H. 1910. "Consultation sur le différend survenu entre la Compagnie N'Goko-Sangha et l'Etat français." Paris: Archives Nationales (Fonds AT 94AP/329, Dossier N'Goko Sangha, 17–3).

Berstein, Serge. 2006. *Léon Blum*. Paris: Fayard.

Bert, Jean-François. 2012. *Marcel Mauss, Henri Hubert et la sociologie des religions: Penser et écrire à deux*. Paris: La cause des livres.

Besnard, Philippe. 1979. "La formation de L'Année sociologique." *Revue française de sociologie*. 20(1): 7–31.

Best, Jacqueline. 2005. *The Limits of Transparency: Ambiguity and the History of International Finance*. Ithaca, NY: Cornell University Press.

Binkley, Robert. 1929. "The 'Guilt' Clause in the Versailles Treaty." *Current History*. 30(2): 194–300.

Binkley, Robert C., and A. C. Mahr. 1926. "A New Interpretation of the 'Responsibility' Clause in the Versailles Treaty." *Current History* 24(3): 398–401.

Birnbaum, Pierre. 1988. *Un mythe politique: la "République juive" de Léon Blum à Pierre Mendès France*. Paris: Fayard.

Blais, Marie-Claude. 2007. *La solidarité: Histoire d'une idée*. Paris: Gallimard.

Blaszkiewicz-Maison, Adeline. 2015. *Albert Thomas: Le socialisme en guerre 1914–1918*. Rennes: Presses universitaires de Rennes.

Blévis, Laure. 2014. "L'invention de l'indigène, Français non citoyen," pp. 212–18 in *Histoire de l'Algérie à la période coloniale*, edited by Abderrahmane Bouchène, Jean-Pierre Peyroulou, Ounassa Siari-Tengour, Tahar Khalfoune, Gilbert Meynier, et al. Paris: La découverte.

Block-Lieb, Susan and Terence Halliday. 2016. "Contracts and Private Law in the Emerging Ecology of International Lawmaking," pp. 350–99 in *Contractual Knowledge: One Hundred Years of Legal Experimentation in Global Markets*, edited by Grégoire Mallard and Jérôme Sgard. New York: Cambridge University Press.

Blum, Léon. 1972 [1923a]. "Discours du 24 mai 1923 au Congrès de l'Internationale socialiste à Hamburg," pp. 272–88 in *L'œuvre, t.2*. Paris: Albin Michel.

1972 [1923b]. "Discours à la Chambre, 14 décembre 1923," pp. 302–7 in *L'œuvre, t.2*. Paris: Albin Michel.

1972 [1924]. "M. Poincaré et les experts. Réponse au discours de Luna Park." *Le populaire*, April 18, pp. 326–8 in *L'œuvre, t.2*. Paris: Albin Michel.
Blyth, Mark. 2013. *Austerity: The History of a Dangerous Idea*. New York: Oxford University Press.
Boltanski, Luc. 1990. *L'amour et la justice comme compétences*. Paris: Métailié.
Bordage, H. 1911. "Letter to Albert Thomas, March 20." Paris: Archives Nationales (Fonds AT 94AP/329, Dossier N'Goko Sangha, 17–2).
Bouglé, Célestin. 1924. *Le solidarisme*. Paris: Marcel Giard.
Bourdieu, Pierre. 1958. *Sociologie de l'Algérie*. Paris: Presses universitaires de France.
1980. *Le sens pratique*. Paris: Minuit.
1990. *Homo Academicus*. Translated by P. Collier. Stanford, CA: Stanford University Press.
1994. *Raisons pratiques. Sur la théorie de l'action*. Paris: Seuil.
2013. *Manet, une révolution symbolique*. Paris: Raisons d'agir.
Bourdieu, Pierre, Jean-Claude Chamboredon, and Jean-Claude Passeron. 1968. *Le métier de sociologue*. Paris: Mouton, pp. 27–80.
Bourdieu, Pierre and Abdelmayek Sayad. 1964. *Le déracinent*. Paris: Minuit.
Bourgeois, Léon. 1919. *Le Traité de paix de Versailles*. Paris: Alcan.
Bouyahia, Malek and Maria Eleonora Sanna. 2013. *La polysémie du voile. Politiques et mobilisations postcoloniales*. Paris: Editions archives contemporaines.
Burnett, Philip Mason. 1965. *Reparations at the Paris Peace Conference. From the Standpoint of the American Delegation*. New York: Octagon Books.
Burrin, Philippe. 1986. *La dérive fasciste, Doriot, Déat, Bergery, 1933–1945*. Paris: Le Seuil.
Byrne, Jeffrey J. 2016. *Mecca of Revolution: Algeria, Decolonization and the Third World Order*. Oxford: Oxford University Press.
Caillé, Alain. 1989. *Critique de la raison utilitaire: manifeste du M.A.U.S.S.* Paris: La découverte.
2005. *Don, intérêt et désintéressement. Bourdieu, Mauss, Platon, et quelques autres*. Paris: La découverte.
Candar, Gilles and Madeleine Rébérioux, eds. 1994. *Jaurès et les intellectuels*. Paris: L'Atelier.
Carabelli, Anna and Mario Cedrini. 2010. "Global Imbalances, Monetary Disorder and Shrinking Policy Space: Keynes' Legacy for Our Troubled World." *Intervention*. 7: 303–23.
Cedrini, Mario. 2010. "What Was Keynes Fighting For?: A Maussian Perspective on Keynes' Economic Diplomacy." Working Paper. Turin: Collegio Carlo Alberto.
Challaye, Félicien. 1906. "*Les deux Congo. Devant la Belgique et devant la France.*" Paris: Cahiers de la Quinzaine.
1911. "Politique internationale et journalisme d'affaire." *Revue du mois*. Paris: Archives Nationales (Fonds AT 94AP/329, Dossier N'Goko Sangha, 17–2).
1912. "Letter to Albert Thomas, Dec. 25." (Fonds AT 94AP/329, Dossier N'Goko Sangha, 17–2).
Charle, Christophe. 1980. *Les hauts fonctionnaires en France au XIXe siècle*. Paris: Gallimard.
1990. *Naissance des « intellectuels » (1880–1900)*. Paris: Minuit.
Chaumont, Charles. 1970. "Cours général de Droit international." *Recueil des cours de l'Académie de droit international*. 1: 335–527.
Chaussade, Pierre. 1958. Que représente l'Algérie pour les finances et l'économie de la métropole? Ministère de l'Algérie (Fonds Soustelle, 112AJ/33).
CNBC. 2017. "ECB's massive bond-buying program is no longer crucial for Greece, prime minister says." June 12. www.cnbc.com/2017/12/06/ecbs-massive-bond-buying-program-is-no-longer-crucial-for-greece-prime-minister-says.html

Cohen, Antonin. 2017. "Pour ou contre un parlement de la zone euro." *Mediapart*. https://blogs.mediapart.fr/antonin-cohen/blog/050717/pour-ou-contre-un-parlement-de-la-zone-euro

Cohen, Antonin and Antoine Vauchez. 2007. "Introduction: Law, Lawyers, and Transnational Politics in the Production of Europe. A Symposium." *Law and Social Inquiry*. 32(1): 75–82.

Cohen, William. 1971. *Rulers of Empire: The French Colonial Service in Africa*. Stanford, CA: Hoover Institute Press.

Cohn, Bernard S. 1996. *Colonialism and Its Form of Knowledge: The British in India*. Princeton, NJ: Princeton University Press.

Cointepas, Michel. 2008. *Arthur Fontaine, 1860–1931: Un réformateur, pacifiste et mécène au sommet de la Troisième République*. Rennes: Presses universitaires de Rennes.

Colliard, Claude-Albert. 1956. *Institutions internationales*. Paris: Droz.

Colombain, M. 1932 "Letter to Mauss, including a report on cooperation in the colonies, January 14." Paris: Collège de France (Fonds Mauss, 57 CDF 56–22).

Colonomos, Ariel and Andrea Armstrong. 2006. "German Reparations to the Jews after World War II: A Turning Point in the History of Reparations," pp. 390–419 in *The Handbook of Reparations*, edited by P. de Greiff. Oxford: Oxford University Press.

Colonomos, Ariel and Grégoire Mallard. 2016. "The *Duty to Repair* in Practice: The Hundred Years History of a Legal Concept," pp. 215–47 in *Contractual Knowledge: One Hundred Years of Legal Experimentation in Global Markets*, edited by Grégoire Mallard and Jérôme Sgard. New York: Cambridge University Press.

Colson Jean-Philippe. 1972. "Le 'groupe des 77' et le problème de l'unité des pays du Tiers Monde." *Tiers-Monde*. 13(52): 813–30.

Colton, Joel. 1966. *Léon Blum: Humanist in Politics*. New York: Knopf.

Commission on the Responsibility of the Authors of the War and on Enforcement of Penalties. 1920. *American Journal of International Law*. 14(1): 95–154

Conklin, Alice. 2013. *In the Museum of Man: Race, Anthropology and Empire in France, 1850–1950*. Ithaca, NY: Cornell University Press.

Couturier, Alain. 2006. *Le Gouverneur et son miroir: Marcel de Coppet (1881–1968)*. Paris: L'Harmattan.

Cox, Robert W. 1979. "Ideologies and the New International Economic Order." *International Organization*. 33(2): 257–302.

Craig, Gordon, and Felix Gilbert. 1963. *The Diplomats 1919–1939*. New York: Atheneum.

Craven, Matthew. 2007. *The Decolonization of International Law: State Succession and the Law of Treaties*. Oxford: Oxford University Press.

David-Weill, David. 1925. "Letter to Mauss, January." Paris: Collège de France (Fonds Mauss, 57 CDF 60–8).

De, Rohit. 2012. "Emasculating the Executive: The Federal Court and Civil Liberties in Late Colonial India: 1942–1944," pp. 59–80 in *Fates of Political Liberalism in the British Post-Colony: The Politics of the Legal Complex*, edited by Terence Halliday, Lucien Karpik, and Malcolm Feeley. New York: Cambridge University Press.

Déat, Marcel. 1932. "Letter to Mauss, May 2." Paris: Collège de France (Fonds Mauss, 57 CDF 60–13).

Dedieu, Jean-Philippe. 2004. "L'intégration des avocats africains dans les barreaux français." *Droit et société*. 56–7(1): 209–29.

De Coppet, Daniel. 1998. "Une monnaie pour une communauté mélanésienne comparée à la nôtre pour l'individu des sociétés modernes," pp. 159–213 in *La monnaie souveraine* edited by Michel Aglietta and André Orléan. Paris: Odile Jacob.

de Gaulle, Charles. 1956. "Letter to Jacques Soustelle, August 19." Paris: Archives Nationales (Fonds Soustelle, 112AJ/3).
de L'estoile, Benoît. 2007. *Le goût des Autres. De l'Exposition coloniale aux Arts premiers*. Paris: Flammarion.
de L'estoile, Benoît, Federico Neiburg, and Lygia Sigaud, eds. 2005. *Empires, Nations and Natives: Anthropology and State-making*. Durham, NC: Duke University Press.
de Rougemont, Guy. 2010. *Lazard Frères: Banquiers des Deux Mondes (1840–1939)*. Paris: Fayard.
Derrida, Jacques. 1991. *Donner le temps, t.1 la fausse monnaie*. Paris: Galilée.
Dezalay, Yves and Bryant Garth. 1996. *Dealing in Virtue: International Commercial Arbitration and the Construction of a Transnational Legal Order*. Chicago: Chicago University Press.
2002. *The Internationalization of Palace Wars: Lawyers, Economists and the Struggle to Transform Latin American States*. Chicago: Chicago University Press.
2010. *Asian Legal Revivals: Lawyers in the Shadow of Empire*. Chicago: Chicago University Press.
2016. "Constructing a Transatlantic Marketplace of Disputes on the Symbolic Foundations of International Justice," pp. 185–215 in *Contractual Knowledge: One Hundred Years of Legal Experimentation in Global Markets*, edited by Grégoire Mallard and Jérôme Sgard. New York: Cambridge University Press.
Drouin, Marcel. 1897. "Letter to Hubert." Paris: Collège de France (Fonds Marcel Mauss, Correspondance Hubert, CDF 123–15).
Drumont, Edouart. 1886. *La France juive: Essai d'histoire contemporaine*. Paris: Flammarion.
Dupuy, René-Jean. 1990. "Le Doyen Claude-Albert Colliard." *Annuaire français de droit international*. 36(1): 7–8.
Durkheim, Emile. 1893. *La division du travail social*. Paris: Alcand.
1991 [1915]. *L'Allemagne au-dessus de tout. La mentalité allemande et la guerre*. Paris: Armand Colin.
1998. *Lettres à Marcel Mauss*, presented by Philippe Besnard and Marcel Fournier. Paris: Presses universitaires de France.
Durkheim, Emile and Ernest Denis. 1915. *Qui a voulu la guerre? Les origines de la guerre d'après les documents diplomatiques*. http://gallica.bnf.fr/ark:/12148/bpt6k113193s.r=qui+a+voulu+la+guerre.langFR
Dzimira, Sylvain. 2007. *Marcel Mauss, savant et politique*. Paris: La découverte.
Eichengreen, Barry and Richard Portes. 1987. "The Anatomy of Financial Crises." NBER Working Paper No. 2126. http://papers.ssrn.com/sol3/papers.cfm?abstract_id=227380
Elbaz, Sharon. 2003. "L'avocat et sa cause en milieu colonial. La défense politique dans le procès de l'Organisation spéciale du Mouvement pour le triomphe des libertés en Algérie (1950–1952)." *Politix*. 16(62): 65–91.
Evian Agreements. 1962, pp. 313–65, in Redha Malek. 1995. *L'Algérie à Evian: Histoire des négociations secrètes*, 1956–1962. Paris: Seuil, http://imedb.blogspot.ch/2008/01/blog-post_25.html
Fanon, Frantz. 1952. *Peau noire, masques blancs*. Paris: Le Seuil.
1961. *Les damnés de la terre*. Paris: Maspéro.
Feldstein, Martin. 1997. "EMU and International Conflict." *Foreign Affairs*. 76: 6.
Ferguson, James and Akhil Gupta 2002. "Spatializing States: Toward an Ethnography of Neoliberal Governmentality." *American Ethnologist*. 29(4): 981–1002.
Firth, Raymond. 1939. *Primitive Polynesian Economy*. London: Routledge.

Flandreau, Marc. 2016. *Anthropologists in the Stock Exchange: A Financial History of Victorian Science*. Chicago: University of Chicago Press.

Florès-Zendejas, Juan. 2016. "Financial Markets, International Organizations and Conditional Lending: A Long-term Perspective," pp. 61–91 in *Contractual Knowledge: One Hundred Years of Legal Experimentation in Global Markets*, edited by Grégoire Mallard and Jérôme Sgard. New York: Cambridge University Press.

Flory, Maurice. 1959. "Algérie et droit international." *Annuaire français de droit international*. 5: 817–44.

1961. "Compte-Rendu de La révolution algérienne et le droit de Mohammed Bedjaoui." *Annuaire français de droit international*. 7(1): 1058–61.

1966. "Décolonisation et succession d'Etats." *Annuaire français de droit international*. 12(1): 577–93.

1973. "Essai de typologie de la coopération bilatérale pour le développement." *Annuaire français de droit international*. 19(1): 696–719.

Flory, Maurice, Gérard Fouilloux, Bruno Etienne, and Jean-Claude Santucci. 1968. *La succession d'Etat en Afrique du Nord*. Paris: CRESM–CNRS éditions.

Foltz, David Albert. 1978. "The War Crimes Issue at the Paris Peace Conference." Dissertation, College of Arts and Sciences, American University, Washington, DC.

Foucault, Michel. 1995. *Discipline and Punish: The Birth of the Prison*. New York: Vintage.

2003. *Society Must Be Defended: Lectures at the Collège de France, 1975–76*. Translated by David Macey. New York: Picador.

2010. *The Birth of Biopolitics: Lectures at the Collège de France, 1978–79*. New York: Picador.

Fourcade Gourinchas, Marion. 2009. *Economists and Societies: Discipline and Profession in the United States, Britain and France, 1890s to 1990s*. Princeton, NJ: Princeton University Press.

Fournier, Marcel. 1994. *Marcel Mauss*. Paris: Fayard.

Francioli, Marc. 2015. *Jacques Soustelle: L'ami qui a défié de Gaulle*. Paris: Rocher.

Frazer, James. 1890. *The Golden Bough: A Study in Magic and Religion*. Oxford: Oxford University Press.

1898. "Letter to Mauss, August 21." Paris: Collège de France (Fonds Mauss, 57 CDF 65–5).

1902. "Letter to Mauss, of May 2." (Fonds Mauss, 57 CDF 65–5).

1929. "Letter to Mauss, March 20." (Fonds Mauss, 57 CDF 65–5).

Freymond, Jacques. 1951. *Lénine et l'impérialisme*. Payot: Lausanne.

Garavini, Giuliano. 2012. *After Empires: European Integration, Decolonization and the Challenge from the Global South 1957–1986*. Oxford: Oxford University Press.

George, David Lloyd. 1939. *Memoirs of the Peace Conference*. New Haven: Yale University Press.

Gide, André. 1927. *Voyage au Congo*. Paris: Pléiade.

1958 [1914]. *Les Caves du Vatican*. Paris: Pléiade.

1958 [1925]. *Les faux monnayeurs*. Paris: Pléiade.

Gide, Charles. 1906. "Letter of July 11, to Mauss." Paris: Collège de France (Fonds Mauss, 57 CDF 66–28).

1932. *La solidarité, Cours au collège de France 1927–8*. Paris: Presses universitaires de France.

Gide, Charles and William Oualid. 1931. "Le bilan de la guerre pour la France," pp. 1–34 in *Histoire économique et sociale de la guerre mondiale*, edited by J. Shotwell. Paris: Presses universitaires de France and Carnegie Endowment for International Peace.

Gilman, Nils. 2003. *Mandarins of the Future: Modernization Theory in Cold War America*. Baltimore: Johns Hopkins University Press.

Girard, René. 1961. *Mensonges romantiques et vérité romanesque*. Paris: Grasset.
1999. *Je vois Satan tomber comme l'éclair*. Paris: Grasset.
Girardet, Raoul. 1972. *L'idée coloniale en France: de 1871 à 1962*. Paris: Editions de la Table Ronde.
Giscard d'Estaing, Edmond. 1937. "Letter to Mauss, Sept. 16." Paris: Collège de France (Fonds Mauss, 57 CDF 60–35).
Go, Julian. 2013. "Decolonizing Bourdieu: Colonial and Post-Colonial Theory in Pierre Bourdieu's Early Work." *Sociological Theory*. 31(1): 49–74.
Godbout, Jacques. 2000. *Le don, la dette et l'identité: Homo donator vs. Homo economicus*. Paris: La découverte.
Graeber, David. 2000. "Give It Away," *In These Times*, April 21. https://inthesetimes.com/issue/24/19/graeber2419.html
2011. *Debt: The First 5,000 Years*. New York: Melville House.
Griaule, Marcel. 1928a. "Letter to Mauss, February 21." Paris: Collège de France (Fonds Mauss, 57 CDF 67–10).
1928b. "Letter to Mauss, June 25." (Fonds Mauss, 57 CDF 67–10).
1930. "Letter to Mauss, November 4." (Fonds Mauss, 57 CDF 67–10).
1931a. "Letter to Mauss, February 16." (Fonds Mauss, 57 CDF 67–10).
1931b. "Letter to Mauss, April 18." (Fonds Mauss, 57 CDF 67–10).
1931c. "Letter to Mauss, December 15." (Fonds Mauss, 57 CDF 67–10).
1931d. "Letter to Mauss, December 23." (Fonds Mauss, 57 CDF 67–10).
Grimaud, Nicole. 1972. "Le conflit pétrolier franco-algérien." *Revue française de science politique*. 22(6): 1276–1307.
Group of 77. 1967. "Charter of Algiers." www.g77.org/doc/algier~1.htm
Groupe Parlementaire de l'Arbitrage. 1913. "Letter to Thomas." Paris: Archives Nationales (Fonds AT 94AP/340).
Guilhot, Nicolas. 2011. "Cyborg Pantocrator: IR Theory from Decisionism to Rational Choice." *Journal of the History of the Behavioral Sciences*. 47(3): 279–301.
Gulati, Mitu and Sarah Ludington. 2008. "A Convenient Untruth: Fact and Fantasy in the Doctrine of Odious Debts." *Virginia Journal of International Law*. 48: 595–639.
Gulati, Mitu and Robert Scott. 2012. *The Three and a Half Minute Transaction: Boilerplate and the Limits of Contract Design*. Chicago: University of Chicago Press.
Guyer, Jane. 2016. "Introduction: The Gift That Keeps on Giving." In Marcel Mauss, *The Gift, Expanded Edition*, translated by Jane Guyer. Chicago: Chicago University Press.
Habermas, Jurgen. 2009. *Europe: The Faltering Project*. New York: Polity.
Halbwachs, Maurice.1917. "Rapport sur les progrès des fabrications de guerre jusqu'à 1917." Ministère de l'Armement et des Fabrications de guerre. June. Paris: Archives Nationales (Fonds AT 94AP/343).
1925. *Les cadres sociaux de la mémoire*. Paris: Alcan.
Halliday, Terence. 2018. "Plausible Folk Theories: Throwing Veils of Plausibility over Zones of Ignorance in Global Governance." *British Journal of Sociology*. https://doi.org/10.1111/1468-4446.12605
Halliday, Terence, Lucien Karpik, and Malcolm Feeley, eds. 2007. *Fighting for Political Freedom: Comparative Studies of the Legal Complex and Political Liberalism*. Oxford: Hart.
2012. *Fates of Political Liberalism in the British Post-Colony: The Politics of the Legal Complex*. New York: Cambridge University Press.
Hardy, George. 1927. "Letter to Mauss, June 6." Paris: Collège de France (Fonds Mauss 57 CDF 68–19).

Hart, Keith. 2007. “Marcel Mauss: Our Guide to the Future.” Memory Bank, March 20. http://thememorybank.co.uk/2007/03/20/marcel-mauss-our-guide-to-the-future

Heilbron, Johan. 1995. *The Rise of Social Theory*. Minneapolis: University of Minnesota Press.

2011. “Practical Foundations of Theorizing in Sociology: The Case of Pierre Bourdieu,” pp. 181–205 in *Social Knowledge in the Making*, edited by Charles Camic, Neil Gross, and Michèle Lamont. Chicago: University of Chicago Press.

Heins, Volker M, Christine Unrau, Kristine Avram. 2018. “Gift-giving and reciprocity in global society: Introducing Marcel Mauss in international studies.” *Journal of International Political Theory*. 14(2): 126–144.

Hennette, Stéphanie, Piketty, Thomas, Sacriste, Guillaume and Antoine Vauchez. 2017. *Pour un traité de democratization de l'Europe*. Paris: Seuil.

Hertz, Robert. 1902. “Letter to Mauss, May 30.” Paris: Collège de France (Fonds Mauss, 57 CDF 69–18).

1908. “Letter to Mauss, February 11.” (Fonds Mauss, 57 CDF 69–18).

1922. *Le Péché et l'expiation dans les sociétés primitives*. http://classiques.uqac.ca/classiques/hertz_robert/peche_expiation/hertz_peche_expiation.pdf

Hubert, Henri. 1911. “Letter of October 4, to Mauss.” Paris: Collège de France (Fonds Mauss, Correspondance Hubert, MAS 6–37).

1922a. “Letter of March 27 to Thomas.” Paris: Archives Nationales (Fonds AT 94AP/381).

1922b. “Letter to Thomas, April.” (Fonds AT 94AP/381).

1923. “Letter to Thomas, December 22.” (Fonds AT 94AP/381).

1925. “Letter to Mauss, December 21.” (Fonds Mauss, Correspondance Hubert, MAS 6–37).

1932. *Les Celtes et l'expansion celtique jusqu'à l'époque de La Tène*. Paris: Albin Michel.

1952. *Les Germains: Cours professé à l'école du Louvre en 1924–1925*. Paris: Albin Michel.

Hubert, Henri and Marcel Mauss. 1899. “Essai sur la nature et la function du sacrifice.” *L'Année sociologique*. 2: 29–138.

1903. “Esquisse d'une théorie générale de la magie.” *L'Année sociologique*. 4: 1–94.

Indigenous Committee [Comité de protection et de défense des indigènes]. 1901. “Letter to the Minister of the Colonies, May 10.” Paris: Collège de France (Fonds Mauss, 57 CDF 58–24).

1906. “Letter to the Minister of the Colonies, February 23.” (Fonds Mauss, 57 CDF 58–24).

International Law Commission (ILC). 1967. *Report of the ILC on the Work of Its Nineteenth Session*. http://legal.un.org/docs/?path=./ilc/documentation/english/reports/a_cn4_199.pdf&lang=EF

1970. *Report of the ILC on the Work of Its Twenty-Second Session*. http://legal.un.org/docs/?path=./ilc/documentation/english/reports/a_cn4_237.pdf&lang=EF

1973. *Report of the ILC on the Work of Its Twenty-Fifth Session*. http://legal.un.org/docs/?path=./ilc/documentation/english/reports/a_9010.pdf&lang=EFS

1976. *Report of the ILC on the Work of Its Twenty-Eighth Session*. http://legal.un.org/ilc/documentation/english/reports/a_31_10.pdf

1981. *Draft Articles on Succession of States in Respect to State Property, Archives, and Debts, with Commentaries*. http://legal.un.org/ilc/texts/instruments/english/commentaries/3_3_1981.pdf

Jèze, Gaston. 1922. *Cours de sciences des finances et de législation financière française*. Paris: Giard.

Journal Officiel. 1911. Débats parlementaires du 7 avril. Paris: Archives Nationales (Fonds AT 94AP/329, Dossier N'Goko Sangha, 17–3).

Judt, Tony. 1998. *The Burden of Responsibility: Blum, Camus, Aron and the French Twentieth Century*. Chicago: Chicago University Press.

Karsenti, Bruno. 1994. *Marcel Mauss, le fait social total*. Paris: Presses universitaires de France.
Kennedy, Duncan. 2006. "Three Globalizations of Law and Legal Thought: 1850–2000," pp. 19–73 in *The New Law and Economic Development: A Critical Appraisal*, edited by David Trubek and Alvaro Santos. Cambridge: Cambridge University Press.
Keynes, John Maynard. 1920. *The Economic Consequences of the Peace*. New York: Harcourt, Brace and Howe.
Kojève Alexandre. 2001. "Colonialism from a European Perspective." *Interpretation*. 29(1): 115–30.
Koskenniemi, Martti. 2001. *The Gentle Civilizer of Nations. The Rise and Fall of International Law*. Cambridge: Cambridge University Press.
Kralfa, Ataouia. 2016. "La profession d'avocat en Algérie coloniale." History of law thesis, Bordeaux University.
Krippner, Greta. 2005. "The Financialisation of the American Economy." *Socio-Economic Review*, 3(2): 173–208.
Labordère, Marcel. 1911a. "L'affaire de la N'Goko-Sangha." *Revue de Paris. Paris*: Archives Nationales (Fonds AT 94AP/329, Dossier N'Goko Sangha, 17–2).
1911b. "Letter to Albert Thomas, January 15." (Fonds AT 94AP/329, Dossier N'Goko Sangha, 17–2).
Lachs, Manfred. 1963. *Report on Succession of States in Respect Other Than Treaties*. International Law Commission. http://legal.un.org/ilc/documentation/english/reports/a_cn4_163.pdf
Lacouture, Jean. 2011. *Le témoignage est un combat*. Paris: Seuil.
Laffont, Pierre. 1960. "Les difficultés du Plan de Constantine." *Echo d'Oran*. June 9. (Fonds Soustelle, 112AJ/36).
Lagrange, Hugues. 2010. *Le déni des cultures*. Paris: Seuil.
Laniol, Vincent. 2012. "Ferdinand Larnaude, un 'délégué technique' à la Conférence de la paix de 1919 entre expertise et Culture de guerre." *Relations Internationales*. (149): 43–55.
Larnaude, Ferdinand. 1917. "La réparation des dommages de guerre. Comment doit s'entendre le droit à la réparation." In *La réparation des dommages de guerre*, edited by H. Berthélemy. Paris: Alcan.
Larnaude, Ferdinand and Albert de Lapradelle. 1918. *Examen de la responsabilité pénale de l'Empereur Guillaume I*. Paris: Imprimerie Nationale.
Lascoumes, Pierre and Patrick Le Galès. 2005. *Gouverner par les instruments*. Paris: Sciences-Po Press.
Latour, Bruno. 1993. *We Have Never Been Modern*. Cambridge, MA: Harvard University Press.
Lavau, Georges. 1989. "Profession politiste, entretiens entre Georges Lavau, Florence Haegel, et Jean-Baptiste Legrave." *Politix*. 2(7): 132–8.
Laville, Jean-Louis (ed.). 2007. *L'économie solidaire: Une perspective internationale*. Paris: Hachette.
Lazard, Didier. 1990. *Max Lazard, ses frères et Lyautey. Lettres (1894–1933)*. Paris: Lazard.
Lazard, Max. 1908. "Letter to Mauss, December 22." Paris: Collège de France (Fonds Mauss, 57 CDF 76–21).
1924. "Letter to Mauss, June 30." (Fonds Mauss, 57 CDF 76–21).
1927a. "Letter to Mauss, January 8." (Fonds Mauss, 57 CDF 76–21).
1927b. "Letter to Thomas, June 13." Paris: Archives Nationales (Fonds AT 94AP/382).
undated. "Letter to Mauss." (Fonds Mauss, 57 CDF 76–21).

Leca, Jean. 2001. "Une relecture cavalière des débuts." *Revue française de science politique*. 51(1): 5–17.

Le Cœur, Charles. 1942. "Letter to Mauss Feb. 16." Paris: Collège de France (Fonds Mauss, 57 CDF 76–27)

Lépinard, Eléonore. 2015. "Migrating Concepts: Migrant Integration and the Regulation of Religious Dress in France and Canada." *Ethnicities*. 15(5): 611–32.

Leroux, M. 1908. "Lettre au Lieutenant Gouverneur du Gabon, August 24." Paris: Archives Nationales (Fonds AT 94AP/329, Dossier N'Goko Sangha, 17–2).

Lévi-Strauss, Claude. 1950. "Introduction à l'œuvre de Marcel Mauss," pp. ix–lii in *Sociologie et anthropologie* by Marcel Mauss. Paris: Presses universitaires de France.

Liebersohn, Harry. 2011. *The Return of the Gift: European History of a Global Idea*. Cambridge: Cambridge University Press.

Lienau, Odette. 2014. *Rethinking Sovereign Debt: Politics, Reputation, and Legitimacy in Modern Finance*. Cambridge, MA: Harvard University Press.

Ligue française et ligue suisse pour la défense des indigènes dans le bassin conventionnel du Congo. 1910. *Bulletin*. (jan.–avril: 4). Paris: Archives Nationales (Fonds AT 94AP/329, Dossier N'Goko Sangha, 17–3).

Loucheur, Louis. 1962. *Carnets Secrets: 1908–1932*. Brussels: Brepols.

Luckau, Alma. 1941. *The German Delegation at the Paris Peace Conference*. New York: Columbia University Press.

Ludington, Sarah, Gulati, Mitu and Alfred Brophy. 2010. "Applied Legal History: Demystifying the Doctrine of Odious Debts." *Theoretical Inquiries in Law*. 11(1): 247–81.

Maier, Charles. 1988. *Recasting Bourgeois Europe: Stabilization in France, Germany and Italy in the Decade after World War I*. Princeton, NJ: Princeton University Press.

2003. "Overcoming the Past? Narrative and Negotiation, Remembering and Reparations Issues at the Interface of History and the Law," pp. 277–94 in *Politics and the Past: On Repairing Historical Injustices*, edited by J. Torpey. New York: Rowman & Littlefield.

Malamoud, Charles. 1998. "Le paiement des actes rituels dans l'Inde védique," pp. 35–52 in *La monnaie souveraine* edited by Michel Aglietta and André Orléan. Paris: Odile Jacob.

Malek, Redha. 1995. *L'Algérie à Evian: Histoire des négociations secrètes, 1956–1962*. Paris: Seuil.

Malinowski, Bronislaw. 1921. "The Primitive Economics of Trobriand Islanders." *Economic Journal*. 31(121): 1–16.

1922. "Letter of December 22, to Mauss." Paris: Collège de France (Fonds Mauss, 57 CDF).

1925. "Letter of November 12, to Mauss." (Fonds Mauss, 57 CDF).

1926. *Crime and Custom in Savage Society*. New York: Harcourt, Brace & Co.

Mallard, Grégoire. 2006. "Quand l'expertise se heurte au pouvoir souverain: La nation américaine face à la prolifération nucléaire, 1945–1953." *Sociologie du Travail*. 48(3): 367–89.

2011. "The Gift Revisited: Marcel Mauss on War, Debt and the Politics of Reparations." *Sociological Theory*. 29(4): 225–47.

2014. *Fallout: Nuclear Diplomacy in an Age of Global Fracture*. Chicago: Chicago University Press.

2017. *European Election Day: Synchronizing National Electoral Cycles and Improving Democracy in Europe*. Report of the conference European Election Day. http://graduateinstitute.ch/files/live/sites/iheid/files/sites/hirschman-centre-on-democracy/docs/EEDay%20Report-05-10-17.pdf

2018. "The Gift as Colonial Ideology: Marcel Mauss and the Solidarist Colonial Policy in the Interwar Period." *Journal of International Political Theory*. 14(2): 183–202.

Mallard, Grégoire and Jérôme Sgard, eds. 2016. *Contractual Knowledge: One Hundred Years of Legal Experimentation in Global Markets*. New York: Cambridge University Press.

Malye, François, and Benjamin Stora. 2012. *François Mitterrand et la guerre d'Algérie*. Paris: Fayard.

Manceron, Gilles. 2003. *Marianne et les colonies: Une introduction à l'histoire coloniale de la France*. Paris: La découverte.

Marks, Sally. 2013. "Mistakes and Myths: The Allies, Germany, and the Versailles Treaty, 1918–1921." *Journal of Modern History*. 85(September): 632–59.

Marseille, Jacques. 1984. *Empire colonial et capitalisme français: Histoire d'un divorce*. Paris: Seuil.

Maupoil, Bernard. 1934a. "Letter to Mauss, July 26." Paris: Collège de France (Fonds Mauss, 57 CDF 81–14).

1934b. "Letter to Mauss, August 22." (Fonds Mauss, 57 CDF 81–14).

1934c. "Letter to Mauss, October 29." (Fonds Mauss, 57 CDF 81–14).

1935a. "Letter to Mauss, Jan. 27." (Fonds Mauss, 57 CDF 81–14).

1935b. "Letter to Mauss, April 22." (Fonds Mauss, 57 CDF 81–14).

1935c. "Letter to Mauss, July 13." (Fonds Mauss, 57 CDF 81–14).

1937a. "Letter to Mauss, May 1." (Fonds Mauss, 57 CDF 81–14).

1937b. "Letter to Mauss, October 2." (Fonds Mauss, 57 CDF 81–14).

1938a. "Letter to Mauss, July 10." (Fonds Mauss, 57 CDF 81–14).

1938b. "Letter to Mauss, July 14." (Fonds Mauss, 57 CDF 81–14).

1938c. "Letter to Mauss, July 23." (Fonds Mauss, 57 CDF 81–14).

Maurois, André. 1931. *Lyautey*. Paris: Plon.

Mauss, Marcel. 1902. "De l'utilité des recherches sociologiques sur l'Indochine française." Paris: Collège de France (Fonds Mauss, 57 CDF 34–2).

1907. "L'ethnographie en France: Une science négligée, un musée à former." (Fonds Mauss, 57 CDF 34–4).

1913a. "Demande de création en Novembre." (Fonds Mauss 57 CDF 48–7).

1913b. "Lettre au Ministre." (Fonds Mauss 57 CDF 48–7).

1914. "Origines de la notion de monnaie." (Fonds Mauss, 57 CDF 32–2).

1921. "Une forme ancienne de contrat chez les Thraces." *Revue des études grecques*. 34: 388–97.

1924a. "Letter to Keynes, November 26." (Fonds Mauss, 57 CDF 74–13).

1924b. "Mélanges à Charles Andler. Gift, Gift." (Fonds Mauss, 57 CDF 32–10).

1925a. "Essai sur le don: Forme et raison de l'échange dans les sociétés archaiques." *L'Année sociologique*. July 1923–July 1924: 31–186.

1925b. "Note sur l'Institut d'ethnologie au Résident Général au Maroc, December 30." (Fonds Mauss, 57 CDF 48–7).

1925c. "Review essay of G. Schwalbe and A. Ploetz." *L'Année sociologique*. July 1923–July 1924: 369–73.

1928. "Letter to Alfred Radcliffe-Brown, January 7." (Fonds Mauss, 57 CDF).

1933. "Letter to Blum, Nov. 6, 1933." (Fonds Mauss, 57 CDF).

1934. "Letter to Griaule, April 29." (Fonds Mauss, 57 CDF 67–10).

1935. "Letter to Marcel Déat, September 18." (Fonds Mauss, 57 CDF 60–13).

1936a. "Letter to Blum, May 5." (Fonds Mauss, 57 CDF).

1936b. "Letter to Roger Bastide, Nov. 7." (Fonds Mauss, 57 CDF).

1937a. "Letter to Charles Le Coeur, Feb. 6." (Fonds Mauss, CDF 132–14).

1937b. "Letter to Charles Seligman, Feb. 29." (Fonds Mauss, 57 CDF).

1937c. "Letter to Bernard Maupoil, April 19." (Fonds Mauss, 57 CDF).

1937d. "Letter to Charles Seligman, Nov. 29." (Fonds Mauss, 57 CDF).

1938. "Letter to Charles Le Coeur, June 21." (Fonds Mauss, CDF 132–14).

1939. "Letter to Germaine Tillion, October 23." (Fonds Mauss, CDF 57).

1940. "Letter to Germaine Tillion, Feb. 8." (Fonds Mauss, 57 CDF).

1950 [1925]. "Essai sur le don," pp. 143–279 in *Sociologie et anthropologie*. Paris: Presses universitaires de France.

1979. "L'œuvre de Mauss par lui-même." *Revue française de sociologie*. 20(1): 209–37.

1990 [1925]. *The Gift: The Form and Reason for Exchange in Archaic Societies*. Translated by W. D. Halls. London: Routledge.

1994 [1896]. "La religion et les origines religieuses du droit penal d'après un livre recent." In *Œuvres 2, Représentations collectives et diversité des civilizations*. Paris: Minuit.

1997 [1905]. "Le Congrès des coopératives anglaises." *L'Humanité*, June 16, 1905, pp. 177–9 in *Ecrits politiques*, edited by Marcel Fournier. Paris: Fayard.

1997 [1913]. "Un coup dirigé contre les coopératives." *L'Humanité*, March 8, 1913, p. 201 in *Ecrits politiques*, edited by Marcel Fournier. Paris: Fayard.

1997 [1920]. "Lettre de l'étranger: Un livre de Webb." *L'action coopérative*, October 30, 1920, pp. 346–50 in *Ecrits politiques*, edited by Marcel Fournier. Paris: Fayard.

1997 [1922a]. "Les changes 1. Etat actuel, la ruine de l'Europe, la crise, les responsables." *Le populaire*, December 4, 1922, pp. 477–9 in *Ecrits politiques*, edited by Marcel Fournier. Paris: Fayard.

1997 [1922b]. "Les changes 2. Une politique, un exemple sinistre, l'Autriche." *Le populaire*, December 5, 1922, pp. 480–3 in *Ecrits politiques*, edited by Marcel Fournier. Paris: Fayard.

1997 [1922c]. "Les changes 3. Danger des mesures arbitraires." *Le populaire*, December 9, 1922, pp. 484–7 in *Ecrits politiques*, edited by Marcel Fournier. Paris: Fayard.

1997 [1922d]. "Les changes 4. La valeur réelle du franc, comment le convertir en or." *Le populaire*, December 11, 1922, pp. 492–4 in *Ecrits politiques*, edited by Marcel Fournier. Paris: Fayard.

1997 [1922e]. "Les changes 5. Comment liquider, comment stabiliser." *Le populaire*, December 13, 1922, pp. 495–7 in *Ecrits politiques*, edited by Marcel Fournier. Paris: Fayard.

1997 [1922f]. "Les changes 6. Pour la conférence de Bruxelles, un précédent." *Le populaire*, December 17, 1922, pp. 499–501 in *Ecrits politiques*, edited by Marcel Fournier. Paris: Fayard.

1997 [1922g]. "Les changes 7. Conclusion." *Le populaire*, December 21, 1922, pp. 502–4 in *Ecrits politiques*, edited by Marcel Fournier. Paris: Fayard.

1997 [1923]. "Observations sur la violence 3, p. La violence bolchevik; bilan de la terreur; son échec." *La vie socialiste*, February 17, 1923, pp. 518–21 in *Ecrits politiques*, edited by Marcel Fournier. Paris: Fayard.

1997 [1924a]. "Appréciation sociologique du bolchevisme." *Revue de métaphysique et de morale*, spring 1924, pp. 537–66 in *Ecrits politiques*, edited by Marcel Fournier. Paris: Fayard.

1997 [1924b]. "Les changes 1. Du calme!" *Le populaire*, January 18, 1924, pp. 566–70 in *Ecrits politiques*, edited by Marcel Fournier. Paris: Fayard.

1997 [1924c]. "Les changes 3. Qui a exporté des francs?" *Le populaire*, January 21, 1924, pp. 571–4 in *Ecrits politiques*, edited by Marcel Fournier. Paris: Fayard.

1997 [1924d]. "Les changes 4. Comment le gouvernement a exporté des francs. Les dépenses militaires et impériales." *Le populaire*, January 22, 1924, pp. 579–82 in *Ecrits politiques*, edited by Marcel Fournier. Paris: Fayard.

1997 [1924e]. "Les changes 5. Politiques d'armement. Situation monnétaire de la France." *Le populaire*, January 24, 1924, pp. 583–6 in *Ecrits politiques*, edited by Marcel Fournier. Paris: Fayard.

1997 [1924f]. "Les changes. L'inflation des prix." *Le populaire*, February 27, 1924, pp. 596–9 in *Ecrits politiques*, edited by Marcel Fournier. Paris: Fayard.

1997 [1924g]. "Les changes. L'inflation fiduciaire, la responsabilité personnelle de Mr. Klotz." *Le populaire*, March 4, 1924, pp. 612–15 in *Ecrits politiques*, edited by Marcel Fournier. Paris: Fayard.

1997 [1924h]. "Les changes. L'inflation fiduciaire, les fautes de Mr. Klotz." *Le populaire*, March 5, 1924, pp. 616–19 in *Ecrits politiques*, edited by Marcel Fournier. Paris: Fayard.

1997 [1924i]. "Les changes. L'inflation fiduciaire: comment le gouvernement Poincaré défendit le franc." *Le populaire*, March 11, 1924, pp. 628–32 in *Ecrits politiques*, edited by Marcel Fournier. Paris: Fayard.

1997 [1924j]. "Les changes. La baisse des devises fortes." *Le populaire*, March 14, 1924, pp. 637–9 in *Ecrits politiques*, edited by Marcel Fournier. Paris: Fayard.

1997 [1924k]. "Les changes. L'action de la finance." *Le populaire*, March 15, 1924, pp. 640–1 in *Ecrits politiques*, edited by Marcel Fournier. Paris: Fayard.

1997 [1924l]. "Les changes. L'inflation fiduciaire." *Le populaire*, March 17, 1924, pp. 647–50 in *Ecrits politiques*, edited by Marcel Fournier. Paris: Fayard.

1997 [1924m]. "Les changes. Raisons d'espérer." *Le populaire*, March 18, 1924, pp. 651–4 in *Ecrits politiques*, edited by Marcel Fournier. Paris: Fayard.

1997 [1924n]. "Les changes. Post-scriptum." *Le populaire*, May 14, 1924, pp. 637–9 in *Ecrits politiques*, edited by Marcel Fournier. Paris: Fayard.

1997 [1928]. "Lucien Herr," pp. 745–7 in *Ecrits politiques*, edited by Marcel Fournier. Paris: Fayard.

1997 [1935]. "François Simiand," pp. 754–7 in *Ecrits politiques*, edited by Marcel Fournier. Paris: Fayard.

2013. *La Nation*, edited by Marcel Fournier and Jean Terrier. Paris: Presses universitaires de France.

2016 [1925]. *The Gift, Expanded Edition*, translated by Jane Guyer. Chicago: Chicago University Press.

Mauss, Rosine. 1918. "Letter to Hubert." Paris: Collège de France (Fonds Mauss, Correspondance Hubert, CDF 132–14).

Mazouz, Sarah. 2017. *La République et ses autres. Politiques de l'altérité dans la France des années 2000*. Lyon: ENS editions.

Mazower, Mark. 2010. *No Enchanted Palace: The End of Empire and the Ideological Origins of the United Nation*. Princeton, NJ: Princeton University Press.

2012. *Governing the World: The History of an Idea*. New York: Penguin.

McGoey, Linsey. 2015. "The Solidarity Conundrum." Discover Society. https://discoversociety.org/2015/10/06/the-solidarity-conundrum

Memmi, Albert. 1957. *Portrait du colonisé précédé du Portrait du colonisateur*. Paris: Corrêa; Buchet/Chastel.

Mérat, Louis. 1927. *L'évolution actuelle du régime financier des colonies: Etudes synthétique et analytique des principales modifications et de quelques applications du décret du 30 décembre 1912*. Paris: Larose.

Minow, Martha. 1998. *Between Vengeance and Forgiveness: Facing History after Genocide and Mass Violence*. Cambridge, MA: Beacon Press.

Mitchell, Timothy. 2002. *Rule of Experts: Egypt, Techno-Politics, Modernity*. Berkeley, CA: University of California Press.

Mitterrand, François. 1957. *Présence française et abandon*. Paris: Plon.

Moatti, Gérard. 2008. "1978–2008 Une brève histoire du CEPII." www.cepii.fr/PDF_PUB/autres/brevehistoireCEPII.pdf

Moutet, Marius. 1909. "Letter to Mauss, March 2." Paris: Collège de France (Fonds Mauss, 57 CDF 84–26).

Nelson, Stephen. 2016. "Market Rules: Social Conventions, Legal Fictions and the Organization of Sovereign Debt Markets in the Long Twentieth Century," pp. 118–52 in *Contractual Knowledge: One Hundred Years of Legal Experimentation in Global Markets*, edited by Grégoire Mallard and Jérôme Sgard. New York: Cambridge University Press.

Noiriel, Gérard. 1988. *Le creuset français, histoire de l'immigration XIXe–XXe siècle*. Paris: Seuil.

Nora, Pierre. 1961. *Les français d'Algérie*. Paris: Julliard.

Olick, Jeffrey and Brenda Coughlin. 2003. "The Politics of Regret: Analytical Frames," pp. 37–62 in *Politics and the Past: On Repairing Historical Injustices*, edited by John Torpey. New York: Rowman & Littlefield.

Olick, Jeffrey and Joyce Robbins. 1998. "Social Memory Studies: From 'Collective Memory' to the Historical Sociology of Mnemonic Practices." *Annual Review of Sociology*. 24: 105–14.

Orléan, André. 2011. "Mon rapport au marxisme." *Revue de la régulation*. 10(2) http://journals.openedition.org/regulation/9502

Oualid, William and Charles Picquenard. 1928. *Salaires, tarifs, conventions collectives et grèves: la politique du Ministère de l'Armement et du Ministère du Travail*. Paris: Presses universitaires de France.

Ouguergouz, Fatsah and Tahar Bownedra. 1999. "Il était une fois … " Pp. 1–13 in *Liber Amicorum: Judge Mohammed Bedjaoui*, edited by Emile Yakpo and Tabar Boumedra. The Hague: Kluwer Law International.

Ozsu, Umut. 2015. "In the Interest of Mankind as a Whole: Mohammed Bedjaoui's International Economic Order." *Humanity*. 129–43.

Pahuja, Sundya. 2011. *Decolonizing International Law: Development, Economic Growth and the Politics of Universality*. Cambridge: Cambridge University Press.

Panizza, Ugo, Federico Sturzenegger, and Jeromin Zettelmeyer. 2009. "The Economics and Law of Sovereign Debt and Default." *Journal of Economic Literature* 47(3): 651–98.

Pauly, Louis W. 1996. "The League of Nations and the Foreshadowing of the International Monetary Fund." *Princeton Series in International Economics*, 1–47.

Pénin, Marc. 1997. *Charles Gide 1847–1932, p. L'esprit critique*. Paris: L'Harmattan.

Pénet, Pierre. 2018. "The IMF Failure That Wasn't: Risk Ignorance during the European Debt Crisis." *British Journal of Sociology*.

Peyrefitte, Alain. 1994. *C'était De Gaulle*. Paris: Fayard.

Pierre, Pénet and Grégoire Mallard. 2014. "From Risk Models to Loan Contracts: Austerity as the Continuation of Calculation by Other Means." Journal of Critical Globalization Studies. 7: 4–50.

Portes, Alejandro and Min Zou. 1993. "The New Second Generation: Segmented Assimilation and Its Variants." *Annals of the American Academy of Political and Social Science*. 530: 74–96.

Prélot, Marcel. 1939. *L'évolution politique du socialisme français, 1789–1934*. Paris: SPES.

Prochasson, Claude. 1993. *Les intellectuels, le socialisme et la guerre*. 1890–1938. Paris: Seuil.

Rajagopal, Balakrishnan. 2003. *International Law from Below: Development, Social Movements and Third World Resistance*. New York: Cambridge University Press.

Rajak, Dinah. 2009. "The Gift of CSR: Power and the Pursuit of Responsibility in the Mining Industry," pp. 190–200 in *Corporate Citizenship in Africa. Lessons from the Past; Paths to the Future*, edited by Wayne Visser, Malcolm McIntosh, and Charlotte Middleton. Sheffield: Greenleaf Publishing.

Ramel, Frédéric. 2004. "Marcel Mauss et l'étude des relations internationales: Un héritage oublié." *Sociologie et sociétés*. 36: 227–45.

Renaudel, Pierre. 1910. "Letter to Mauss, November 22." Paris: Collège de France (Fonds Mauss, CDF 87–30).

Ribi-Forclaz, Amalia. 2015. *Humanitarian Imperialism: The Politics of Anti-Slavery Activism 1880–1940*. Oxford: Oxford University Press.

Riles, Annelise. 2011. *Collateral Knowledge: Legal Reasoning in Global Financial Markets*. Chicago: University of Chicago Press.

Rist, Charles. 1930. "Letter to Mauss, November." Paris: Collège de France (Fonds Mauss, 57 CDF 88–19).

Rist, Gilbert. 1996. *The History of Development: From Western Origins to Global Faith*. New York: Zed.

2002. "Le prix des mots," pp. 9–24 in *Les mots du pouvoir: Sens et non-sens de la rhétorique internationale, Cahiers de l'IUED*, 13, edited by Gilbert Rist. Geneva: Graduate Institute Publications.

Rivière, Georges Henri. 1930. "Letter to Mauss, September." Paris: Collège de France (Fonds Mauss, 57 CDF 88–24).

Rockefeller Foundation. 1930. "Letter to Mauss, October." Paris: Collège de France (Fonds Mauss, 57 CDF 89–6).

Rosenberg, Clifford. 2002. "Albert Sarraut and Republican Racial Thought." *French Politics, Culture and Society*. 20(3): 97–114.

Rostow, Walt W. 1960. *The Stages of Economic Growth. A Non-Communist Manifesto*. New York: Cambridge University Press.

Rothbard, Murray Newton. 1963. *America's Great Depression*. New York: Nash.

Saada, Emmanuelle. 2003. "Citoyens et sujets de l'Empire français: Les usages du droit en situation coloniale." *Genèses*. 53(4): 4–24.

Sack, Alexander 1927. *Les effets des transformations des Etats sur leurs dettes publiques et autres obligations financières: traité juridique et financier*. Paris: Recueil Sirey.

Sacriste, Fabien. 2011. *Germaine Tillion, Jacques Berque, Jean Servier et Pierre Bourdieu: des ethnologues dans la guerre d'indépendance algérienne*. Paris: L'Harmattan.

Sahlins, Marshall. 1974. "The Spirit of the Gift," pp. 149–83 in *Stone Age Economics*. London: Tavistock.

Sarraut, Albert. 1931. *Grandeurs et servitudes coloniales*. Paris: Le Sagittaire.

Schmitt, Carl. 2003 [1950]. *The Nomos of the Earth in the International Law of the Jus Publicum Europaeum*. New York: Telos.

Schrijver, Nico. 1997. *Permanent Sovereignty over Natural Resources*. Cambridge: Cambridge University Press.

Schuker, Stephen A. 1988. *American "Reparations" to Germany, 1919–1933*. Princeton, NJ: International Finance Section, Dept. of Economics, Princeton University.

Schulte-Tenckhoff, Isabelle. 2001. "Misrepresenting the Potlatch," pp. 167–87 in *Expanding the Economic Concept of Exchange*, edited by Caroline Gerschlager. Boston: Kluwer Academic.

Seligman, Charles Gabriel. 1938. "Letter to Mauss, July 1." Paris: Collège de France (Fonds Marcel Mauss, 57 CDF 91–2).

Servet, Jean-Michel. 1980. "Gratuité, dons, économie politique et économistes." *Recherches et documents du Centre Thomas More*. 26: 51–64.

1984 *Numismata: Etat et origines de la monnaie*. Lyon: Presses universitaires de Lyon.

1998. "Démonétarisation et remonétarisation en Afrique Occidentale et Equatoriale (XIXe–XXe siècles)," pp. 289–324 in *La monnaie souveraine* edited by Michel Aglietta and André Orléan. Paris: Odile Jacob.

1999. *Une économie sans argent, les systèmes d'échange local*. Paris: Seuil.

2016. "Entretien avec Grégoire Mallard, June 16." Geneva.

Shaffer, Gregory and Michael Waibel. "The Rise and Fall of Trade and Monetary Legal Orders: From the Interwar Period to Today's Global Imbalances," pp. 289–324 in *Contractual Knowledge: One Hundred Years of Legal Experimentation in Global Markets*, edited by Grégoire Mallard and Jérôme Sgard. New York: Cambridge University Press.

Shapin, Steven and Simon Shaffer. 1989. *Leviathan and the Air-Pump: Hobbes, Boyle, and the Experimental Life*. Princeton, NJ: Princeton University Press.

Shepard, Todd. 2008. *The Invention of Decolonization: The Algerian War and the Remaking of France*. Ithaca, NY: Cornell University Press.

Sibeud, Emmanuelle. 2004. "Marcel Mauss: Projet de présentation d'un bureau d'ethnologie." *Revue d'histoire des sciences humaines*. 10(1): 105–15.

2009. "Une libre pensée impériale? Le Comité de protection et de défense des indigènes (1892–1914)." *1900: Revue d'histoire intellectuelle*. 27(1): 57–74.

Sigaud, Lygia. 2002. "The Vicissitudes of The Gift." *Social Anthropology*. 10(3): 335–58.

Simiand, François. 1917. "Note du 8 février." Ministère de l'Armement et des Fabrications de guerre. Paris: Archives Nationales (Fonds AT 94AP/351).

1924. "Letter to Mauss, January." Paris: Collège de France (Fonds Mauss, 57 CDF 91–12).

1925. "Review essay of J. M. Keynes." *L'Année sociologique*. July 1923–July 1924: 778–9.

Singaravélou, Pierre. 2011. *Professer l'Empire. Les "Sciences coloniales" en France sous la IIIe République*. Paris: La Sorbonne.

Soustelle, Jacques. 1955. "Lettre d'un intellectuel à quelques autres à propos de la guerre d'Algérie, Nov. 14." Saint Denis: Archives Nationales (Fonds Soustelle, 112AJ/35).

1956a. "Création de l'Union pour le Salut et le Renouveau de l'Algérie Française (USRAF), July." (Fonds Soustelle, 112AJ/3).

1956b. "Letter to a MP, October 5." (Fonds Soustelle, 112AJ/3).

1957a. "Avant-rapport sur les problèmes relatifs au futur statut de l'Algérie pour le Comité directeur de l'USRAF." (Fonds Soustelle, 112AJ/36).

1957b. *Le drame algérien et la décadence française: Réponse à Raymond Aron*. Paris: Plon.

1957c. "Notes sur le projet de loi-cadre, Sept. 3." (Fonds Soustelle, 112AJ/36).

1958. "Notes sur l'Assemblée générale de l'USRAF, Feb. 2." (Fonds Soustelle, 112AJ/35).

1959a. "Note, March 26." (Fonds Soustelle, 112AJ/23).

1959b. "Press conference, April 7." (Fonds Soustelle, 112AJ/23).

1959c. "Letter to P.L. Darnar, May 26." (Fonds Soustelle, 112AJ/3).

1959d. "Note on 'self-determination' sent to Michel Debré, Sept. 8." (Fonds Soustelle, 112AJ/36).

1959e. "Letter to Michel Debré, Sept. 12." (Fonds Soustelle, 112AJ/36).

1962. *L'espérance trahie*. Paris: Editions de l'Alma.

1963. *A New Road for France*. New York: Robert Speller.

1967. *Les Quatre soleils*. Paris: Terre Humaine.

1975. *Rapport sur la recherche française en anthropologie et en archéologie*. La Documentation française (Fonds Soustelle, 112AJ/68).

1986. "Mémoires, entretiens avec George Suffert." (Fonds Soustelle, 112AJ/88).

Steiner, Philippe. 2005. *L'école durkheimienne et l'économie*. Paris: Droz.

Steinmetz, George. 2007. *The Devil's Handwriting: Precoloniality and the German Colonial State in Qingdao, Samoa and Southwest Africa*. Chicago: University of Chicago Press.

2008. "The Colonial State as a Social Field: Ethnographic Capital and Native Policy in the German Overseas Empire before 1914." *American Sociological Review*. 73(4): 589–612.

2013. "Major Contributions to Sociological Theory and Research on Empire 1830s–present," pp. 1–52, in *Sociology and Empire: The Imperial Entanglements of a Discipline*, edited by George Steinmetz. Durham, NC: Duke University Press.

Tardieu, André. 1910. "L'affaire N'Goko Sangha, December 21." *Le Temps*. Paris: Archives Nationales (Fonds AT 94AP/329, Dossier N'Goko Sangha, 17–2).

Tarot, Camille. 1999. *De Durkheim à Mauss, l'invention du symbolique, sociologie et science des religions*. Paris: La Découverte/MAUSS.

Taussig, Michael. 1980. *The Devil and Commodity Fetishism in South America*. Chapel Hill, NC: University of North Carolina Press.

Terrier, Jean and Marcel Fournier. 2013. "Présentation: La Nation, une expédition dans le domaine du normatif," pp. 1–42 in *La Nation*, by Marcel Mauss. Paris: Presses universitaires de France.

Teubner, Gunther. 1996. "Global Bukowina: Legal Pluralism in the World-Society." In *Global Law without a State*, edited by Gunther Teubner. London: Dartsmouth.

Thénault, Sylvie. 2001. *Une drôle de justice: les magistrats dans la guerre d'Algérie*. Paris: Découverte.

2012. *Violence ordinaire dans l'Algérie coloniale. Camps, internements, assignations à résidence*. Paris: Odile Jacob.

Thiveaud, Jean-Marie. 1998. "Fait financier et instrument monétaire entre souveraineté et légitimité: l'institution financière des sociétés archaïques," pp. 85–128 in *La monnaie souveraine* edited by Michel Aglietta and André Orléan. Paris: Odile Jacob.

Thomas, Albert. 1911a. "Note à la Commission du Budget." (Fonds AT 94AP/329, Dossier N'Goko Sangha, 17–2).

1911b. "Note sur le duel au fromager." Paris: Archives Nationales (Fonds AT 94AP/329, Dossier N'Goko Sangha, 17–2).

1911c. "Note sur le nouveau cahier des charges." (Fonds AT 94AP/329, Dossier N'Goko Sangha, 17–2).

1911d. "Note sur le scandale de la N'Goko Sangha." (Fonds AT 94AP/329, Dossier N'Goko Sangha, 17–2).

1919. *La Coopération et les usines de Guerre*. Paris: Bibliothèque de l'École Coopérative.

1920. "Lettre au Ministre pour demande de légion d'honneur à Hubert." September. (Fonds AT 94AP/381).

1922a. "Letter of April 4, to Hubert." (Fonds AT 94AP/381).

1922b. "Letter of August 26, to Hubert." (Fonds AT 94AP/381).

1922c. "Letter of September 14, to Hubert." (Fonds AT 94AP/381).

1924. "Letter of January 24, to Hubert." Paris: Collège de France (Fonds Mauss, 57 CDF 139–4).

1925. "Letter of March 24, to Mauss, with the Report of the ILO's Department on Cooperation." (Fonds Mauss, CDF 56–22).

1926. "Letter of December 14, to A. Gide." (Fonds AT 94AP/380).

1928. "Letter of February 17, to A. Gide." (Fonds AT 94AP/380).

1929. "Letter of July 3, to A. Gide." (Fonds AT 94AP/380).
Thomas, Martin. 2005. "Albert Sarraut, French Colonial Development, and the Communist Threat, 1919–1930." *Journal of Modern History*. 77(4): 917–55.
Tillion, Germaine. 1937. "Letter to Mauss, March 6." Paris: Collège de France (Fonds Mauss 57 CDF 93–22).
1939. "Letter to Mauss, May 9." (Fonds Mauss 57 CDF 93–22).
1960 [1957]. "L'Algérie en 1957." In *L'Afrique bascule vers l'avenir*. Paris: Editions de Minuit.
2005. *Les ennemis complémentaires: Guerre d'Algérie*. Paris: Tirésias.
2009. *Fragments de vie*. Paris: Seuil.
2015. *Il était une fois l'ethnographie*. Paris: Seuil.
Tomuschat, Christian. 2004. "The 1871 Peace Treaty and the 1919 Versailles Treaty." In *Peace Treaties and International in European History*, edited by R. Lesaffer. Cambridge: Cambridge University Press.
Topalov, Christian, ed. 1999. *Laboratoires du nouveau siècle: La nébuleuse réformatrice en France et ses réseaux (1880–1914)*. Paris: EHESS.
Torpey, John. 2003. "Introduction: Politics and the Past," pp. 1–36 in *Politics and the Past: On Repairing Historical Injustices*, edited by J. Torpey. New York: Rowman & Littlefield.
2006. *Making Whole What Has Been Smashed: On Reparations Politics*. Cambridge, MA: Harvard University Press.
Toussaint, Eric. 2017a. *Le système dette*. Paris: Les liens qui libèrent.
2017b. "Les propositions de Varoufakis qui menaient à l'échec." www.cadtm.org/Les-propositions-de-Varoufakis-qui
2017c. "Comment la BCE a gagné 7,8 milliards d'euros grâce à la dette grecque." *Le Monde*. October 10. www.lemonde.fr/economie/article/2017/10/26/comment-la-bce-a-gagne-7–8-milliards-d-euros-grace-a-la-dette-grecque_5206484_3234.html
Trachtenberg, Marc. 1979. Reparation at the Paris Peace Conference. *Journal of Modern History*. 51(21): 24–55.
United Nations. 1983a. "Summary Records of the Plenary Meetings and of the Meetings of the Committee of the Whole." Vol. I of *Official Records of the United Nations Conference on Succession of States in Respect of State Property, Archives and Debts*. Vienna, March 1–April 8. A/CONF.117/16. http://legal.un.org/diplomaticconferences/1983_succession/vol1.shtml
1983b. "Vienna Convention on Succession of States in Respect of State Property, Archives and Debts." Vol. II of *Official Records of the United Nations Conference on Succession of States in Respect of State Property, Archives and Debts*. Vienna, April 8. A/CONF.117/16. http://legal.un.org/ilc/texts/instruments/english/conventions/3_3_1983.pdf
United Nations General Assembly (UNGA). 1974a. Resolution 3201 (S-VI), May 1. Declaration on the Establishment of a New International Economic Order. www.un-documents.net/s6r3201.htm
1974b. Resolution 3201 (S-VI), May 1. Programme of Action on the Establishment of a New International Economic Order. www.un-documents.net/s6r3202.htm
1974c. Resolution 32/81, Dec. 12. Resolution Containing the Charter of Economic Rights and Duties of States. www.un-documents.net/a29r3281.htm
1979. Resolution 34/138, Dec. 14. Global negotiations relating to international economic co-operation for development. www.un-documents.net/a34r138.htm
Varoufakis, Yanis. 2017. *Adults in the Room: My Battle with Europe's Deep Establishment*. London: Random House.
Vauchez, Antoine. 2013. *L'union par le droit: L'invention d'un programme institutionnel pour l'Europe*. Paris: Presses de Sciences Po.

2014. *Démocratiser l'Europe*. Paris: Seuil.
Vergès, Jacques. 1968. *De la stratégie judiciaire*. Paris: Editions de Minuit.
Waibel, Michael. 2011. *Sovereign Defaults before International Courts and Tribunals*. New York: Cambridge University Press.
Weber, Maurice. 2007 [1927]. "Lettre ouverte à André Gide." *Le Populaire*, reproduced in *Voyage au Congo*, by André Gide. Paris: Gallimard.
Weber, Max. 1978 [1922]. *Economy and Society*. Berkeley, CA: University of California Press.
Willis, James F. 1982. *Prologue to Nuremberg. The Politics and Diplomacy of Punishing War Criminals of the First World War*. Westport, CT: Greenwood Press.
Winock, Michel. 1992. *Le socialisme en France et en Europe*. Paris: Seuil.
Zelizer, Viviana. 1994. *The Social Meaning of Money: Pin Money, Paychecks, Poor Relief and Other Currencies*. Princeton, NJ: Princeton University Press.
Zettelmeyer, Jeromin, and Kenneth Rogoff. 2002. "Bankruptcy Procedures for Sovereigns: A History of Ideas, 1976–2001." IMF Staff Papers, 49(3): 470–507. Washington, DC: International Monetary Fund Staff Papers 49(3).

Index

CPSIA information can be obtained
at www.ICGtesting.com
Printed in the USA
LVHW021311281220
675134LV00011B/302

9 781108 453486